Not since the classic Christian annotations of the *Lectionary* has there been such a worthwhile and important tool for God's people. Since many Christians no longer read through the Bible using the *Lectionary*, which was based on the traditional readings of the church and the synagogue, *Around the Word in 365 Days* is just what is needed. It will help believers to better know God so that they can better make Him known. Thank you, Linda Sommer, for this terrific resource!

—DR. TED BAEHR
CEO OF THE CHRISTIAN FILM AND TELEVISION COMMISSION AND
PUBLISHER OF *MOVIEGUIDE*®

Linda Sommer and her husband, Tom, have been dear friends of mine for many years. They both have a heart for God and missions. Reading these devotions by Linda has enriched my life and ministry. As you read these rich spiritual nuggets, you will be blessed and inspired.

—SYVELL PHILLIPS
FOUNDER, EVANGEL BIBLE TRANSLATORS

Linda Sommer has crafted a practical, hands-on tool that will greatly enrich your reading of the Bible. Her daily devotionals provide clarity, encouragement and real-life applications of key passages throughout the Scriptures.

—DR. KENNETH BOA
PRESIDENT, REFLECTIONS MINISTRIES

A DAILY NAVIGATIONAL GUIDE
FOR READING THE BIBLE IN A YEAR

AROUND THE WORD IN 365 DAYS

LINDA SOMMER

CREATION
HOUSE
PRESS

AROUND THE WORD IN 365 DAYS by Linda Sommer
Published by Creation House Press
A part of Strang Communications Company
600 Rinehart Road
Lake Mary, Florida 32746
www.creationhouse.com

Unless otherwise noted, all Scripture quotations are from the New King James Version of the Bible. Copyright © 1979, 1980, 1982, 1984 by Thomas Nelson, Inc., publishers. Used by permission.

Scripture quotations marked KJV are from the King James Version of the Bible.

The One Year ® plan © 1991 is printed by permission of Tyndale House Publishers, Inc. All rights reserved.
The One Year is a registered trademark of Tyndale House Publishers, Inc.

Edited by Jonda Crews and Max Morris
Copyright © 2002 by Linda Sommers
All rights reserved

Library of Congress Control Number: 2001097462
International Standard Book Number: 0-88419-849-9

02 03 04 05   8 7 6 5 4 3 2 1
Printed in the United States of America

DEDICATION

I dedicate this book to my husband, Tom, who has been the heartbeat of the final publication of this book. He had been my business partner throughout this project.

We have been married forty-two years. Tom took early retirement from BellSouth at the age of fifty-five and has helped me full time in the work of God's kingdom. We are both so grateful God has granted us these golden years to colabor together in this last great harvest.

ACKNOWLEDGMENTS

My loving appreciation to. . .

The Three in One:

My loving heavenly Father, who revealed His heart to me as I wrote.

Jesus Christ, the lover of my soul, who imparted His love to me every morning as we met together to agree in prayer for this book.

The Holy Spirit, who took so many of the things of Jesus Christ and showed them to me as I read through the Scriptures.

Tyndale House, who published the One Year Bible that has so blessed me over the years.

Those who encouraged me to seek professional publication of these devotionals.

Landmark Church for their cooperation and prayers in the process of this final publication.

Allen Quain, manager of Creation House Press, who has been so delightful to work with throughout this project.

The whole staff at Strang Communications who have spent many hours of labor under the pressure of a tight schedule.

Richard Parker for the early editing of these monthly devotionals.

Dr. Max F. Morris and his wife for the final editing of the book. The foreword he wrote for this book was appreciated and contained exactly the message I wanted to convey to the reader.

My three sons and their wives—Russ and Marianne, Ron and Mary Virginia, and Ray and Teri—who have encouraged me throughout this project. Russ, who is called to be a bridge between races; Ron, who is called to be a bridge between nations; and Ray, who is called to be a bridge between families (joining the Jew and Gentile together in God's kingdom) have inspired many of the stories shared in this book.

All those who have invested their finances and prayers in this project.

Contents

Foreword

According to a recent Gallup poll, 87 percent of professing Christians admit that they do not read the Bible regularly. This sad statistic indicates that many Christians may be biblically illiterate and spiritually undernourished. When Christians are asked why they do not read the Scriptures on a daily basis, they offer two excuses: First, they do not have the time to read the Bible. Second, they do not understand the Bible when they read it.

Years ago, the *One Year Bible* was published to encourage and enable Christians to read the entire Bible in one year. It selects related passages of both the Old and New Testaments and divides these passages into 365 days. Thus, with about fifteen minutes of daily reading, a person can read the entire Bible in one year. The *One Year Bible* has been a blessing to thousands of Christians.

Still, the shocking statistic of 87 percent of nonreaders remains.

Around the Word in 365 Days adds an exciting new dimension to Bible reading that will motivate Christians to read the Bible every day! By ingeniously utilizing the *One Year Bible* reading plan, Linda Sommer highlights a scripture passage for each day of the year and provides the reader with an insightful commentary on that particular passage. She makes each passage come alive! The reader is given a practical, down-to-earth daily devotional related directly to God's Word.

Mrs. Sommer has been a Christian for over fifty years, but she does not write from the perspective of a learned theologian or Bible scholar tucked away in a cloister of higher learning. Rather, she writes from the perspective of a Christian wife and dedicated mother who has reared three boys. In clear, understandable language, she shares practical illustrations and refreshing anecdotes drawn from her many years as a church member, wife and mom.

Anyone who desires to read the Bible consistently and grow in the knowledge of God's Word will be encouraged and inspired by *Around the Word in 365 Days*.

—Dr. Max F. Morris
Inventor of the Kwickscan™ Reading System
and Kwickscan Bible™

Introduction

At the beginning of every New Year, I look forward to reading the Bible through in the year. For at least thirty of my more than fifty years as a Christian, I have had the joy of reading God's Word daily. When I first began reading the Bible through I began with Genesis and ended with Revelation. This program of daily Bible reading at times was tedious. Usually when I reached Leviticus I found myself struggling to get through the required readings. I was so blessed when the One Year Bible was published. One of the most outstanding features of the One Year Bible is the convenience and variety found in it. The text is divided into daily readings. For each day there is a portion of the Old Testament, the New Testament, the Psalms and Proverbs grouped on consecutive pages. This arrangement in the *One Year Bible* gives freshness and diversity to each day's reading. At the end of the day the reader has received a flavor of how the Holy Spirit speaks to us in the pages of the entire Bible. Personally, I believe this arrangement gives the whole counsel of God's Word on a daily basis. The One Year Bible is available in the following versions: King James, The Living Bible, New American Standard, New International, New Revised Standard and The New King James.

It has been such a blessing for me to use the *One Year Bible*, and I wanted to share this blessing with others. To encourage others to use this method of Bible reading, I have written a devotional highlighting one of the daily readings listed in *One Year Bible*. In these devotionals I share from my heart an experience or a lesson the reading brings to my mind.

You may say to yourself, "But I don't have time to do this daily." Then I must respond to this statement with a very important question: "How much time do you spend reading the newspaper every day or watching television?" David said, "Thy word have I hid in my heart, that I might not sin against thee"(Ps. 119:11, KJV). On the next page you will see the reasons for reading the Word daily and what the Word of God will do for the reader. It takes fifteen to twenty minutes daily of your time to read the Bible through in a year. You may desire to read the Old Testament and New Testament readings in the morning and the Psalm and Proverb in the evening. Surely you can set aside the amount of time daily to read the Manufacturer's Handbook. So many go through life without a clue about how to live the abundant life promised to us by our Lord. The Manufacturer's Handbook has all the wisdom, knowledge and instruction you need to live life to its fullest capacity. A life filled with joy, love, peace, grace, wisdom, knowledge, understanding and instruction awaits you. What are you waiting for?

Spiritual leaders of all generations have agreed upon the importance of daily Bible reading as a vital means of growth and maturity. Many Bible readers have wished for a method that would help them with the discipline of regular, systematic study of God's inspired Word. I challenge you to allow the Holy Spirit to be your teacher as you read through the Bible this year. Write down the thoughts He gives you as you read, and share these thoughts with your loved ones. Your life will be enriched, and you will encourage others. *Happy new year and happy reading.*

What the Word of God does for us: Psalm 119
  The Word of God keeps us from defilement (v. 1).
  The Word of God causes us to be blessed (v. 2).
  The Word of God keeps us from shame (v. 6).
  The Word of God helps cleanse us (v. 9).
  The Word of God keeps us from sin (v. 11).
  The Word of God gives us joy (v. 14).
  The Word of God removes us from reproach and contempt (v. 22).
  The Word of God gives us counsel (v. 24).
  The Word of God quickens us (v. 25).
  The Word of God gives us understanding (v. 27).
  The Word of God strengthens us (v. 28).
  The Word of God enlarges our heart (v. 32).
  The Word of God show us salvation (v. 41).
  The Word of God gives us an answer for those
      who reproach us (v. 42).
  The Word of God gives us hope (v. 43).
  The Word of God gives us liberty (v. 45).
  The Word of God comforts us (v. 50).
  The Word of God gives us new songs (v. 54).
  The Word of God imparts mercy (v. 58).
  The Word of God gives us good judgment (v. 66).
  The Word of God gives us soundness of heart (v. 80).
  The Word of God shows us God's faithfulness (v. 90).
  The Word of God keeps us through affliction (v. 92).
  The Word of God gives us good meditation (v. 97).
  The Word of God gives us wisdom (v. 98).
  The Word of God keeps us from speaking evil (v. 101).
  The Word of God keeps us from error (v. 104).
  The Word of God gives us direction and
      shines light on our path (v. 105).
  The Word of God upholds us (v. 116).
  The Word of God gives us safety (v. 117).
  The Word of God keeps iniquity from
      having dominion over us (v. 133).
  The Word of God keeps us pure (v. 140).
  The Word of God relays truth to us (v. 151).
  The Word of God gives us peace (v. 165).
  The Word of God gives us deliverance (v. 170).
  The Word of God helps us (v. 173).

AROUND THE
WORD IN
365
DAYS

January 1

Walk, Stand, Sit
Psalm 1:1–6

The psalmist reverses the natural way we learn to walk. A baby first learns to sit up and then gradually pulls himself up to the standing position. Finally, when he feels steady on his feet, he ventures to take the first step. God has not called us to a **natural way** of walking. He has called us to a **supernatural walk**. We walk in His ways, we stand in His righteousness, and we sit in His presence.

WE WALK IN HIS WAYS. ⚬ First comes the desire in our lives to walk in His ways. We know the way we are going is not fruitful and that there must be a better way. Then we discover the way. Jesus said, "I am the Way, the Truth, and the Life." We recognize our own inability to walk in joy and peace, and we come to Jesus in our desperation. We discover that in our own strength we cannot take another step in this life. A divine exchange happens when we ask Jesus to forgive us for the way we have walked before (our own natural thinking and rationalization) and we confess our desire to walk as Jesus walked. Every unrighteous act, word or thought in our lives at that moment is cleansed. As far as the east is from the west, so far does God wipe away all of our transgressions, iniquities and sin. Our unrighteousness is exchanged for His righteousness. We are now able to stand in His righteousness, and we enter into His kingdom. His kingdom is not meat or drink, but righteousness, peace and joy in the Holy Spirit.

WE STAND IN HIS RIGHTEOUSNESS. ⚬ The desire to walk in His ways grows stronger and stronger as we receive more and more of the Lord's strength into our lives. In all the areas of our weakness, He is able to come into our lives and be our strength. As we look to Jesus for our daily strength and His Word for our daily food, we are able to stand in His righteousness. We become steadfast in Him, and faithfulness and longsuffering begin to develop in our lives. The joy of the Lord becomes our daily strength, and we realize we are steady on our feet. We have the faith to begin to walk in the Spirit and be led by the Spirit, rather than having our natural or carnal minds control our way of walking in this life.

WE SIT IN HIS PRESENCE. ⚬ The more we walk in His ways, the more the desire comes into our lives to sit in His presence. We realize that without Him we are helpless and can do nothing of eternal consequence in our lives. Our souls cry out to be more like Jesus. We know in order for this transformation to take place, we must spend more quiet time with Him. In His presence are fullness of joy and pleasures forever more. When we begin to walk in the Spirit, we enter His classroom of life; we have to still ourselves to learn of Him. The invitation is extended to us to find rest for our souls if we daily come to Jesus and let the Great Teacher, His Holy Spirit, instruct us in meekness and lowliness of heart. The more we daily still ourselves and stay our minds upon Jesus and His Word, the more we become like Him.

1

READ: *Genesis 3:1–4:26; Matthew 2:13–3:6; Psalm 2:1–12; Proverbs 1:7–9*

Three Temptations
Genesis 3:1–4:26

There are only three ways the enemy can tempt us. When God created Adam and Eve, they had three beautiful desires: the desire to worship God in all of His holiness, the desire to enjoy God and all of His creation, and the desire to glorify God or make His presence manifest on earth to all of creation. All the desires in the souls of Adam and Eve were directed toward God, and only God could satisfy those desires. These desires were perverted after the Fall into three lustful areas in our souls: The desire to worship God was perverted into the lust of the eyes (greedy longings in our minds); the desire to enjoy God was perverted into the lust of the flesh (seeking to satisfy our five senses through overindulgence); and the desire to glorify God was perverted into the pride of life (trusting in our own resources and ourselves more than we trust in God). These are the three buttons Satan always tries to push in us because he knows we will always have these weaknesses in our souls.

THE LUST OF THE EYES ∼ Satan offered Adam and Eve temporary and immediate satisfaction of these desires when he tempted them in the garden. Everything in the garden was beautiful, and all the fruit trees were designed for consumption except for the tree of the knowledge of good and evil. God forbade Adam and Eve to eat from this tree, or they would die. The first temptation Eve received was the temptation in her mind to doubt that God's word was true. If Satan is able to put any doubt in our minds at all about God's, Word then he has access to the rest of our souls—our emotions and our wills. Eve's mind was seduced by Satan's suggestions, and the lust of the eyes developed in her mind. Now the emotional part of her soul was about to be seduced.

THE LUST OF THE FLESH ∼ Eve looked at the fruit and saw that it was good for food and pleasant to her eyes. Her thinking probably went like this: "Surely God created this also for my pleasure, and nothing will happen to me if I eat this." This type of thinking has seduced millions into addictive habits. People who take drugs or become alcoholics never think of the consequences. They only think of the immediate satisfaction. Satan knows just how to tantalize our senses to actually crave what would be harmful to us if used unwisely or used to the extreme. God created us with the desire first to hunger and thirst after Him and for us to find pleasure first in Him, not in His creation. Counselors will tell us that most addiction is rooted in deep emotional needs that have not been fulfilled. The addicted person seeks to fill his soul through substance abuse. The emotional area of Eve's soul was seduced.

THE PRIDE OF LIFE ∼ Eve also thought the fruit would make her as wise as God. God wants us to be like Him because we were originally created in His image. God knew, however, if Adam and Eve knew about evil, they would no longer be led by the Spirit of God, and their spirits would die. The will area of Eve's soul was touched. She trusted herself more than she trusted God's Word, and pride entered. What caused Satan's downfall caused hers.

Overcoming the World
Matthew 3:7–4:11

We describe people as worldly when they are consumed with their own lusts. First John 2:16 tells us what these three lusts are: the lust of the eyes (greedy longings in our minds), the lust of the flesh (seeking sensual pleasure in obsessive, indulgent ways) and the pride of life (trusting in our own selves and our resources more than we trust in God). This verse says that these lusts are not of the Father, but they are of the world. Jesus, however, through His victory over temptation and through His death, burial and resurrection from the dead, has overcome the world. In this story of the temptation of Jesus we see Satan tempting Jesus as he tempted Eve in the areas of the three beautiful desires—to enjoy God, to glorify God and to worship God. Satan thought he would also succeed in seducing Jesus. He forgot one very important fact: Jesus was the Word of God made flesh. The Word is the offensive sword of the Spirit against Satan, and Jesus wielded this sword effectively against the enemy. We can do the same.

TO ENJOY GOD AND HIS CREATION ~ In Matthew 4:1–4, Jesus had been fasting for forty days, and He was extremely hungry. Satan tempted Jesus to turn the stone into bread. At the thought of bread, Jesus remembered how bread tasted, and as He did, His salivary glands were alerted. He remembered how bread smelled, looked and felt. Even the sound of bread being chewed in His mouth came to Him. Jesus, however, did not give in to the cravings of His five senses. Satan was seeking to gain control over the emotional area of the soul of Jesus, but Jesus spoke aloud, "It is written, man shall not live by bread alone, but by every word that proceeds out of the mouth of God." Satan was stabbed by the sword, but he did not give up the battle for the soul of Jesus.

TO GLORIFY GOD ~ In Matthew 4:5–7, Satan recognized the power of God's Word after the first temptation. He used the Word, but misquoted it to Jesus in an attempt to gain control of Jesus' will. Satan tempted Jesus to jump off the pinnacle of the temple to prove that the angels would bear Him up. Satan quoted from Psalm 91:11–12, but he left off the phrase "to keep thee in all thy ways." Angels will come to our assistance if we are walking in God's ways, not our own. Jesus was God in the flesh, and if He fell for this temptation, Jesus would be walking in Satan's way, not God's way, because God the Father had a plan for God the Son—to die on the cross and to be resurrected. Jesus knew this, and He said, "It is written, you shall not tempt the Lord your God." Another stab wound was delivered to Satan.

TO WORSHIP GOD ~ In Matthew 4:8, Satan attempted to gain control of the mind area of Jesus' soul by showing Jesus the kingdoms of this world. He offered them to Jesus if He would bow down and worship him. Jesus said simply, "You shall worship the Lord your God, and Him only shall you serve." The devil then left him for a season.

3

Protecting the Gates
Proverbs 1:20–23

In ancient times most cities were walled cities. Jerusalem, for example, had twelve gates and high, thick walls. These walls were created to keep the enemies of the city from entering and destroying the city. Proverbs 16:32 says, "He who is slow to anger is better than the mighty, and he who rules his spirit than he who takes a city." Proverbs 25:28 says, "Whoever has no rule over his own spirit is like a city broken down, without walls."

Our inner person—**soul and spirit**—is compared to a city. The outer walls of this city are our bodies. The eyes, ears, nose, tongue and skin are the outer gates to the city, and the inner gates to the city are the five senses—touch, taste, see, hear and smell. **The place of chief concourse of Proverbs 1:21 is the mind.**

Our enemy, Satan, can only enter the soul—**mind, will and emotion**—through the outer gates. We hear his voice daily shouting at us through the radio, television, Internet, reading material, movies, music and thoughts. There is a voice, however, that is also shouting at the gates of our inner person. That voice is the voice of wisdom, and this voice needs to be heard above the roar of the enemy. Wisdom will tell us when we need to shut the eye, ear, nose, tongue and touch gates to our minds. We need to listen carefully to this voice, and if we obey, we will keep our souls from many troubles. For example, there is another proverb that says, "In the multitude of words sin is not lacking, but he who restrains his lips is wise" (Prov. 10:19).

Our daily commitment should be to listen to the voice of wisdom. If we will listen to this voice and shut out the voice of the enemy, we will be able to rule the city within us—our souls and spirits. Satan is a thief, and he sometimes even tries to climb over the walls and sneak into our thought life.

One night when I was going to sleep, I heard a voice saying, "There is a thief in your house." I woke my husband immediately, and he said, "I hear nothing." Then I recognized the voice of wisdom. "Lord, is this You?" I asked. Then He spoke to me the following: "The thief in your house is your television. It is robbing you of valuable time with your family, and it is distracting your children from their call."

The next day my mother called to tell me her television was broken. I offered her ours, and we have been without a television since that time. Our children were all under twelve years of age when we heard the voice of wisdom, and our children thank us today for hearing that voice of wisdom. Jesus is wisdom personified. First Corinthians 1:30 says, "Christ Jesus, who became for us wisdom from God—and righteousness and sanctification and redemption." When we listen to the voice of Jesus Christ within, we will always hear wisdom speaking to us.

January 5

Let Your Light Shine
Matthew 5:1–26

One of the scriptures that always comes to my remembrance when I pray is, "Let your light so shine before men, that they may see your good works and glorify your Father which is in heaven" (Matt. 5:16.) We are exhorted in the Scriptures to challenge one another to love and good works (Heb. 10:24).

When we were in India, one of the Indian pastors our church supports was under observation by the police. The pastor's neighbors called the police to report that Mr. Raju was having much activity at his home and they suspected he was drug dealing. A police inspector was assigned to follow Mr. Raju. After following Mr. Raju for two weeks, the policeman knocked on Mr. Raju's door. "May I come in?" the police inspector asked John Raju. John let the policeman in, and then the inspector confessed he had been following John for two weeks. The inspector said, "I have a question to ask you, Mr. Raju. What causes you to do so many good things for so many people?" In the two weeks the inspector had followed John he saw John visiting leper colonies, feeding orphans and widows and doing many other good works.

John replied to the inspector's question, "My Boss instructs me to do these good works."

The inspector then asked enthusiastically, "Who is your boss? I would like to meet him." John then shared the gospel with the inspector and introduced him to Jesus Christ, his Boss, and on that day Jesus gained another eternal employee. We had the privilege of seeing the inspector baptized while we were in India.

Let His light shine through you today, and others will see His good works through you and glorify God in heaven. Your main work today above all other work is to trust and love Jesus with all of your heart and allow His love to flow through you to others. Join me in a prayer I pray almost every morning:

Lord, help me to love as You love.

Let There Be No Strife
Genesis 13:5–15:21

The herdsmen of Abraham's cattle and the herdsmen of Lot's cattle were in strife. Each of them probably thought the other had more grazing land than he did. Abraham's response to this strife was, "Is not the whole land before you?" There was plenty of land for both.

Strife is caused by two basic roots of all sin—pride and jealousy. Proverbs 13:10 tells us that by pride comes contention. James, which is the book of wisdom in the New Testament, says, "For where envying and strife is, there is confusion and every evil work" (James 3:16, KJV).

Yesterday we talked about letting our light shine before men by demonstrating God's love through good works. Today we hear, "Let there be no strife." Strife is always an evil work because it opens the door to demonic activity. The Lord gave me a vivid picture of what happens when we get into strife with one another. I saw a husband and wife in a boxing ring together. Instead of pounding one another with gloved hands, they were striking one another with their tongues. The audience was cheering each time they wounded one another.

Centering my attention from the ring to the audience, I was shocked to see that the audience was every kind of grotesque demon imaginable. One yelled, "Hit her again. Tell her about the time she hurt you." Then I heard another yell to the wife, "Tell him he is a wimp and can't do anything right." I'll never forget this vivid vision.

When we get into strife, all of Satan's demons rejoice because they get to take a vacation. We do their wounding work for them with our own tongues. We glorify our Father when we let our light shine before men that they may see our good works. We glorify the devil when we allow ourselves to get into strife because we are doing his evil work for him. Proverbs 20:3 says, "It is an honour for a man to cease from strife" (KJV). Proverbs also makes it clear that it is an angry person who stirs up strife. A person becomes angry when he is jealous or prideful. Daily we need to hear the Holy Spirit remind us to cease from strife. If we obey this admonition, we will have a blessed day. Let there be no strife in your life today.

Heavenly Father, help me to seek peace today. If I find myself beginning to have words with anyone at work, in the community or at home, help me to listen to the umpire of my spirit and soul, the Holy Spirit, as He reminds me to cease from strife. Then give me the strength to shut my mouth. Above all, I confess any pride or jealousy in my heart that makes me vulnerable to strife. Cleanse me of these two things that cause me to get into strife. Help me to esteem others higher than myself; this will bring down both of these strongholds in my life. Amen.

READ: Genesis 16:1–18:19; Matthew 6:1–24; Psalm 7:1–17; Proverbs 2:1–5

Taking Care of Ashes
Matthew 6:1–24

Jesus tells us not to lay up treasures on this earth where moth and rust corrupt and where thieves break in and steal; instead we are to lay up for ourselves treasures in heaven where moth and rust will not corrupt, and where thieves will not break through to steal. Whatever we treasure is what we give our heart and soul to keep. This exhortation of Jesus caused me to examine my own life and ask myself these questions: "Where is my treasure? Is it on earth, or is it in heaven?"

I discovered the answer to this question when I was touring Israel. Our tour was at Megiddo, and we were observing the twenty or more layers of civilization. Each civilization was reduced to little more than one inch of ash. As I looked at this amazing phenomenon, the Lord spoke this to my heart:

Why do you spend so much time taking care of ashes?

I realized how much of my time is spent tending earthly things that will ultimately burn. I was challenged to invest my life into three eternal things—faith, hope and love. These will last forever because they represent the eternal soul of Jesus—His mind, emotions and will. Jesus' mind was filled with faith, His emotions were anchored in hope, and His will was motivated by His love for His heavenly Father.

When I invest in **growing in faith, hope and love,** I am laying up for myself treasures in heaven. When I go to heaven there are a few things I can take with me. I will take my soul and spirit, the Word of God I have hidden in my heart, the prayers I have prayed on earth and the people I have witnessed to. These glorious treasures will increase in the exact measure that I increase in faith, hope and love. We are exhorted in Psalm 2 to ask for the heathen, and God will give them to us as our inheritance. What more rewarding treasure could there be than to meet someone in heaven who is there because you witnessed in word and deed to him? Are you adding to your inheritance daily?

Let this be your prayer today:

Lord, there is only one stock market that is reliable. That stock market is Your kingdom, because only Your kingdom is unmovable, unshakable and eternal. Help me today to invest in kingdom things—Your Word, growing in faith, hope and love, sharing Your gospel and love with others, and praying.

Divine Bodyguards
Proverbs 2:6–17

We witnessed in our church a dramatic conversion. A bodyguard for the Mafia was saved, and he shared with us some of his assignments as a bodyguard to Mafia leaders. He was charged to defend the Mafia leader with his own life. He was to check out where the Mafia leaders were to eat, sleep and travel to be sure there would be no way someone could get to that leader to do him harm. He stayed awake all night to guard the leader. This passage in Proverbs reveals several divine bodyguards we have as we walk in the path God sets before us. These bodyguards preserve our way and keep us from traveling on the path that leads to destruction.

Every day when I awaken I am conscious of these bodyguards. I know that if I acknowledge their presence and stick close with them all day, I will be protected from making mistakes that would bring destruction and disaster. God is a buckler to those who walk uprightly, but to walk uprightly daily we must look to these bodyguards. These bodyguards are:

- WISDOM
- KNOWLEDGE
- UNDERSTANDING
- DISCRETION
- PRUDENCE

Five is the number of grace, and it is so comforting to know that we have five bodyguards on duty night and day to preserve, protect and keep us walking in God's path of righteousness. All of these bodyguards are under the instruction of the Captain of the Heavenly Hosts—Jesus Christ.

Daily we have choices. Will we listen to these bodyguards when they warn us not to go down the dark path? We can listen to them daily as we search out God's Word, because all of these bodyguards are found in God's Word. Wisdom, knowledge, understanding, discretion and prudence will only be on duty in our lives if we have submitted to the instructions they give in God's Word. Have you looked into the faces of your bodyguards today? God shines a light on their faces as we turn on the lamp of God's Word every morning. Let this be your prayer this morning:

Your Word is a lamp to my feet and a light to my path. Help me to turn this lamp on today as I spend time in Your Word. Thank You for wisdom, knowledge, understanding, discretion and prudence, who will watch over me and keep me safe from the enemy who seeks my destruction. I will listen carefully as they instruct me today.

We Must Be Willing to Give
Genesis 20:1–22:24

The father was patiently instructing his seven-year-old son how to be an effective outfielder in baseball. He gave the following instructions: "First, son, you have to stand with your glove ready to receive the ball, and keep your eye on the ball. As the ball is falling, you need to run to where the ball is and try to catch it before it reaches the ground. If the ball hits the ground, scoop it up quickly and throw it to the base…"

The young boy looked puzzled as he reviewed the instructions. "Dad, why can't I keep the ball? After all, I caught it."

Can you imagine the puzzled expression on Isaac's face as his father tied him and laid him on the wood for a sacrifice? Isaac was about to learn one of the greatest lessons of living a life of blessing. His father obeyed God's instructions to sacrifice his own son. He was able to do this because he trusted in God's goodness. Abraham had already tasted the Lord, and he knew He was good. He knew that whatever God told him to do would be the best thing he could do even if he did not understand the instructions. Abraham never questioned God; he only obeyed, and because he believed God knew what was best for him, his belief was counted as righteousness to him.

Abraham was willing to give his own son if this was God's requirement. He was willing to do this because he believed that God had the power to resurrect his son. He made a great faith statement to his servants: "Abide ye here with the ass, and I and the lad will go yonder and worship, and come again to you" (Gen. 22:5, KJV). As they were climbing the mountain, Isaac asked his father where the lamb for the burnt offering was. Abraham made another faith statement, "My son, God will provide himself a lamb for a burnt offering"(v. 8). Abraham believed that God would provide.

Just as a young boy cannot catch or throw a ball with a closed hand, we cannot receive from or give a blessing to others with a closed hand. Only those things we give to God will be blessed. Those things we withhold from Him will never be blessed. The first step is to believe that God will provide as we are willing to give. Everything we receive in this life from the hand of our heavenly Father we must hold lightly, and we must be ready at any time to throw it heavenward by investing it in His kingdom here on earth.

Today pray with me:

Lord, help me to hold on to nothing but You today. You are all I need. Amen.

January 10

Read: Genesis 23:1–24:51; Matthew 8:1–7; Psalm 9:13–20; Proverbs 3:1–6

God's Word Brings Blessing
Proverbs 3:1–6

The story is told of a man who bought a ticket for a cruise to the Caribbean. He climbed on board and looked forward to the four-day cruise. He had carefully packed for the trip and had included all the food he would need for each meal during the cruise.

After the second night of the cruise it was brought to the captain's attention that one of the passengers had not shown up for even one meal during the trip. The captain looked into the situation and went to visit the cabin of this passenger. He knocked on the door, and a young man opened the door. The captain asked, "Sir, why have you not shown up for any of the meals on this ship?"

The man looked surprised and replied, "Captain, I simply cannot afford to pay for the meals, so I brought my own food."

The captain responded, "Sir, your meals are included in the price of the ticket."

Embarrassed, the passenger said, "Sir, no one explained this to me." The conversation ended with the captain's invitation to sit with him at his table that evening.

We have God's invitation daily to dine at the table He has set before us. At this table is food that will add long life, length of days and peace. The food God offers us is His Word. Have you been missing some meals lately because you were ignorant of the fact that God's table is laden with food that lasts eternally? None of us can afford to miss a meal that gives us all we need for our daily sustenance.

Lord, I want to dine with You today. The dishes You have prepared for me today far surpass anything I could cook up myself. Take over the kitchen of my heart, and I will wait expectantly for the delights You have prepared for me to eat today.

READ: Genesis 24:52–26:16; Matthew 8:18–34; Psalm 10:1–15; Proverbs 3:7–8

Being Led by the Holy Spirit
Genesis 24:52–26:16

This Genesis passage gives a beautiful picture of how the Holy Spirit seeks us, chooses us to be the bride of Christ and leads us. The servant who sought a bride for Isaac is a type of the Holy Spirit. The servant was given the assignment to find a bride for Isaac. He found Rebekah, but before he could take Rebekah to Isaac he had to have her permission. When the servant knew Rebekah was the chosen one for Isaac, he wasted no time. He presented gifts of gold, jewels and raiment to Rebekah. Then he asked Rebekah's parents for her to go with him to marry Isaac. Rebekah's parents were hesitant and asked if Rebekah could remain with them at least ten days. The servant shared how the Lord had prospered him in his way, and now he was ready to take Rebekah home with him to meet Isaac. The parents then said they would ask Rebekah. Rebekah's reply was immediate and positive. "And they called Rebekah, and said unto her, Wilt thou go with this man? And she said, I will go" (Gen. 24:58, KJV).

The Holy Spirit seeks and chooses us. His first act toward us is to give us gifts. Remember the account in Acts when the 120 gathered together, and they received the gift of speaking in tongues and the sevenfold anointing (the spirit of wisdom and understanding, might and counsel, the fear of the Lord and knowledge and the spirit of the Lord). Those gathered together on that great day when the church (the bride of Christ) was birthed received gifts and were empowered by the Holy Spirit to be witnesses in this world. They could have chosen to remain within closed doors and use and exercise these gifts among themselves. The whole purpose of this empowering, however, was to equip those early disciples for ministry and to be witnesses. They not only received the gifts, buy they also were willing to go into all the world to share the gospel and to make disciples of many. Notice in this story Rebekah's immediate and quick response of "yes" to the invitation of the servant, even though her parents wished she could stay with them for a period of time. She also took all of her damsels and servants with her.

What would have happened if Rebekah had decided to wait the ten days her parents desired? She still would have been Isaac's bride, but she, by her own choice, would have delayed the marriage. We have been chosen to be the bride of Christ. We have been given gifts by the Holy Spirit. Now the Father asks us this question, "Will you go with this servant (the Holy Spirit)? Will you let the Holy Spirit lead you?" We have a choice. We can delay that wedding day by refusing to be led by the Holy Spirit, or we can hasten the day of that wedding by our obedient readiness to be led by the Holy Spirit. Could it be that the Lord has not come for His bride yet because there are those who are not following the commission found in Matthew 28:19–20. "Go ye therefore, and teach all nations, baptizing them in the name of the Father, and of the Son, and of the Holy Ghost: teaching them to observe all things whatsoever I have commanded you..." (KJV).

READ: *Genesis 26:17–27:46; Matthew 9:1–17; Psalm 10:16–18; Proverbs 3:9–10*

Listening to the Heart
Matthew 9:1–17

Jesus' response to the scribes who accused Him in their hearts of blasphemy was, "And Jesus knowing their thoughts said, Wherefore think ye evil in your hearts? For whether is easier, to say, Thy sins be forgiven thee; or to say, Arise, and walk? But that ye may know that the Son of man hath power on earth to forgive sins, (then saith he to the sick of the palsy,) Arise, take up thy bed, and go unto thine house" (Matt. 9:4–6, KJV).

Our hearts speak louder to Jesus than our words. The scribes never said audibly, "You are a blasphemer," but they said it within themselves, and Jesus heard their thoughts. The Bible says, "As he [a man] thinks in his heart, so is he" (Prov. 23:7).

God knows the thoughts of your heart. Does this scare you? This would only scare you if you are holding on to evil thoughts in your heart. All through our lives our enemy, Satan, will bombard our minds with temptations, but we have the power to reject these thoughts. Satan will give us mental images also that will stir lusts in our hearts, but we have the choice to pull the shade down within us and say, "No, I will not look at that."

When these thoughts are allowed to remain in our minds for a length of time, they can become longings. The lust of the eye is greedy longings in our minds like fantasies and vain imaginations. Looking at pornographic material can cause greedy longings in our minds. Even if we never see such material with our natural eyes, Satan has the power to give such images to our minds.

God destroyed the whole earth except for one family of eight because of the wicked imaginations in the hearts of men. Are these wicked imaginations in our heart today? Satan will send these imaginations, but the moment the image comes, we have to shine the light of Jesus upon that dark image. How do we do this? We say aloud, "I will worship the Lord my God, and Him only will I serve." This is the sword of the Spirit to wield as a mighty weapon to dispel the wicked images Satan sends you. All worship is based upon imaginations.

Which God will you worship today—false gods or the one true God? Jesus is the divine expressed image of the invisible God. We need to keep His face ever before us, and then our imaginations will be touched with His purity. If the eyes of our minds (our imaginations) are single upon Jesus, then our whole bodies will be filled with light.

Father, give me holy imaginations today. Cleanse my mind and give me Your thoughts.

READ: Genesis 28:28:1–29:35; Matthew 9:18–38; Psalm 11:1–7; Proverbs 3:11–12

Jacob's Ladder
Genesis 28:28:1–29:35

As a child I remember singing, "We are climbing Jacob's ladder." In the song was the phrase, "Every rung goes higher, higher." Jacob experienced a divine connection between heaven and earth. In his dream he saw a ladder between heaven and earth, and he saw angels ascending and descending this ladder. The Lord stood above the ladder, and He spoke to Jacob and told him how the families of the earth would be blessed through his seed. He promised Jacob that He would keep him wherever he went, and that the time would come when He would bring him again to the land He promised Abraham, his great grandfather. When Jacob woke up, he said "Surely the Lord is in this place."

The good news is that if we never dream a dream as Jacob did, we can still experience daily the same divine connection between heaven and earth. We may not see angels ascending and descending a ladder from heaven, but we can daily say, "Surely God is in this place."

Where does God dwell? I remember asking my mother that question as she gave me a spot bath one Saturday evening in preparation for Sunday church the next day. "Mommy, where does Jesus live?" My mother wisely answered, "Jesus lives in heaven, and He also lives in your heart." Later as an adult I understood completely how correct her answer was. I now know that Jesus is seated on the right hand of God the Father. He has been raised from the dead, and He is in a glorified body, one that has the ability to defy matter. This would have been too much for a girl of seven to understand, but I could understand that He is in heaven and also in my heart. As a young child I invited Jesus to come into my heart, and He did. My picture of Him in my heart was what a child would have. I pictured Jesus sitting at a desk, and there was a list He was checking. It had two columns that said "Good and Bad." Above the columns was my name, "Linda." He was checking the list twice to see if I had been naughty or nice that day. My view of Jesus at that time was a "Santa Clause image." Unfortunately many adults still have this Santa Clause image of God—He blesses us when we are good and curses us when we are bad. Thank God I now understand more about God than I did as a child.

I don't have to climb a ladder of success now to reach heaven. I don't have to prove to God my love for Him by what I do or don't do. He loves me just as I am. He is for me, not against me, and He is not checking up on me to see if I am misbehaving. When Jesus died on the cross for my sins, and when I received this as true and asked forgiveness for my sins, there was no separation between me and my heavenly Father. The Scriptures say, "Behold, I stand at the door and knock. If anyone hears My voice and opens the door, I will come in to him and will dine with him, and he with Me" (Rev. 3:20).

Is heaven in your heart today? I trust that you will know for sure that God lives in the home of your heart.

How to Be Happy
Proverbs 3:13–15

Everyone in this life is searching for happiness. The word *happy* in Hebrew is the same word for "blessed." We all want blessings in our lives, and yet so many fail to live a happy, blessed life. This passage in Proverbs gives the secret to a continual life of happiness or blessedness. "Happy is the man who finds wisdom, and the man who gains understanding"(Prov. 3:13).

All the treasures of wisdom are hidden in Jesus Christ. Unless a man comes into this knowledge of Jesus Christ, he will always lack the wisdom that brings happiness. Chances are also he will seek happiness in the wrong places.

There are two kinds of wisdom—the wisdom of this world, which comes from below, and the wisdom of God, which comes from above. James tells us about these two kinds of wisdom: "Who is a wise man and endued with knowledge among you? Let him show out of a good conversation his works with meekness of wisdom. But if ye have bitter envying and strife in your hearts, glory not, and lie not against the truth. This wisdom descendeth not from above, but is earthly, sensual, devilish. For where envying and strife is, there is confusion and every evil work. But the wisdom that is from above is first pure, then peaceable, gentle, and easy to be entreated, full of mercy and good fruits, without partiality, and without hypocrisy" (James 3:13, KJV).

Which wisdom will you choose to walk in today? If you choose the wisdom from above, you will have a happy, blessed day no matter what circumstances you encounter.

Lord, You are all wisdom, and I will grow in heavenly wisdom only as I stay close to You, talk with You and listen to Your Word. You are the way that leads me to all the hidden treasures of wisdom. Your Word is the road map that instructs me as I follow this way. Help me as I go searching for hidden treasures today in Your Word, and help me to operate in heavenly wisdom today in all of my relationships with others. Thank You. Amen.

The Benefits of Wisdom
Proverbs 3:16–18

The benefits of wisdom are not just happiness. This passage lists some of the benefits we will experience if we will live our lives in the wisdom from above.

~ We will have length of days.
~ We will have honor.
~ We will have wealth.
~ We will experience pleasant lives.
~ We will have peace.

The above is a list of what all men desire. They want to live long lives, have honor and wealth. They want to experience peace and live pleasant lives. The man who seeks the wisdom from above will experience these benefits.

A man of wisdom will learn to be content or happy in whatever state he finds himself. Happiness is not based on our circumstances. Happiness is based upon our character. If our character grows daily to be more like the character of Jesus Christ, we will be blessed every day of our lives.

Does this mean we have no problems if we live in the wisdom from above, which is peaceable and pure, full of good fruits and without partiality and hypocrisy? Wisdom does not protect us from troubles, because Jesus is all wisdom and He experienced many troubles while on earth. He also said, "In the world you will have tribulation; but be of good cheer, I have overcome the world" (John 16:33). Operating in the wisdom from above guarantees us that we will come through each trial, each testing, each temptation we face victorious, but only if we depend upon Jesus through troubled times. The moment we try to take control of troubled times without consulting and inquiring of the Lord who is all wisdom, we will experience misery instead of joy in the midst of troubled times. We have no idea what is facing us this day, but God already knows. Take time to ask Him for the wisdom from above to face every problem, person and circumstance you may encounter today.

Lord, help me to seek You today with all my heart. Help me to look to You today for wisdom in every problem, circumstance and relationship today. Thank You for overcoming the world so I can be of good cheer and not be overwhelmed by the troubles in this world. I desire to live in peace and contentedness today no matter what I face. You are my peace and joy. Amen.

READ: Genesis 32:13–34:31; Matthew 11:7–30; Psalm 14:1–7; Proverbs 3:19–20

Come Unto Me
Matthew 11:7–30

The invitation extended throughout the Word of God is "Come unto Me." We live in a world that is burdened and heavy-laden, a world where men have no rest for their souls. Men everywhere seek peace of mind and long to have joy in living. They run to drugs for pseudo peace and alcohol for temporary highs, but there is no lasting peace or joy apart from the Lord. Only the Shepherd and Bishop of our souls, Jesus Christ, can offer eternal peace and joy and right standing with God the Father. He gives us the invitation today, "Come to Me, and learn of Me meekness and lowliness of heart."

Daily we have the choice to accept His gracious invitation or to reject it. He alone can teach us meekness and lowliness of heart, but we must open the textbook, which is His Word. As we read His Word, He teaches us and transforms our restless souls into rest filled-souls—souls filled with His joy, His peace, His righteousness. How can we ever refuse to enter His classroom daily? Each day we attend class, we will learn more, and we will grow more like our great Teacher.

I have seen restless souls, and it is not a pleasant sight. Restless souls run from conference to conference, ever seeking to learn the truth and to gain knowledge. But they return from these conferences the same as they were before they went. Restless souls are not willing to spend time in the classroom. They are always looking for recess—the time in the day when they can feel something—some thrill or excitement in the game of life. These restless souls are lovers of pleasure more than lovers of God. They have never learned the truth that in the presence of the Lord is fullness of joy and pleasures forever more.

So many of us are guilty from time to time of seeking the feeling instead of the Person. Every day I take time to be with the lover of my soul, Jesus, who is my spiritual husband. If I spend quality time with Him, my soul is always touched. I may not have a thrill, but knowing His nearness is enough for me. I listen intently as He teaches me meekness and lowliness of heart, and I make sure I do not miss one of His classes. Every day I have the privilege of sitting at the feet of the greatest lecturer and teacher in the whole world—Jesus Christ.

Are you going to attend class every day this week?

Thank You, Lord Jesus, for teaching me meekness and lowliness of heart. If I learn the lessons You teach, I will pass every lab test I encounter in this life. Help me to be attentive today to Your words, and don't let my mind wander to recess time.

January 17

The Lord Shall Be Your Confidence
Proverbs 3:21–26

So often in life we are found in situations where we feel a lack of confidence. It may be the first day on a new job, the big interview for a job or simply a test we're taking in school. It is at these times we rely on this verse in Proverbs 3:26: "For the LORD shall be your confidence."

When we place our confidence in the Lord rather than ourselves, we are saying to ourselves, "I can't, but He can." Where we are weak, He is strong. I have found that it is in my weakest moment that the Lord is able to be my strength. Often when I place confidence in myself or my own abilities, I fall on my face and blow it. My focus is on my own ability instead of His ability. One of the definitions of *responsibility* is responding to His ability within us. We are totally dependent upon God. In fact, the whole world is totally dependent upon God. However, many do not realize this. They do not realize that the whole world holds together by God's Word, and they could not take another breath without God giving it to them.

Pride will always cause a fall in our lives. Paul wrote, "Let him who thinks he stands take heed lest he fall" (1 Cor. 10:12). The moment we begin to stand in any situation in our own strength, we are standing in pride. Humility is recognizing our inability and applauding His ability through us. It is seeing ourselves as God sees us. He sees us as worthy of the death of His Son and created in His image. These facts, however, should not instill pride in us, but rather a deep sense of awe of God's greatness and gratefulness to Him for choosing us. The treasure of His glory is in our earthen vessels so that He can show His excellency through us.

One of the most liberating scriptures in the Bible is Jesus' words, "Without Me you can do nothing" (John 15:5). When we recognize our total dependence upon God and that it is God who works within us both to will and to do of His good pleasure, we are set free from our struggle to get everything just right in this life. Perfectionism is a prison in which many find themselves locked, and the only key to freedom is Jesus Christ, the perfect One. You've heard many say, "Well, nobody is perfect." There is Somebody who is perfect, and He wants to perfect everything in our lives. We may blow it when we trust in ourselves more than we trust in God in certain situations, but the good news is that Jesus Christ is not only perfect, but He is the perfect redeemer. He is able to take our mess-ups and redeem them if we will turn to Him and ask Him to forgive our pride and arrogance and release what we have messed up to Him.

The apostle Paul had a great battle with pride because he was so skilled in so many areas. He speaks of this in his letters to the churches often when he makes the statement, "I could glory, but I will not." Then he tells us he has learned to glory in his infirmities. He was saying he was thankful for all of his weak areas because he had to rely on Jesus' strength.

Today is a day of great opportunity for the Lord to show Himself strong on our behalf. The only thing that would hinder this is our pride.

Idle Word Room
Matthew 12:22–45

I have a friend who said she would probably spend the first 10,000 years in heaven in the "idle word room." It would take that long for the Lord to judge all of her idle words. Jesus said in Matthew 12:35–37, "A good man out of the good treasure of the heart brings forth good things, and an evil man out of the evil treasure brings forth evil things. But I say to you that for every idle word men may speak, they will give account of it in the day of judgment. For by your words you will be justified, and by your words you will be condemned."

Thank God there is no "idle word room" in heaven, but this passage should be a wake-up call to us all. We need to be careful about what we speak aloud. It is important to remember that Satan cannot read our minds, but he can send us many evil thoughts. Our responsibility is to take those thoughts captive to Jesus Christ before we speak them aloud. I would not be married today if I spoke aloud every thought the enemy gave me about my husband. Satan is the accuser of the brethren, and his language is always critical, judgmental and negative.

I recall one night soaking in the bathtub after a long day of hard work in the home cleaning and watching after our three sons. Some of the thoughts running through my mind were so negative. I can still remember thinking, *Nobody cares in this household; nobody helps me. I'm just a slave. My husband never helps around the house.* Suddenly while I was drowning in this pool of negative words in my mind, I heard the Lord speak to my spirit. He said, "Don't let the enemy take advantage of you." Then I realized Satan wanted me to speak all those thoughts aloud to my husband. I resisted Satan then and said aloud to him, "If you think I'm going to repeat the thoughts you just gave me to my husband, you have another think coming. I release these thoughts right now to the Lord Jesus Christ, and I refuse to allow these thoughts to ever be spoken as words out of my mouth." The thoughts stopped immediately.

Our mouth can be compared to a gun. A Wall Street article compares the mouth to a gun. It said, "Sometimes you may blurt out something you really don't mean. But words once spoken, like bullets once fired, cannot be recalled, and they can wound."

Don't blast anyone today by pulling the trigger of your tongue. In a multitude of words is sin.

READ: Genesis 39:1–41:16; Matthew 12:46–13:23; Psalm 17:1–15; Proverbs 3:33–35

Heavenly Rain
Proverbs 3:33–35

Again in our readings for the month of January we see the wicked person's life compared to the life of a just person (one who has been justified by God). God's Word tells us that the rain falls on the just and the unjust. I have always interpreted that to mean troubles fall upon the just and the unjust. However, I see in the Bible where rain is usually a symbol of the blessings of God. When the people of a land are pleasing God, He sends the early and latter rains upon the land. When they are disobedient, He withholds the rain. I believe God is always sending showers of blessings upon the earth. The wicked, however, have the umbrella of pride over them, and they never receive the blessings. Today's passage from Proverbs confirms this.

The curse of the Lord is on the house of the wicked. The Book of James tells us that God resists the proud, but gives grace to the humble. The wicked in their pride cause a curse to come upon themselves. They raise the umbrella of pride daily and block the refreshing rain of the Holy Spirit and God's blessings upon them. God longs for the wicked to humble themselves and turn toward Him so His blessings will come to them unhindered, but instead, the wicked seek to be blessed by the world and its system rather than by God. The blessings the world offers may appear to be showers that refresh, but in reality these showers are short-lived. These worldly showers never satiate the thirsty land of the soul as God's blessings do, and soon the land of the soul of the wicked is thirsty again. The wicked never see God's blessings in their lives because they believe they obtain blessings through their own efforts. "God helps those who help themselves" is their motto. The truth is that God helps those who know they cannot help themselves. He is looking to bless the contrite, humble-hearted man who is totally dependent upon Him.

The blessings of the Lord flow naturally unhindered to those of a contrite, humble and grateful heart. Grace abounds to the grateful. The wicked never are grateful and therefore never receive the grace God wants to deliver to them. We used to sing a song called "Showers of Blessings." The theme of the song is, "Count your blessings, name them one by one, and then you will see what the Lord has done." One of my joys is keeping a record of what the Lord does daily in my life. He never fails to surprise me. Each day I live is always a good day. I can always find something to thank God for because He is so faithful. I am humbled when I think that God, the Creator of the universe, is looking each day for new, wonderful ways to bless me. Not only are grace and blessings flowing daily from His throne room, but mercy is also a continual soaking shower. Mercy drops are flowing toward you today, and God wants to perfect everything that is a concern to you.

Today let His blessings, grace and mercy flow freely upon us and satiate our souls. Refuse to block the flow of His refreshing, supernatural rain by forgetting to be grateful to Him. The moment we feel we have the day in our hands and under our control, we have opened the umbrella of pride, and we will not experience the soaking of our souls with heavenly rain.

READ: Genesis 41:17–42:17; Matthew 13:24–46; Psalm 18:1–15; Proverbs 4:1–6

The Pearl
Matthew 13:24–46

Jesus compared the kingdom of heaven to a merchant man who sought good pearls. When he found one of a great price, he sold all that he had and bought it. In this passage Jesus shared four parables about the kingdom of heaven. The last parable is about the pearl. He does not explain this parable, so the hearer or reader must interpret it himself.

The pearl of great price I believe is the person who needs salvation. Recently I heard a speaker share an even deeper interpretation of this parable. Just before Jesus gave the parable about the pearl, He shared the parable about a man finding a treasure hidden in a field and how he sold everything he had to buy the whole field so he could possess the treasure. The speaker explained that the Jews understood the parable about the treasure because they knew they were God's treasure. Over and over again God speaks of Israel as His treasure. They, however, did not appreciate the parable about the pearl. Pearls to the Jew are unclean because they come from oysters. You will never see an orthodox Jewish lady wearing pearls. The pearl in this parable represents the Gentiles, who are considered unclean by the Jewish people. Jesus was saying, "He came to earth and purchased the world by His shed blood in order to save all those who would believe in Him, and this includes both Jew and Gentile (the whole family of God). 'For God so loved the world, that he gave his only begotten Son, that whosoever believeth in him should not perish, but have everlasting life' (John 3:16, KJV)."

The price God gave to purchase both the treasure (the Jewish believers) and the pearl (the Gentile believers) was His own Son, who died and shed His blood to forgive and cleanse us from all unrighteousness. While we were yet sinners, Christ died for us. How could the man know about the hidden treasure and about the pearl that was hidden inside an oyster shell? The man had to have supernatural x-ray eyes to see these priceless treasures. God is the man in the parable, and He has x-ray eyes. He humbles Himself to look at the hearts of men, and He sees the hearts that will receive Him even when we are still sinners. The hearts of both Jews and Gentiles who will believe in His Son are hidden treasures and costly pearls.

Do you understand that you have been bought with a great price? That great price was the blood of Jesus. Do not ever feel worthless, because God sees you as worth the death of His only Son. He loves you. Receive the revelation and fullness of His great love today.

READ: Genesis 42:18–43:34; Matthew 13:47–14:13; Psalm 18:16–34; Proverbs 4:7–10

The Release of Children
Genesis 42:18–43:34

Jacob's first response to his sons' appeals to send Benjamin to Egypt as Joseph required was a definite no. He was not about to lose another son as he thought he had lost Joseph. Later in the passage we see Jacob's heart turn. Famine was once again a plague on the land where Jacob lived, and he knew the only way he could save his family was to meet the demands of the Egyptian leader to send Benjamin back with his brothers. He was willing to take the risk of never seeing Benjamin again if that was the only way he could save the rest of the family. Jacob says, "And God Almighty give you mercy before the man, that he may send away your other brother, and Benjamin. If I be bereaved of my children, I am bereaved" (Gen. 43:14, KJV).

One of the hardest things a parent can face is the loss of a child. Jacob thought Joseph was dead, and now he faced the possibility of losing two more of his children—Benjamin and Simeon.

How can parents come to a place of releasing their children to the Lord? Only the Lord can work this in the hearts of parents as He did in my heart.

When my three sons were two, six and nine, I was faced with the tormenting fear that I would die young and leave my children. For two weeks this thought caused me to have sleepless nights. Finally one morning I asked the Lord, "Lord, where is this thought coming from? Is it from You, the devil or me?"

His response to this question was as follows: "So what if you did die young and leave your children without you? Do you believe I could take care of them as well as you, and I could fulfill My plans for their lives without your being on the scene?"

I was shocked by this answer I heard with my spiritual ears. Then I realized I truly had not released my children to the Lord. I still was possessive of them, and I needed to ask the Lord to forgive me for my lack of trust in Him. I prayed, "Lord, forgive me for not trusting You with my children. They are not my children. They are Your children, and You lent them to me. I give up my control and possession of them, and I trust You to keep them in Your hands always even if I leave this earth before they do."

On that day I felt as if I died, and I did. Yes, I died to the possession of my children, and now I am still alive and have lived to see all three sons married to wonderful wives. I am also the grandmother of blessings who have been lent by the Lord. The tormenting whisper I heard that said, "You're going to die young," was the devil because it struck fear in my heart. God, however, used what Satan meant for evil for good. When I totally surrendered my children, Satan lost. What we give to God, Satan will never ultimately possess.

READ: Genesis 44:1–45:28; Matthew 14:14–36; Psalm 18:35–50; Proverbs 4:11–13

Sure Footing
Psalm 18:35–50

We have everything going for us if we choose to go the way of the Lord. He leads us in paths of righteousness for His name's sake. He goes before us to lead the way, but remember, His face is turned toward us, and He never turns His back on us. God turned His back to Jesus on the cross because He could not look upon the sins of the world that were laid upon Jesus, the Lamb slain for our sin. Since the cross, however, we have God's promise as spoken by Jesus, "I will never leave you nor forsake you." Thank God for the cross that bridged the gap between God the Father and us, and made the way for us to enter His throne room daily and find grace in time of need. Jesus is now seated at the right hand of God the Father, and He daily is making intercession for you. He is watching your every move and is there to catch you if you begin to fall. Your part is to keep looking into the face of Jesus. If you daily seek His face, you will keep walking forward in Him and you will not backslide.

The image of the face of Jesus was ever before David. He shares in this psalm, "You have given me the shield of your salvation, and your right hand holds me up, and your gentleness has made me great."

Then David speaks of how the Lord has enlarged his steps so his feet would not slip. What a joy to know that as you walk in the ways of the Lord, He daily is enlarging your steps. One day as I was walking with my husband on our daily walk I fell. I was talking with him, and suddenly my feet slipped under me. I found myself sprawled on the asphalt road. I slipped on an acorn that caused me to fall forward. If my husband and I had been holding hands, I think my fall could have been prevented. Daily Satan will put acorns in your path to trip you up, but Jesus' right hand is holding you up. What security to know Jesus has His face turned toward you and His right hand is pulling you forward. If you begin to stumble, you will fall right into His arms.

I trust you will today know that security in your walk with Jesus. He is enlarging your steps and placing you on solid ground today. Remember, your part is to keep looking into His face and to keep holding His hand.

> Lord, I take Your hand outstretched to me today. I look into Your face and see Your twinkling eyes coaxing me to keep moving forward toward you. I know You will catch me if Satan tries to trip me up. Thank You for Your everlasting arms of love.

January 23

Tradition
Matthew 15:1–28

Remember the song from *Fiddler on the Roof* called "Tradition"? We all have our traditions. I recall one Christmas hosting my older sister and her family from Seattle. She and her family have their special Christmas traditions, and so does our family. We had a time trying to fit in both family traditions on Christmas day. Traditions are not bad, but they can become a hindrance to God's Word. In fact, if we hold to our religious traditions more than we hold to God's Word, we can make the Word of God have no effect in our lives.

In our church we have heard some say, "But we cannot change this part of the service because we have always done it this way." God is always doing something new. He has not stopped creating. Traditions will often block the new fresh move of the Holy Spirit. It is mind-boggling to realize that the Word of God, which is more powerful than a two-edged sword, can be blocked by tradition.

We are exhorted in the Bible to take up the shield of faith daily as a part of our full armor. Faith mixed with the Word daily will have a lasting effect upon our lives. However, if we choose to take up the shield of tradition rather than the shield of faith, the Word of God will be blocked from touching us and changing us. The Pharisees and Sadducees in Jesus' day were avid readers of the Law. Jesus said they searched the Scriptures but would not come to Him. The Pharisees and Sadducees were looking for the answers in the Scriptures, but they had no idea the answer to all of their questions was standing right in front of them. Jesus is all wisdom and all knowledge, and His Holy Spirit is the great teacher. Tradition is based upon the past. Faith, however, can only operate in the present. The change in our hearts and minds as we read and hear the Word will only come when faith is exercised. Faith and tradition can never mix together. They are like oil and water.

Is there something in the past you are holding on to? Is there a way that you always have your quiet time in the morning, and it hasn't changed for years? Maybe the traditional way of spending time with the Lord needs to be shaken so you can exercise faith as you read God's Word.

Be open to new fresh ways of spending time with the Lord. He wants to do a new thing in your life. Don't block it by continuing to do the same old, same old. By the way, I am preaching to myself.

Lord, help me to get out of the rut. I heard once that a rut is a grave with both ends open. Help me to climb out of routine and tradition and wait for the fresh wind You have for me by Your Holy Spirit. If I stay in the rut, I will never feel the sometimes powerful and sometimes gentle wind of Your Holy Spirit. Holy Spirit, breathe a refreshing breeze upon me today. In Jesus' name I pray.

January 24

READ: Genesis 48:1–49:33; Matthew 15:29–16:12; Psalm 20:1–9; Proverbs 4:20–27

Our Heritage
Genesis 48:1–49:33

Just recently I had the joy of discovering the genealogy of my family on the side of my maternal grandfather. I had the history of my father back to the 1600s, but I had no knowledge of the ancestry of my mother. Some people are really into their heritage, and I'm thankful for people who keep records and research genealogies, because it is rewarding to know our heritage.

In this passage in Genesis we learn our common heritage as Gentiles. It is easy to find the heritage of the Jewish people, which traces back to Abraham, but what about the Gentiles? We can trace our family line as Gentiles back to Joseph. Joseph had two sons by his Egyptian wife. Their names were Manasseh and Ephraim. Even though Joseph was Jewish, his children were considered Gentile because they had a mother who was not Jewish.

As we read this passage, we see that Ephraim, the second born, received the blessing that always was awarded to the first-born son. When Jacob laid his hands on the two sons of Joseph to bless them, his right hand crossed over his left hand and rested upon the head of Ephraim. The blessing of the first born always was transferred by using the right hand. Joseph tried to correct his father, but Jacob said he knew what he was doing. He said the younger would be greater than the older and his seed would become a multitude of nations. The word *Gentile* in Hebrew is *goy*, which means "nations."

Our forefather as Gentiles was Ephraim, and in Ezekiel 37:15–20, we see God's plan to join in the last days the two families of God (Jew and Gentile) into one. God instructs Ezekiel to write on one stick "Ephraim" and on the other stick "Judah." Then God tells Ezekiel to take the two sticks and join them together as one. Few understand this glorious plan of God, but Paul speaks of this plan clearly in Romans 9–11.

As Gentiles, we not only know our heritage, but we also know our future. God is forming one glorious church made of Jewish and Gentile believers in the Messiah Jesus Christ. God eagerly awaits that great day when all of His family will be gathered unto His Son Jesus. As a mother it gives me such pleasure to be with all three of my sons and their wives and children at one time.

Just imagine the joy our heavenly Father will have when we will be joined with our Jewish brethren and all feast at His table together. We are seeing the beginning of this in our day, which tells us the Lord is coming soon.

Thank You, Father, for your great plans for a glorious family reunion. Help me to share this good news with my Jewish brothers and sisters who do not yet know Your great plan. Amen.

January 25

READ: Genesis 50:1–Exodus 2:10; Matthew 16:13–17:9; Psalm 21:1–13; Proverbs 5:1–6

God Meant It for Good
Genesis 50:1–Exodus 2:10

Throughout our lives circumstances and situations occur that we just do not understand. For example, I have been praying this week for two dear saints of the Lord who have been stricken with cancer. They both love the Lord with all of their hearts, and yet they are facing a severe test of faith. Why would God allow such a thing to occur? I often see how we blame God for our troubles, but we have to remember the "trouble maker" is not God. The "trouble maker" is Satan, and his plan is to destroy us. God's plan is to give us life and give it to us more abundantly. My husband had two heart attacks, and during that time, he held on to the scripture in Jeremiah 29:11: "For I know the thoughts that I think toward you, saith the LORD, thoughts of peace, and not of evil, to give you an expected end" (KJV).

Joseph did not have this verse of Scripture to hold on to when he went through many severe testings of his faith. He was almost murdered by his brothers, sold into slavery, accused falsely and imprisoned, yet Joseph never became bitter. He only became better. In this passage we see how afraid his brothers are because now their father was dead and they expected Joseph to seek retribution for their sin against him. After all, they were the ones who sold him into slavery and started his cycle of suffering. Some of the most amazing words in the Bible are recorded as Joseph talks with his brothers: "And Joseph said unto them, Fear not: for am I in the place of God? But as for you, ye thought evil against me; but God meant it unto good, to bring to pass, as it is this day, to save much people alive. Now therefore fear ye not: I will nourish you, and your little ones. And he comforted them, and spake kindly unto them" (Gen. 50:19–21, KJV).

Joseph knew his place, and he knew God's place. It was not his place to bring retribution upon his brothers. He released all judgment of them to God. He forgave them, and he even encouraged them and promised to nourish and take care of them the rest of their lives. Joseph understood the sovereignty of God. He knew as long as he was faithful to God and loved God with all of his heart, God would ultimately work everything for good in his life. Joseph knew this in his spirit, but we have an advantage over Joseph. This revelation that God works everything for the good for those who love Him and are called according to His purpose is clearly written by Paul to us in Romans 8:28. If we love God with all of our hearts and know we are walking in the calling of God, we can have the deep assurance that whatever trial we face in this life, God's ultimate plan is to work it for good in our lives.

READ: Exodus 2:11–22; Matthew 17:10–27; Psalm 22:1–18; Proverbs 5:7–14

Why Have You Forsaken Me?
Psalm 22:1–18

Some of the most traumatic feelings a person can experience is being abandoned. Abandonment rocks our emotions with feelings of insecurity, fear, doubt, loneliness, failure, rejection, grief, sorrow and unworthiness, just to name a few. I've never experienced abandonment, but I know people who have. I know a fifty-year-old man who is still being healed emotionally of the abandonment he experienced as a young boy. Both his mother and father were alcoholics, and they would leave their two young boys on the beach alone at night while they partied at the bars. Later this man's father killed his mother. Imagine the trauma of abandonment he felt.

Can God heal such deep emotional consequences of abandonment? The good news is that Jesus Christ on the cross provided the healing needed for abandonment. The psalm today is a prophetic psalm that David received in the spirit. It describes in detail the death of Jesus and even relates how His garments were parted and had lots cast for them after He gave His spirit into the hands of God the Father. On the cross, Jesus quotes the first verse of this psalm, "My God, My God, why have You forsaken Me?" The reason God turned His back on Jesus and separated Himself for a moment from Him was because God has purer eyes than to behold evil. In that moment in time when all of our sins were laid upon Jesus, He who knew no sin became sin for us so that we could be made the righteousness of God in Him. This act is more than our human minds can comprehend. Jesus was abandoned by the Father for all those who have experienced abandonment in their lives so that they can be accepted by the Father and never experience the feelings of abandonment again.

The fifty-year-old man who was abandoned can find healing for his soul. The first step he must take is to believe Jesus purchased this healing for him on the cross. The next step is to see himself crucified with Christ. Each pain of abandonment he experiences today is a deception from the enemy. The enemy wants this man to remain wounded, fearful and in self-hatred. This man is in a prison of deception that can only be penetrated by the truth. He will know the truth, and the truth will set him free. The key to his healing is to believe Jesus bore his abandonment on the cross and receive the acceptance and the love the Father has for him. Jesus gave a condition to receiving the truth that will set anyone free. He said, "If you abide in My word, you are My disciples indeed. And you shall know the truth, and the truth shall make you free" (John 8:31–32). Jesus speaks these words of truth to all who have experienced abandonment "Lo, I am with you always, even to the end of the age. Amen" (Matt. 20:20).

The Value of a Prayer Partner
Matthew 18:1–22

It has been my privilege over my fifty-plus years as a Christian to always have a prayer partner. There are so many advantages in having a prayer partner. This passage in Matthew gives two very important reasons for us to pray with others. Jesus tells us, "Again I say unto you, that if two of you shall agree on earth as touching any thing that they shall ask, it shall be done for them of my Father which is in heaven. For where two or three are gathered together in my name, there am I in the midst of them" (Matt. 18:19–20, KJV).

Whenever we pray in agreement with another person, God promises to answer our requests, and He promises to be in the midst of us as we pray with two or more people. There is great power in agreement. For years I had my own quiet time and Tom had his. We only prayed together when there was an emergency. One Sunday morning during communion, the Lord spoke this to my heart: "The days ahead are going to be difficult. If you do not pray in agreement with your husband, you will not be able to get through these days. I want you to pray daily together first for your nation and leaders, then pray for yourselves, your family, your church and others."

We had been married for twenty-five years when I received that exhortation from the Lord. We have seen miracles happen over and over again as we have agreed together in prayer about the things listed above. We have seen our son delivered from drugs, three beautiful daughter-in-laws who love the Lord with all their hearts and who simply adore their husbands, deliverance from serious injury in a car accident, healing of a heart problem, just to name a few. If none of our requests had been answered, however, just experiencing the presence of the Lord as we prayed was gift enough to keep us praying in agreement together. God promised to hear every prayer request for others as we touched them through prayer and prayed for their concerns.

One of the greatest joys of my life has been to meet with several neighborhood ladies to pray every Monday night. We have been meeting for more than seventeen years and have seen so many answers to prayers for our families, for one another and others. I look forward to going to church on Wednesday nights when our whole church meets to pray in agreement for those things that concern us. If the prayer of one righteous man avails much, just think about what the prayers of two or more righteous people will accomplish.

Unforgiveness—a Luxury No One Can Afford
Matthew 18:23–19:12

In this passage in Matthew, Jesus tells the story of the servant who had been forgiven all his debt by his master, but this servant was unwilling to forgive another the debt he was owed. The conclusion to this story is the following statement: "And his lord was wroth, and delivered him to the tormentors, till he should pay all that was due unto him. So likewise shall my heavenly Father do also unto ye, if you from ye hearts forgive not every one his brother their trespasses" (Matt. 18:34–35, KJV).

Unforgiveness is a luxury none of us can afford. If we are not willing to forgive our brother, then God will allow us to be tormented. I have seen people who are not willing to forgive; even their countenance reflects torment. Unforgiving people run the risk of having both physical and emotional torment.

Corrie ten Boom was imprisoned in a concentration camp during World War II because her family helped hide Jewish people from the Nazis. Corrie was the only one who survived the imprisonment, and after the war she traveled to Germany and spoke at many churches to share a message of forgiveness and reconciliation. On one of these occasions she had to live out all she spoke about in her messages. After a night of sharing, a German came up to her and asked her forgiveness. As she looked into his face she was shocked as she recalled he was one of the German guards who severely persecuted her family. He reached his hand out toward her to receive her forgiveness, and she froze. She silently prayed, "Lord, I cannot forgive this man." Then she heard the Lord instruct her, "Reach out your hand in faith to him, and I will do the rest." Reluctantly, but by faith, she reached out her hand to the former guard, and suddenly a rush of compassion filled her for this man, and she was able to forgive him from her heart. Her heart was changed in an instant because she was willing to act in faith, and then forgiveness followed.

Forgiveness is not an emotion. Forgiveness is an act of our will. All God requires from us is our willingness to act in faith to forgive, and He supplies the supernatural gift of forgiveness.

Is there someone you have been unwilling to forgive? Reach out in faith and allow the Lord to forgive this person through you. I am convinced that total forgiveness is a supernatural gift of God, but He can only grant this gift if we are willing to forgive in faith. He will do the rest.

READ: Exodus 8:1–9:35; Matthew 19:13–30; Psalm 24:1–10; Proverbs 6:1–5

Lift Up Your Head and Hearts
Psalm 24:1–10

This psalm has special meaning to me because it is one of the psalms I memorized when I was in grammar school. The first thing we did each morning in school was pray the Lord's Prayer together, read a psalm and work on memorizing it, pledge allegiance to the flag and sing the national anthem. Can you imagine the stir this would cause in public schools today if this was done? It is illogical that God and country have been removed from our children's education when education has its roots in Christianity. The first schools that existed in our country were church schools. How I pray that one day we will be able to once again have freedom of speech that includes praying aloud in public schools. Until that time we as parents can teach our children the importance of honor for country and the value of the Word of God. We need to exhort our children to memorize Scriptures because the Word that is hidden in children's hearts at a young age will be with them always. I actually paid my boys to learn Proverbs. They were given $1 for every verse in Proverbs they memorized. When our Russian son took this on as a challenge, he just about broke me.

The verse I remember in this psalm is as follows: "Lift up your heads, O ye gates; even lift them up, ye everlasting doors; and the King of glory shall come in" (Ps. 24:9, KJV).

I have always wondered what that verse meant, but now I think the Holy Spirit has helped me to understand it. We are the temple of the living God, and there are gates and doors to that temple. We are a spirit, we have a soul, and we live in a body. The spirit is the holy of holies part of our tripart being. This is where we commune with God in the spirit. The soul has three parts—mind, will and emotions. The soul represents the inner court of the temple, and the body represents the outer court of the temple. The gates to our soul are our five senses—touch, taste, see, smell and hear. Everything that enters our souls enters through those gates. We have a responsibility to God to be careful about the material that enters these gates to our soul. This psalm also exhorts us not to lift up our souls unto vanity. Instead we are to lift our souls daily up to the Lord. This is what "Lift up your heads, O ye gates" means.

We are also to lift up or open up the doors to the Lord, and the promise is the King of glory will come in. The holy of holies in the physical temple was blocked from anyone entering except the high priest, and he was only allowed to enter once a year on the Day of Atonement. The mercy seat was behind a huge veil in the holy of holies. It was here at the mercy seat that the high priest communed with God and saw and felt His presence. We also have doors to our spirit (the holy of holies in our tripart being). Those doors are our hearts. We are to worship the Lord our God with all our minds and all our hearts. When we open the doors of our hearts to the Lord, we go boldly to the mercy seat and find grace in time of need.

January 30

READ: Exodus 10:1–12:13; Matthew 20:1–28; Psalm 25:1–11; Proverbs 6:6–11

Lifting Up Your Soul
Psalm 25:1–11

Yesterday's reading talked about lifting up our heads and hearts to the Lord. We discovered that the spirit of man represents the holy of holies in the temple of God. We are now the temple of the Holy Spirit. The soul (mind, will and emotions) of man represents the inner court of our temple. The body represents the outer court of the temple, and the gates to that temple are our five senses. When Jesus died on the cross and gave His spirit into the hands of the Father, the veil of the temple was rent in two. The mercy seat of God now became available to not only the high priest, but to all who would believe and receive Jesus as their Lord and Savior.

How can we lift up our souls daily to the Lord? We do this through prayer. Daily in prayer we can surrender our body, soul and spirit to the Lord. Every day in my early morning prayer time I do this. Later this year we will talk about how to surrender our spirit and body to the Lord, but today's devotion is about lifting up our souls to the Lord. The soul includes the mind, the emotions and the will. It has been my practice to pray the following prayer as I lift up my soul to the Lord:

Father, I lift up my mind to You today. I bind my mind to the mind of Christ. Help me to take every thought captive to You today and keep my mind from wandering. Help me to focus on You today. I ask You to give me wisdom, understanding and knowledge today as I read and hear Your Word. I ask You to give me divine imaginations and help me to refuse vain imaginations. Father, I lift up my emotions to You today. Help my emotions to be anchored in hope. Your Son Jesus Christ is my hope. Christ in me is my hope of glory. I dress myself in the garment of praise today so that all heaviness in my emotions has to flee. I receive the joy of the Lord, which is my strength. I receive the peace that only You can give, peace that passes my understanding. I will seek peace and pursue it today. Thank You for causing my emotions to be stable today. Father, I lift up my will today to You. I bind my will to the way You want me to walk. I commit my way to You so that You can bring Your will to pass in my life. I thank You that You work within me today, both to will and to do of Your good pleasure. Cause my will to always operate in Your love just as Jesus' will was controlled completely by You because He loved You. Let my words and deeds today reflect Your love.

Let this be a daily prayer in your life, and He will be glorified in your life today.

January 31

READ: Exodus 12:14-13:16; Matthew 20:29-21:22; Psalm 25:12-22; Proverbs 6:12-15

The Fear of the Lord
Psalm 25:12-22

There are many benefits that come to those who fear the Lord. This passage lists only a few of them. What does it mean to fear the Lord? The fear of the Lord is an awesome respect that causes us to honor and worship the Lord with all of our being. When we fear the Lord, we will desire to walk in His ways. The good news is that all those who fear the Lord will be taught the ways of God.

The children of Israel did not have the fear of the Lord in a perfect way when they exited Egypt. They did not understand the ways of the Lord. Only Moses seemed to have this understanding, and it was because he obeyed God. The children of Israel had to wander in the wilderness for forty years because of their disobedience to God. God offered the Promised Land to them and told them they could go in and possess it, but they doubted His word. They became fearful. One of the main manifestations in a person's life who does not fear the Lord is fear of many things (fear of the future, fear of the unknown, fear of failure and hurt, etc.). The children of Israel feared all of these things instead of fearing the Lord. Even after seeing the mighty works of the Lord, like the parting of the Red Sea, they still were fearful. They only knew God's mighty works, but they had no understanding of His mighty ways. God was able to teach Moses His mighty ways because Moses had an obedient heart.

This psalm tells us that the promise to those who fear the Lord is that their soul shall dwell at ease and their seed will inherit the earth. What a great benefit, but there is even more promised in this psalm. Those who fear the Lord will know the Lord's secrets, and His covenant will be revealed to them.

We live in a society now where the fear of the Lord is not taught. People have lost their awesome respect for God. Could it be many have no fear of the Lord because their hearts are not obedient? God gave instruction to us to have no other gods before Him and to love Him with all of our hearts and minds. We live in a land now where the majority are lovers of pleasure more than lovers of God. Thank God there is a remnant left who still fear the Lord. I pray you are a part of that remnant, and if you are, you can look forward to being taught of the Lord His ways.

When we know His ways, all fear leaves.

Lord, help me today to fear You with all my heart. I want to know Your ways, not just Your works in my life. When I come to know Your ways, I will not have to fear anything because I will be assured that You desire only for my good. I do not even have to fear what man would do to me, because I know You are my shield and my salvation. Teach me Your ways, O Lord, and help me to walk in Your truths. Unite my heart to fear Your name, and I will glorify You today and forever.

31

READ: Exodus 13:17–15:19; Matthew 21:23–46; Psalm 26:1–12; Proverbs 6:16–19

The Lord Shall Fight for You!
Exodus 13:17–15:19

One of my favorite expressions is, "The victory is ours, and the battle is the Lord's." There have been many trials in my life, as there are in all of our lives. Jesus said that in the world we would have tribulation, but His exhortation was to be of good cheer, for He has overcome the world. James tells us to count it all joy when we have trials because these trials will form patience and other character traits of God in us.

When we enter trials, we need to think of the word *traits*. When we change the *l* to *t* in the word *trials*, the word *traits* appears. Trials will always be turned into godly traits in us when we trust in the Lord no matter how hard the trial is.

God allowed the children of Israel to experience trials as they traveled through the wilderness because He wanted their character traits to change. He knew they would have a tendency to want to go back to the land of Egypt (the land of bondage) when the going got rough. He knew their character, and we see the children of Israel murmuring and complaining to Moses. They said, "It had been better for us to serve the Egyptians, than we should die in the wilderness" (Exod. 14:12, KJV).

In every trial, we face the temptation to go back into the land of bondage. The enemy always whispers, "You were better off before you trusted in the Lord." The truth, however, is this: The Lord will fight for us if we hold our peace.

In the midst of our trials we need to position ourselves in the cleft of the Rock (Jesus Christ) and watch Him do battle for us. Our place is to wait upon Him, trusting in Him with all of our hearts. When we trust in Him and surrender to His control of the trial, peace will always come. The Word of God says, "I will keep him in perfect peace whose mind is stayed upon the Lord." The Lord is our strength and song, and He has become our salvation.

The next time you are in a trial, ask the Lord what character traits of God He is trying to form in you. It may be one of the fruit of the spirit: love, joy, peace, longsuffering, gentleness, goodness, faith, meekness, self-control. Then position yourself in the cleft of the Rock (Jesus Christ) and trust Him. The victory is ours, and the battle is the Lord's.

The Pavilion of Peace
Psalm 27:1–7

For in time of trouble he shall hide me in his pavilion: in the secret of his tabernacle shall he hide me; he shall set me upon a rock. And now shall mine head be lifted up above mine enemies round about me: therefore will I offer in his tabernacle sacrifices of joy; I will sing, yea, I will sing praises unto the LORD" (Ps. 27:5–6, KJV). What an encouraging word David wrote about times of trouble.

Yesterday we talked about positioning ourselves in the Rock (Jesus Christ) and trusting in Him in times of trouble. Peace comes to our souls when we do this. James 1:2–3 says, "My brethren, count it all joy when ye fall into divers temptations [trials]; knowing this, that the trying of your faith worketh patience" (KJV).

In this psalm, David talks about offering the sacrifice of joy and singing and praising God in the midst of trouble. David reveals the reason he is able to keep praising God in the midst of every trial. He shares that God Himself has set him upon Rock (Jesus Christ) and He has hidden him in His pavilion. I have experienced this pavilion on a trip to India, and nothing can compare with it.

On our second trip to India we discovered the secret pavilion of God. People in the church gathered around us and prayed for us. As they laid hands upon us to send us forth in India, one person had a vision. She said, "I see mighty angels standing in a circle around you. Their backs are toward you, and they are facing outward into the darkness. They are holding what looks like thick clear shields, and you are in an invisible gazebo of protection." We were encapsulated in this pavilion the whole time we were in India on our second trip. This time we did not feel the great heaviness caused by demonic forces in the atmosphere. India is a land of great idol worship, and the over 300 million gods that are worshiped in India are actually demonic spirits. Those demonic spirits were incapable of penetrating the pavilion of peace placed around us because of the prayers of others.

Each morning you awaken and have your quiet time with the Lord, you can place yourself and your whole family in this secret pavilion of God's peace. How can you do this? You can pray this prayer:

Thank You, Lord, for Your secret pavilion that protects my family and me. Your Word says, "The angels of the Lord are encamped around those who fear you." I know they are on duty this day to protect my family from all the schemes of the enemy. Thank You.

A Peculiar, Precious People
Exodus 17:8–19:15

God instructed Moses to speak to the children of Israel these words: "Now, therefore, if ye will obey my voice indeed, and keep my covenant, then ye shall be a peculiar treasure unto me above all people: for all the earth is mine: And you shall be unto me a kingdom of priests, and an holy nation" (Exod. 19:5–6, KJV).

Similar words were spoken by Paul in his letter in Titus. "Who gave himself for us, that he might redeem us from all iniquity, and purify unto himself a peculiar people, zealous of good works" (Titus 2:14, KJV).

Peter also speaks of a peculiar people in 1 Peter 2:9. "But ye are a chosen generation, a royal priesthood, an holy nation, a peculiar people; that ye should shew forth the praises of him who hath called you out of darkness into his marvelous light" (KJV).

The Exodus passage speaks of Israel as a peculiar people. Paul and Peter speak of believers in Jesus Christ (both Jew and Gentile) as peculiar people. The Hebrew word for *peculiar* is "a jewel, a treasure, good, and proper." The Greek work for *peculiar* is "being beyond usual, a special purchased possession, and set apart for a purpose."

It never bothers me for people to say I'm a little different or I'm religious. In fact, I have the reputation in my neighborhood as the lady who prays or "the church lady." A neighbor I hardly knew asked me to pray for her husband who needed surgery. As believers we are set apart for a purpose, and God sees us as a precious treasure purchased by Him when Jesus died on the cross for us.

We had the privilege of hosting two missionaries in our guest room. The couple had given up everything to be on the mission field, including a very successful dental practice. This dentist and his wife were available to go wherever the Lord wanted to send them. All they wanted to do while they visited us was to be out witnessing and sharing the gospel with others. The Lord spoke to me one night as I was going to sleep, and only a wall separated the head of their bed from the head of our bed. The Lord said, "You are hosting two of My precious, peculiar people." I didn't understand what that meant then, but I do now.

You Would Not
Matthew 23:13–39

Jesus expresses the heartcry of the Father in this passage. He would that none perish, but that all should come to repentance. As Jesus looked from the temple mount upon Jerusalem, He cried out, "How often would I have gathered thy children together, even as a hen gathereth her chickens under her wings, and ye would not" (Matt. 23:37, KJV).

As a mother I know how comforting it is to have all my children (my little chickens) under my roof. When the boys were older, I always breathed a sigh of relief when they were all tucked safe in their beds for the night.

In this last hour the Father is gathering His chickens. He will not be satisfied until all of His children come to dwell in His house. As I read this heartcry, I wondered how often the Father has wanted to direct me by His Holy Spirit or speak to me through His Word, and I would not. Every morning if I listen intently I can hear the invitation, "Come sup with Me." Every morning the Lord is waiting to have fellowship with me.

I heard a marvelous sermon by Seville Phillips on the words Jesus spoke on the cross. Jesus said, "I thirst." The main point of his message was that the God of the universe, tented in flesh, had a need. He was thirsty. His thirst, however, was not just physical. He thirsted for fellowship with the Father and His disciples. He wanted to be satiated by love. The separation from the Father He experienced on the cross was more than He could bear. God has purer eyes than to behold evil, so He had to turn away from Jesus for a moment in time because even though Jesus knew no sin, He became sin for us. That separation broke Jesus' heart. Jesus' heart burst under the burden.

This morning spend time supping with Jesus. He longs and thirsts to have fellowship with you. He bids you to come. He wants to gather you into His arms as a mother chicken gathers her brood under her wings. Will you respond to His invitation? Don't break His heart.

Lord, forgive me for the times I have refused Your invitation to fellowship with You. I know You wait daily to have a conversation with me. There are love letters from You I haven't even taken the time to read. I remember when I was courting my husband, how daily I waited at the mailbox for his letter to arrive when we were separated because of his job. The moment the letter came, I tore into it and sat down and read and reread it. O Lord, create in my heart the same eagerness to read Your Word. You have loving things to say to me daily in Your Word, and so often I fail to daily open these love letters. I've been too busy to read them. I am so sorry.

READ: Exodus 21:22–23:13; Matthew 24:1–28; Psalm 29:1–11; Proverbs 7:6–23

Like Lightning
Matthew 24:1–28

Suddenly without warning a flash of lightning bolts through the sky. The Second Coming of the Lord will be just that sudden. Does this strike fear in your heart?

Fear was my reaction when David Wilkerson interrupted his message when he was speaking at the Savannah Civic Center with this message: "Jesus just walked in the back door of this auditorium. Look! He is here!"

The audience turned to look, and then he asked us, "What did you feel when I said this?" It was a dramatic illustration of how suddenly the Lord can return. My first thought was, *I'm not ready.* The bride has the responsibility to make herself ready for the Lord's return. I realized that I must prepare myself. However, no matter how well we prepare, we will never be totally ready. My only hope of being presentable as the bride to my husband, the Lord Jesus Christ, is found in the scripture below: "Beloved, now are we the sons of God, and it doth not yet appear what we shall be: but we know that, when he shall appear, we shall be like him; for we shall see him as he is. And every man that hath this hope in him purifieth himself, even as he is pure" (1 John 3:2–3, KJV).

With this hope of being like Jesus when He appears, we have no more fear. Faith is the evidence of things not seen, the substance of things hoped for. The substance of hope for us is the promises of God written in His Word. What a great promise to hold to until He comes. I do not have to be fearful about His coming, but I do have the responsibility to purify myself daily. How do I do this? Daily I sin, and often I am not even sure of all the ways I have sinned. The Word of God says, "If we confess our sins, he is faithful and just to forgive us our sins, and to cleanse us from all unrighteousness" (1 John 1:9, KJV).

I can purify myself daily by confessing my sins, both known and those I do not know about, to the Lord. I also ask Him for the strength to overcome the next time I am tempted to sin. Each day I pray, "Lead me not into temptation, but deliver me from evil." Jesus is the only One who can cleanse me and get me ready for His coming. I will be ready if my heart is daily turned to Him.

Lord, I confess my sins to You today. Cleanse me and help me to walk in Your ways. Thank You for Your purity. Purify my heart today.

READ: Exodus 23:14–25:40; Matthew 24:29–51; Psalm 30:1–12; Proverbs 7:24–27

You Can't Take It With You!
Matthew 24:29–51

There is an expectancy of the Lord's soon return that only the Holy Spirit can give. Paul had this expectancy, and nearly two thousand years later men and women all over the world believe in Jesus and are anticipating His return.

Our two youngest sons had their own unique way of expressing their expectancy of the Lord's return. Our youngest son, Ray, shared his eagerness for the Lord's return by standing almost daily in our carport. I asked him, "Ray, what are you doing?" As he looked up to the sky he said enthusiastically, "Today may be the day Jesus comes!"

One night when we were having family devotion, my husband read this passage from Matthew about the Lord's return. As Tom closed his Bible, our middle son, Ron, responded to the reading with a question. "Dad, will we leave this earth wearing clothes?" You could tell Ron was intently thinking of the day we would meet Jesus in the sky. My husband paused for a moment to get his thoughts together, and then Tom said, "No, Ron, we will not have clothes on because naked we come into the world and naked we will leave the world." Then Ron said, "That's cool, streakers in the sky!" This was a nine-year-old's view of the rapture.

Are you eagerly awaiting this Lord's return? It may be today.

Lord, I want to have this expectancy in my heart every day. Help me to order my day as if it were the last day I would spend on earth. Thank You for another day to give Your Word voice on this earth, and thank You for the excitement You are now stirring in my heart about Your soon return.

Being Ready for the Bridegroom
Matthew 25:1–30

We used to lead a "Lamp Lighters" group when my husband was in the army. The children in this group were junior high age, and I loved hearing them sing. "Give me oil in my lamp, keep me burning till the break of day." This story of the ten virgins is about being ready for the Lord's return. One has to understand the Jewish betrothal customs to receive the full impact of what is being conveyed in this passage.

Betrothal was a Jewish custom that occurred before the consummation of a marriage. We would call it today an engagement period, but betrothal was a much deeper commitment than an engagement. During the betrothal period, which was usually a year, the bride was given all the rights of a wife, including all of her future husband's income and inheritance. During this year of betrothal the bridegroom would prepare a place for his bride to live. The day would come when he would call for his bride, and this was done in a unique way.

Every year in the small villages on the Judean hillsides, as many as ten virgins or more could be betrothed. Their duty was to be prepared at all times for the trumpet sound and the shout, "The bridegroom comes!" At that moment the virgins were to light their lamps so the bridegrooms could find them. Usually the shout would come in the midnight hour. All the bridegrooms would then travel down the hillside to find their respective bride, and thus would begin the time of celebration before the wedding supper and the consummation of their marriages. The virgins would usually know the season of their betrothal, but they would never know the exact day. They were to have sufficient oil daily to keep their lamps ready for that special night. In this story five of the expectant virgins went out to meet their bridegrooms, and they also carried vessels of oil with them. The other five failed to have sufficient oil with them, and their lights went out because their bridegrooms tarried for awhile. The virgins who were not prepared asked for oil from the prepared virgins, but the prepared virgins told the unprepared to go out and buy some more oil. While the unprepared were purchasing more oil, the marriage took place and the door was shut to them.

Our bridegroom Jesus is coming soon, and it is our responsibility to stay filled with the oil of the Holy Spirit so our lights will not go out before He comes for us. We are the only light the world has now, and it seems the darkness around us becomes more intense as we await the coming of our Lord. The question to ask ourselves is, Are we receiving daily a fresh filling of this oil of anointing from the Holy Spirit? The Holy Spirit always has sufficient oil, but do we receive it? Daily I pray this prayer, and you may want to pray it today with me:

Lord, I ask for a double portion of Your anointing. Fill me with Your Holy Spirit today.

The Book of Wisdom
Proverbs 8:11–13

Proverbs is called the Book of Wisdom. Solomon wrote Proverbs, and one can find the golden threads of wisdom woven throughout the thirty-one chapters. You have probably heard the expression, "Eat an apple a day and keep the doctor away." Reading a chapter of Proverbs every day will keep the devil away. We were inspired to begin this daily exercise of reading the proverb for the day to our three sons when we saw the great results this brought to a family down the street. This family had three boys and a girl, and the father read the proverb for the day aloud to his children as they gathered for breakfast every morning. All of these children never departed from the ways of the Lord because they learned much wisdom through the proverbs.

Later we challenged our three sons to memorize as many proverbs as possible. We promised them one dollar for every verse they memorized. Later, when we had a Russian exchange student come live with us, we also challenged him in memorize the proverbs. Vladimir became like a son to us and had been with us for seven years. He just about broke us, however, because he memorized so many proverbs.

I believe that God will supply two very special bodyguards to us if we will daily hide the proverbs in our hearts. These two bodyguards are called "Wisdom" and "Prudence." They will protect us from making wrong decisions and thus being ensnared by the enemy. Two of our sons did wander into the world for a season, but I believe it was the proverbs they hid in their hearts that kept them from going too far astray.

Proverbs was especially directed toward young men. If you have sons, I would highly recommend this practice of reading one proverb a day aloud to your family as you gather together. Daughters also can benefit greatly from such a practice. Recently someone gave me a testimony of how memorizing verses from Proverbs had helped her daughter. Her daughter was attending a very difficult school, and she was having problems studying and doing well on tests. Her mother suggested that she read a chapter in Proverbs a day and memorize at least two verses from that chapter. Soon after her daughter began this daily regimen, she noticed marked improvement in her grades. Her mind was being renewed daily, and she was able to study better, learn and retain more knowledge than ever before.

Today would be a great day to start such a regimen. I challenge you before you go to bed tonight to read Proverbs 8 and commit at least two verses to your memory.

The Quiet Place
Psalm 31:19–24

Imagine being in a pavilion set in a green meadow sprinkled with wild flowers. As you view the bright blue sky, the only sounds you hear are the birds singing, the quiet flow of the stream beside you and the Holy Spirit making melody in your heart. We can enter such a place daily as we walk in the Spirit. David knew this secret. "Thou shalt hide them in the secret of thy presence from the pride of man: thou shalt keep them secretly in a pavilion far from the strife of tongues" (Ps. 31:20, KJV).

Every morning I lie on the sofa in our sunroom and look at the sky through the sky light above me. On the table beside me is a decorative sign that says "The Quiet Place." The only sounds I hear are the birds singing and leaves gently falling with the breeze. As I sink into the sofa, I climb into the quiet place God has promised me. It is just a time for my Maker and me. It is our time of intimacy. Here my Good Shepherd stills my soul, and I find strength for the day that lies ahead of me. Here I hear His still, quiet voice speaking to me, and I rejoice in Him. Sometimes I sing songs to Him, and sometimes I hear with my spiritual ears His songs to me. Often I hear Him say, "Linda, I love you." No sound is able to break the silence of my soul as I wait upon Him. I know I will soon have to arise from this quiet pavilion and get about the duties of being a wife, homemaker and teacher in the kingdom. Before I arise, however, I ask the Lord to keep my soul and spirit in this quiet place all the day long. I want to be able to hear His voice during the day as He instructs me and teaches me. I want to make melody in my heart to Him all the day long.

The promise of our Lord is that if we would come to Him daily and learn of Him meekness and lowliness of heart, we will be able to remain in this quiet pavilion far away from the strife of tongues. Here we will find rest for our souls, and nothing that is spoken to us will offend us. Every word spoken in strife against us will bounce off this pavilion that is cushioned with His grace and perfect love.

I have come to recognize the instant I walk out of this quiet place by my own free will. My soul becomes troubled, and things others say against me impact my mind and emotions. When this happens, once again I think of that pavilion in the green meadow by the stream, and I say, "Lead me by the still waters, Lord, and comfort my soul." The quiet place is established once again, and I can continue the day with settled emotions. Join me in this quiet place today by responding to His invitation: "Come unto me, all ye that labour and are heavy laden; and I will give you rest. Take my yoke upon you, and learn of me; for I am meek and lowly in heart: and ye shall find rest unto your souls" (Matt. 11:28–29, KJV).

February 10

Peace in the Presence of the Lord
Psalm 32:1-11

David knew the secret of the quiet place, and he had to constantly focus to remain in this quiet place. He writes, "Thou preparest a table for me in the presence of mine enemies" (Ps. 23:5, KJV). David had many enemies. However, he knew he was not fighting against flesh and blood. He knew his true enemy was Satan. David knew the secret to overcoming Satan. When Saul chased after him to kill him, David wrote, "Where can I flee from Your presence?" (Ps. 139:7). The presence of the Lord was always much stronger than the presence of the enemy to David. No matter what difficult situation David encountered, he knew the Lord was ever before him. He wrote, "Your face is ever before me."

For over seven years David had to flee from Saul, and his favorite hiding place was Engedi. We have visited Engedi many times on our trips to Israel, and it was easy to see why David chose such a spot for his hiding place. It is an oasis in the middle of the area around the Dead Sea where flowing falls cascade from cliffs laden with lush green trees. Each cliff contains a multitude of caves. Saul knew this was David's secret refuge, and it was at Engedi that David cut the hem of Saul's garment while he was asleep. David later repented for touching God's anointed.

Could it be that as we hide ourselves in our special pavilion of God's presence the enemy is surrounding us, watching our every move? It is true that we are not only surrounded by a host of angels, but we are also surrounded by hosts of demonic spirits that seek to destroy us. Yet, in the midst of our enemies, God has prepared a feast for us, and the presence of the Lord is so bright at this table He has prepared for us that we are not even aware of the darkness that surrounds us. As long as we remain at this table where we feast on His Word and talk with the Lord, the enemy is helpless to penetrate the shield of light that surrounds us. In the presence of the Lord is joy and pleasures forever more. Even though the enemy surrounds us, we are also compassed about by the Lord's songs of deliverance. David writes, "Thou art my hiding place; thou shalt preserve me from trouble" (Ps. 32:7, KJV).

Nothing can separate us from the love of God—neither death, nor life, neither principalities nor powers. What a comfort it is to know His presence in the midst of our enemies. We can be at peace.

Thank You, Lord, for Your abiding peace.

READ: Exodus 32:1–33:23; Matthew 26:69–27:14; Psalm 33:1–11; Proverbs 8:33–36

His Word Is Steadfast
Psalm 33:1–11

God spoke, and it was done; He commanded, and it stood fast. God is not a man that He should lie. I've heard it said the only thing God cannot do is lie. His Word is truth, and this psalm says His Word is right and all His works are done in truth. His Word not only is right, but it also has creative power. God spoke into being all of creation.

I can remember looking up to the night sky near Phoenix, Arizona. I saw stars I did not know existed, and I knew there were probably universes not yet discovered by man. The heavens do declare the glory of God, and we cannot help but stand in awe of His great power. The day will come soon, however, when the stars will fall and all of heaven will be rolled up like a scroll. There is only one thing that will last forever—His Word. All that can be shaken will be shaken as the day comes near to His coming, but His Word will remain steadfast.

These thoughts challenge me to daily read His Word because His Word is eternal. There are only a few things we can take to heaven with us when we leave this earth, and one of them is the Word of God that we have hidden in our hearts.

We live in a world that often is chaotic and unstable. We all need something we can trust that never changes. God's Word is steadfast. Jesus is the living Word, or the Word made flesh, and we can go to Him the moment we feel shaky or tossed about by the circumstances we experience.

I know what a comfort it is to me to have my husband hold me closely and speak comforting words when I am shaking from some trauma in my life. Several years ago as I was driving in my own neighborhood, I hit a little child riding his bike. The boy almost died. My husband was not with me at the time, but as soon as I reached home, I fell into his arms. The strength of his arms supported me, and the comfort of his words calmed my trembling body. I felt secure and safe, and the peace of God submerged me.

We have a faithful God whose Word is steadfast. Jesus, the Word made flesh, is always with us in every circumstance of life. The moment we need an anchor for our troubled souls, He is reaching out to us to hold us close to Him, and He longs to comfort us with His words. The sad reality of life is that many do not turn to Him or His Word for strength and stability in this life. He is our only hope when things look hopeless. Run to Him and hear His Word whenever you need something to hold on to in this life. He longs to hold you throughout every trial.

Lord, teach me to quickly turn to You the moment I feel shaky. You are my solid rock, my strong tower, my only hope in times of trouble.

READ: Exodus 34:1–35:9; Matthew 27:15–34; Psalm 33:12–22; Proverbs 9:1–6

The Seven Pillars of Wisdom
Proverbs 9:1–6

I've always wondered what the seven pillars of wisdom were. After studying the sevenfold anointing spoken of in Isaiah 11:2, I concluded that the seven pillars of wisdom must be the seven aspects of the Holy Spirit of the Lord. Isaiah 11:2 says, "And the spirit of the LORD shall rest upon him, the spirit of wisdom and understanding, the spirit of counsel and might, the spirit of knowledge and the fear of the LORD" (KJV).

Jesus Christ is all wisdom. He was anointed with seven wonderful aspects of the Holy Spirit—wisdom and understanding, the spirit of counsel and might, and the spirit of knowledge and the fear of the Lord. The Spirit of the Lord contained all of these strong pillars. The number seven means complete. Jesus operated in the complete anointing of the Holy Spirit. The Bible tells us that God's Word is what holds the earth in place. These seven aspects of the Holy Spirit are the pillars that give support to mankind on earth. If these pillars did not exist in some people on earth, we would have utter chaos.

The seven pillars of wisdom were established even before the foundation of the world. God holds this world together by His Word, and the seven pillars of wisdom give mankind the ability to hold on in faith, no matter if the whole earth is shaken. In the last days the Bible says everything that can be shaken will be shaken. Those who are operating in God's wisdom will not be shaken. Revelation tells us that those who overcome will be made pillars in the temple of the living God. If we depend upon the Holy Spirit daily as Jesus did while He was on earth, we will be those pillars in eternity.

Don't you want to be a pillar, someone who overcomes in every circumstance? You can be if you operate daily in the wisdom that comes from God. This wisdom is described in James 3:17: "But the wisdom from above is first pure, then peaceable, gentle, willing to yield, full of mercy and good fruits, without partiality and without hypocrisy." We also have to refuse to operate in worldly wisdom. Worldly wisdom is full of strife, envy, confusion and every evil work. Which wisdom will be your mode of operation today?

Lord, help me to operate in Your wisdom today. Thank You for Your secure pillars of wisdom that give me strength in a world that seems to be falling apart.

READ: Exodus 35:10–36:38; Matthew 27:35–66; Psalm 34:1–10; Proverbs 9:7–8

A Willing Heart
Exodus 35:10–36:38

"And they came, every one whose heart stirred him up, and every one whom his spirit made willing, and they brought the LORD's offering to the work of the tabernacle of the congregation, and for all his service, and for the holy garments" (Exod. 35:21, KJV). This is a beautiful story of how the people had a willing heart to give, to work and to serve. We learn in the next chapter how willing the people actually were. Exodus 36:5 says, "And they spake unto Moses, saying, The people bring much more than enough for the service of the work, which the LORD commanded to make" (KJV).

Often in this passage we see the phrase, "their hearts were stirred up." When we have a willing heart, the Lord by the power of His Holy Spirit is able to stir our hearts. The great encourager, the Holy Spirit, stirs us with an anointing and a vision to give generously. All He is waiting for is a willing heart.

Recently I received a letter from a YWAM missionary who told a modern-day version of this passage in Exodus. The YWAM base in Africa was hosting a school of prayer where people came from all nations. At one of the meetings it was announced that a special offering would be taken to raise the monies needed for a high-tech video machine that would enable interactive teaching through the video. The price was $17,000. No one that night came prepared to give an offering, but this did not discourage the willing hearts present at this meeting. God moved upon the young people present to give precious jewelry, stereos, guitars, etc. Possessions worth $11,000 were given. A man from Taiwan then offered to pay the balance, but later the Lord moved on this same man's heart to give the full amount of $17,000. All the precious items were returned to their owners because this man was stirred in his heart to give the total amount needed. What a story of redemption.

When we have a willing heart, we are stirred up to give by the Holy Spirit. Then our heavenly Father is stirred to return to us in some way far more than we thought possible. He has already redeemed us as His precious possession.

Lord, give me a willing heart, and then enable me by the power of the Holy Spirit to give generously. Stir me up to give, and thank You for enabling me to be a faithful giver.

The Greatest Love Story
Matthew 28:1–20

This is the day men give candy and roses to their wives or sweethearts. For me it usually means a dinner out or a weekend away. This day of celebration is in honor of the love between a man and a woman. It is interesting that the symbol of this day is a heart and the colors used to decorate are red and white. The greatest love story ever told also involves the heart and the colors red and white. On the cross Jesus died because the weight of our sin broke His heart, but because of His sacrifice, we now can have our broken hearts mended. The red blood of Jesus poured upon the ground and was offered as an atonement for all sins, which satisfied God's requirements for a penalty for sin. Jesus, who knew no sin, became sin for us that we might be made the righteousness of God in Him. Though our sins were as scarlet, they became white as snow. On that day over two thousand years ago, the greatest love story was revealed to mankind. This story continues to unfold as we look forward to the day that we will sit at the table of the lover of our souls. There will be a marriage of the Bridegroom (Jesus) with the bride (the church), and the celebration will continue for all eternity.

In this passage today we see a portion of this great love story. First Mary Magdalene and Mary discover the empty tomb at dawn on the first day of the week. These women loved Jesus as both mother and friend, but soon this love would deepen into a supernatural love that would far exceed any human love. God was in Christ Jesus reconciling the world to Himself. God's love is inexpressible, but God's love found expression through Jesus Christ. The height of God's love is His grace, the depth of God's love is His forgiveness, the length of God's love is His mercy, and the width of God's love is His truth. All these four aspects of God's love were fully expressed in Jesus Christ, who is the express image of the invisible Father. When the angel appeared to the two Marys, they were first fearful. But then, when they heard the message, "He is not here, for He is risen, as He said," they were filled with great joy and ran to tell the disciples. This story of God's love expressed through the death, burial and resurrection of Jesus Christ had to be shared with others.

Whenever we experience a loving act in our lives, we like to share it with others. On this special dawn, the two Marys could not wait to tell their friends. Their response to this great news should be our response today. Later Jesus spoke to His disciples and said, "All power is given unto me in heaven and in earth. Go ye therefore, and teach all nations, baptizing them in the name of the Father, and of the Son, and of the Holy Ghost: Teaching them to observe all things whatsoever I have commanded you: and lo, I am with you alway, even unto the end of the world" (Matt. 28:18–20, KJV).

Is there someone you need to tell the greatest love story to today?

READ: Exodus 39:1–40:38; Mark 1:1–28; Psalm 35:1–16; Proverbs 9:11–12

God's Occupation
Mark 1:1–28

In order to follow someone or something, one has to leave something or someone. When Jesus said to Simon and Andrew, "Come, and I will make you fishers of men," they did just that. They forsook their nets and followed Him.

One morning I asked my heavenly Father why those fishermen left instantly when Jesus asked them to follow Him. The response I heard in my spirit was that Jesus had a compelling compassion for people. God became a man, and He dwelled among us to identify with our weakness. Jesus was touched with the feelings of all our weak areas. When He saw Simon and Andrew, His heart was moved with compassion. That love was instantly transmitted to them, and they could not help but follow Him. The love of Jesus compelled them like a magnet, and their focus was no longer on their occupation, but on Jesus.

The invitation was clear, "Come after me, and I will make you fishers of men." People are much more important than jobs and money. To fish for men is an eternal occupation that pays eternal dividends. People are God's special treasure and His inheritance. We are His inheritance, and He has invested His all in us. Jesus was asking Andrew and Simon to become investors in this eternal inheritance-people.

Are you a people person? When you have seen Jesus in the spirit, there is only one response you can have. Your heart will leap within you, but that is not all. Your heart will be moved with compassion for all the people you know, and even some you do not know. When you see Jesus in the Spirit, you will leave behind your focus on your job and money, and your new eternal occupation will be fishing—fishing for men. As you fish for men, all you have to do is throw out the line with the bait. God by His Holy Spirit will pull the fish (people) into the net of His kingdom. The line you throw out is prayer for that person you want to come to know Jesus as Lord and Savior. The bait is God's Word. God's Word never returns void. It always accomplishes the things it is sent out to do. The Spirit of God does the rest. Remember to share with the person you are witnessing to that God cleans His fish after He catches them. So many people resist accepting Jesus Christ as Lord and Savior because they think they have to clean up their act. Only God by the power of His Holy Spirit can do the cleansing needed in a life, and the cleansing agent is the blood of Jesus. If we confess our sins, He is faithful to forgive us of our sins and to cleanse us from all unrighteousness. Want to go fishing with me today?

Jesus, sometimes I lose my focus, and I forget why I am here on earth. I am here to be a fisher of men, and I need You to help me to stay focused. Help me to see each person I meet today as Your special treasure. Help me to be co-investor with You in their lives.

Our First Love
Mark 1:29–2:12

And Jesus, moved with compassion, put forth his hand, and touched him, and saith unto him, I will; be thou clean" (Mark 1:40, KJV). The motivating force in Jesus was to do the will of the Father. His first love was the Father, and everything He did on earth was first to please His heavenly Father. In this passage we see Jesus' great love for the Father as He put the Father and His will first and obeyed the Father. Many people came to Jesus for healing and deliverance, and He healed all who came to Him, but He knew that His Father had called Him to preach. First He obeyed the Father in fulfilling His call, but He also was moved with love for the people. When the leper approached Him, he was moved with compassion.

Jesus had a soul even as we do because He was both man and God. He had a mind, emotions and a will. His will was motivated always by love. The actions we do daily should stem from our love first for the Father and then toward others. God has given us many gifts, but if those gifts are released from our lives with any other motivation in our hearts but love, they are wood, hay and stubble in God's sight. All the works we do on earth that are not motivated by love will be burned when our works are judged in heaven.

I had a perfect illustration of how love is to be the channel for every word, deed and gift in our lives. I was standing in the kitchen washing dishes when suddenly the whole kitchen faucet flew off, and the water became a geyser that reached the ceiling and splashed down on me. I panicked, but the Holy Spirit prompted me to turn off the water so I could screw the faucet on again. As I screwed the faucet on tightly and then turned the water on gently, I clearly saw the purpose of a faucet. A faucet channels water in such a way that it is effective. The flow of water now had direction and purpose, when before it just got me all wet because the faucet was missing and there was no direction. As I pondered this, I heard God speak to my heart. "I have given gifts to men, but these gifts must be channeled through My love. If love is not the motivating force in your words and deeds, then what you say and do daily is in vain. For your life to have direction and purpose, your words and deeds must always be channeled through My love. My power and gifts can easily be misdirected and misused with others if love for Me first is not the motivating force of your will. Disastrous results can occur when I am not your first love. If the power of My Spirit is not channeled through loving actions, people you minister to will experience power without purpose. My purpose is to refresh and change them eternally by My Spirit."

READ: Leviticus 4:1–5:19; Mark 2:13–3:6; Psalm 36:1–12; Proverbs 10:1–2

The Character of God
Psalm 36:1–12

This psalm says so much about the character of God. One of the tactics of Satan is to try to bring doubt in our hearts about God's goodness. So many times I have heard the enemy whisper, "If God is so good, why did He let this happen?" To defend ourselves against this tactic we need to know what the Bible says about the character of God. This psalm gives a great character sketch of God.

The verses in this psalm reveal that God is merciful, faithful, righteous and excellent in loving-kindness. He is our protector and provider. When we become grounded in scriptures like this, we will not be overwhelmed when trials and tribulations come our way. We know that because God is good, His desire is to bring eternal good out of every situation we face in life. You have heard this expression: We have to accept the bitter with the sweet in this life. God desires to work everything for the good in the lives of those that love Him and are called according to His purpose. When we love the Lord and respond to His call and purpose for our lives, we can rest assured that all He allows in our lives will ultimately work for our good.

The best illustration I heard about how things work together in our lives for the good was shared in a Bible study I attended. The teacher shared that life is like baking a cake. First, all the ingredients are laid out; if you taste each ingredient separately, you would doubt these ingredients create a delicious cake. The salt is salty, the flour and eggs are tasteless, the baking powder is bland, and the vanilla that gives flavor to the cake tastes bitter. When all the ingredients are stirred together and then baked, out of the oven comes a delicacy that tastes, looks and smells delightful. Two steps are essential for a good cake—all the ingredients must be blended carefully, and the temperature of the oven and the time the cake is left in the oven have to be correct.

We have the Master Baker, and He is blending the different situations, trials, testing and circumstances of our lives with loving care. He will make sure that when we go through fiery trials, the heat will not burn us. He will never allow us to be tested above that which we are able to stand. What will help us the most when we are in the oven of testing is to remember God's character and review His marvelous acts through the years. David knew the secret of this. Circumstances and situations may change in our lives, and sometimes things may look very dark, but God dwells in the midst of darkness. When you put a cake in the oven, unless you turn on a light, the only light you see is the cooking element. God's Word is a lamp to our feet and a light to our path. When we go through fiery trials in our lives, the key to overcoming is to shine the light of God's Word on the trial. Then we can clearly see that God is working, and in His timing the results of this trial will be good simply because God is a good, caring God. Remember, God's character is formed in us when we turn to Him in our trials.

READ: Leviticus 6:1–7:27; Mark 3:7–30; Psalm 37:1–11; Proverbs 10:3–4

The Character of a Meek Person
Psalm 37:1–11

Yesterday the psalm we read shared about God's character. Today Psalm 37 shares about the character of a meek person. Two people in the Bible are spoken of as meek men. The Bible tells us that Moses was the meekest man that ever lived. Of course, Moses was not divine as Jesus is. But we also know that if we want to see the complete character trait of meekness demonstrated, we must look to Jesus. Jesus exhorted us to learn of Him because He is meek and lowly of heart. Can we learn meekness? As we observe the lives of Jesus and Moses in the Bible, we can learn much about meekness. However, the key to learning about meekness is to come to Jesus. Jesus issues the invitation for us to come to Him daily and let the Holy Spirit teach us all about meekness. Meekness will only be formed in our own lives as we submit ourselves to growing in intimacy with the Lord by spending quality time with Him daily. This psalm tells us the benefits of meekness and exactly how meekness is demonstrated in our lives.

Listen to the promise issued to the meek: "The meek shall inherit the earth; and shall delight themselves in the abundance of peace" (Ps. 37:11, KJV). That phrase "abundance of peace" ignites the desire in me to grow in the fruit of the Spirit called "meekness." What are the character traits of a meek person? This psalm lists eight character traits. A meek person frets not, trusts in the Lord, does good, delights in the Lord, commits his way to the Lord, rests in the Lord, waits upon the Lord and ceases from anger and forsakes wrath.

A meek person responds to people instead of acting out against them. We know that Moses did on one occasion come against God and the children of Israel, and it cost him a great blessing—the blessing of living in the Promised Land. Because a meek person trusts in the Lord, he does not fret, but instead rests and waits upon the Lord. This fruit of the Spirit can be cultivated in our lives, but there is a key condition we must fulfill for meekness to grow in our lives. The key to cultivating all nine fruit of the Spirit in our lives is spending time with the Master Gardener—Jesus. We have to take time for the preparation of the soil of our hearts to receive the seed of the Word of God, and then we have to continue to fertilize that seed daily with more of the Word of God. We must allow time in our daily lives to receive the refreshing water of the Holy Spirit. One of the tactics of the enemy in the last days is to wear out the saints, and lately I have observed many worn-out and dry Christians. When we are weary, that is a clear sign that we are not spending enough quality time with the Lord.

Fruitfulness
Mark 3:31–4:25

We learned yesterday about how fruit is cultivated in our lives. The key to cultivating any of the nine fruit of the spirit listed in Galatians 5:22–23 is to spend quality time with Jesus daily. This is how we prepare the soil of our hearts to receive His Word. Only the Holy Spirit can water the seed of God's Word and cause it to grow and produce.

Every farmer knows the most effective rain a crop can receive is a gentle, steady rain that daily showers his fields before the heat of the afternoon sun. We can receive such a shower from the Holy Spirit every morning as we study God's Word if we allow the Holy Spirit to enlighten our understanding. The water of the Holy Spirit will cause the seed of God's Word to germinate and grow and eventually produce a bumper crop of the fruit of the Spirit in our lives. It is essential that our souls be watered and refreshed by the Holy Spirit daily and that we are able to keep the soil of our hearts moist with His Spirit all the day long. How do we do this? Paul tells us in Ephesians 5:18–21 exactly how to stay filled with the Holy Spirit. He tells us to:

1. Speak to one another in psalms, hymns and spiritual songs.
2. Sing and make melody in your heart to the Lord.
3. Give thanks always for all things to God the Father in the name of Jesus.
4. Submit to one another in the fear of God.

In this passage in Mark, Jesus tells us what will cause the soil of our souls or hearts to become parched and dry. He tells us exactly about the weeds that will choke out fruitfulness in our lives. He lists three lusts of the world that choke out fruitfulness in our lives: the cares of this world, the deceitfulness of riches and the lusts of other things. John expresses these lusts clearly: "For all that is in the world, the lust of the flesh, and the lust of the eyes, and the pride of life, is not of the Father, but is of the world" (1 John 2:16, KJV). Whenever we allow the cares of the world to overwhelm us, we are operating in the pride of life, which is trusting in ourselves more than we trust in God. If we truly trusted God, we would release all of our cares to Him and not worry about anything. Whenever we become absorbed in making money and accumulating wealth, we are operating in the lust of the flesh, which is seeking to satisfy our fleshly desires with more and better food, drink, clothing, entertainment, etc. Whenever we begin to covet other things and have our focus on things rather than God, we are operating in the lust of the eyes, which is greedy longings in our minds. God no longer is our focus. Material things and satisfying our five senses becomes our chief goal.

When we walk in the Spirit and daily stay filled with the Spirit, these lusts of the world will not be able to choke out our fruitfulness in the Lord. The worldly cravings of our souls or lusts will have to take a back seat because we will be filled with God's Spirit.

Faith Overcomes Fear
Mark 4:26–5:20

When we look at Jesus and the life He lived on earth, we see His mind was filled with faith. Worry and doubt were not part of His life. He was able to sleep through the storm because He trusted in the Father, whom He knew controls the storms of this life. Fear overcame the disciples in the boat because their focus was on the storm instead of their heavenly Father, who sits on and even rides upon the clouds. Faith comes when we learn to glance at the storms (the trials and testing in our lives) and gaze upon Jesus. The moment we encounter a difficulty on this earth we need to look at it briefly and then focus our eyes heavenward. Paul exhorts us to set our affections upon things above.

I learned through a great trial I experienced what to do when my faith was being overwhelmed by fear and doubt. A little boy I hit with my car was lying in a hospital bed battling for his life. He was experiencing a breathing problem, and the doctors were not sure he would survive. When I learned of his condition one morning when I visited the hospital, my heart sank, and I was paralyzed with fear. By the power of God's spirit I was able to compose myself long enough to make a few calls to prayer warriors. I knew who would faithfully intercede for Richey. As Richey continued his battle for life, I continued my battle for faith. I kept hearing, "If Richey died, I could not live."

One of those faithful friends I called came immediately to the hospital to pray for Richey. We first knelt in the intensive care waiting room and prayed with Richey's mother. Then we excused ourselves to go to the chapel. After a season of prayer, my friend had to leave, and I was alone again to face these doubts and fears that attacked my faith. I entered the elevator to return to the waiting room, and no one but the Lord was in the elevator with me. I cried out to the Lord, "Lord, I believe; help my unbelief." As I pressed the button to go down, I heard the Lord say, "All you need is one finger of faith. Lift that finger heavenward, and the ocean of My love will support you and keep you from sinking."

My mind raced back to when my dad taught me how to float in the swimming pool. His strong hands held me up on the surface of the water, but slowly he withdrew one finger at a time until only one of his fingers was supporting me. Then he withdrew that finger. When I realized his finger was no longer supporting me, I began to sink. Immediately my father placed his strong hands under my back to get me above the surface of the water again. He said, "Relax, I will not let you sink. Look up at the clouds and the blue sky and concentrate on their beauty." As I focused heavenward, once again Dad's hands were withdrawn, but I did not sink this time. I felt all tension leaving my body, and a peace overwhelmed me. I was floating, and I knew if I began to sink again, Dad would quickly catch me. Faith began to fill me and doubt left. When the doors of the elevator opened, I was greeted with the news that Richey's breathing crisis had passed.

Which Is the Right Way?

Proverbs 10:8-9

Recently I seemed to be hopelessly lost in a town that I knew nothing about. My only hope was to stop at a gas station to ask for directions. What a feeling of relief I had when I knew how to reach my destination. I knew the road signs and landmarks to watch for as I made each turn. Before I asked for directions, it seemed that every turn I made was wrong, and I was going further away from my destination instead of closer to it.

Life is a journey, and often we think we are on the right road only to find that we missed a turn somewhere and are going in the wrong direction. There is a proverb that says, "There is a way that seems right to a man, but its end [the final destination] is the way of death" (Prov. 14:12).

Today's proverb says the wise in heart receives commandments, and he that walks uprightly walks surely. The commandments of God are like that gas station where I finally received the correct directions. I had to listen carefully to the directions, and then I had to follow the signs and landmarks as I traveled to my destination. God's directions to us are His commandments and the signposts are His promises.

When I obey His commands and walk in His promises, I will be on the right road, and I will safely and surely reach the final destination of my life that is heaven. I began my journey heavenward when I received Jesus as my Lord and Savior, and I will continue on the right road as long as I love Jesus and keep His commandments. Receiving the instructions from the gas station manager was easy. The hard part awaited me. Each time I made the right turn, I breathed a sigh of relief because I knew the promise of reaching my final destination was being fulfilled. All the promises in God's Word are "yes and amen" through Jesus Christ. When I was driving, I did not have the visible presence of the gas station manager in the car with me, but I remembered his words. "Turn right at the light and go three blocks, then make a left turn at the convenience store and follow that road five miles. At the second stop sign you will see a Texaco station, take a left and your road will be the next street on the right." Even though we do not have the visible presence of Jesus with us, we can hear the voice of His Spirit, saying, "This is the way; walk in it."

Have you lost your direction in this life? Are you doubting that you will reach your final destination? Go to the filling station (your quiet time where you pray and read God's Word), and you will receive your bearings and once again be on the right path.

Lord, help me to go to the filling station every morning to get my directions for the journey of the day facing me. I want to walk in the path You have prepared for me. Don't let me get diverted and make any wrong turns.

52

READ: Leviticus 13:1–59; Mark 6:1–29; Psalm 39:1–13; Proverbs 10:10

The Tongue—a Mighty Weapon
Psalm 39:1–13

The tongue is a mighty weapon that can be used for good or for evil. When I was in Mexico teaching some young children, I asked them if they would like to disarm the devil. They all shouted, "Yes, we hate the devil." Then I instructed them to stick out their tongues. They followed those instructions. Then I gave them an instruction they could not follow. "Now," I said, "pull out your tongue." Laughter broke out as some of them did yank on their tongues. Of course, we cannot pull our tongues out, but if we could, we would disarm the devil.

One of the most powerful weapons Satan has is our tongue. The mouth can be compared to the barrel of a gun, and the trigger is the tongue. The bullets are the words we speak. Satan wants us to pull the trigger of our tongues to shoot harmful words to others and to ourselves. Unfortunately, Satan is all too successful in using this weapon; when we receive his bullets (the thoughts he sends us), we often pull the trigger of our tongues and start firing.

David knew this when he wrote this psalm. He said, "I will take heed to my ways, that I sin not with my tongue: I will keep my mouth with a bridle, while the wicked is before me" (Ps. 39:1, KJV). David knew that if he came against his enemies with his tongue, he risked having his words backfire. If he judged, criticized or cursed his enemies, he was cooperating with Satan; others would be hurt, and he also would be hurt. The truth is, when we speak evil of any man, we are doing Satan's dirty work for him.

Over the years my husband and I have received a few letters that had harsh words written against one or both of us. Usually the writer of these letters would say something like this, "I am writing this in love to share with you in a constructive way some things you need to know about yourselves." Then as we read the letter, somewhere along the way was the phrase, "I am so angry for what you did." Even if some of what the letter shared was the truth, in most cases the Holy Spirit had already convicted us of these things. Words do not have to be spoken to harm people. They also can be written. We would be wise not to give people a piece of our minds when we speak or write, because when we do, we lose a piece of our own minds. Our own minds are affected by the anger, and we have strife in our minds that eventually can cause a lot of confusion and open the door to other evil work in our own lives. We experience backfire.

Daily I pray to the Lord, "Let the words of my mouth and the meditations of my heart be acceptable in Your sight, O Lord, my Strength and my Redeemer." Would you like to join me in this prayer this morning?

Lord, forgive me for the times I have cooperated with Satan and used the trigger of my tongue to harm others. Help me not to speak in haste.

A Miracle a Day
Mark 6:30–56

The disciples had just witnessed the miracle of the multiplication of the loaves and fishes. They saw over five thousand people fed from five loaves and two fishes. Now they were in the boat rowing to the other side when the winds came against them. Suddenly they saw Jesus walking upon the sea. They thought it was a spirit, and they were afraid. They were amazed when the winds ceased after Jesus boarded the boat. Mark records, "And they were sore amazed in themselves beyond measure, and wondered. For they considered not the miracle of the loaves: for their heart was hardened" (Mark 6:51–52, KJV).

Life has a way of hardening our hearts if we let it. We go from day to day, experience to experience, routine after routine, and if we do not keep our focus on Jesus, we can easily be overwhelmed by the storms of this life. Our hearts can even become hardened because we are not grateful for every breath we take. We take too much for granted. Every time we take a breath, we experience a miracle from God.

Today, instead of becoming impatient when you miss a light and have to wait for what seems like an eternity for it to change, take ten deep breaths. After each breath say, "Thank You, Lord, for the miracle of life." Your whole day will then become a miracle.

Forgive me, Lord, for taking the gift of life for granted. Life truly is a miracle. Keep me in an attitude of gratitude all this day long so my heart will not be hardened. Give me eyes to see and ears to hear Your creative miracles all the day long. Thank You, Lord, for breath today so I can live another day in Your presence here on earth. I can hear one of Your miracles now as the birds sing loudly while the sunrise unfolds. You cause the evenings and the mornings to rejoice. Cause me to rejoice always also, because this is the day You have made, and I will rejoice in it.

February 24

READ: Leviticus 15:1–16:28; Mark 7:1–23; Psalm 40:11–17; Proverbs 10:13–14

Tradition
Mark 7:1–23

There was a song in the musical *Fiddler on the Roof* called "Tradition." As this Jewish father sang this song, this message was immediately conveyed: Life is full of traditions. Traditions can be meaningful, but sometimes they get in the way of the effectiveness of God's Word in our lives. I can remember one Christmas when my sister Nancy and her husband visited us. We knocked ourselves out trying to fulfill all the traditions her family and mine always observed during this season. Keeping traditions can sometimes become very burdensome. As you listen to the song "Tradition" in the film, you can hear the frustration and weariness in the voice of the father. He too had worn himself out trying to keep all the traditions. Keeping traditions can also sometimes prevent us from seeing the newness and freshness of life.

In this passage Jesus makes an amazing statement. He says, "You make the word of God of none effect through your tradition, which you have delivered and many like things that you do." (See verse 13.) Traditions occur simply when we keep repeating the same thing over and over again. God offers much more to us than tradition. He offers newness of life. His Word is life; however, we can quench the life in the Word through our own traditions.

Religions are full of traditions, and Christianity has many. There were certain experiences God did instruct us to repeat over and over again. One of these is the partaking of the Lord's supper on a regular basis. When a tradition overshadows the life-giving Word of God, the Word of God is not effective. How many times have you sung the doxology or repeated the Lord's Prayer? If we are not careful, even the words we speak and sing can be repeated so often that we take them for granted and are not affected by them.

Our goal as we daily walk with the Lord is to keep our spiritual eyes and ears open to the new fresh things He wants to impart to us. Each day He seeks to give us fresh manna, but if we leave the Word on the shelf and do not partake of it, it will have no effect upon us. Never allow the way you worship God to become tradition. Worship in church should never be the "same old, same old." Each time we gather corporately to worship the Lord, there should be an expectancy of something new from God's Word or the songs we sing that will touch and change our hearts. Guard yourself against letting your worship and quiet times becoming simply routine.

Lord, each day You have something new for me. Help me to have ears to hear and eyes to see the new things You want to speak to me and show me. I enter this day with excitement because it is a new day, and You make all things new.

READ: Leviticus 16:29–18:30; Mark 7:24–8:9; Psalm 41:1–13; Proverbs 10:15–16

Giving to the Poor
Psalm 41:1–13

Our church has always given to some ministry that feeds the poor, and often members of our church will go down to the inner city and serve meals to the poor. We also have orphanages in India and Mexico that house many children who otherwise would be living in poverty on the streets. I believe the fact we have always been faithful in giving to the poor is the reason we have never experienced any financial crisis of consequence.

There is a proverb that says, "When you give to the poor, you are lending to God." When you lend to God, He does not have to pay any interest, but instead He pays great dividends. The dividends acquired when we lend to God by giving to the poor are without measure. I can remember seeing a little Indian preacher jump up and down for joy when he received his first pair of shoes. He was forty years old and never wore shoes. At Christmas time I always had a party at my home in honor of a dear friend who had a ministry with the poor. Those invited were to bring an offering to her so she could distribute gifts and clothing to the poor at Christmas. I couldn't wait till everyone finally left the house so my friend and I could total up the offering. We were always so blessed to see the giving spirit of all those invited.

You also will receive a blessing when you give to the poor in spirit. Whenever we impart a drink of spiritual water and a portion of God's Word to thirsty and hungry souls, we will experience great blessing. Remember, Jesus came to preach the gospel to the poor.

Lord, help me to look for ways I can lend to You by giving to the poor. There are so many needy people whom You want to bless financially and spiritually. I want to be a co-laborer with You in the ministry to the poor.

Hope in God
Psalm 42:1–11

David wrote this psalm when he was going through a depressed state. He says, "Why art thou cast down, O my soul? And why art thou disquieted in me? Hope thou in God: for I shall yet praise him, who is the help of my countenance" (Ps. 42:11, KJV). David is telling himself to praise God even when he does not feel like it. The world has grabbed this principle, and motivational seminars usually include a section on "self talk." God's Word relates this principle often. An example is, "Let the weak say I am strong" (Joel 3:10, KJV). There has been an emphasis over the years on making positive confessions rather than negative ones. Sometimes if we are not careful, we curse ourselves by declaring negative things over us. I know when I keep saying I'm tired, it seems I get more tired. David tells himself to hope in God.

What is hope? Hope is the substance that faith is made of. We are able to partake of this substance through the Word of God. "Faith is the substance of things hoped for, the evidence of things not seen" (Heb. 11:1, KJV). How can we build ourselves up in hope when we are having down days? David reveals the secret in this psalm. Even though things were not going David's way and he was depressed about it, he remembered that no matter what the circumstances were or how he felt, the Lord was still commanding His love toward him. "Yet the LORD will command his lovingkindness in the daytime, and in the night his song shall be with me, and my prayer unto the God of my life" (Ps. 42:8, KJV).

There was enough substance of faith (God's Word) hidden in David's heart to give him hope even at his lowest moment. He describes the physical, mental and emotional pain he is experiencing, yet in that tremendous time of pain, he makes the decision of his will to praise the Lord in the midst of all he was encountering. He tells himself to hope in God. If we put our hope in circumstances or our feelings, we will easily lose faith and begin to sink into a depressed state. However, if we put our hope in God, His Word and His promises, we will eventually come out of the slump. David praised the Lord for the help and health of His countenance (presence). We can also praise the Lord for the hope of His countenance. I believe when David was down, he pulled out his harp, began to sing songs to the Lord and entered into the presence of the Lord. David prayed, sang songs and remembered the times when his soul was lifted through praise and worship. He also remembered the lovingkindness of the Lord. This is how he encouraged himself in the Lord. We can do the same.

Lord, help me to put all of my hope in You. When the storms of life are about to drown me, help me to anchor my soul in hope. You are the bishop of my soul, and only You can be the glory and lifter of my head when life gets me down.

READ: Leviticus 20:22–22:20; Mark 9:1–29; Psalm 43:1–5; Proverbs 10:18

Oppression Leads to Depression
Psalm 43:1–5

Yesterday we saw the emotional, mental and physical pain David was experiencing because his enemies were coming against him. He was depressed, but he made the decision with his will to praise the Lord even in the midst of a very low time in his life. All depression is caused by some kind of oppression. Granted, depression can be caused by a chemical imbalance in our system, and this can be treated medically. However, whether we are depressed because of a chemical imbalance in our system or circumstances that surround us, Satan takes advantage of us in our weakened state. He oppresses us with all kinds of deceptive thoughts.

Throughout the psalms and also 1 and 2 Samuel, we see how David was constantly surrounded by enemies. David spent most of his life either fighting or fleeing. We have to remember, however, that even though we may be oppressed by physical human beings, we are not fighting a flesh-and-blood battle. Paul tells us clearly in Ephesians 6 that our battle is not with flesh and blood, but with principalities, powers, rulers of darkness and wickedness in high places that control flesh and blood. For example, Derek Prince, a well-known Bible teacher, fought a constant battle with depression for most of his life. Finally, as he was praying one day, he got the victory in this battle. He realized he was not in a flesh-and-blood battle, but he was experiencing a spiritual battle. As he was reading Isaiah 62:3 he saw that God had provided the garment of praise to lift the spirit of heaviness. He recognized then that he had to come against the spirit of heaviness by praising the Lord. He bound the spirit of heaviness and loosed his soul to praise the Lord. He continued to do this faithfully whenever he felt heaviness coming upon him again. It worked, and he was delivered from the stronghold of depression in his life.

In the psalm, David prays a powerful prayer that released him from depression. He asked the Lord to do the following:

1. Judge him (see if there was anything he needed to confess to the Lord).
2. Plead his cause against his enemies.
3. Deliver him from deceitful and unjust men.
4. Send His light and truth to him.
5. Lead and bring him to the place of worship and fellowship again.

God heard David's prayer, and the results were many of the joyous songs David wrote that we use today to praise and worship the Lord. Exceeding joy awaited David, but first he had to make a decision to praise the Lord, pray to the Lord and sing songs to the Lord even when he was oppressed by Satan and his spirit was down. You may want to pray as David prayed: "Lord, search me and show me if there is any sin I need to confess. Plead and do battle for me against Satan and deliver me from his deceptive thoughts by sending Your light and truth to me. Restore to me the joy of my salvation."

Victory Over Depression
Psalm 44:1–7

We end our readings for the month of February on a very positive note. In this psalm David reveals what sustained him throughout his life of trials and temptations. What sustained David was his love and trust relationship with the Lord. Because David was secure in his relationship to the Lord, he was able to release all into the hands of the Lord. There were times when David felt distant from God, but the truth that God commanded His lovingkindness always toward David gave David the anchor he needed to keep him from being overwhelmed by his circumstances. He constantly rehearsed and reviewed the marvelous works of the Lord and all the times the Lord had strengthened him.

In the first part of this psalm David reviews how it was not by its own strength or its own sword that Israel was able to drive out the heathen from the Promised Land. He gave all the credit to the Lord: "For they got not the land in possession by their own sword, neither did their own arm save them: but thy right hand, and thine arm, and the light of thy countenance, because thou hadst a favour unto them" (Ps. 44:3, KJV).

David was confident that God not only commanded His lovingkindness toward him, but also that God commanded deliverance for him and the children of Israel. Listen to this great statement of victory that David makes: "Through thee will we push down our enemies: through thy name will we tread them under that rise up against us" (v. 5, KJV).

Then David shares the key to victory in every circumstance. That key is trusting the Lord rather than trusting in our own strength or intelligence. He says, "For I will not trust in my bow, neither shall my sword save me. But thou hast saved us from our enemies, and hast put them to shame that hated us" (vv. 6–7, KJV).

We see in this psalm that David has come through his time of depression because he kept putting his trust in the Lord. He knew that the victory was his and the battle was the Lord's. When we put our trust in the Lord Jesus, Captain of the heavenly hosts, He fights our battles, and we can stand and see the salvation and deliverance of the Lord. If God be for me, who can be against me? Jesus is always able to put oppression to flight and remove it far from us. Paul tells us that Jesus through the cross spoiled principalities and powers and made a show of them, openly triumphing over them (Col. 2:15).

THE GIFT OF A DAY

The burden of the day is often enough in our thoughts, and the duty of the day is not likely to lie forgotten. But what we constantly overlook is the much happier, and equally true idea, of the gift of a day. We receive a valuable present every morning—for the most part, thanklessly. We ask God to give us this day our daily bread, and we return thanks for that when it is set before us. But which of us remembers that He gives, not only the bread, but the day as well?

Stevenson declares that when a man who has got well beyond seventy lays his old bones in bed for the night, there is an overwhelming probability that he will never see the day. Even for the most youthful, however, sleep is a hazardous adventure. Our personality dies every twenty-four hours. Yet the spirit returns to its tabernacle; we wake again exactly to what we left last night, with never a gap in the seam to show the joining. What brings me back? Perfectly sure am I that I had nothing to do with it. I received a precious gift this morning. Someone has given me this day. Moreover, it is not yesterday that we get back, but a new day. You went to bed last night tired and worn. And when God brought you His gift this morning, behold, He had smoothed out all the weariness and had added strength and energy.

When we think of what a day brings, we are compelled to recognize the pure unmerited grace of giving. When our eyes open on a spring morning, how boundless are the riches within the reach of the poorest of us. The air, the sky, the song of the birds, the colors—all priceless things, and your entire very own, if you can only take them. There's nobody so poor that he cannot afford a spring day. Each morning we rise to a clean sheet on which we may write what we please. We have a chance to work, be kind, learn and pray. This morning was a blank check, valid for just as much as we liked to take.

And while we look with shame upon the time that we have wasted, every morning God in His mercy lets us begin again. Yesterday you were sad and gloomy. Today is your chance to prove yourself an unconquerable soul. Yesterday you spoke unkindly to a friend. Today you can go and tell him you are sorry. Every morning, God in His mercy lets us begin again.

Perhaps there is a hidden blessing in the fact that God's gift is only a day, that we are tenants of life only between sleeps. Around His gift God built a fence of night and unconsciousness as if each day were meant to stand by itself.

> Build a little fence of trust just around today;
> Fill the space with loving work, and therein stay.
> Look not through the sheltering bars upon tomorrow.
> God will help thee bear whatever comes of joy or sorrow.
>
> AUTHOR UNKNOWN

The gift of a day being what it is, surely we cannot maintain an indifferent attitude toward the Giver of it. What we receive each morning, indeed, is a sacred and solemn trust. How base were it then to abase it and abuse it, to spend any part of our day in ways from which He who gives it must avert His Face! Let's ask Him to help us to use it as He wills.

Silver Tongue
Proverbs 10:20–21

When you go to the doctor, usually the first thing he says is, "Stick out your tongue." Your physical condition often will be shown by the condition of your tongue. The same is true about your spiritual condition. What you speak with your tongue reveals what is hidden in your heart. Some of the spiritual diseases that are revealed by what we speak are bitterness, jealousy, pride, anger and so forth.

This proverb says the tongue of the just is as choice silver. Silver is a metal that must be fired at a high temperature to remove all the impurities. The dross will come to the surface as the silver is fired. The dross or impurities of our lives will often surface when we go through fiery trials. When the pressure is on in our lives, our true nature is usually expressed by what we say. Could it be that this is one of the reasons the Lord allows fiery trials in our lives? He desires for our tongues to be pure and holy.

The daily challenge is to guard our tongues, but no man can tame the tongue. Only the Holy Spirit can do this. In order to heal some of the other diseases of the tongue, we must spend time with the Lord, our Great Physician, for He alone can heal them. We must then take the medicine prescribed for these tongue conditions:

- Critical, judgmental words—Titus 3:1–2
- Flattery—Proverbs 26:28; 29:5
- Lies—Proverbs 6:16–19; 12:22; Revelation 21:8
- Idle words—Matthew 12:36; 5:37
- Murmuring and complaining—Philippians 2:14–15; 1 Corinthians 10:10
- Negative words—Ephesians 4:29
- Cursing and suggestive words (caused by seducing spirits)—1 Timothy 4:1
- Angry, argumentative words—James 3:16; Proverbs 13:10
- Gossip—Proverbs 20:19; 18:8; 11:13; 26:20; Leviticus 19:16
- Hasty words—Ecclesiastes 5:3, Proverbs 10:32; 17:28; 29:20; Psalm 106:32–33
- Excessive words—Ecclesiastes 5:3; Proverbs 10:19; James 3:8

When we take the prescribed medicine from a doctor, we expect results. I believe if you will meditate on the scriptures above, you will soon be healed of whatever tongue disease you may have. Let the prayer of David in Psalm 17:3 be yours today:

I am purposed that my mouth shall not transgress.

God's Blessings

Leviticus 25:47–27:13

We used to sing the song, "There Shall Be Showers of Blessing." This passage in Leviticus tells of the showers of God's blessings that will flow from His throne room upon us. However, all the blessings listed here are conditional. Most of the promises of God are conditional. He promises so much in His Word to us, but for the promises to be fulfilled in our lives we have a part. Both the Old Testament and New Testament have the same main condition expressed for the fulfillment of the blessings and promises. The condition we must meet is to walk in God's ways and keep His commandments.

In the New Testament Jesus gives only two commandments that we must fulfill: To love the Lord God with all of our hearts, and to love our neighbor as ourselves. All the Law, Jesus says, is based on these two commandments. The good news is that Jesus came to fulfill the Law so that we now are capable in His strength of obeying the Law. Many people claim the promises of God without fulfilling the conditions.

Listen to all the blessings that will come to those who walk in God's ways and keep His commandments to obey them.

1. Rain in due season (Lev. 26:4)
2. Fruitful land (Lev. 26:4)
3. Fruitful trees (Lev. 26:4)
4. Abundance—vintage crops (Lev. 26:5)
5. Plenty of bread to eat (Lev. 26:5)
6. Safety (Lev. 26:5)
7. Peace in the land (Lev. 26:6)
8. No fear of enemies (Lev. 26:6)
9. Evil beast will not be a threat (Lev. 26:6)
10. The sword of enemies will not be a threat (Lev. 26:6)
11. Victory over enemies (Lev. 26:7)
12. Old things will pass away and newness will replace it (Lev. 26:8)
13. Fertility (Lev. 26:9)
14. God's presence (Lev. 26:11)
15. God's favor (Lev. 26:12)

What a list of blessings! This list challenges me to walk in the ways of the Lord every day. When the Lord is our shepherd, goodness and mercy will always follow us. Let this be your prayer today:

Lord, lead me in Your paths of righteousness for Your name's sake. Teach me Your ways that I might fear and glorify Your name today.

READ: Leviticus 27:14–Numbers 1:54; Mark 11:1–26; Psalm 46:1–11; Proverbs 10:23

The Wings of Prayer
Mark 11:1–26

The question often is asked, "Why are some prayers never answered?" The answer to this question is that God does answer every prayer that reaches His throne room and every prayer He hears. Some prayers, however, never reach His throne room. Prayers prayed in unbelief do not avail anything. James tells us that a double-minded man can expect to receive nothing from God.

In this passage in Mark we learn the wings of prayer that send our prayers directly into God's throne room. The wings of prayer are faith and forgiveness. When we pray, we must do two things to set our prayers soaring into God's throne room. We must believe that He hears us, and we must forgive all. If we are in unforgiveness, God will not hear our prayers. Also, we must be careful to pray according to the will of God. How do we know what is the will of God? As long as we are praying according to the Word of God, we will be praying in God's will. His will is His Word. There is a great promise in 1 John 5:14–15: "Now this is the confidence that we have in Him, that if we ask anything according to His will, He hears us. And if we know that He hears us, whatever we ask, we know that we have the petitions that we have asked of Him."

The Bible tells us that if a man regards iniquity in his heart, God will not hear his prayers (Ps. 66:18). The word *regard* here means "to see." If we see a sin in our own lives and refuse to confess it and receive God's forgiveness for it, then we have regarded iniquity in our hearts, and God will not hear us. Prayer is a waste of breath and time if we have unforgiveness in our hearts toward anyone, or if we know we have sinned and refuse to confess this to the Lord and receive His forgiveness and cleansing.

Confession and cleansing are key ingredients necessary for our prayers to be heard. I like the ACTS method of prayer that many use—Adore the Lord, Confess your sins, Thank the Lord, Supplicate and make your requests known unto the Lord. This morning before you pray, spend some time first in adoration to the Lord. This is a way of declaring your faith in Him. Then confess your sins and also ask the Lord if there is anyone you need to forgive. If the Holy Spirit brings a name to your mind of a person you need to forgive you can pray a prayer of forgiveness like this: "Lord, I forgive ____, and I ask You to bless ____." Remember forgiveness is not a feeling. It is an act of your will. Make the decision this morning to forgive all who have wronged you. Now you are ready to make your supplications and requests known to the Lord, and do this with thanksgiving. If you follow this simple way of praying, you can have confidence that God will hear your prayers and you will have the petitions you desire of Him. Have a blessed time this morning as you send your prayers soaring on the wings of faith and forgiveness…

Who Is the Owner?
Mark 11:27-12:17

We have had the privilege of having two exchange students live with us—a Chinese girl and a Russian boy. Both became like a daughter and son to us, and they called us Mom and Dad. Our Chinese daughter has returned to China where she lives with her parents and sister. What a joy it has been to be enriched by two of God's precious treasures. People are God's inheritance, and we have learned over the years that in order for us to fully enjoy God, we must also take pleasure in His treasures.

I'll never forget one night when I shared my heart with my Russian son. He had become a little frustrated with me since I took his things out of the dryer in order to dry some of my things. His response was, "Don't touch my things." I went upstairs and prayed, and later that night I asked him, "Who owns this house?" He responded, "You do." Then I asked, "Who owns this dryer?" He responded, "You and Dad do." Then I shared, "You are wrong on both counts, because Dad and I own nothing. We are only stewards of God's treasures on earth." Then I shared with him that we learned the hard way to hold all we enjoy on this earth with an open hand, because everything we think we possess in this life—houses, family, etc.—in reality belongs to the Lord.

In this passage in Mark, Jesus' response to the Pharisees' and Herodians' question, "Shall we give or not give tribute to Caesar?", reveals how God views true ownership. Jesus responded, "Render to Caesar the things that are Caesar's and to God the things that are God's." They marveled at Him. Jesus with this answer was saying that all things on this earth are of Him, for Him and by Him because He created all things. Caesar owned nothing. He created Caesar and all Caesar thought he owned. When we recognize true ownership, the right we thought we had to ownership of our possessions on this earth will be erased.

When we recognize that God owns the cattle on a thousand hills and created all things for His pleasure, then jealousy, covetousness, pride and greed are dealt a severe blow. We begin to have a thankful heart for even the smallest things God has allowed us to be stewards of on this earth. A steward only has to take care of the things he is lent for a season. He is not burdened down with all the details the owner has to deal with daily. God owns us and everything we enjoy on this earth. But He is never burdened down with having to see to the details about all that concerns us. In fact, the Bible says His burden is light. God is the owner of all, and He enjoys caring for all that is a concern to us. Peter tells us the way we can humble ourselves before God is to cast all of our cares upon Him. I have often said, "The more a person has, the more he has to take care of, and sometimes it becomes a burden." This problem can easily be solved when we recognize true ownership. I now say, "The more a person has, the more he has to release to God for Him to care for, and He knows how to perfect everything that is a concern to us." What a relief to know I do not have to hold on possessively to anything in this life. I am set free to take pleasure in all God has lent me on earth even as He takes pleasure in all He has created.

March 5

READ: Numbers 4:1–5:31; Mark 12:18–37; Psalm 48:1–14; Proverbs 10:26

The Importance of Covering
Numbers 4:1–5:31

As I read this scripture I saw something I missed in my former readings over the years. All the treasures and holy things that were used in the service of the Lord were covered first with a blue or purple cloth, and then were covered with badgers' skin. The covering had to be placed upon the instruments of sacrifice and worship before they could be taken to another location. This action of covering is symbolic of how important covering is in our lives. We are living sacrifices, and our act of worship is to daily offer our bodies to the Lord as instruments of His righteousness, peace, love and joy.

The blue or purple cloth that first was wrapped around the holy things in the tabernacle represents God's setting us apart as a holy thing before Him. Many call this process sanctification. The word prefix *sanct-* means "saint," and the suffix *-ification* means "being made." We are being made saints as we live our lives out on earth. The covering of the badgers' skin represents the shedding of blood that gives us remission of sins and places us in a position of authority. Leviticus tells us without the shedding of blood there is no remission of sins. Before the holy things in the tabernacle could be moved to another location, they had to be covered with both the blue or purple cloth and the badgers' skin.

Daily we are set apart as instruments for the Lord's service. Before we move from our quiet place to go outside our home into the world, it is important that we too are covered with the anointing of the Holy Spirit and the blood of Jesus. We are God's treasures, and we are His holy instruments of service. In the morning I try to pray the following prayer that places me under His anointing and the covering of His blood:

> *Lord, I lift my body, soul (mind, will and emotions) and spirit up to You. Use me as an instrument of Your peace, love and joy. I offer the members of my body as instruments of righteousness today. I cover my family members and myself today with the blood of Jesus. Thank You for the blood of Jesus that sanctifies me, forgives me, cleanses me, heals me and justifies me. Amen.*

I did not realize until this morning as I read this passage in Numbers that for years through praying this prayer I have been preparing myself and my family members to be taken to wherever God wants to use us. This may be the reason two of our children have been sent to distant lands to be used as instruments of service in those lands.

Moment by Moment
Psalm 49:1–20

Their inward thought is, that their houses shall continue for ever, and their dwelling places to all generations" (Ps. 49:11, KJV). It is the nature of man to feel he will never die. That inward thought says, "You'll never die."

The phrase "you shall not die" was first used by Satan in the garden to deceive Eve, and he has been using that phrase ever since to deceive us. If Satan can get us to swallow that lie, we will always think there will be a tomorrow, and we will live our lives accordingly. We will be subject to procrastination and to apathy about where we will spend eternity.

I learned when I almost lost my life how God wants us to see our days. There is a psalm that says, "Teach us to number our days that we might apply our hearts unto wisdom." I almost hemorrhaged to death, and in that moment when I felt my spirit leave my body, I knew that if God did not intervene I would die. God did intervene, and I lived. After this experience with near death I learned a great lesson. God not only wants us to number our days, He desires also that we live in the moment because this is all we have. So many in this life play the "when, then game." They think that when they retire or when they get a new job, then they will be able to do certain things. Many look forward to the Lord releasing them into ministry when in reality the only ministry they have is now. Faith can only operate in the now. Our ministry is in the moment. Moment by moment we need to be led by the Spirit, and whomever we are facing or whatever we are facing in each moment is our ministry.

I remember hearing a dynamic speaker when I lived in Savannah, Georgia. After her talk, several ladies went forward to be prayed for by the speaker. I heard one lady ask the speaker, "What do you think my ministry is?" The speaker was very wise in her response. She said, "Are you a housewife and do you have children?" The lady replied, "Yes." Then the speaker said, "Your ministry is faith and forgiveness…hand and minister to those around you. Your ministry is loving your husband and your children, and your call for the day may be as simple as baking cookies for your children." Don't miss the ministry of the moment.

Forgive me, Lord, for missing out on the many opportunities You give me each day to share Your love and good news with others. So often I'm so busy thinking ahead that I forget what is right before me. Help me to be sensitive to the needs of my own family, and help me to listen for the guidance of Your Holy Spirit. I do not want to miss out on any divine appointments You may have for me today. Amen.

The Tongue and Troubles
Psalm 50:1–23

There is one promise of God that will be fulfilled in every life. Jesus said, "In the world you will have tribulation; but be of good cheer, I have overcome the world" (John 16:33). Because we live in a fallen world, there will always be trouble. This psalm reveals two important responses we should have when trouble comes our way. Verse 15 exhorts us to call upon the Lord in our day of trouble. Verse 23 exhorts us to praise the Lord and to order our conversation aright.

If we will call upon the Lord in the day of trouble, the promise is He will deliver us. If we will praise the Lord and order our conversation aright in the day of trouble, He will show us His salvation.

The moment we enter troublesome times, we should first pray—and then we should be careful about what we say. God will be glorified when we do these two things. If we fail to call upon God in our troubled times, the hope of being delivered through or out of the trouble will be slim.

Preventative medicine is better than a cure. A lot of the trouble we find ourselves in is self-inflicted. We have submitted to fleshly lusts instead of following the Spirit. The preventative medicine to keep us out of trouble is God's Word and prayer. We can prevent the majority of troubles in our lives if we are not anxious about anything, but instead pray about everything. If we stay in God's Word daily, chances are we will be able to discern the origin of the thoughts we have throughout the day. Our thoughts usually come from three sources: God, our own flesh or the devil. We will only be able to recognize the counterfeit if we know the Truth, and we find that in God's Word. We only can take those thoughts captive to Jesus if we recognize who gave us those thoughts.

Another preventative medicine is to be careful about what we speak. There is a proverb that says, "He that keepeth his lips is wise; he keeps his soul from troubles." We get into trouble many times just because we have not been wise in our speech. David, when he wrote this psalm, knew that the only way God could be glorified in our lives was if we learned to order our conversations aright. The tongue is the red carpet we throw out to Satan to walk right into our lives with his special delivery of troubles.

Even if we guard our tongues, pray about everything and stay in God's Word, some troubles will come our way simply because we live in a corrupt world. Tribulation is in the world and always will be until the Lord sets up His kingdom on earth. The moment trouble comes knocking on your door, you need to begin to praise the Lord because you know He is in control. His plan is to work good out of what Satan means for evil. The moment you begin to praise the Lord, a glory shield is placed around you because you have ordered your conversation aright. You will not be overwhelmed by whatever trial is facing you. You will be at peace and can even experience fullness of joy in the presence of the Lord.

A Heart After God
Psalm 51:1–19

Davavid is described as a man after God's own heart. He was not perfect by any means, but there was something in him that attracted God. It was his heart. David had a contrite and humble heart. The Bible tells us that God will not despise a contrite heart. David had just committed adultery when he wrote this psalm, and this psalm instructs us how to confess our sins. First John 1:9 says, "If we confess our sins, he is faithful and just to forgive us our sins, and to cleanse us from all unrighteousness" (KJV). We have another scripture in James 5:16: "Confess your faults [shortcomings and sins] one to another, and pray one for another, that ye may be healed. The effectual fervent prayer of a righteous man availeth much" (KJV).

Since the Protestant Reformation, there has almost been a neglect of the power of confession. The Catholic Church requires that confession be made to a priest for one's sins. Just because we consider ourselves mature Christians does not negate our need for a daily time of confession. Remember the form of prayer suggested previously called ACTS. Our private and group prayer times would be much more effective if we followed this little outline:

A dore the Lord; spend time in telling the Lord how much you love Him.

C onfess your sins; ask the Holy Spirit if there is anything you need to confess.

T hank the Lord and enter into praise.

S upplicate and make your requests known unto God with thanksgiving.

David knew the power of confession, and he gives us an outline that includes the major ingredients of confession in Psalm 51:

1. Have mercy on me—appeal to God's mercy (v. 1)

2. Blot out my transgressions—acknowledge the loving kindness of the Lord (v. 1)

3. Wash me thoroughly from my iniquity—iniquity is "the want to or desire to sin" (v. 2)

4. Cleanse me from my sin—we are cleansed by the blood of Jesus (v. 2)

5. I acknowledge my transgression—transgression is how we have hurt others (v. 3)

6. Against You only have I sinned—when we sin we grieve God (v. 4)

7. Behold, You desire truth—we need to be honest with God concerning our sin (v. 6)

8. Make me to know wisdom—wisdom is what keeps us from sinning (v. 6)

9. Purge me with hyssop—hyssop was used to apply the blood to the door post (v. 7)

10. Make me to hear joy and gladness—restore the joy of my salvation (v. 8)

11. Create within me a clean heart and renew a right spirit—restore my spirit (v. 10)

12. Open my lips to praise You and tell of Your wonders—restore my witness (v. 15)

We see in this psalm that the sacrifice God is pleased with is a broken, contrite heart. Such a heart always attracts God, and He always is willing to cleanse and restore us if we will only confess our sins to Him. Spend a little time in confession this morning.

Green Means Go—Red Means Stop
Psalm 52:1–9

I remember my mother teaching me how to obey the traffic signals when I was a child. "Green means go," she would say, "and red means stop." In this passage we see the comparison between red and green. The tongue is red, and it is, as shared earlier, a red carpet we roll out to Satan whenever we allow him to use our tongues. David speaks about the tongue of an evil man and how it devises mischief and even has the power to devour. The end of the evil man who cannot control his tongue is destruction. There is a proverb that says, "Death and life are in the power of the tongue." When we see a red light, we immediately put on the brakes of our car or stop at the curb if we are walking. If we would stop to think before we speak and wait for the green light of the Holy Spirit to lead our conversation, we would be extremely wise.

This psalm goes on to speak of a person who loves the Lord and wants to obey Him in word and deed. He is like a green olive tree in the house of God that trusts in the mercy of God forever and ever. He praises the Lord and waits upon Him. Green is a color used often to represent peace. There is even a movement today called "Green Peace." If we will trust in the Lord with all of our hearts, praise Him and wait upon Him, we will have peace and will be like green olive trees. An olive tree never dies. In the gardens on the Mount of Olives in Israel today, there are olive trees that have sprung from the roots of trees growing during the time of Jesus. Our kind, prayerful, thoughtful words have the power to last forever from generation to generation. On the negative side, our murmuring, complaining and word curses have the power to go on for generations. We forget the power of words to penetrate the airwaves and remain forever. Satan knows this, and this is why he is sometimes called "the Prince and Power of the Air."

Remember, "Red means stop; green means go." The next time you are about to open your mouth, don't roll the red carpet of your tongue out for Satan by speaking unwisely. We are exhorted in the Word to always allow our speech to be seasoned with grace and to only speak those things that edify. We are also told to speak evil of no man. Ask the Holy Spirit to hold your hand today as you cross the streets of this life. You will feel His gentle hand restraining you if the light is not green and you are about to speak something unwise.

> Lord, I want to order my conversation aright. I do not want to roll out the red carpet of my tongue to allow Satan to walk into my life. Help me to obey the gentle restraining hand of the Holy Spirit when I am about to say something I should not. I want to keep my soul from troubles. Help me to glorify You with my speech today. Amen.

The Glory of God
Numbers 14:1–15:16

God told Moses, "As truly as I live, all the earth shall be filled with the glory of the Lord." Moses was pleading with God not to destroy the Israelites for their disobedience. He made his appeal on the basis that all of Israel's enemies would see their destruction and would believe that God was not able to save them. God's response was that His ultimate plan for the earth would be fulfilled no matter how disobedient man was. He told Moses that the day will come when His glory will fill the whole earth.

When I was Presbyterian, I had to learn the Presbyterian Catechism. One of the questions asked in the Catechism was, "What is the chief end of man?" The answer that we memorized was, "The chief end of man is to glorify God and enjoy Him forever." This answer gives us our part on earth. We were created for God's glory, and the whole earth will only be filled with His glory if we cooperate with His Holy Spirit.

As God views the earth, He sees particles of light here and there on the dark surface of the earth. These lights shining in the midst of darkness are people who allow God's glory light to shine through them. One day God will look upon the earth, and He will see no darkness at all because the whole earth will be filled with His glory—people who allow His glory to shine through them. I don't believe this will happen in all of its fullness until the millennium when Jesus reigns on earth. It is exciting, however, to know that we can brighten the corner where we are.

When New Jerusalem descends from heaven, the whole earth will be filled with God's glory. New Jerusalem has no need for a light, because the glory of the Lord will be a light for the people. Until that day, we can let our lights shine brightly each day of our lives. "This little light of mine, I'm going to let it shine."

Father, Your glory will shine throughout the earth and fill it one day. In the meantime, help me to stay lit with the fire of Your Holy Spirit. Help me to shine brighter and brighter as the day draws near to Your coming. I desire to brighten every room I enter, every person I meet, every situation I encounter today. Never let me walk in darkness. Help me to always walk in Your light and carry Your light to others. Amen.

Pleasing Men
Mark 15:1–47

This passage in Mark gives the details of what led to the crucifixion of our Lord. Pilate was warned by his wife in a dream not to harm Jesus, but Pilate was a man pleaser. We hear these chilling words: "And so Pilate, willing to content the people, released Barabbas unto them, and delivered Jesus, when he had scourged him, to be crucified" (Mark 15:15, KJV).

Pilate listened to the people, and he put their desires above anything else. He wanted to be popular with the people, and so he gave into their demands. One might say that Pilate was subject to peer pressure.

Peer pressure is one of the main causes for teenagers to get into drugs. Our youngest son, Ray, got into drugs because he wanted to have friends. He was rejected in his late grammar school days because of his faith in Jesus. When he reached high school, he found a group of friends who accepted him, but unfortunately they were drug users. It was not long before Ray got into drugs. Even though he knew the Bible and had been raised in a Christian home where prayers went up for him daily, he got into drugs. Why? The answer is that he wanted to be popular with the people. When Pilate chose to please man over pleasing God or his wife, the result was the crucifixion of Jesus Christ.

When we choose to please men above God, we are in a sense crucifying Christ afresh. We are exhorted to crucify our own flesh or reckon it dead daily so that we might be alive to Jesus Christ. Just the opposite happens when we choose to please men rather than God. We reckon ourselves alive to sin and dead to Christ whenever we willfully please men rather than God.

The good report is that God is a redeemer and restorer, and He sent Jesus Christ to make a way of escape when we are tempted. God in his mercy redeemed and restored Ray, and he now is serving Christ in Budapest, Hungary as a missionary with his wife. The fear of the Lord became evident in Ray's life when he wanted to please God more than himself or other people. Could it be that "peer pressure" is one of the reasons for America's steady moral decay? The Bible speaks about how in the last days men will be lovers of pleasure more than lovers of God and they will seek their own rather than the welfare of others. Some politicians are even willing to sell their soul for the almighty vote.

There is only one vote I am concerned about in this life, and that is God's vote. Is He for me and will He support me when the campaign of life gets rough? The answer is "yes," because He said, "I will never leave you or forsake you." Even though Ray for a season was seeking the vote of acceptance from his peers, God was giving him His vote of confidence. God knew that Ray would turn back to Him, and God was with Ray even during his rebellious season of life. Whose vote are you seeking? Are you seeking God's approval or man's approval? The truth is that God already approves of you. After all, He gave His only begotten Son to save you. If you were the only person living on the earth, God would still have sent His Son to die for you.

The Perfect Sin Sacrifice
Mark 16:1–20

God is a God of infinite detail. He made sure that Jesus fulfilled every requirement for a sin sacrifice according to His laws. The account in Mark of Mary Magdalene bringing sweet spices on the Sabbath to anoint Jesus' body reveals a very important fact about Jesus' burial.

Jesus died around 3 P.M. in the afternoon just before sundown on a Friday. At sundown the Sabbath would begin, and the body could not be prepared on that day. When Jesus delivered His spirit into the hands of the Father and died, He was taken off the cross and wrapped for burial. There was not sufficient time to prepare His body completely for burial because those tending Him were rushing to get the job done before sundown.

When the Sabbath was past, the two Marys brought sweet spices to anoint the body of Jesus and thus complete the embalming process that could not be completed before the Sabbath. Along with these sweet spices I believe frankincense was included. Frankincense is a sweet white gum that comes from a tree in Israel. It has a sweet odor and was mixed with other sweet spices to make the holy perfume mentioned in Exodus 30:34. Frankincense was used with oil to cover most of the sacrificial offerings required by the Levitical law. There was one sacrifice, however, upon which frankincense was forbidden for anointing. This sacrifice was the sin offering. We find this in Leviticus 5:11: "He shall put no oil upon it, neither shall he put any frankincense thereon: for it is a sin offering" (KJV).

God is a God of infinite detail. He made sure frankincense was never laid on the body of Jesus, because if it had been, He would not have fulfilled the requirements as the perfect sin sacrifice. I believe Mary was carrying the very frankincense that was given to her by the Magi on the night Jesus was born. She probably kept it in a safe place and treasured it for years.

The scriptures do not tell us that Mary was carrying frankincense, but it is a natural assumption since she was carrying sweet spices. I believe this was the case and that it proves how awesome our God is. He has marked the heavens with the span of His hand and can hold all the waters on earth in the hollow of His hand (Isa. 40:12), yet He humbles Himself to number the hairs on our heads and to see the hearts of men. He has named every star in the universes (Ps. 147:4–5), and yet He saw the need to prevent frankincense from being applied to the body of our Lord, which would have nullified His acceptance as the perfect sin sacrifice.

All we have talked about this morning should give us strong confidence that God can meet our needs through Jesus Christ because He loves us. Jesus fulfilled every requirement to be the perfect sin offering for our sake, and because He did, we now can have access to the throne room of God through prayer and can approach His throne of grace and find help in time of need. So what are you worried about?

When to Trust in the Lord
Psalm 56:1–13

The Bible exhorts us in many verses to trust in the Lord at all times. There is, however, a special time when we need to say aloud, "I trust in the Lord." That special time is when fear comes upon us. David writes in this psalm, "What time I am afraid, I will trust in You." If you are familiar with David's history, you will know he was provided with many opportunities to be afraid. He constantly was surrounded by enemies, and in the psalms David reveals some of the secrets to overcoming fear. He certainly became an expert at this. David was quite sure that fear would always present its cold, clammy handshake throughout his life. David, however, learned not to shake hands with the devil and receive fear.

Fear is the frontal assault the enemy uses against us. If he can get us in fear, then he has neutralized any effort of ours to overcome him. We must have faith to overcome the enemy, and fear always negates faith. Fear is the anesthesia Satan uses to paralyze so he can then perform his surgery on his victims. If we learn to refuse fear, we will spare ourselves from much of what Satan would love to accomplish in our lives. Jesus said, "Fear not," and the words "be not afraid" and "fear not" are written over 365 times in the Bible. We see over and over again people who began in faith, but then were overwhelmed by fear. The moment fear entered in, they were neutralized in their effectiveness. An example of this, of course, was Peter when he was walking on the water. Everything was going fine until Peter took his eyes off Jesus and looked at the angry sea. He was overcome with fear and began to sink.

In this psalm David tells us what to do when fear comes. David knew that Satan would never stop trying to put fear on him, but David learned how to resist Satan when he came knocking at the door of his heart with the special delivery marked "FEAR." The moment fear knocked, David said, "I will trust in the Lord." Not one of us is skillful enough to overcome Satan's tactics in our own strength. If, however, we put our trust in the Lord to fight our battles for us, we will have the victory every time.

The next time fear comes knocking at your door, say aloud, "I will trust in the Lord and not be afraid." The moment these words leave your mouth, you will feel a surge of faith and strength rising within you. The Bible tells us not to be anxious about anything, but instead to pray about everything. We have learned today not to be fearful in anything, but to trust the Lord in everything. When we do this, the peace of God will mount guard over our hearts with His peace. Fear always attacks the heart and upper part of the body. Fear causes our hearts to race, and also causes that sinking feeling in the pit of our stomachs. The moment you feel either of these sensations, immediately say aloud, "I will trust in the Lord and not be afraid." A blanket of God's peace will flow over you, and you will be able to fulfill all God desires for you on this earth.

March 14

READ: Numbers 21:1–22:20; Luke 1:26–56; Psalm 57:1–11; Proverbs 11:9–11

When Nothing Is Impossible
Luke 1:26–56

We like to quote so often the phrase in this passage, "For with God nothing shall be impossible." If God did not have to work through men, His power on earth would be unlimited. However, even though nothing is impossible with God and He does all things well, the stark reality is that we as Christians do not allow Him to do the impossible in our lives because of our lack of faith. The story comes to mind when the disciples came to Jesus for help in casting a deaf and dumb spirit out of a little boy. Jesus told them they were unable to do this because of their lack of faith. Then He said, "O faithless generation." Nothing is impossible with God when we put our complete faith and trust in Him.

Mary in this passage is a prime example of complete faith and trust. The angel told her, "Fear not." As we studied yesterday, fear has to be dealt with or we will lose our effectiveness in overcoming the devil. Mary had no fear. Then when Mary heard all that would be done to her in the conception of Jesus Christ, she had faith. She said simply, "Be it unto me according to Your word." Now the way was paved for God to do the impossible. Nothing is impossible when we overcome fear through faith and trust in God.

We hear of report after report of miracles happening in countries like Africa and Indonesia, yet we seem to have a famine in the United States of miracles. Why? We as Christians in America often do not display the simple childlike faith that people in other countries do.

What has choked out our faith? I believe it is the materialism and the instant gratification syndrome that have overtaken many of us. We are not willing to spend time in prayer and the Word to build our faith. Faith comes by hearing and hearing by the Word of God. Often in these small villages in other lands where there is no TV, no Walmart, we see mighty miracles. The people in these villages are not distracted from what is most important—doing the will of God and believing Him when they pray. Jesus said that unless a man became like a little child, he could not enter the kingdom of heaven. A small baby is completely dependent upon his parents for every need, and he trusts his parents to meet them. Is this where God wants every Christian? If we could strip ourselves of all the materialism and business in our lives, perhaps we could become as a little child—totally dependent upon God for everything and ever hanging on His Word.

Nothing is impossible with God when we trust in His Word and fear not.

Lord, I earnestly pray, be it done unto me today according to Your Word. Place within me the faith of a little child, and give me the courage to step out in faith. Faith was the substance Peter walked on when he was coming toward You on the sea. Help me to walk in faith today.

READ: Numbers 22:21–23:30; Luke 1:57–80; Psalm 58:1–11; Proverbs 11:12–13

God Said It, I Believe It, I Receive It
Numbers 22:21–23:30

This passage relates the story of Balaam, a prophet who was certainly not perfect, but a prophet who knew God was true to His Word. Balaam said, "God is not a man, that he should lie; neither the son of man, that he should repent: Hath he said, and shall he not do it? or hath he spoken, and shall he not make it good? (Num. 23:19, KJV).

God always makes His Word good. He keeps His Word, and He performs His Word. He makes His Word good. When we believe this about God's character, we will be able to trust Him and trust His Word. The only reason why we would hesitate to trust the Lord would be that we believe somehow that He will not do what He has said He will do. If we doubt His trustworthiness, then we will not trust Him.

How can we build our trust in the Lord? The only way this will happen is if we read His Word and see His faithfulness to His own Word to perform it throughout history. When we read God's Word, we will see that His Word always performs that which it is sent out to do. When we know this, we can trust Him.

Father, You have proven over and over again in Your Word that You are trustworthy. You never lie, and all of Your promises are "yes and amen" through Jesus Christ. As I read through the Bible this year, help me to be built up in faith. I never want to doubt Your Word, because Your Word is Truth. Amen.

The Lord Is My Defense
Psalm 59:1–17

When we were in St. Petersburg, Russia, for an evangelical music festival designed to reach Jewish people, one of the musicians sang a song that I'll never forget. The phrase "He is my defense" was repeated over and over again in the song. That phrase still resounds in my spiritual ears. God truly is our defense, and David knew this even though his enemies surrounded him and used their tongues as swords against him. He knew that God was his strong defense. David said, "God shall let me see my desire upon my enemies."

David also knew the secret of dressing himself in the garment of praise continually. After reviewing what he wanted God to do to defeat his enemies, he said, "But I will sing of Your power; yes, I will sing aloud of Your mercy in the morning; for You have been my defense and refuge in the day of my trouble…for God is my defense" (Ps. 59:16–17). When we sing aloud to the Lord, demons are put to confusion, and all of our enemies have to flee. Praise is the devil's death knell. When we praise the Lord, we place an invisible shield around us, and we can say with David, "You prepare a table before me in the presence of my enemies" (Ps. 23:5).

My twin sister one time had a vivid picture of just how the Lord's table looks as it is prepared in the midst of our enemies. She saw a table beautifully set with gold and silver, and laden with different kinds of fruits. The Lord Himself was at the head of this huge table. Above Him and all the people gathered was a shield that resembled a glass enclosure. The shield was in reality just a shelter of light. It was God's glory shield over all those present at His table. Just past this shield was total darkness. The people gathered, however, could see through the darkness, and they saw that although Satan with all of his demonic spirits was trying to penetrate this shield—they could not. Those dining were singing beautiful songs of praise as they partook of their wonderful feast.

God is our defense. He is our rock, our high tower and our hiding place. The clothing worn by the guests at this wonderful feast were garments of light that glistened brighter as the guests began to praise the Lord. These were the garments of praise mentioned in Isaiah 61:3—the garment of praise for the spirit of heaviness. The Bible tells us that God dwells in the midst of our praises. Something supernatural happens when we praise the Lord. As we praise Him, we are dressed in these special glory garments. We cannot see it, but Satan sees it, and he hates it because he knows he is unable to get to us. One morning as I was singing an old hymn, "Oh worship the King all glorious above," the phrase "pavilioned in splendor, and girded with praise" stood out to me. At that moment I heard the Lord speak this to my spirit: "Yes, I do dwell in the midst of the praises of My people. As they praise Me, I too am dressed with the glory garments of praise. My glory intensifies as My saints on earth praise Me."

77

March 17

A Good Prayer for Children
Luke 2:36–52

From the time my boys were very young I prayed they would all have the same excellent spirit that Daniel had. Daniel had favor with man, and he had much wisdom. He also lived to be an old man. In this passage we see Jesus as a young boy honoring both His heavenly Father and His earthly father. Even though He knew He had to be about His Father's business, He was willing to subject Himself to Mary and Joseph and return with them to their home when they found Him in the temple. Our pastor recently preached a good sermon about how Mary should have first looked in the temple for Jesus because it was considered the house of God. She knew Jesus was the Son of God. After looking for three days, Mary and Joseph finally found Jesus among the doctors in the temple. He was intently listening, but He also shared with them some of His thoughts. They were astonished at His wisdom. The Bible tells us that Jesus returned to Nazareth and increased in wisdom and stature and favor with God and man.

In this passage, we discover a wonderful prayer we can pray for our children. Combining verses 40 and 52, we can pray the following effective prayer for our children:

> *Father, in the name of Jesus we pray that our children will wax strong in the spirit and that they will be filled with wisdom. May Your grace be upon them always. May our children be subject to God and to us as parents, and may they increase not only in stature, but also in wisdom and favor with God and man. Amen.*

March 18

READ: Numbers 26:52-28:14; Luke 3:1-22; Psalm 61:1-8; Proverbs 11:16-17

Jochebed
Numbers 26:52-28:14

One morning I was waking from a night's sleep, and I heard the name "Jochebed" in my spirit. I knew it was the Lord calling me Jochebed. I got up and looked up the name in the *Strong's Concordance* and found that Jochebed was the mother of two sons and a daughter. Both of her sons were priests. She was the mother of Moses, Aaron and Miriam. The name *Jochebed* in Hebrew means "the Lord glorified."

For over a year I pondered about why God would call me Jochebed. One night coming home from church I was listening to Chuck Swindoll on my car radio as he shared the Hebrew meaning for priests. He said that the word *priests* in Hebrew means "bridge builder." When my boys were very young I asked the Lord to show me their call in life. He was faithful to do this and spoke to me the following:

~ Your oldest son, Russ, will be a bridge between races.
~ Your middle son, Ron, will be a bridge between nations.
~ Your youngest son, Ray, will be a bridge between families. He is a peacemaker.

This prophetic word has been fulfilled in all three of my son's lives. Russ has had many opportunities to bridge the races, and Ron and his wife and two children left for China in 2001 to teach English as a second language to Chinese college students. Ray and his wife, Teri, are reaching out to Jewish people in Budapest, Hungary. Through their witness to the Jewish people, they are joining the two families of God—Jew and Gentile—together as one.

The Lord called me Jochebed because I too am a mother of priests—bridge builders in the kingdom of God. If you have children or grandchildren, why don't you spend some time seeking the Lord about their call in life? I know God will be faithful to reveal this to you.

Lord, Your Word tells me that there are works You have prepared for me to do even before I was born. The same is true of my children and grandchildren. I desire to know what these works are so that my whole family can walk in every work You have prepared. Show me clearly the call You have on each of my loved ones. Thank You.

Casting Our Cares Upon Jesus
Psalm 62:1–12

David gives excellent advice in the psalm. He exhorts us to trust in the Lord at all times and to pour out our concerns and cares before Him. I learned how much God does love for us to cast our cares upon Him several years ago.

My usual time with the Lord is in the early morning. For some reason I missed my usual time and did not have this special time with the Lord until it was 2 P.M. As I went to prayer, the Lord spoke the following to my heart: "Linda, I love you because you cast every care upon Me. Thank you."

At that moment, I saw with my spiritual eyes my cares wrapped as gift-wrapped packages. They were ascending to the throne room, and Jesus was there to catch each package. He held the gifts of my cares to His bosom and danced around heaven rejoicing because now He could perfect all those things that concerned me. One of the cares I cast upon the Lord was my concern for my boys to marry wonderful Christian girls who were also called to be laborers in God's vineyard. Five minutes after I released this to the Lord, I received a telephone call from one of my "daughters in the Lord." I had grown weary of waiting for daughters-in-law, so I adopted and mentored several younger women I knew. Rebecca, one of these special daughters, called and said, "Linda, I believe I have a message for you from the Lord. I really wrestled with the Lord about calling you since I knew I would be seeing you this afternoon at 4 at our prayer time. But when I was in a Christian bookstore I saw a sign that I knew was a message for you. The sign said, 'Daughters-in-law are worth waiting for.'" The timing of this call was too perfect to be a coincidence. I believe God dropped a post card from heaven through Rebecca to me telling me to be patient. The daughters-in-law were on the way. Today I have three of the most beautiful daughters-in-law, and they all adore God and their husbands. They all are servants in God's vineyard.

Is there a burden or care this morning that you want to cast upon the Lord? He is waiting expectantly to receive it, and He will perfect all those things that are a concern to you.

Lord, forgive me for not pouring out my heart to You. Help me to cast every care upon You, because I know You do care for me. Amen.

READ: Numbers 30:1-31:54; Luke 4:1-32; Psalm 63:1-11; Proverbs 11:20-21

The Anointing for Ministry
Luke 4:1-32

So many in this day are seeking the anointing, but few realize that we already have the anointing. We have the same anointing for ministry that Jesus had. Isaiah lists seven aspects of this anointing of the Holy Spirit in Isaiah 11:1-2:

~ The Spirit of Wisdom and Understanding
~ The Spirit of Counsel and Might
~ The Spirit of Knowledge and the Fear of the Lord
~ The Spirit of the Lord

In this passage in Luke Jesus tells how the Spirit of the Lord anointed Him for ministry. He then lists six things this anointing will enable Him to do:

1. Preach the gospel to the poor
2. Heal the brokenhearted
3. Preach deliverance to the captives
4. Recovering of the sight to the blind
5. Set at liberty those who are bruised
6. Preach the acceptable year of the Lord

The anointing of the Holy Spirit is what enabled Jesus to fulfill these six ministries. The Spirit of Counsel and Might enabled Jesus to heal the souls of the people. He was able to counsel those who were brokenhearted, and He also set at liberty all that were bruised in their souls. The Spirit of Wisdom and Understanding enabled Him to preach the gospel to the poor in spirit who needed wisdom and understanding, and the Spirit of the Fear of the Lord and Knowledge enabled Him to preach the acceptable year of the Lord.

We have this same anointing. The Spirit of the Lord is upon you today. To whom will you minister today?

Lord, forgive me for seeking an anointing that I already have. Because Jesus lives in me, I have the same anointing He experienced when He was on earth. Why do I hesitate to move out in this anointing to minister to others? Help me to get rid of all of my fear and self-awareness and allow the Holy Spirit to minister through me today. Amen.

March 21

READ: Numbers 32:1–33:39; Luke 4:33–5:11; Psalm 64:1–10; Proverbs 11:22

Discretion
Proverbs 11:22

Today's proverb is one of my favorites. Whenever I meet a woman who lacks discretion, immediately I have this mental picture of a pig with a beautiful gold-jeweled ring in her snout. Sometimes I have to battle this image in my mind, because it does cause me to be closed to anything this woman might have to say.

What is discretion? Webster's defines *discretion* as "the power to discern and judge, the freedom to make decisions and choices, being careful about what one does and says, prudence." I have mentioned before how wisdom, prudence and discretion are usually linked together. They are like God-assigned bodyguards who keep us out of trouble.

Over the years I have met a few women who lack discretion. If you are reading this and think you might be one of these women in my life, don't worry. The fact that you are reading this devotional means that you do have some discretion. When I meet a woman or a man who lacks discretion, I know exactly how to pray for them. I pray they will grow in the wisdom that comes from above. James 3:17 says, "But the wisdom that is from above is first pure, then peaceable, gentle, and willing to yield, full of mercy and good fruits, without partiality and without hypocrisy."

A person who operates in the wisdom that comes from above will be a discreet person who knows when to speak and when not to speak. To put it bluntly, a discreet person knows when to keep his mouth shut.

The other day I was so excited about going to an event where I would meet some new Christians. I always love fellowshiping with Christians because the subject we always share in common is the Lord and what He is doing in our lives. As I entered the home, several groups were already gathered while we enjoyed refreshments. As I floated from group to group, I was so disappointed. One group was discussing a recent murder in Atlanta. Another group was discussing an interview with a sports figure on TV that was less than edifying. Everything being discussed was what these ladies had seen on TV the night before. I thought to myself, *Garbage in, garbage out.* We speak what we have filled our minds with, and so often it is just garbage.

To grow in discretion, we must submit ourselves daily to a fresh washing of the Word of God. The world around us is so cluttered with garbage and filth that if we do not do this, our minds will never be renewed and the thoughts we think and the things we say and do will lack discretion.

Lord, help me to fill my mind with Your Word and to develop discretion.

March 22

READ: Numbers 33:40–35:34; Luke 5:12–28; Psalm 65:1–13; Proverbs 11:23

Choosing to Enter God's Presence
Psalm 65:1-13

It was a cold wintry day, and someone was knocking violently at my door. I looked through the peephole to discover two frightened young ladies who seemed desperate. Then I heard dogs barking in the background. I opened the door, and they said, "Please let us in!! Some dogs are chasing us!!" They were going door to door selling magazines, and some neighborhood dogs were following them. I let them in quickly, and they ended up staying with me for two hours. They were so relieved to find a refuge in my home. After some conversation and some hot tea, one of the ladies asked, "Don't you get lonely in this big house?" My husband was at work, and my children were at school. I answered, "No, I never get lonely because the Father, Son and Holy Spirit are always with me, and we have a tea party every day." Suddenly one of the ladies said with urgency in her voice, "We've got to go now." I guess they thought I was crazy, but at least my statement finally made them leave.

This incident reminds me of the times I have chosen to enter God's presence, His dwelling place, just to find refuge and comfort because I am desperate. So often I neglect my quiet times in the morning when things are going well in my life, but I would not dream of missing time with the Lord when I am going through hard times.

This psalm speaks of the blessing that awaits those who approach God. "Blessed is the man You choose and cause to approach unto You, that he may dwell in Your courts. We shall be satisfied with the goodness of Your house, of Your holy temple" (v. 4).

Note it was God who chose and caused the man in this psalm to approach Him. This offers hope for me in the discipline of a daily quiet time. Sometimes I just don't feel I have the time to spend alone with the Lord, and frankly sometimes I just don't want to take the time. When those times come in my life now, I can pray this prayer:

> Lord, cause me to approach Your throne. Don't let anything stop me from entering into Your presence. Give me the excitement and expectancy I need to draw me faithfully into Your presence. Amen.

READ: Numbers 36:1–Deuteronomy 1:46; Luke 5:29–6:11; Psalm 66:1–20; Proverbs 11:24–26

God's Divine Meat Grinder
Psalm 66:1–20

Have you ever been through God's divine meat grinder? Some people today do not believe that God tests us, but the Bible says clearly that we are tested by the Lord. The request by God for Abraham to sacrifice Isaac was clearly a test from God. God, however, is not the tempter. James tells us that we are led astray by our own lusts and then tempted. He says, "Let no one say when he is tempted, 'I am tempted by God'; for God cannot be tempted by evil" (James 1:13).

Temptation is the devil's business, and make no mistake, he is an expert at his job. Testing, however, is God's business, and sometimes God will allow Satan to tempt us simply because God wants us to learn to overcome temptation. If God never allowed Satan to tempt us, we would never grow in the skills of spiritual warfare. It is important to recognize that God has Satan on a leash. If we are walking faithfully with the Lord and our hearts are continually turned toward Him with the desire to keep walking in His ways, we can rest assured that whatever comes our way in the form of temptation or trial is ultimately going to work for our good. We also have to recognize that a lot of the troubles we get into and sins we commit are simply because we give into our fleshly lusts. We definitely cannot blame God for those times we have made stupid mistakes, been hasty in our decisions or willfully chosen the world's way instead of God's way. We learn in Job that Satan had to ask permission from God to tempt Job because Job was a righteous man.

Psalm 66:1–20 tells us clearly that God does allow affliction sometimes in our lives. We have only to look at the story of Israel to discover this truth. God is purifying us and forming His character in our lives, and to have this happen, we all will go through some type of fiery trial. God the Father allowed Jesus to be tempted forty days and forty nights, so we would be presumptuous to believe that we will never be tempted. The good news is that God will not put us in His divine meat grinder unless He knows we will come out as steak. God's meat grinder is designed to mold us into something better than what went into the grinder. David says in this psalm, "For You, O God, have tested us; You have refined us as silver is refined" (v. 10).

The truth is, God will not give us more than we can bear, and with every temptation He will give us a way of escape. That way of escape is Jesus. Does this mean that the moment we call upon Jesus, He will instantly deliver us when we are going through severe trials and testings? God will allow us to remain in His divine meat grinder just long enough to make us come out like steak. The next time you experience trials, don't ask, "Why, Lord?" Instead, ask, "What, Lord? What do You want to develop in me through this trial?" Remember, tribulation works patience in our lives, and there truly is no other way for this fruit to be developed in us.

Prayer Vigils
Luke 6:12–38

Over the years I have experienced many prayer vigils. One particularly comes to mind. Our little neighborhood women's prayer group decided to spend all night in prayer at my home. We tried to pray from 8 at night to 8 in the morning. We failed miserably. We kept falling asleep, and often we talked more than we prayed simply because we knew if we closed our eyes we would be off to sleep again. Jesus, however, did not have any problem spending a whole night in prayer. This scripture says Jesus continued all night in prayer.

Recently I heard someone say that they make appointments with God. They set aside a whole day to spend in prayer with Him, and if anyone calls them, they just say, "Today is my day apart with the Lord; I'll call you back tomorrow." I think I could do this. I am an early morning person, and I could pray for eight hours during the day. If I started at 6 A.M. and stayed in that special prayer place until 4 when I had to fix dinner, this would be eight hours.

God, however, is not interested in our keeping a timetable for prayer. He just wants us to pray without ceasing and to ever commune with Him. There are times, however, when we need to set aside special seasons of prayer. My husband, for example, went to Stone Mountain for the day and prayed all afternoon. It was during this time of prayer that he understood his call to be a Joseph in these end days. In fact, he heard with his spiritual ears God call him Joseph. His father's middle name was Joseph. Joseph means "provider," and all the Josephs in the Bible were providers. First there was Joseph who went into Egypt ahead of his brothers to prepare for a time of famine. Then Jesus' earthly daddy or guardian was named Joseph. This Joseph provided a safe, loving environment for Jesus in His childhood. And then there was Joseph of Arimathea, who provided the tomb for Jesus. Blessed insights like this come to us when we are willing to set time apart to be with the Lord.

It has been a long time since I took a day apart, and I am challenged this morning to make an appointment with God in the near future to just spend a day with Him. Maybe you are a night person, and you could spend a whole night in prayer. Whatever works for you. Just do it.

> *Father, forgive me for not making appointments with You. I make appointments with my husband all the time to have little getaways together. Help me to remember that You long for a little getaway with me. Show me the time that would be best for You and me. Thanks.*

READ: Deuteronomy 4:1–49; Luke 6:39–7:10; Psalm 68:1–18; Proverbs 11:28

What We See in Others Is in Ourselves
Luke 6:39–7:10

So often I stand in judgment of others, and soon discover I am guilty of the very same things I see critically in others. You've heard the old expression, "When you point your finger at someone, four fingers are pointing back at you." Isaiah 58 speaks of God's chosen fast, and one of the things listed we need to fast from is the pointing of the finger. If our church could go on such a fast, we would have unity in the church.

Jesus tells us that we often see the mote (a tiny splinter) in the eye of others and neglect to see the beam that is in our own eye. It has been my experience that the things that really bug me in some people are the very things I am struggling to overcome in my own life. The moment I get irritated by another person, I quietly pray, "Lord, is this in me?" The answer always comes back, "Yes." Then I have to pray, "Lord, forgive me for seeing this so quickly in another and refusing to see this in myself. I confess this as sin and ask You to cleanse me." Now I am in a position to effectively pray for the person I criticized or the person who irritated me.

Most critical, judgmental people have a lot of insecurity. They are always pointing the finger to keep from examining their own lives for fear they will discover they too are not perfect. I have found that most critical, judgmental people are perfectionists. They are afraid of having their imperfections discovered, so they criticize all those they encounter in life.

Today you might want to ask the Lord, "Is there a beam in my own eye I need to see and with Your help remove?"

> *Lord, forgive me for being judgmental and critical of others. I need to recognize my own faults and to see I am the one who needs to change. Help me to look at myself honestly first, and then I will be able to accept others just the way they are. Amen.*

The Lord Is One God
Deuteronomy 5:1–6:25

The Jewish people say this phrase, "Hear, O Israel: The Lord our God is one Lord," whenever they are gathered together at a temple or synagogue. Jewish people and Christians do have much in common. Both are sons of Abraham, both are believers in the God of Abraham, Isaac and Jacob, and both are chosen by God to be a special people.

Some Jewish people mistakenly believe that Christians believe in three Gods because we believe in the Trinity. The *Shama*, "The Lord our God is one Lord," has been a stumbling block for years to the Jewish people, and it has prevented them from seeing the truth that Jesus truly is their Messiah. If they understood the meaning of *one* in this passage, they would see that truly God is three in one. The word for *one* in Hebrew in this passage is *echad,* which means a cluster—like a cluster of grapes. The Trinity is not three Gods, but one God—God the Father, God the Son and God the Holy Spirit.

I recall a dream I had years ago when we were preparing to go to India on a missions journey. This dream caused me to think we should be going to Israel instead of India. In the dream I was in Jerusalem at the time of the Feast of Tabernacles. At this time Jewish people build little booths outside their homes and eat their meals there as a family for seven days. I dreamed that I went from booth to booth explaining that the God that Christians serve is the same God they serve. The God that Christians serve is not three Gods. The Lord opened the eyes of their understanding, and they believed and accepted Jesus as their Messiah. The major difference between Jewish people and Christians is that Christians know God as their heavenly Father, not just creator God. We came to this knowledge after we accepted Jesus as our Lord and Savior. No man can know the Father unless the Son of God reveals this to them. We can pray for our Jewish brethren this way:

Father, draw these dear people to You by revealing Your Son to them. Pull the veil off their eyes and open the eyes of their understanding to see You as their heavenly Father. Let them receive Your Son Jesus so He can reveal You as their heavenly Father. Amen.

He That Is Forgiven Much Loves Much
Luke 7:36–8:3

In response to the those who questioned His willingness to allow a woman who was a sinner to wash His feet, Jesus told a parable: "There was a certain creditor which had two debtors: the one owed five hundred pence, and the other fifty. And when they had nothing to pay, he frankly forgave them both. Tell me therefore, which of them will love him most? Simon answered and said, I suppose that he, to whom he forgave most. And he said unto him, Thou hast rightly judged" (Luke 7:41–43, KJV).

Over the years I have heard many testimonies of people who have been delivered from drugs, prostitution, homosexuality, alcoholism, etc. These people who have had such dramatic conversions from worldliness to holiness have such a deep love for God. There is a man in our church who was delivered out of the homosexual lifestyle and healed of AIDS. He has a deep love for Jesus. Another man and his wife in our church had been into everything—drugs, alcohol, sex outside of marriage, etc. We have the opportunity to pray with this man often at our little prayer groups in the church, and he just weeps when he prays. He is so grateful to God for what He has done in his life. He is so expressive in his love for Jesus.

He and his wife are so in love with Jesus because they have been forgiven much. I also know a man who was lifted off of the streets of Atlanta, delivered from cocaine and alcoholism, taught to read and who now is a master plumber. Every time I see him I think, *Look what the Lord has done! It is marvelous in our eyes!!* He also has a deep love for Jesus.

If we really thought about it, we could all say we have been forgiven much. Even though our testimonies may not be as dramatic as the ones shared above, we all were sinners, and Christ forgave us. We all were prisoners, and Jesus set us free. We all were bruised in our souls, and Jesus set us at liberty and healed our broken hearts. Jesus has forgiven us all of every sin. Remember, there are no degrees of sin with God. The major sin that leads to all other sins is unbelief. We have all been guilty of this. Jesus loves us much, He forgives us much, and our response is a grateful heart that loves Him much.

> *Lord, help me never take for granted where I have come from and where I am going because You have forgiven me and canceled the debt I owed. I love You, Jesus.*

The Stiff-Necked Disease
Deuteronomy 9:1–10:22

We all suffer from pride from time to time. God has a special name for the ailment of pride in our lives. He calls it the "Stiff-necked Disease." We catch the "Stiff-necked Disease" when we have unbending wills and refuse to submit to God. Pride is the root of this disease, and humility is the cure. A little boy was asked to sit down and be quiet by his mother.

He did sit down, but he replied angrily, "I'm sitting down on the outside, but I'm standing up on the inside." God is not as concerned about outward obedience as He is our inward obedience and the motivation for our obedience. Do we obey God with a willing heart out of love, or do we obey Him grudgingly with murmuring and complaining? The little boy in the story was still in control of his attitude. He had not submitted his attitude to God. He was in rebellion even though his outward actions indicated that he was obedient. If we obey outwardly, but still have an ungrateful, rebellious attitude on the inside, we are victims of the "Stiff-necked Disease."

When people have a stiff neck in the physical, they usually cannot turn their heads. The neck determines the moment of the head. When we are stiff-necked spiritually and refuse to go God's way, Jesus Christ, who is the head of the church, cannot move in our lives.

Moses and God were in agreement. They both called Israel a stiff-necked people. I pray God does not see me this way. Only our great physician, Jesus, can deliver and heal us from the "Stiff-necked Disease." Jesus is the only one who can teach us meekness and lowliness of heart, and we can only learn this lesson as we sit at His feet. When we are in pride, we have two enemies—God and the devil. God resists the proud, and the devil uses pride to bring strife, confusion and every evil work into our lives.

Will you listen and answer Jesus' call to you today? "Come unto me, all ye that labour and are heavy laden, and I will give you rest. Take my yoke upon you, and learn of me; for I am meek and lowly in heart; and ye shall find rest unto your souls. For my yoke is easy, and my burden is light" (Matt. 11:28–30, KJV).

March 29

Where Is Your Faith?
Luke 8:22–40

We have had the opportunity to cross the Sea of Galilee many times. Our guide usually points out the fact that storms can come up quite suddenly on the sea because of the Golan Heights that surround the sea. Jesus was peacefully sleeping through the storm while His disciples were frantically bailing water out of the boat. Jesus rebuked the wind and the raging waters and suddenly all was calm. Then Jesus asked them, "Where is your faith?"

I think of the many times in my life when Jesus probably asked, "Where is her faith?" Faith is the evidence of things not seen and the substance of things hoped for. The disciples in the boat were afraid, and this killed their faith. Whenever we let fear overwhelm us, our faith goes out the window. Note that I said that our faith goes out the window. There is another faith that will never leave us, and this is the faith we need to tap into when fear is overwhelming us. This faith is the faith of Jesus Christ. Paul said, "I am crucified with Christ: nevertheless I live; yet not I, but Christ liveth in me: and the life which I now live in the flesh I live by the faith of the Son of God, who loved me, and gave himself for me" (Gal. 2:20, KJV).

What a comfort to know I have a deeper level of faith that resides in me—the very faith of Jesus Christ. On that stormy day on the Sea of Galilee, the disciples had Jesus in the flesh with them. Now we have Jesus in the spirit with us, and He has promised never to leave us nor forsake us. Jesus now can travel with us through every storm of life, and His faith within us enables us to say, "Peace, be still," to the raging waves of trials and tribulations we encounter.

Where is your faith? You have the very faith of the Son of God indwelling you. With that kind of faith, you can move mountains and calm every storm.

Thank You, Lord, for indwelling me with Your faith. When my own faith fails, I can tap into Your faith. I believe; help Thou my unbelief.

March 30

READ: Deuteronomy 13:1–15:23; Luke 8:41–9:6; Psalm 71:1–24; Proverbs 12:5–7

Fear Not, Believe Only
Luke 8:41–9:6

Jairus had just heard the news that his daughter was dead. Can you imagine his amazement when he heard Jesus say, "Fear not, believe only?" This story has a happy ending because Jesus raised Jairus' daughter from the dead.

As we have studied earlier, fear always nullifies faith. The product of fear is unbelief. The product of faith is hope, and we all need hope. Have you heard people say, "Now don't get your hopes up, because you may be disappointed"? What a statement of unbelief this is. If we are afraid to get our hopes up because we fear that we will be disappointed, what is controlling us? Fear is controlling us.

If we knew the author and finisher of our faith a little better, we would always have our hopes up. Jesus is the author and finisher of our faith, and He also is the bishop of our souls. Hope is an anchor for our souls, and Jesus is our only hope. When we place our hope in Jesus instead of circumstances, we will always have our hopes up. Our hope is built on nothing else than Jesus and His righteousness. We stand on Christ our solid rock, who alone can keep us from the sinking sands of unbelief and discouragement.

I believe that Jairus was able to fear not and believe only because he kept his eyes on Jesus. He probably did not even look at his dead daughter. He looked at Jesus, and then he knew that Jesus was able to even raise his daughter from the dead.

Lord, help me to always put my hope in You. You are the author and finisher of my faith, and You do all things well.

READ: *Deuteronomy 16:1–17:20; Luke 9:7–27; Psalm 72:1–20; Proverbs 12:8–9*

Like Rain on Fresh Mown Grass
Psalm 72:1–20

Vladimir, our Russian son, has been our gardener for the seven years he has lived with us. I remember the first time he cut the grass; he was so very proud of his accomplishment. Shortly after the grass was mowed, a shower came; we both stood in the carport and breathed in the elegant smell of rain on freshly mowed grass. There is nothing to compare with this smell. This psalm gives a beautiful description of what will happen to people who fear the Lord. One of the promises of God to those who fear Him is, "They shall fear thee as long as the sun and moon endure, throughout all generations. He shall come down like rain upon the mown grass: as showers that water the earth" (vv. 5–6, KJV).

What a promise to those who fear the Lord this is! I believe the psalmist is saying that when we fear the Lord, we will receive showers of blessings and our lives will have the clean fresh smell of newly mown grass after a shower. Another verse in Scripture says the fear of the Lord is clean and pure.

What happens when showers come and water the earth? All the vegetation begins to grow. As we fear the Lord, we will be soaked in the refreshing shower of the Holy Spirit and the water of His Word. We will grow into trees of righteousness, the plantings of the Lord.

The opposite is true of those who do not fear the Lord. In fact, their lives have an odor about them that is not good. I have been in places where I knew there was a lot of demonic activity; the whole place had a stench of death about it. When we stay close to the Lord, we will bring refreshing showers to others when they are experiencing draught in their lives. This psalm continues to share more promises given to those who fear the Lord. God promises them righteous days and abundance of peace. This psalm is the last of the prayers written by David and recorded in the Scriptures. David ends his writings with these verses, "His name shall endure forever: his name shall be continued as long as the sun: and men shall be blessed in him: all nations shall call him blessed. Blessed be the LORD God, the God of Israel, who only doeth wondrous things. And blessed be his glorious name forever: and let the whole earth be filled with his glory; Amen, and Amen" (vv. 17–19, KJV).

What a great way to end our March readings!

April 1

Focus
Psalm 73:1-28

Where will your focus be today? Here the psalmist looks at the people around him. He compares himself with those who are ungodly and realizes they seem to be better off than he is. He reminds God of how he has cleansed his own heart, but he cannot see the benefits of living a righteous life. His complaint to God is the same as that of many Christians today: "What's the use in trying to be good and going God's way when nothing is working out?" But then he goes into the sanctuary and draws near to God. He realizes that the wicked will eventually perish, but he will not. He thanks God for His faithfulness in holding his hand through hard times, for His guidance, counsel and strength. Then he shares this wonderful statement: "It is good to draw near to God; to put our trust in Him and to declare His works." The psalmist first sees only the people who are close to him and the circumstances around him. At the end of this psalm, he is given a supernatural pair of glasses to see beyond those things he is experiencing. He focuses on the God who is in control of all things. To receive healing for his eyesight, however, he had to go into the sanctuary and draw near to God. He had to retreat from his circumstances and the people who surrounded him and get alone with God. In the sanctuary there were no distractions and his attention was focused only on God.

Several years ago, I visited a monastery where the monks belonged to an order that required a vow of silence. They passed one another without greeting and spent most of their time in prayer. You may be thinking, *If I could only live in a monastery, then I would have no trouble drawing near to God. This world is too filled with distractions, and I'm not able to focus.* We listened to one of the monks who had permission to talk since he daily went into town to purchase things. He exclaimed, "It is extremely difficult to be shut in with God twenty-four hours a day without any communication with others except God. There is no escape." Restricting your communication with others is unnatural. My husband tried a vow of silence for one day, and he broke it within one hour.

God desires fellowship with us continually, no matter what our day holds, but He also designed us to fellowship with others. Granted we live in a world where it is difficult to have constant communion with God because of the distractions around us. Another monk found the secret to keeping his eyes focused on the Lord. His name was Brother Lawrence, and he wrote a book called *Practicing the Presence of God.* He shares in his book how he used his everyday tasks and people he saw to remind him of God and His love. As he washed dishes, he thought about the cleansing of Jesus' blood and the water of His Word. When he saw different people during the day, he would quietly pray for them. I challenge you today to practice the presence of God and then declare to others God's works. When you do this, you will always be in the sanctuary. I guarantee you will have a good day, because your focus will be on a good God. HAVE A GOOD DAY!!

Laborers for the Harvest
Luke 9:51–10:12

From the time my three sons were toddlers, I prayed that all three would be used as laborers in the last great harvest. Jesus exhorts us to pray for the Lord of the harvest to send forth laborers. The harvest is great, but the laborers are few. The Lord sends the laborers. He speaks to the potential laborer and gives him the call for his special field.

Our part daily is to pray for laborers for the harvest. The Lord heard my prayers over the years, and two of our sons have gone to foreign countries, while one is active as a laborer in the harvest in Atlanta. Our middle son, Ron, got his call as a laborer in a very unusual way. He was working on the work crew for a Young Life Camp when suddenly his chores were interrupted by the voice of the Lord. He didn't hear an audible voice. but he heard this statement with his spiritual ears: "Ron, you are going to China." This call was confirmed in the next half hour when the work crew had devotionals. The young man leading the devotions that night had a devotion on Hudson Taylor, who ministered in China. Ron knew he was to go as a laborer to China, and he has already spent three years in China and plans to go back.

Ray, our youngest son, was drawn to minister to the Jewish people. He met his wife, who also was called to be a laborer, and she felt drawn to Eastern Europe. One day as she was in the room of one of her friends at school, she saw a map of Budapest. She could not get that beautiful city off her heart and shared with Ray, who at that time was engaged to her, that maybe they should go to Budapest. Ray's positive response was based on research he made to discover that Budapest has the third largest Jewish population of any city in Eastern Europe. I also received a confirmation for his call fifteen years ago. Upon waking from a nap, I saw an unusual flag in my mind. It was green, white and red with horizontal stripes. I knew it was not Mexico or Italy, since the stripes were horizontal, so I looked it up in the encyclopedia. It was the flag of Hungary, and for years I thought I would have to go to Hungary. I never shared this vision with Ray, but after he told me he was going to Hungary, I shared with him. This was a confirmation to his call. Russ, our oldest son, is called to be a bridge between races in Atlanta, Georgia.

The fields are truly ready for harvesting. Today ask the Lord where your field is. I believe we all have our fields, and many may not be overseas. Your field may be in your own neighborhood or your own family. Today pray for laborers for the harvest, and I believe you also will receive your own call as a laborer in the fields God has chosen for you.

Lord, I know there are works You have designed especially for me from the foundation of the earth. Help me not to miss out on any of these good works. I want to always be in the right place at the right time so the fields You have chosen for me will always be fruitful and provide a great harvest.

April 3

READ: Deuteronomy 23:1–25:19; Luke 10:13–37; Psalm 75:1–10; Proverbs 12:12–14

What You Say Is What You Get
Proverbs 12:12–14

One of my constant prayers is that the law of kindness would be upon my tongue and that my conversations would be seasoned with grace. There is a proverb that says that pleasant words are health to our bones. This proverb says that we are satisfied with good by the fruit of our lips.

Everyone desires to live a pleasant and good life. Whether we attain this depends on what we speak. If we are critical, judgmental and always murmur and complain, we will not be satisfied with good. The fruit of our lips will taste bitter. If we have a grateful heart and look for ways to exhort people to love and good works by our words, we will be satisfied with good fruit.

Each day we live we will be able to taste the goodness of the Lord. The Bible says to taste and see that the Lord is good. It is interesting to me that most digestive problems have to do with an overproduction of acid in our stomach. The Bible also warns against the gall of bitterness. Bitterness in the heart will always cause bitter words to come out of our mouths, and this may ultimately affect our physical bodies. When we are critical and judgmental of others, acid words can come out of our mouths that will eat away at our joy and the joy of others.

Nothing feels better than having been satisfied with a good meal. When we are satisfied, we feel a great sense of peace and well-being. When we speak kind, uplifting words to others, we also will have that sense of peace and well-being. What we speak has the power to set the atmosphere at the dinner table. Have you ever thought about that? Most counselors suggest that people not argue at the dinner table because it brings stress to their digestive systems. Communication at the dinner table should be uplifting and peaceful. Meal time should be a time of not only giving thanks before the meal, but also of thanking the Lord for one another during the meal. Sadly to say, many households spend little time at the dinner table together. TV, activities and the computer have stolen our times together as a family at the table. Eating together should be an experience that we look forward to. It is just not time to "slop the hogs," as some people say.

Tonight make a special effort to gather together the whole family around the dinner table. Make something special, and then think of sharing with each person present an uplifting and encouraging word. If you live alone and eat your meals alone, use your meal time to read some of God's Word. Make a practice of these dinner habits, and I believe your digestive problems will be solved.

Lord, forgive me for being so busy with outside activities that I seldom eat with the entire family and have time for conversations. Relationships are very important to You, and sometimes I trade relationships for activities. Help me to daily taste and see that the Lord is good, and then share Your goodness with others at meal time. Amen.

One Thing Is Needed
Luke 10:38–11:13

Our pastor has said that we have to remember to keep the main thing the main thing. When we look at our lives, we have to ask ourselves, "What is the main thing?" I had a friend who put on her refrigerator a sign that said, "What difference will this make 10,000 years from now?" Priorities change when we realize that our life here on earth is but a hands breadth. Those who know Jesus Christ personally will live forever with Him. Jesus told Martha that she was careful and troubled about many things, but Mary had chosen the one thing needful. Mary chose to sit at His feet and learn of Him. Without Him we can do nothing. When we realize this, we will spend more time sitting at His feet as Mary did.

Each morning Jesus gives us this invitation, "Come learn of me, for I am meek and lowly of heart, and you shall find rest for your soul." Martha had no rest for her soul. She was busy and anxious about many things, and this stole her peace. In fact, she was so concerned about her dinner that her attitude toward Mary was negatively affected. She saw Mary with critical eyes because Mary was not doing what she wanted her to do. Has this ever happened to you?

Daily we are challenged to keep the main thing the main thing. The main thing is our relationship with the Lord and then with others. Yesterday we talked about the value of spending time with our family at the dinner table. Breaking bread together was a regular occurrence in the early church, and most of their meetings involved sitting at a table. In this busy culture in which we live, many have lost the gift of hospitality. However, if we become so concerned about our dinner preparations that we fail to spend time with our guests, we have failed miserably as a hostess. People are always more important than appearances, food and things. Over the years I have learned to entertain without making a fuss about having things just right. Things will always be just right as we exercise the gift of hospitality if we keep the main thing the main thing.

The Holy Spirit can give us wisdom about how to have a dinner party without being so worn out that we are not good company. Often it is the fear of man (caring too much about what others think) that compels us to overdo in our hospitality. The people who come to our homes desire to talk with us and listen also to our news. This is their first priority. Good conversation at the dinner table always makes up for what may be lacking in the finer dinner or an immaculate house. Next time you entertain, turn the lights down low and no one will notice if you missed cleaning somewhere. Cook something that smells great and keep it simple. If your guest offers to bring something, always let them. It will make it easier on you, and you will have more time with your guests. These are just a few ideas to KEEP THE MAIN THING THE MAIN THING. Your life as well as your entertaining will always be a delight when the presence of the Lord and people are more important than your presentation.

Jesus Redeems Our Mistakes
Luke 11:14–36

One of the favorite expressions in our family is, "Well, nobody is perfect." We all make mistakes, and I am so ever grateful for our Lord Jesus Christ, who is our redeemer. He is able to take our messes and make something worthwhile out of them. As I was reading this morning about another ministry Jesus had, I recalled an incident I experienced in India.

India is a land filled with demons, and some people have physical manifestations in their body caused by the work of demons. Our pastor, his wife and we were in India ministering to the sick, unsaved and demon-possessed. Often the same people whom we ministered to would be in the line each night because they just wanted another touch from God. On one night I especially remember praying for a mother who carried a four-year-old boy in her arms. The boy was lame. On that same night another mother of a boy of four presented her son for prayer, and he was dumb and deaf. I prayed for them both. Nothing happened that night. On the next night the same mothers with their four-year-old sons were in line to be prayed for again, and I got them mixed up. I prayed for the dumb boy to walk, and I prayed for the lame boy to talk. It was not until we were in the taxi on the way back to the hotel that I realized my mistake. I prayed, "Lord, You'll have to redeem my mistake." He did!! The following night the mother of the dumb and deaf boy said her son spoke his first word. God saw my mistake, but He heard my heart and prayer, and He delivered the dumb boy.

Today's reading in Luke tells us that dumb people spoke when Jesus cast out demons. Of course not everyone who is hearing impaired has a demon, but there is such a thing as a dumb and deaf spirit that can affect our speech. The good news is that Jesus has all power and authority over the power of the enemy, and He also has given us that same authority in His name. When Jesus cast out the demon in this passage, some accused Him of having a devil Himself. His response was that He cast out demons with the finger of God, which revealed the kingdom of God had come. Jesus was and is that kingdom. Jesus came to set the captives free, and it is exciting to know we have that same power to liberate people. It truly is God who gives us such power. This should challenge us all to pray for people who are bound by demons. We can do all things through Christ who gives us the strength, and this includes liberating people from demon harassment and possession. What a privilege to see people set free.

Lord, help me to operate in all the fullness of Your power. Your desire is to set people free from any influence of the enemy. Use me to set the captives free.

April 6

READ: Deuteronomy 29:1–30:20; Luke 11:37–12:7; Psalm 78:1–25; Proverbs 12:19–20

Peace Brings Joy
Proverbs 12:19–20

Counselors of peace have joy." Romans 14:17 tells us, "For the kingdom of God is not eating and drinking, but righteousness and peace and joy in the Holy Spirit." In yesterday's reading we learned that Jesus is the kingdom of God. He is all righteousness, all peace and all joy, and we can enter into the kingdom when we ask Jesus to come into our hearts and take over our lives. I do not know a person on earth who does not desire to be right with God and his fellowman, to have peace and to experience joy. Jesus came preaching the kingdom of God, and sometimes we forget this is our message also. In addition to preaching the kingdom, we also now can tell of the crucifixion, death, burial and resurrection of Jesus Christ, who now sits in heaven making intercession for us. The gospel should contain all of these facts.

Jesus preached the kingdom of God, and our first appeal to people as we share the gospel is to introduce them to the kingdom and then to the King. When we ask a person if he wants to be right with God and others, to have peace and to experience joy every day of his life, you will definitely get his attention. We live in a very troubled world, and the possibility of experiencing joy and peace daily appeals to us. The fruit of righteousness is peace, and the manifestation of peace is always joy.

This proverb tells us that the counselors of peace have joy. Jesus said, "Blessed are the peacemakers, for they shall be called sons of God" (Matt. 5:9). Most children under the age of six are joyful. They love to play and laugh. Jesus also said, "Except you become as a little child, you shall not enter the kingdom of God." (See Matthew 8:3.) A little child is totally dependent upon his parents, and God desires for us to be totally dependent upon Him. A little child also trusts his parents. God wants our complete trust. Could it be that if we totally trusted God with everything we face in this life and were dependent upon Him at all times, we also would experience joy every day of our lives?

To be a counselor of peace one has to be dependent upon God, because only God can impart lasting peace to the soul. The counselor of peace is able to receive from God whatever the one counseled needs, and then he is able to transmit those things to the one he counsels. In reality Jesus Christ, who is the kingdom of God in its fullness, is all a person ever needs. Jesus said, "My peace I give to you, not as the world gives do I give to you" (John 14:27). Jesus has already given us His peace, but some people need to know how to receive it. The first requirement to receiving His peace is to enter into His kingdom by becoming a little child. Once we have taken this step, then it is even possible that we may become a counselor of peace. Today you may meet someone who desperately needs peace in his life. I recently had a dream in which I was witnessing to a very anxious and troubled woman. I told her what she needed was Jesus. Isn't that what we all need? He is truly all we need, and we must make the decision to choose the one thing that is needed.

God's Pleasure
Luke 12:8–34

My life verse is Philippians 2:13: "It is God who works in you both to will and to do for His good pleasure." It was such a joy to have this understanding when I was twenty-six years old. I was at a retreat, and our leader instructed us to go out by the lakeside and be quiet and still before the Lord. We were instructed to ask the Lord questions and then wait for answers. Waiting for an answer when I prayed was a new experience for me, as usually all my prayers were one-way conversations with the Lord. What happened in a twenty-minute span of time changed my whole life.

As I sat on a log by the lakeside, I asked the Lord what was wrong with my life. I was not experiencing the joy other Christian friends seemed to have. He answered in a still quiet voice within my soul. "Linda, what is wrong with your life is you have been trying to earn My love. My love is free. I gave it to you two thousand years ago. Receive My love today; rest in My love and relax. Instead of working for Me, allow Me to work through you. If you did nothing but sit on that log the rest of your life, I would still love you."

When He shared His answer with me, I was bathed not only by the sunlight around me, but also by His love that was so unconditional. I realized I did not have to prove myself to God. No longer would I have to try to emulate the life of Jesus. He now was my life. I could say with Paul, "I am crucified with Christ: nevertheless I live, yet not I, but Christ liveth in me: and the life I now live in the flesh I live by the faith of the Son of God, who loved me, and gave himself for me" (Gal. 2:20, KJV). On that day I was set free from my own efforts to follow Jesus, to a life of yielding to His grace. Paul said, "It is grace that labors through me." On that day I ceased from my own labor and entered what is called the Sabbath rest. The only labor I experienced after that day was prayer, which is our spiritual exercise and obedience, which requires the laying down of my own will and desires. I was set free now to do the good pleasure of God.

What is the good pleasure of God? Today's reading in Luke reveals the answer to this question. "Do not fear, little flock, for it is your Father's good pleasure to give you the kingdom" (Luke 12:32).

The kingdom of God is righteousness, peace and joy in the Holy Ghost. I will be doing God's pleasure when I share with others God's kingdom, which is found in Christ Jesus.

Coming Ready or Not
Luke 12:35–59

R emember the game "hide and seek"? One child closes his eyes and counts to ten while the other child hides. At the count of ten, the child opens his eyes and begins his search by saying, "Coming ready or not!" Then this child diligently searches high and low to find where the other child is hiding. I recall being a child hiding, and the moment the one who sought me found me, my heart jumped and I always yelled loudly "Boo" to scare him.

Jesus is coming ready or not! He is seeking after faithful people who will be ready for His coming. In my earlier years as a Christian the thought of Jesus' coming frightened me. I always felt I was not ready, and I prayed, "Lord, just give me a little more time to get it together before You come." I felt that I had to be perfect in every way, and I knew I was not. I remembered what the Scriptures said about Jesus coming for a bride (the church) who was without spot, wrinkle or blemish. I knew I had all three.

It was not until later in my Christian walk that I became excited instead of fearful when I thought of Jesus' return. What happened to change my attitude? I realized that no matter how much I tried, I would never have it all together. Only Jesus could perfect those things in my life that concerned me. After all, He is the author and finisher of my faith. The word *author* means "the source or well-spring of all things." If He authored my faith, He surely planned to finish it. He never leaves the book of our lives half finished. Whatever He had written in my book of life, He planned to accomplish. My part is to stay filled with the Spirit and faithful to His calling.

In this passage in Luke Jesus speaks of the faithful steward: "Who then is that wise and faithful steward, whom his master will make ruler over his household, to give them their portion of food in due season?" (v. 42).

Jesus said, "My meat is to do the will of the Father." Just yesterday, we learned what the Father's good pleasure is. We are to share the good news of the kingdom with others and dispense the meat of God's Word in the proper portion to others. The wise steward is able to discern just the amount of meat his household needs. My constant prayer as a Bible teacher is:

> Lord, help me to give those who hear my teaching just the right portion of Your Word at just the right time.

"Coming ready or not!" You will be ready for His coming if you are faithful in your sharing His Word with others. Jesus will finish your book of life, and you will be found faithful.

Fertilizing the Seed
Luke 13:1–22

This passage in Luke has special meaning to me because the plea of the vine dresser became a prayer my husband and I prayed for a church we were attending. In this church the pastor was open to the things of the Spirit, but most of his congregation were not. They did not want any changes. We were in this church for three years when we attended a Sunday school retreat. The retreat was in Calloway Gardens in South Georgia, and we were in charge of getting the speaker.

The first night of the retreat the speaker delivered a powerful message about his work in Indonesia. He shared many of the miracles he had seen with his own eyes in this land. Many of those present were not able to receive what the speaker shared, and some even packed their things and left to return to Atlanta. The Bible speaks of people who have a form of religion, but who deny the power thereof. Whenever a person denies the power of the Holy Spirit to work in the church today, he usually is bound by religion and tradition. Needless to say, my husband and I were discouraged and even wondered if anyone would be present to hear the speaker the following morning.

That night we prayed with a preacher friend of ours whom we had invited to come to the retreat. He was the pastor of another church. We asked him if he felt the time was right for us to move on to another church since the one we were in seemed to not want to move in the things of the Holy Spirit. He drew aside and prayed alone about our situation and then read us Luke 13 and shared a word to us from the Lord. As we read this passage together we were struck with the fact that the vine dresser had worked with this fig tree for three years, and we had been in this church for three years. The Lord of the vineyard wanted to cut it down, but the vine dresser asked permission to dig the tree for one more year and then if it did not bear fruit, he would cut it down. We were led by this word to stay one more year at this church and see what happened.

We knew our assignment was to attempt to plow up the hard ground around the hearts of the people in this church. The only way to do this was to keep teaching God's uncompromising Word no matter what people thought. Our hope was that the hearts would be softened and would receive the seed of God's Word and that seed would then germinate, grow roots and then spring up and eventually produce fruit. We fulfilled our assignment, and sadly at the end of one year all those who seemed to begin to grow in their faith because of the Word left the church; those who remained stayed closed to the Spirit of God. They even dismissed the pastor who was open to the things of the Holy Spirit. We also felt led to leave just before this pastor was dismissed because we knew our assignment in this church was over. I still pray this church will begin to grow in God's Word and Spirit. Be sure this morning you have a soft heart to receive God's Word.

Prosperity and Success
Deuteronomy 34:1–Joshua 2:24

So many seek success and desire to prosper. Financial seminars are held to teach people how to invest and make the most of their money. Training seminars on selling yourself to the interviewer are attended by those who desire to advance in the business world. The Lord sees prosperity and success totally opposite of the way the world sees it.

To be successful in God's sight one must do the will of the Father. God is one who promotes and demotes. The most successful person in God's sight is the one who is a servant to many. The way up is the way down in the sight of the God. The person who humbles himself will be exalted.

I heard a wonderful definition of prosperity once. Prosperity is having enough to meet your own needs and to give to others. Money in God's sight is only a means of exchange. The real treasures in God's sight are people in His kingdom who are righteous and have peace and joy in the Holy Spirit. These treasures are eternal. We are prosperous in God's sight when we enter into His kingdom and when we share His kingdom with others.

So many spend their whole life climbing the ladder of success, only to find in the end they have been climbing the wrong ladder. The ladder of worldly success causes the one climbing to step on others to make it to the top. The ladder God wants us to climb causes us to lift up others in order to make it to the top. We have to esteem others higher than ourselves or God will never consider our lives as successful.

When asked how he would have spent his time better on earth, a dying man replied, "I wish I had spent more time with my family and friends and reading God's Word and less time watching TV, playing golf and working." This man realized he had been climbing the wrong ladder.

Lord, forgive me for climbing the wrong ladder of success. I want to climb Your ladder of success. Forgive me for times I spent on the golf greens or watching TV instead of spending time with those I love. Help me to share Your good news with others and help me begin to meditate on Your Word day and night. I know when I do this I will be making an investment of time that will go with me into eternity.

The Cost of Discipleship
Luke 14:7–35

Jesus shares in this passage the cost of discipleship. He says clearly that discipleship requires forsaking all. He shares the parable about the man who prepared a great supper and invited many to come. Those invited had excuses for not attending the dinner. One man was too busy with his possessions, another was too busy with his business, and another was too busy with his family.

If the devil cannot make us sin morally, he will keep us so busy with things that we are of no value in the kingdom of God. We are the salt of the earth, and when we are too busy to do the Father's will, we lose our savor. Others see our lives, and we are no different from the people in the world. We can even be so busy with church work that we are not a good witness to our next door neighbor.

Jesus told His mother at the temple when He was twelve years old that He had to be about His Father's business. He, however, did not leave His family as a young boy of twelve. He returned to His family and grew in stature and favor with God and man. Jesus could not skip the discipline of being in a home where He received instruction from both parents and was required to obey. We know little of Jesus' childhood days, but He had to go through every stage a child goes through, even the teen years. This is why He can identify with us so well. He knows everything about maturing from infancy to adulthood. It was not until He was thirty that He began His earthly ministry.

When Jesus says in verse 26 that "if anyone comes to Me and does not hate his father and mother, wife and children, brothers and sisters, yes, and his own life also, he cannot be My disciple," He is sharing simply that He must come first in our lives.

To be a disciple of Christ does not mean that we no longer value our business, our possessions, our family, etc., but they should not be our top priority. Our first allegiance is to the Lord and to seek Him first in all areas of our lives. What Jesus wants us to forsake is our own will to busy ourselves instead of seeking Him first. Remember also that Jesus set us the example of submitting to His family through the years of His childhood and early adulthood until His ministry began. If we neglect our own family to do what we feel is the will of God, I believe we are not doing the will of God. He desires for our families to be growing together in His kingdom.

Today, I challenge you to be about the Father's business, which is to do His good pleasure (sharing His kingdom) in the work place, market place, family and neighborhood. Be willing to forsake your busy life to spend time with the One who should be number one in your life. Then spend quality time with your family sharing the together God's Word, His wonders and His works.

April 12

Cooking Is a Curse
Psalm 81:1–16

Today's reading includes a promise of God I've been claiming for years: "I removed his shoulder from the burden: his hands were delivered from the pots" (v. 6, KJV).

I am the mother of three sons, and I have spent forty years in the kitchen cooking. If there is such a thing as a cross to bear, I guess this might be one of mine. With four hungry men to satisfy, I often felt that I was one giant feed bag. Saturday was not my favorite day, because I would just get through serving a big breakfast when one of the boys would always ask, "What's for lunch?" I could feel the tingles of resentment crawling up my spine when this was asked, and I always had to pray, "Lord, give me strength."

We had the opportunity to have a Russian exchange student live with us, and I was hoping we would get a girl who could help me in the kitchen. After reviewing several essays written by Russian students, the Lord led us to choose a boy. We got a boy who could eat instead of a girl who could cook. We have had Vladimir with us now for seven years, and he is a bodybuilder who can put away the food. I'm still standing on this promise, but I have yet to be delivered from the pots.

It was only after the fall of man in the Garden of Eden that cooking was necessary. God originally gave only the herb-bearing seed and every tree that yielded fruit as meat in the diet of Adam and Eve. When He killed the beast to cover Adam's and Eve's nakedness, man became meat eaters and cooking became necessary. Mankind received the curse of having to cook. Although this was not spelled out as a curse for Eve, I believe it was. Laboring over a hot stove is not as hard as laboring to have a baby, but it is still labor. Adam also received his curse, which was to toil in the fields when before the fields only needed tending. Weeds now grew, and if they were not pulled, the good seed would be choked and not bear fruit.

Recently I released my bad attitude about cooking to the Lord, and an interesting thing happened. I began to enjoy cooking, and what was a curse to me became a special calling. God always blesses whatever we release to Him, and He can cause our cares and burdens to become blessings.

Is there a burden or something you consider a curse in your life? Do you feel your work is a curse? Today release every care and whatever you feel you are cursed with to the Lord. You will find what seemed to be a curse can become a special calling in your life.

You May Have to Eat Your Words
Proverbs 13:2-3

We learned earlier that a man is satisfied by the fruit of his lips. Today's proverb conveys this same thought when it says, "A man shall eat well by the fruit of his mouth." Then this proverb adds a special exhortation "He who guards his mouth preserves his life, but he who opens wide his lips shall have destruction."

In World War II they had an expression, "Loose lips sink ships." This was an exhortation to factory workers and all who were working in the war effort to be careful about what they said to others. There is another proverb that says we are snared by the words of our mouth. Still another proverb tells us that the man who guards and keeps his mouth keeps his soul from troubles. All these proverbs convey the message that a wise man is a man of few words.

God created us with two ears and one mouth for a reason. We would be wise if we listened twice as much as we talked. We will always put our foot in our mouth if we have it opened all the time. My mother told me if I did not have something good to say, I shouldn't say it. Many words can lead to meaninglessness and even hurt.

Where is a person's focus who talks constantly? His focus is on himself. If we truly love people and are concerned about them, we will want to hear what is going on in their lives instead of monopolizing the conversation with what is going on in our own life. If we could hear a recording of some of our conversations with others, I believe we would all make a pledge to be a person of few words.

Jesus said, "Let your yes be yes and your no be no. Anything more than this tends to evil." His exhortation was for us to be direct, decisive and thoughtful in our speech. Today make it your goal to think before you open your mouth. Philippians 4:8 tells us those things we are to think about "Finally, brethren, whatsoever things are true, whatsoever things are honest, whatsoever things are just, whatsoever things are pure, whatsoever things are lovely, whatsoever things are of a good report; if there be any virtue, and if there be any praise, think on these things" (KJV).

Ask yourself if what you are about to say is lovely, of good report, pure, virtuous, etc. If the words you are about to speak fail the think test, then do not speak them to others.

Do You Believe in Hell?
Luke 16:19–17:10

I had a frightening dream one night, and it changed my life. In the dream I saw masses of blindfolded people walking off a cliff into a fiery ravine. Then I saw Jesus standing close by. I cried out, "Jesus, stop them, stop them!! They are perishing." Then I heard Jesus say, "I cannot stop them. I am in My resurrected form in heaven, but you as the church are My body on earth. On earth My spirit indwells you and desires to use the vessel of your body to do My will. You are My hands, eyes, mouth and feet on earth, and for the Holy Spirit to do His work, you must submit your body to be used by Him. Unless you use your own voice to warn these people, they will all perish."

Today's reading in Luke tells the story of the rich man and Lazarus, a poor beggar man. Both were dead. The rich man was in a place of torment, and Lazarus was in Abraham's bosom (the holding place for all who died believing in the promise of salvation). When the rich man saw Lazarus, he asked Abraham to send Lazarus to dip the tip of his finger in water and cool his tongue. Abraham explained there was a great chasm between him and Lazarus, and this could not be crossed. When the rich man realized he would not be delivered out of his torment, he then asked Abraham to send Lazarus to warn his family about this place of torment. Abraham replied that if his relatives did not receive Moses and the prophets, they would not receive this warning even if someone who was raised from the dead was sent to tell them.

We now have Jesus who was raised from the dead, and the good news is that no one has to go to hell unless he chooses to do so. The whole world seems to be going to hell in a hand basket, but we have the words of life to share with the world: "You don't have to go to hell!" Will you give voice to this message today? There are many who are perishing.

Lord, I offer my body to You today for the Holy Spirit to use the members of my body to do Your will. I have the words of life. Help me to boldly declare to others the gospel so they will not have to experience eternal torment in hell.

A Grateful Heart
Luke 17:11–37

Thanks seems to be a word that is used less and less in this culture. People seem to expect to be served, and it doesn't cross their minds to thank the person serving them. This passage in Luke tells the story of ten lepers who were cleansed by Jesus. Only one returned to thank Jesus for healing him. Jesus asked where the other nine were, and then He told the leper who thanked Him that his faith had made him whole. Did something else occur when this leper gave thanks to Jesus? Wasn't he already made whole when Jesus healed the ten lepers?

I believe the one who gave thanks received a deeper healing than just the skin on his body. He received a healing in his heart. His heart was made whole, and he received the love of God in all of its fullness when he made the effort to return and give thanks to the Lord. We too will always receive a healing for our hearts when we give thanks to the Lord in everything.

We are exhorted in the Word to give thanks in everything and for everything. I used to resist the verse that exhorted us to give thanks for all things, because it was difficult for me to give thanks for some of the trials I experienced in this life. However, when I look back at these trials, I realize that God used them to build character in me and to also cause others to see God's glory through me as I went through fiery trials without being burned or bitter. Now I can give thanks for all things, even those things God allows Satan to use against me. I have to remember that no weapon that is formed against me will prosper, and ultimately the very weapons Satan uses against me will be used for my good to bring me into a deeper understanding of spiritual warfare or to build more of God's character into my life.

Grace abounds through thanksgiving, and when I have a grateful heart no matter what I am experiencing, I place myself in the position to receive more of God's grace. No matter what we are going through, we can always find something to be grateful for. I heard someone say if you can't find something to thank God for, just thank Him for the fluid in your eyeballs. We take so much for granted in this life, but a grateful heart will take nothing for granted. The one who has a grateful heart sees everything as a gift from God and he gives God the glory. I would much rather be around people who are grateful than people who murmur and complain all the time. Griping charges the atmosphere with the negative, but a grateful heart gifts the atmosphere with grace, love and joy.

We used to sing a song, "Accentuate the positive, eliminate the negative, latch on to the affirmative and don't mess with Mr. In Between." Mr. In Between is the devil, and we latch on to him every time we murmur and complain instead of being grateful.

Lord, help me always to have a grateful heart.

April 16

Give Me the Mountain
Joshua 13:1–14:15

Caleb was forty years old when Moses sent Joshua, him and others to spy out the land of Canaan. Joshua and Caleb were the only two who came back with a good report and were the only two adult men who survived the wilderness experience for forty years. They survived because they were men of faith. God honored their faith by granting them the privilege of entering into the Promised Land. Without faith it is impossible to please God, and nothing pleases God more than to see a man of faith. Caleb was a great man of faith.

Faith is acting upon what God has said is true. Faith is seeing things as God sees them. Faith is believing, receiving and acting upon all God has promised. When Caleb was eighty-five years old, he was still a man of faith. He saw the mountain he wanted, and he was bold enough to ask for it.

The faith that pleases God asks God for great things, things that in the natural would seem impossible. Notice Caleb made his appeal to Joshua for this mountain based upon his past record of obedience to the Lord. He said about himself, "I wholly followed the Lord my God." Many presumptuously ask God for big things, but they do not receive them because they have not fulfilled a very important condition—obedience to God's Word. Others ask God for big things, and they do not receive them because they ask amiss with a desire to fulfill their own lusts.

Caleb also based his request for the mountain on what Moses had promised him. He reminded Joshua of how Moses swore on that day Joshua and Caleb gave their good report that they would possess the land wherever they had trodden.

In order to possess this mountain, Caleb had to conquer it. He was eighty-five years old, but he had confidence in the strength the Lord had given him over the years. He told Joshua that he would be able to drive out the enemies on the mountain and possess it. Joshua granted Caleb's request, and Caleb did take the mountain. The mountain was in an area now called Hebron, where all the patriarchs are buried. It is symbolic for Abraham, the father of our faith, to be buried in the specific place where Joshua and Caleb first tread. Caleb finally possessed the mountain and drove out the most feared enemies of Israel—the Anakims, who were giants.

Is there a mountain you want to claim as your own today? This mountain is something that in the natural seems insurmountable to you. You can ask God to let you climb and claim this mountain. Remember, however, a battle may await you and you will have to drive out the enemies who have formerly possessed this mountain. Has Satan robbed you of something that you want to reclaim? You have the power and authority to drive him off what rightfully belongs to you because of the cross of Jesus Christ. According to your faith be it done unto you.

Who Then Can Be Saved?
Luke 18:18–43

Salvation is a gift from God. We cannot earn it, and we do not deserve it. Everyone needs to know about this priceless gift, which includes forgiveness of sins and love that lead us into wholeness in this life. The question is, "Who then can be saved?" Anyone who comes to Jesus because the Father has drawn him can be saved.

Is there someone you have been praying for years to be saved and nothing has happened? Things that are impossible with you are possible with God. No man can save a soul, but any man who is led by God's Spirit can give the gift of salvation to even the hardest heart. The Scriptures tell us he who wins souls is wise. The Holy Spirit needs a voice on earth to share this great gift of salvation with others. He softens the hard heart and prepares it to receive the seed of God's Word. Your intercessory prayers work in cooperation with the Holy Spirit to remove the obstacles standing in the way of a person's salvation, obstacles such as religious tradition, wrong beliefs, pride, unbelief, fear and generational bondages. Someone must then deliver the Word to this person, so you also can pray for laborers to be sent to witness to the person. You must, however, pray believing that it is God's will to save this person.

A lady training me in sharing the gospel with others doubted that it was God's will to save her son, who was strung out on drugs. She had prayed for him for years and nothing had happened. I read her the verse that tells us that God's will is that none perish, but that all should come to repentance and the knowledge of His Son. As I shared with her, she confessed her unbelief as sin, and we prayed in faith for her son. One year later a young lady who was visiting Atlanta came up to me after a Bible study I taught in my church. She said, "You do not know me, but you know my mother-in-law. She came with a group of people to train others in sharing the gospel, and she was your trainer. You prayed together for her son. I am her new daughter-in-law. Before I married her son he was delivered from drugs and committed his life to Jesus Christ."

Another lady shared with me that she had been praying for her father's salvation for years. He was now in his eighties. One morning when she was in prayer the Lord spoke to her heart, "Do you fear that your father will not be saved before he dies?" She responded with a yes and then confessed her sin of fear to the Lord and asked Him with faith to save her father. Two weeks later she got a call from someone in her home town who shared that her father had responded to the invitation to receive Jesus and was gloriously saved in the church she attended as a child.

Scriptures tell us if we pray anything according to the will of the Father, He hears us and he will grant the petitions we desire of Him (1 John 5:15). You can rest assured that when you pray for the unsaved to be saved, you are praying according to God's will. This morning with faith and no fear pray for those who need to receive the gift of salvation.

To Seek and to Save
Luke 19:1–27

One of my favorite songs I sing to children is "Zacchaeus." It goes like this: "Zacchaeus was a wee little man, a wee little man was he. He climbed up in the sycamore tree, the Lord he wanted to see. And when the Lord came passing by He looked up in the tree and said, 'Zacchaeus, you come down. For I'm going to your house today. I'm going to your house today.'" This passage tells us that Zacchaeus made haste and came down from the tree and received Jesus joyfully. Jesus was on His way to have lunch with Zacchaeus, and those around began to complain because He was going to the home of a sinner. Jesus says, "This day is salvation come to this house, forsomuch as he also is a son of Abraham. For the Son of man is come to seek and to save that which was lost" (vv. 9–10, KJV).

The other night we were talking with our Russian son about *Touched by An Angel,* our favorite program on TV. In fact, it is the only one we watch. We always enjoy this show because it has so much Scripture in it and it always has a good story line.

Vladimir told us that some Christians do not like the show. I asked him why, and he said, "Because the angels in the show reach out to people who are not saved." I could not believe that some would object to angels reaching out to the lost because after all, isn't that what Jesus came to do? He came to seek and save the lost. My guess is that those who murmur about reaching out to the lost are probably also lost. They may have a form of religion and may call themselves Christians, but they could be compared to the religious leaders in Jesus' day.

Christianity is not a religion. It is a relationship with the living Jesus Christ. The religious leaders in Jesus' day were always opposed to Jesus. Today in America many have religion, but few have an abiding relationship with Jesus Christ. The Scriptures tell us that in the End Times people will have a form of religion, but will deny the power of God.

Zacchaeus was seeking a relationship with Jesus, and this is why Jesus invited Himself to his home. Jesus said, "Zacchaeus, hurry up and come down; I'm going to your house today." Zacchaeus responded joyfully to Jesus' invitation, and he also repented for all of his wrongdoing and promised to restore fourfold to all who he had taken from because he accused them falsely. When we meet Jesus, we have no choice but to repent and ask forgiveness.

Daily Jesus gives this invitation to all. He says, "I must abide at your house." If we have only a form of religion, we will never know the joy of having Jesus abide in our home (our hearts). When we hear His voice, we have to come down from the pride, religion and other strongholds that hold us, and then we must repent of these things. The result will be joyful.

April 19

Hope
Proverbs 13:12–14

Hope is the expression of something good. Have you ever heard someone say, "I'm hoping for the bad"? Hope is the substance of faith. Faith is not a wispy substance that floats in the air. By faith the children of Israel walked on water across the Jordan. The moment the first priest put his foot in the water, the water held him up. Jesus walked on water. Peter walked on water. How were they able to do these mighty miracles? They were walking on a very real substance called faith. Faith solidifies everything that would ordinarily drown us—the circumstances of life, the trials and tribulations we encounter when God tests us or Satan tempts us.

Faith is solid because it is made of an upholding substance called hope. Hope provides the invisible stepping stones that allow us to cross the most treacherous seas of this life. This hope is different from the hope the world experiences. This hope is based on the Word of God and the living Word, Jesus Christ. Remember the song, "My hope is built on nothing less than Jesus and His righteousness." Then it continues, "On Christ the solid rock I stand, all other ground is sinking sand, all other ground is sinking sand."

Hope is the substance of faith, and this substance consists of building blocks called the promises of God. The highway to heaven is called "FAITH," and this highway is paved with HOPE. When we were in Israel, our guide led us back from visiting Tel Dan on a very strange path. The path was a stream with rocks placed just enough distance from one another enabling us to leap from rock to rock. To leap from rock to rock, we had to have faith that we would not slip on the next rock and that we had the strength to make the leap. The Christian walk is like this. We take leaps of faith all of our lives, and we trust the next rock will be there for us.

Today's passage in Proverbs says, "Hope deferred makes the heart sick" (v. 12). You have heard the saying, "Now don't get your hopes up because you will be disappointed." If we place our hope in circumstances or people, we will always be disappointed, but if we place our hope in God's promises, we will never be disappointed. I heard someone say, "The way to never be disappointed is to never expect anything." Can you imagine a life without expecting good—a life without hope? Hope that does not produce the desired results will make a person sick at heart.

There was a song that went this way, "You've got to have hope, miles and miles of hope." We can have miles and miles of hope if we will base our hope on the solid rock, Jesus, and on the solid promises of God in His Word. When we place our hope in Jesus and His Word, we will never be disappointed. HAVE A GOOD DAY (A DAY FILLED WITH HOPE)!

Lord, help me today to base my hopes on Your Son Jesus and Your Word.

Great Is His Faithfulness
Psalm 89:1–13

One of my favorite hymns is "Great Is Thy Faithfulness." We sang this at my oldest son's wedding. As we sang this song, I thought of how faithful the Lord was in hearing and answering my prayers for wives for my sons. For years I prayed two things for my future daughters-in-law. I prayed they would first love the Lord with all of their heart, and second, they would simply adore my sons. After many years of waiting, I saw all three sons married in a nine-month period of time to the most wonderful young Christian ladies. They are just as beautiful on the outside as they are on the inside.

Psalm 89 is about God's faithfulness. He extends, establishes and encircles us with His faithfulness. When we are not faithful, He is faithful. When we look at the word *faithful* and reverse this syllables, we see "full faith." We have the faith of Jesus who works within us to cause us to have full faith. None of us have this power to remain faithful, except through the Holy Spirit who provides us the abiding presence of Jesus Christ in our hearts.

Yesterday we talked about the substance of faith, which is hope. Jesus Christ is our hope, and more than that He is our very faith. Paul writes in Galatians 2:20, "I am crucified with Christ: nevertheless I live; yet not I, but Christ liveth in me: and the life which I now live in the flesh I live by the faith of the Son of God, who loved me, and gave himself for me" (KJV).

There is a chorus I love that says, "I walk by faith, every step I take, I walk by faith." Remember we are walking on the sure substance of faith called hope. Some people say, "I don't have enough faith to believe for this miracle (it may be healing, financial provision, a job)." We all need these kinds of miracles in our lives, and often we feel so lacking in faith. The truth is we never lack faith if we have invited Jesus to come and abide in our hearts. Jesus Christ Himself is our faith. He is the faithful One who enables us to remain faithful. Great is His faithfulness, and His great faithfulness is imparted to us by Jesus Christ. If we abide in Jesus and His Word abides in us, God's own character of faithfulness will be formed within us and displayed out of our lives.

Just this week I heard a testimony of a missionary in Sudan who saw her husband and five children killed by Muslim radicals. They cut her throat and left her for dead. She survived. Her picture was passed around our ladies meeting so we could pray for her. As I looked in her face I was awed at the glory of God that shone through her face. She did not look hopeless. She was radiant. Wouldn't you think her first thought would be to leave Sudan immediately and never return? This was not the case. She chose to remain in Sudan to finish the call she and her husband had to this war-torn land. How could she remain? She has the faithful One.

A Faithful Ambassador
Proverbs 13:17–19

We talked about faithfulness yesterday and how it is the Lord who enables us to remain faithful (full of faith). This proverb speaks of the faithful ambassador. Verse 17 says, "A faithful ambassador brings health." We are all called to be ambassadors for Christ. We are passing through a foreign land because as believers we have a new citizenship in heaven. When we are faithful in our role as ambassadors for Christ, we will bring health to others. There are many sick souls on this earth who are wanting healing. Only the ambassador for Christ can introduce these sick souls to the great physician Jesus who can heal every sin-sick soul. He is the healing balm that is poured upon the soul.

Ambassadors usually are assigned to specific countries where they take up residence. They are official representatives of their own country, and one of their charges is to inform people about their country and its policies. Think about it for a moment. If our citizenship is in heaven and we are ambassadors for Christ, then our duty is to inform others on earth about the country in which we have our citizenship—heaven.

Some people on earth picture heaven as a place where the saints ride on clouds and play harps.

Heaven is a real place. I remember hearing Betty Maltz give her testimony of what she saw in heaven when she died on a hospital bed and then revived. She said heaven is very much like earth, but everything is perfect. Nothing decays or dies, and there is no pollution. She noticed that much building was going on in heaven and Jesus was the foreman for all the buildings in heaven. Didn't He say, "I go to prepare a place for you"? Everything in heaven was focused on the Triune God—Father, Son and Holy Spirit. There was no sorrow or tears in heaven, only abundance of joy, love and peace. There is only one policy in heaven: "Love the Lord and those around you, and worship the Lord your God with all your heart." There are a lot of people in heaven to love.

When an ambassador goes to a foreign land, he is on assignment. As Christians we are strangers and pilgrims in the land, and we also are on assignment as ambassadors for Christ. Your assignment may be your own family, your neighborhood, your civic club, your garden club, your work place—wherever you find yourself during the day where other people are is your assignment.

What is your assignment? You must be faithful in your call as an ambassador for Christ and tell those who are sick where they can find healing, those who are brokenhearted where they can find hope, those who are heavy hearted where they can find joy, and those who are troubled in heart where they can find peace. The truth is everyone can experience heaven on earth if they daily obey the King of our country. His name is Jesus.

Without a Test There Is No Testimony
Luke 21:1–28

In this passage of Luke Jesus warns His disciples about all the troubles they are going to experience in the future. He tells them that they will be persecuted, but it shall turn for them for a testimony. Whenever we go through trials and testings we add to our testimony.

Recently I heard a volunteer who works for an organization called "Voice of the Martyrs." She and her husband go to various countries where there is persecution of Christians, and they obtain the testimonies of those being persecuted. They bring their testimonies back to the church in America and ask for us to pray for these ones who are going through such trials.

When she visited our church, this volunteer showed pictures of those who had been tortured in the Sudan by the Muslim radicals. These Christians were tormented until they recanted their faith. But most refused to recant. They remained strong for Jesus Christ, and what is most amazing, most of these Christians have never seen a Bible. They have had the Word preached to them, and just based on that Word, they feared the Lord and refused to deny their faith.

After teaching an eight-week session on "Growing in the Fear of the Lord," I came to the understanding that one of the main ways to grow in the fear of the Lord is to hide God's Word in your heart and meditate on it day and night. I exhorted the ladies I was teaching to read their Bibles daily. These Christians in Sudan, however, do not own Bibles, so how can they grow in the fear of the Lord? These Christians have hidden the Word in their hearts, and the Word is written on the tablets of their hearts. It does not take volumes of God's Word to help us grow in the fear of the Lord. It only takes enough Word to build our faith, and then every time we remember that promise that built our faith, we become even stronger in our faith.

No one could face the tests and trials those Christians in the Sudan faced without having the hope of God's promises securely in place in their hearts. The Word of God says we overcome Satan by the blood of the Lamb and the word of our testimony. Testimonies are powerful, and this is why Satan tries so hard to ruin our testimony by trying to get us to sin. We have seen too much success lately in this tactic of the enemy.

Every testimony is based upon a trial of our faith, and when we reach heaven, these trials will turn to gold. Peter writes, "In this you greatly rejoice, though now for a little while, if need be, you have been grieved by various trials, that the genuineness of faith, being much more precious than gold that perishes, though it is tested by fire, may be found to praise, honor, and glory at the revelation of Jesus Christ" (1 Pet. 1:6–7).

Today make it your goal to share your testimony with another, and Satan will not have success with you today. Your testimony is a mighty weapon against the enemy.

Follow the Man
Luke 21:29–22:13

Recently I heard Derek Prince talk about his life of over fifty years in the ministry. He has buried two wives and has traveled the world fulfilling the Great Commission. He shares that all he did these fifty years and more was to follow the Man. He shared then in great detail about the scripture we read today in Luke. It was the time of the Passover, and it also was the time Jesus would soon be betrayed and crucified. Jesus wanted to spend the Passover with His disciples because He knew His time on earth was short. He sent Peter and John to go ahead of Him and the other disciples to prepare the Passover for them, and He gave them these instructions: "Behold when ye are entered into the city, there shall a man meet you, bearing a pitcher of water; follow him into the house where he entereth in" (Luke 22:10, KJV).

Derek shared that the man who bore the pitcher of water stood out in the crowd because in Jesus' day only women carried pitchers of water. This man evidently was told by the Holy Spirit to get ready for a very important dinner, and he prepared a room to be used by the Master.

Derek continued, "All my life I have followed the Man, and He has never failed to go ahead of me and prepare the way." Remember Jesus said, "In My Father's house are many mansions: if it were not so I would have told you: I go to prepare a place for you." (See John 14.)

Derek shared how the Holy Spirit knew he would lose his second wife and would need provision of care when she died. He went ahead and prepared a lovely apartment in the home of a family his wife had befriended in Jerusalem.

The man with the pitcher in this passage represents the Holy Spirit who always leads us and guides us. Jesus said about the Holy Spirit, "He will lead you into all truth." Those who are led by the Holy Spirit are called sons of God. Like Derek, all through my over fifty years as a Christian I have seen God's faithfulness to send the Holy Spirit ahead of me to prepare me for every situation in life. Some of the rooms of life I have experienced have involved great trials, but before I reached those rooms, the Holy Spirit prepared me ahead of time to be ready. One very difficult room of life I experienced was when the car I was driving hit a little eight-year-old boy who was seriously injured. We didn't know whether he would live or die, but thanks to the Lord, the boy was spared. I was even given the opportunity to lead him to the Lord. Six months before this great trial happened, the Lord spoke to me during communion and said, "You are going to go through a fiery trial, but just like Shadrach, Meshach and Abednego, you also will go through the fire and I will be with you, and you will come out of the fire without the smell of smoke on you." It was this message that got me through this room in my life. Follow the Man, and the Man, the Holy Spirit, will always prepare a way for you where there seems to be no way.

A Wise Woman Builds Her House
Proverbs 14:1–2

This proverb says every wise woman builds her house, but the foolish plucks it down with her hands. The building blocks a woman uses to build her house are her words. Proverbs tells us that life and death are in the power of the tongue. Every day a woman has the choice to build her house with her words or to tear her house down with her words.

One of the main duties of a wife is to give honor to her husband. If she tears him down with critical, judgmental words, she is coming against her very own personhood because she and her husband are one. As a mother a woman has the charge to encourage her children and to teach them the ways of the Lord. She has the opportunity every day to sow the good seed of God's Word into her children. When she walks with them, she can share about God's beauty and creative power as demonstrated in nature. When they eat together, she can give thanks to God for His blessings and provision. When she puts their clothes on, she can talk about the full armor of God. When she puts them to bed, she can pray with her children and read Scripture to them.

A woman can commit herself to let her conversations glorify God daily by ordering her conversation aright. She has to be careful not to gossip and be determined to only speak kindly of others. The law of kindness needs to be on her lips, and her daily prayer should be, "Lord, set a guard over my lips that I might not sin with the words I speak." Daily I pray, "Let the words of my mouth and the meditations of my heart be acceptable in Thy sight, O Lord, my strength and my redeemer. May everything I say today glorify You and sow good seed into the lives of others. Amen."

As a housekeeper, a woman has the duty of not just looking after the home, but she also has the privilege of charging the atmosphere of her home with her praises, her hymns and spiritual songs to the Lord. Her praises can fill her home with an aroma that is better than any deodorizing spray. She will be a wise woman if she will choose her words carefully and always seek to season her conversations with grace and edifying words. The foolish woman will be negative, critical, judgmental and will tear her home down with her words.

Today you have a choice. Whether you are a man or a woman, you also can build a very special building with your words. You have the great privilege of building a sanctuary for the Lord's presence wherever you are—in the market place, on the job, in the gym, in your neighborhood, at your school, in your church, in your family. The building blocks for this sanctuary are the words you speak. As you sing psalms, spiritual songs, hymns and make melody in your heart continually all the day long, you will be building this special sanctuary where God's presence will bring great joy not only to you, but also to all those around you. How is your sanctuary construction coming along today?

That Sinking Feeling
Psalm 94:1–23

Everyone during their lifetime experiences that sinking feeling. It may be fear that usually hits us with a racing heart and a sinking feeling in the pit of our stomachs. It may be discouragement. The saying goes that when the devil created the tool of discouragement, he then ceased from his works. We may have that sinking feeling when we are experiencing the loss of a loved one. When we receive the report we have been turned down for an interview, once again that sinking feeling overwhelms us. The psalmist David was quite familiar with the sinking feeling. Flight and fight were his constant companions during his lifetime. In this psalm he reveals how he was able to survive the sinking feeling. He writes, "Unless the LORD had been my help, my soul had almost dwelt in silence. When I said, My foot slippeth; thy mercy, O LORD, held me up. In the multitude of my thoughts within me thy comforts delight my soul... They gather themselves together against the soul of the righteous, and condemn the innocent blood. But the LORD is my defence; and my God is the rock of my refuge" (vv. 17–19, 21–22, KJV).

David knew to whom he could turn when he had that sinking feeling. In an earlier devotion I shared about the vision a friend had about how the Lord walks with us through life. She said the Lord never turns His back on us. He is face to face with us always, and as we walk through life, He is walking only a few steps in front of us with His hands outstretched to catch us if we start to fall. As she shared this vision, I pictured a loving father teaching his year-old child how to walk. Lovingly he stretches his arms out toward the child, and he stoops to eye level with the child. Then he coaxes the child by saying, "Come on, you can do it. Daddy is here to catch you if you begin to fall." Then slowly the father moves backward so the child will move forward to be near him.

When you have that sinking feeling, Jesus is face to face with you with His arms outstretched to catch you when you start to slip down. In Psalm 26:1 David prays, "Vindicate me, O LORD; for I have walked in my integrity. I have also trusted in the LORD; I shall not slip."

In Psalm 37:31 David speaks of a righteous man: "The law of his God is in his heart; none of his steps shall slide."

Today remember the Lord is your help, your defense, and in His mercy He will not let you sink.

READ: Judges 6:1–40; Luke 22:55–23:10; Psalm 95:1–96:13; Proverbs 14:5–6

A Sinking Heart
Luke 22:55–23:10

This passage in Luke tells about Peter's denial of Jesus. Yesterday we talked about the sinking feeling we experience when we face certain difficult situations. Fear and discouragement can cause the sinking feeling. Today we see an even deeper level of emotional turmoil. When Peter denied Jesus, he had more than a sinking feeling. He had a sinking heart. His heart was broken. When the Lord turned and looked at Peter after the cock crowed, Peter remembered the word of the Lord and how He told him that before the cock crowed he would deny Him three times. Peter left the scene and wept bitterly.

Peter had a broken heart, but more was broken in Peter than his heart. Something broke in Peter that changed his life. Earlier Jesus warned Peter that Satan wanted to sift him as wheat. Jesus said, "Simon, Simon, behold, Satan hath desired to have you, that he may sift you as wheat: But I have prayed for thee, that thy faith fail not: and when thou art converted, strengthen thy brethren" (v. 31–32, KJV).

Peter responded confidently, "Lord I am ready to go with thee, both into prison, and to death" (v. 33, KJV).

What did Jesus mean when he told Peter "when you are converted, strengthen the brethren"?

Wasn't Peter already converted? After all, he was the very disciple who confessed exactly who Jesus was by saying, "Thou art the Christ, the Son of the living God." Then why did Peter have to be converted? On that fateful day when Peter denied Christ three times, more than his heart broke. Peter's pride was broken. He was converted from the confident, independent Peter to the broken, dependent Peter. On that day Peter experienced his own crucifixion—the crucifixion of his own flesh.

It is not easy to die to ourselves. Daily we are exhorted to reckon ourselves dead to sin and alive to Jesus Christ. When the Holy Spirit reveals who we are without Christ, the picture is overwhelming and we have a sinking heart. We sigh and ask, "Lord, am I that wicked?"

Just as Jesus went to the cross and Peter had his cross experience on the day he denied Jesus, we must also have our cross experience. It happens when we lay down our self-sufficiency, pride and independence, and when we recognize that without Jesus we have the capability of being just as wicked as Charles Manson the murderer. It is only when we recognize our weakness that we can then turn to Jesus to be our strength. A broken, contrite heart Jesus will not despise. We all have our appointment with the cross when we die to ourselves so we can live in the resurrection power of Jesus Christ. Have you been converted?

April 27

The Inheritance of the Righteous
Psalm 97:1–98:9

Our own righteousness is as filthy rags, but the Lord's righteousness is filled with blessing upon blessing. We can only tap into the Lord's righteousness when we accept Jesus Christ as our Lord and Savior. From that moment on we are considered righteous, not because of our own righteous deeds, but because of the blood of Jesus Christ that was shed for us. Because of His blood that provided our forgiveness, cleansing, justification, sanctification, glorification and righteousness (right standing with God), we are now dressed in His robe of righteousness. We begin a life journey of blessing if we continue to abide in His Word and His love and obey His commandments. Of course, we will experience trials and temptations (and probably many of them) before we go to heaven, but Jesus the Righteous One will fight our battles, and the ultimate victory will be ours.

Here are some of the things we inherit because we have been made righteous through Jesus Christ:

1. Preservation of our souls
2. Deliverance from the hand of the wicked
3. Light that is always shone on our path
4. Gladness always in our hearts
5. Rejoicing in the Lord a part of our daily lives
6. Only our deeds and words judged for reward, but we ourselves saved eternally

This should make our hearts (which may sink from time to time) sing for joy. God has a wonderful word for us when we feel condemnation. This is always the tactic of the enemy. First he tempts you to sin, and then he makes you feel guilty because you had such a thought. Another great inheritance of the righteous is freedom from condemnation. John tells us, "For if our heart condemns us, God is greater than our heart, and knoweth all things. Beloved, if our heart condemn us not, then have we confidence toward God. And whatsoever we ask, we receive of him, because we keep his commandments, and do those things that are pleasing in his sight. And this is his commandment, That we should believe on the name of his Son Jesus Christ, and love one another, as he gave us commandment" (1 John 3:20–23, KJV).

Isaiah 54:17 gives us the most powerful weapon against condemnation, and it is the fact that our righteousness is of the Lord and this is our inheritance as His servants. Joy! Joy!

Joseph—the Provider
Luke 23:44–24:12

This passage tells about Joseph of Arimathea, who provided the sepulchre for Jesus' burial place. Luke describes Joseph of Arimathea as a counselor, a good and just man. He also had refused to condemn Jesus. The name *Joseph* in Hebrew means "provider."

My husband had a precious experience when he went to be alone for a day at Stone Mountain. He felt it was time to seek the Lord about some things and he just wanted to be alone in the presence of the Lord. As he was praying, he heard the Lord say, "I call you Joseph." It was not an audible voice, but Tom heard it with his spiritual ears. When he came home and shared this experience with me, I began to do research on the name Joseph in the Bible and discovered that all the Josephs mentioned were providers.

There are three Josephs mentioned in the Word of God: Joseph, the son of Israel who was sold into slavery, went ahead of his brothers to Egypt and was able to provide food during famine not only for his brothers, but also for all of Egypt. Joseph, the guardian father of Jesus, provided a safe childhood, family and home for Jesus. Joseph of Arimathea provided the burial place for Jesus.

God has a special name for each one of His children. If we miss finding out what this name is on earth, we will know it in heaven. We learn in Revelation that those who overcome will be given a white stone, and on the stone will be written a name (Rev. 2:17). The Lord knows each one of us personally, and it is His joy to give a special name to each of His children. My husband truly is a "Joseph" because his motivational gift is "giving." I joke with people and tell them my motivational gift is spending, so we make a good team. Whatever name Jesus has chosen for you, I am sure it will reveal your special calling here on earth. I know one name He has chosen for each of us, and that is "Precious."

> *Lord, it is so wonderful to know You love me so much and Your delight is to give me a new name. Names are so important to You, but more important to You are the people who bear those names. I'm so glad to be called by Your name (a Christian and a child of God).*

April 29

READ: Judges 9:22–10:18; Luke 24:13–53; Psalm 100:1–5; Proverbs 14:11–12

Quiet Time
Psalm 100:1–5

Every morning I try to have an hour with the Lord. Many people call this time their devotional time or their prayer time, and some call it their quiet time. My quiet time is not very quiet.

During my quiet time I am doing every thing listed in this psalm. This psalm tells us how to enter into God's presence, and it is interesting to see the sequence of steps. They are as follows:

1. *Make a joyful noise unto the Lord.* The call to worship was the shofar, which was blown loudly several times.
2. *Serve the Lord with gladness.* We need to approach the Lord with a servant attitude by offering ourselves to our Master to do His service.
3. *Know you that the Lord He is God.* We cannot know the Lord apart from His Word. A portion of our quiet time needs to be spent in God's Word.
4. *Acknowledge that you belong to God.* We are the sheep of His pasture. We did not make ourselves. We all have our agenda for the day, but we must recognize who is our main boss. Without the Lord we can do nothing. He created us to glorify Him on earth, not to do our own thing.
5. *Enter His gates with thanksgiving.* We need to be grateful and thankful. The Jesus attitude is one of gratitude. I thank Him for many things in the morning. Grace abounds to us through thanksgiving.
6. *Enter into His courts with praise.* Praise is the next step into His courts. When we praise the Lord we are not just thanking Him for what He has done for us. We are praising Him for who He is.
7. *Bless His name.* I try to review the names of God like Jehovah Shalom (the Lord my peace), and Jehovah Jireh (the Lord my provider). I'm thankful His name is higher than any name named on this earth.
8. *Think of His character.* I review His name and His character. He is good, and His truth endures to all generations.

I usually am up with the sunrise, and I always notice how the birds are singing very loudly as the sun comes up. They are praising God, and I am so privileged to be able to join their serenade of praise. Make a joyful noise this morning to the Lord, praise and bless His holy name, and give thanks to Him. He is worthy.

Jesus Is the Light
John 1:1–28

John begins his letter with the words "In the beginning was the Word." The Word was Jesus. He is the living Word. The Father is a Spirit. The Holy Spirit is the breath of God and Jesus is the Word of God. The Word of God took the form of flesh and came to live here on earth. I like to say God decided to put on an earth suit so He could come live with us. Jesus was with the Father from the foundation of the earth. When God said, "Let there be light," the light of Jesus began to shine on this earth. Jesus is the true Light that lights every man who comes into the world.

Science is always proving the Bible to be correct. With the recent development of test tube babies, an interesting occurrence happens at the time sperm meets with egg. Observers noticed that the moment sperm meets egg, a flash of light occurs. That light is the Light that lights every man who comes into the world. Jesus is present at every conception because He is life. At the moment of conception Light has shown into darkness. The sad part is that many have chosen to walk in darkness.

Jesus is still bringing the light of His countenance to us daily. In my witnessing to people I have noticed that those who receive Christ suddenly glow like a light bulb. Jesus has shone out of darkness into their hearts to give them light of the knowledge of the glory of God in the face of Jesus Christ. When I had a vision of Jesus' face, I asked Him why I could not take a picture of His face to the whole world because I knew when they saw the love in His eyes they would instantly repent. He spoke this to my heart: "I have not chosen to reveal Myself in this way to the world. I have chosen to reveal Myself through My body on earth (the church). You are the one to show My face through your face to the world."

David writes that the Lord is the light of His countenance. When our son Ron was in China teaching, several of his students would come up and ask him, "What makes your face shine?" Ron was shining the light of Jesus to China, a very dark land. "For God, who commanded the light to shine out of darkness, hath shined in our hearts, to give the light of the knowledge of the glory of God in the face of Jesus Christ. But we have this treasure in earthen vessels, that the excellency of the power may be of God, and not of us" (2 Cor. 4:6–7, KJV).

> Lord, let the light of Your countenance always be upon me. Today I want to allow Your light to shine out of my heart and face to others.

May 1

READ: Judges 13:1–14:20; John 1:29–51; Psalm 102:1–28; Proverbs 14:15–16

He Knows You
John 1:29–51

How many times have you called a person, only to receive a taped message? Because of great advancements in the technology of the computer and satellites, we have become a faceless society. At the same time we also have a society in which there is no privacy. Even though my face may not be known to others because I never have face-to-face communication with them, my whole life is known to others. Via the computer and satellite others know all about me—my buying habits, how much money I have in the bank, my age and the number in my family.

This is why I take comfort in our reading for today. In this passage of John, we see how the Lord Jesus knows everything about us. Even though today we do not have face-to-face communication with Him, He sees us and knows us. He even counts the number of hairs on your head. Jesus knows your character, your strengths, your weaknesses and your secret desires. Most importantly, He knows your heart. This passage in John tells us how Jesus knew everything about His disciples before they even met Him. The moment He saw Simon, He called him by name: "Thou art Simon the son of Jona: thou shalt be called Cephas, which is by interpretation, A stone" (v. 42, KJV). Then Jesus saw Nathaniel and said, "Behold an Israelite indeed, in which is no guile!" Nathaniel asked Jesus how He knew him, and Jesus said to him, "Before that Philip called thee, when thou wast under the fig tree, I saw thee." Nathaniel responded with this great confession, "Rabbi, thou art the Son of God, thou art the King of Israel" (vv. 47–49, KJV).

What is so exciting about this personal knowledge Jesus has of each one of us is that we can tap into this knowledge daily through prayer. If we will seek Him as we intercede for others, He will tell us many things about those we are praying for, such as the strongholds in their lives that need to be pulled down. We can also daily ask Him to show us ways we can better serve those around us. One of the questions I ask Jesus daily is, "How can I make life easier for my husband, my sons and their wives, and all those I will see today?" He never fails to give me inspiration and instruction about little things I can do that will make their day better. Often my family members will ask me, "How did you know I needed that?" I usually don't reveal my source of information, but now you know my secret.

Jesus was touched with the feelings of our infirmities (weaknesses), and He was tempted in every way we are tempted, yet He never sinned. Ask Him today to share with you how you can make life easier for those around you.

Lord, show me little things I can do that will help brighten the day for others.

Just Do It
John 2:1–25

My husband and I lead tours to Israel, and we are about to take our sixth trip together there. We always make sure we do not miss the lovely chapel that now marks the place where Jesus turned the water into wine at the wedding of Cana. The presence of the Lord is always so strong in this place.

One of the greatest mysteries on earth is marriage, and it is not surprising Jesus performed His first miracle at a wedding since He is our bridegroom. It is always our custom when visiting this chapel to take a few moments to pray in the courtyard before we go into the chapel. We pray for marriages, and we also pray for the singles who want to be married. The scripture we always pray for the singles is one I found in Isaiah: "Search from the book of the LORD, and read: not one of these shall fail; not one shall lack her mate. For My mouth has commanded it, and His Spirit has gathered them" (Isa. 34:16).

After praying this at the Cana chapel on several trips to Israel, I decided to look that scripture up again. When I read it in context, I got a good chuckle. This promise is not for people, but for birds. The verse before this promise speaks of gathering owls and vultures. Of course, I never told our lovely singles about my discovery, and in spite of my mistake, many of those we prayed for got married. Wedding wine is sold just outside the chapel, and our tour people always insisted I buy some for the wedding of our three sons. I always said, "That wine will turn to vinegar before the boys get married." God is faithful, however, and all three of our sons were married in a space of nine months, and we now have grandchildren. The oldest son was thirty-five when he married.

Mary said something we should all take note of and heed. When the wine ran out she said, "Whatever He says to you, do it." David DuPlessis (often called Mr. Pentecost) tells of having a private audience with the pope. In this meeting he shared with the pope that even though their faiths differed a little, they did have one thing in common. He said, "We both believe in doing whatever Mary tells us to do." He was referring to these words Mary spoke just after Jesus began His public ministry. We all need for these words to resound in our ears daily. "Do whatever Jesus tells you to do."

> Lord, help me to listen carefully to Your instructions daily. Most of Your instructions to me are found in Your Word, but You also speak quietly to my heart by Your Holy Spirit. Don't let me miss out on anything You want me to do. When I hear what You want me to do, empower me by Your Spirit to do it.

The Earth Is Full of His Riches
Psalm 104:1–24

This psalm is so beautiful in its description of the majesty of God. This would be a great psalm to read when you are at a low point in your life. As I read about the creative power and manifold works of our God, confidence welled up within me, and I knew without a doubt that God could handle my every problem.

Let's look at some of the statements made about our mighty God in this psalm. Let the verses settle deep in your spirit, and meditate on them all day long. Meditation is like worry in the sense that you keep thinking about the same thing over and over again. However, meditation is creative and restorative, and worry is destructive. When we establish a pattern of meditating on God's Word all the day long, we will have little time to worry.

- God covers Himself with light as with a garment. God literally inhabits our praises, and as we praise Him, the intensity of the light around Him increases because He girds Himself with praise. We have the privilege every day to dress God with garments of praise.

- God stretches out the heavens like a curtain. Isaiah 40:12 tells us that God measures the heavens with the span of His hand. God is big, and He can perfect everything that is a concern to you today.

- God lays the beams of His chamber in the waters. Isaiah 40:12 also tells us that God can hold all the waters on earth in the hollow of His hand. God is big enough to handle every problem you may face today.

The psalm continues listing all of God's marvelous works, with verse 24 summing it all up: "O Lord, how manifold are Your works! In wisdom You have made them all. The earth is full of your possessions."

After reviewing all of God's riches on earth, we can only end with praise as the psalmist does: "I will sing to the Lord as long as I live; I will sing praise to my God while I have my being. May my meditation of Him be sweet to Him; I will be glad in the Lord" (vv. 33–34).

Let your meditation of Him be sweet today as you meditate on Psalm 104.

Loose Lips Sink Ships
Proverbs 14:22–24

In a previous devotional we talked about the saying "Loose lips sink ships," which was a by-word in World War II. Those who were working in the war effort were cautioned to be extremely careful about what they shared with others. They didn't want any information to leak out to the enemy. We also have an enemy, and he uses our very own words as ammunition against us. We forget that the devil cannot read our minds, but he can give us thoughts and can hear what we say. A lot of the time we do his dirty work for him just by being careless in our words.

This proverb says that the talk of lips tends to poverty. Another proverb says he that keeps his lips keeps his soul from troubles. When we speak too much, we often let out information to the enemy that he will use against us. We serve a God who owns all the cattle on the hills and the entire universe. He is rich and wants to bless us with many of His resources, but often we rob ourselves of His blessings by speaking the wrong things. I have caught myself actually speaking curses over my own life by the words I say. I will say things like, "We'll never have enough money to do this or that." I also can bring poverty to my own soul by speaking things like, "I'm so depressed," or "I'm an emotional wreck." Pretty soon our souls will pick up on what we are saying, and the emotional area of our souls will respond to our words.

We can enrich our souls by what we speak also. David learned this lesson, and he often spoke to his soul: "Why are you cast down, O my soul; hope in God." We can speak encouraging words to our soul when we feel down. The Bible teaches us to speak in faith and often calls for us to call those things that are not as though they are. The Bible says, "Let the weak say they are strong." I've tried to practice this in my life, and if I am having negative feelings, I try to speak just the opposite. People sometimes feel this is not being honest, but when we are weak, in the Lord we are strong. When we are down, in the Lord we are joyful. When we are confused, in the Lord we have peace of mind. We need to speak what the Lord is in our lives no matter how we feel. Emotions are deceptive, and often the enemy wants us to wallow in our emotions rather than confess the Word of God in faith.

Many of the troubles we have are brought upon ourselves by what we speak. Make it your goal today not to speak any negative words. Ask the Holy Spirit to stop you if you begin to speak negatively. A prayer I pray almost every morning is:

Lord, let the words of my mouth and the meditations of my heart be acceptable to You. You are my strength and my redeemer. Amen.

Spirit of Truth
John 4:5–42

Immediately after Jesus told the woman of Samaria that she had five husbands and that the man she now had was not her husband, she changed the subject. She saw that this Man knew well her history, but she was not willing to go into it with Him. She proceeded to ask Him a theological question. How like human nature. When someone is getting too close to the truth in our own lives—our own sin and shortcomings—we want to change the subject. The woman asked Jesus where He believed was the correct place of worship. The answer Jesus gave is revealing. "Woman, believe Me, the hour is coming when you will neither on this mountain, nor in Jerusalem, worship the Father. You worship what you do not know; we know what we worship, for salvation is of the Jews. But the hour is coming, and now is, when the true worshipers will worship the Father in spirit and truth; for the Father is seeking such to worship Him" (vv. 21–23).

True worship is not dependent upon the location. It is dependent upon our being led by the Spirit of God. Where the Spirit of the Lord is, there is liberty. The Father seeks those who will worship Him in spirit and truth. What does this mean? We must allow the Holy Spirit to interpret God's truth to us. Without Him the Word of God is just black words on white paper. It is the Holy Spirit that ignites the Word in our hearts. I recently went to a wedding, and it was lovely. The pastor read from Scripture, and it was good, but it lacked the anointing. He was just reading words without submitting to the power of the Holy Spirit who is able to make every word in God's Word have dynamite power. The Holy Spirit is able to impart faith to us, and faith must be mixed with the Word for it to avail anything.

Our pastor is well aware of the importance of the Spirit of Truth conveying God's truth to us. One Sunday as usual he had prepared for his message, but as he began to read the Word, he knew there was something missing. The anointing that breaks every yoke of bondage was not there, so he closed his Bible and told us to go home and seek the Lord on our own. This was probably the best thing that ever happened to some of us because we saw how we cannot be dependent upon a pastor. We must be dependent upon the Holy Spirit to be our teacher and our worship leader. Worship without the anointing of the Holy Spirit is not pleasing in God's sight. He desires for us to worship Him in both spirit and truth. The Holy Spirit is the Spirit of Truth, and only He can impart God's Word to us and lead our worship in the way that pleases God.

Lord, let me be led by the Holy Spirit as I worship You.

The Fear of the Lord
Proverbs 14:26–27

This proverb tells us that the fear of the Lord will give us strong confidence, and our children will have safety because they have a place of refuge. One of the major problems in America is that our children are not being taught to fear the Lord. I just recently taught an eight-week study on the fear of the Lord, and we learned that the fear of the Lord is not caught; it is taught. Parental instruction in the Word of God seems to be waning, and we are reaping the consequences. We see the shootings in the high schools in America, and recently there was even one in the first grade. We learn in this proverb that the fear of the Lord is a fountain of life and keeps us from the snare of death.

Teaching our children to fear the Lord is a vital part of their training. Deuteronomy 7:1–2 exhorts Israel to teach the commandments, the statues and the judgments of the Lord to the generations to come. The promises in Deuteronomy 7:2–3 given to those who obey the commandments are that they will increase mightily and things will go well with them; their days will be prolonged. Most children who were raised in church cannot quote the Ten Commandments. Is this the fault of the church? No, it is the fault of parents. They are instructed by God to teach the commandments to their children when they are walking and sitting and in every activity.

The question to ask yourself is, "Can I recite the Ten Commandments?" If you cannot, then today make it your goal to memorize and meditate on the Ten Commandments this week. Just recently I heard of how a whole church came into revival simply because the pastor exhorted his congregation to meditate daily on the Ten Commandments. He suggested that parents have the Ten Commandments framed on a wall near their dining table so that they can discuss one or more commandments at meal times.

I challenge you to look up every blessing that is promised to those who fear the Lord. I know if you do this, you will want to instruct others in the fear of the Lord.

Lord, I confess my neglect of learning and teaching the Ten Commandments. It is not too late for me to make this a top priority in my life and the life of my family. Help me to be diligent to teach the fear of the Lord to others.

None Holy As the Lord
1 Samuel 1:1–2:21

It was not until this morning that I realized I have been singing often in my private worship time Hannah's song. When Hannah brought Samuel to the temple to lend him to the Lord as her thanks to God for the conception and delivery of this precious son, she prayed a powerful prayer that acknowledged the sovereignty and power of God: "There is none holy as the LORD: for there is none beside thee: neither is there any rock like our God" (1 Sam. 2:2, KJV).

Often in the morning I sing this song, and my heart is comforted because I know He is sovereign. In the midst of troubles, He is in control, and because He is my rock, I have a refuge to run to when the going gets rough. There truly is none holy as the Lord. As I hear the birds praise the Lord every morning as the sun comes up, I am overwhelmed by His awesome power. This is my time in the morning to meditate on His holiness, and I think of the angels, saints and every creature in heaven and earth praising and singing in unison in one great symphony of praise. They are all singing, "Holy, holy, holy. Holy is the Lord."

I recently heard the testimony of a man who had a vision of heaven. He saw the cherubim and seraphim circling the throne of God, and they were saying, "Holy, holy, holy." He asked the Lord if the seraphim and cherubim got tired of circling the throne. The Lord responded, "No, they never tire of circling the throne of God, because every time they circle it, they discover a new attribute or aspect of God they never knew before." We have not even begun to search the depths that are in our mighty heavenly Father, but we can make a beginning this morning. Try singing that old familiar song, "Holy, Holy, Holy." It goes like this: "Holy, holy, holy, all the saints adore thee. Casting down their golden crowns around the glassy sea. Only thou art holy, there is none beside thee. Perfect in power, love and purity." There are many more words to this great hymn. Learn them and join the cherubim and seraphim, the saints, and every creature on earth every morning as they sing, "Holy, holy, holy."

Envy
Proverbs 14:30–31

This proverb says that envy is rottenness to the bones. Envy is a sin that brings only evil consequences. Some sins are a pleasure for a season, but of course, sin always births death in our lives in some way. The Bible tells us that the person who commits adultery kills his own soul. It may be years before we reap what we have sown, but beware, our sins will find us out. If we do not confess our sins and turn from them, there will be eternal consequences also. We will not lose our salvation unless we commit the sin of denying our faith in Christ, but we will lose some rewards in heaven if we do not deal honestly and openly with our sins here on earth. When we confess our sins, God is faithful and just not only to forgive our sins, but also to cleanse us from all unrighteousness. We can go to heaven with a clean slate if we have not hidden iniquity in our hearts by refusing to confess our sins and turn from them.

Envy is a sin that will cause even physical consequences. It will cause our bones to rot. The death in our lives that is caused by envy is experienced right away. Envy causes a death to our relationships. The first murder in the Bible was caused by envy. Cain envied Abel because God favored Abel's sacrifice over his own. Envy will also bring death to peace in our lives. Envy always causes strife. James tells us, "But if you have bitter envy and self-seeking in your hearts, do not boast and lie against the truth. This wisdom does not descend from above, but is earthy, sensual, demonic. For where envy and self-seeking exist, confusion and every evil thing are there" (James 3:14–16).

When envy is present, strife will soon occur; this then opens the door to confusion and every evil work. The spirit of jealousy is what caused the first murder, so whenever we are jealous of another, in a sense we may wish that person dead. Envy occurs when we feel we have not been treated fairly. The way we can kill envy instead of allowing it to kill us is to humble ourselves.

We need to esteem others higher than ourselves. If we do, we will never be envious. Pride is the root of envy, and we destroy pride when we gladly take upon ourselves the form of a servant just as Jesus did. Life is not fair. Some people have more than others in intelligence, wealth, meaningful relationships, etc. God is just and merciful, however, and if you determine to humble yourself under the mighty hand of God, He promises to lift you up.

At the foot of the cross, we are all at the same level. We need to remain at the foot of the cross daily, and envy will never invade our lives to destroy it.

Lord, keep me near the foot of Your cross. Help me to operate with Your mind today. You humbled Yourself, came as a servant and made yourself of no reputation. Give me a servant spirit today.

READ: 1 Samuel 5:1–7:17; John 6:1–21; Psalm 106:13–31; Proverbs 14:32–33

Leanness When We Lust
Psalm 106:13–31

All mankind has three things in common. We all have three major lusts in our souls: the lust of the flesh (seeking to fulfill our five senses in an overindulgent way); the lust of the eye (greedy longings in the mind that can cause greed and covetousness; pornography is caused by this lust); and the pride of life, which is trusting our own resources and ourselves more than we trust in God. All of these lusts are located in our souls—our minds, wills and emotions. These three lusts are the buttons Satan is constantly pressing with his seducing spirits. James tells us that God never tempts us, but we are led astray by our own lusts. The devil cannot make us do anything. We first have to open the door to him through one or more of these lusts.

When we lust for certain things, God may allow us to experience what we lust for as He did with the children of Israel. They asked for food other than manna, which was God's provision. Because they were not grateful and lusted for more than God's provision, God sent leanness to their soul. We forget that the first step in the cycle of sin is an ungrateful heart. Romans 1 tells us all about the downhill spiral of sin. When we fulfill our own lusts, we may be satisfied for a season, but soon we will be empty again. Leanness will come to our souls. Many of us suffer from bulimic souls. We have stuffed ourselves through fulfilling our own lusts, but we are anemic spiritually because we have neglected the things of God that really count. When we fill ourselves full of God's Spirit and His Word, we will be fulfilled, or filled full. If we walk in the spirit, we will not fulfill the lust of the flesh.

Lord, forgive me for seeking my own pleasure, for filling my mind with the wrong things and for trusting in myself more than I trust in You. I want to be filled with Your Spirit daily, and then I will not fulfill my own lusts. Help me today, Lord, to stay close to You.

May 10

READ: 1 Samuel 8:1–9:27; John 6:22–46; Psalm 106:32–48; Proverbs 14:34–35

I Need Some Bread
John 6:22–46

I'll never forget hosting a Russian Jewish lady on her birthday. The table was set with the finest china, and fresh flowers provided the centerpiece for the table. All the food was presented well, and I felt everything was near perfect. The moment I sat down at the table after much diligent preparation in the kitchen, the guest of honor said in her heavy Russian accent, "I need some bread. Where is the bread?" She sincerely felt she could not even begin her meal unless bread was on the table. I later found out why she was desperate for bread. Her hands were arthritic, and she used bread to help push things on her fork. Often she would just forget to use the fork and raised her food to her mouth on pieces of bread.

Wouldn't it be wonderful if we had the same desperate desire for the bread of life—Jesus Christ? In this passage Jesus identifies Himself as the true bread of God sent from heaven to give life to the world. He said, "I am the bread of life." It is interesting that Jesus was born in Bethlehem, which means "House of Bread" in Hebrew. Bread is often called the staff of life. Jesus is the bread that is the staff of life in this life and the next. He is the only One who can give us lasting sustenance that will sustain us through all the circumstances of life. Every Lord's Supper we partake of the bread, remembering His body that was broken for us. There is nothing that smells any better than fresh baked bread. One of my happiest memories about my college years was the smell of the Colonial Bread Company that was located on my drive to college. The smell of fresh bread baking, however, cannot compete with the sweet aroma of the Lord's presence.

Today you will probably eat bread with every meal. When you eat your bread at mealtime, think of Jesus, the bread of life, and how much you need Him in your life. Jesus, the bread come down from heaven, will give strength not only to your physical body, but also to your soul and spirit.

Lord, I need You to sustain me today. Only You can satisfy my longing soul, and only You can give me the spiritual food that lasts forever. Help me not to miss any meals with You today.

O That Men Would Praise the Lord
Psalm 107:1–43

A grateful heart is one of the keys to a joyful life. If we look carefully at the moments of our day, we will always see things worthy of our praise. This psalm lists many reasons to praise the Lord. If we do not see His hand in the moments of our lives, then we can praise Him for His very character and His works. Praise comes before worship, and one of the roots of this word is "worth." God's character and works are always worthy of praise. Praise is the first step we have to take when we enter His presence. Let's look the steps the priests had to take to enter the holy of holies in the tabernacle.

Just as priests of Israel had to enter into the holy of holies by a special pattern given them by God, we also enter into His presence using this same pattern. In the early days of the tabernacle, only the high priest could enter into the holy of holies. He entered first into the tabernacle through the eastern gate. The psalmist wrote, "Enter into His gates with thanksgiving and into His courts with praise" (Ps. 100:4). Our first time in God's presence should be spent in thanksgiving, then this should flow into praise.

After entering the eastern gate the priest offered the offerings on the brazen alter. These included a burnt offering, a meat offering, a peace offering, a sin offering and a trespass offering. This represents a time in which we offer our bodies as a living sacrifice to be used by Him that day. After this we can enter a time of confession so that we may receive the cleansing of the Lord. After all the offerings on the brazen altar, the priests washed, themselves in a laver filled with water. This laver was made of polished brass, which was used to make mirrors in the early days. Before washing, the priests could clearly see their own reflection in the shiny brass. We all need a time of reflection and judging ourselves before we continue our progress into the presence of the Lord.

The priests then entered a section of the tabernacle called the holy place. Here was a lamp, a table with twelve loaves of bread and an altar of incense. I believe the bread and the lamp represent His Word, which is a lamp to our feet and a light to our path. The lamp also represents the sevenfold anointing of the Holy Spirit. Jesus said, "Man shall not live by bread alone, but by every Word of God." Before we make our requests known unto the Lord, it might be well to spend some time in God's Word. To pray according to God's will, we must know His Word because His Word is His will. Then the altar of incense represents our petitions and supplications to the Lord. Finally we enter into the holy of holies where we commune with Him. There is no veil of separation now because Jesus rent the veil. We can boldly enter His throne of grace through the blood of Jesus and find help in time of need. Remember we begin this journey by entering His gates with thanksgiving and His courts with praise. Use Psalm 107 to begin your journey today. You can praise the Lord for His character—He is good, merciful, loving and kind. You can praise the Lord for His works—He redeems us, delivers us, guides us, satisfies our souls and breaks our bondages.

The Tongue
Proverbs 15:4

You have heard the phrase, "Divide and conquer." When there is division of any kind that disturbs unity, we are much more vulnerable to the enemy. The enemy does not have to use mighty weapons against us in order to divide us. Instead, he uses the mightiest member of our body, our own tongue, to divide and conquer. Death and life are in the power of the tongue. James tells us the tongue is like the rudder on a ship and the bit in a horse's mouth; this tiny member of our body has the power to control our whole body.

A person's tongue also can affect his spirit. This proverb tells us that "a wholesome tongue is a tree of life, but perverseness in it breaks the spirit." When we are perverse in our speech, we can cause a division in our spirit. It is called a divided heart. Some meanings for the word *perverse* are "crooked, wicked, false, froward, rash, rebellious" just to name a few.

You've also heard the expression, "He speaks with a forked tongue." This means a person's tongue is divided. Whenever we lie, are rash, rebellious or froward, we are speaking with a "forked tongue." Our words not only can cause division in the lives of others, but also in our own lives.

One of my callings is to minister to the brokenhearted, and almost every brokenhearted person I counsel has had perverse words spoken over them. These perverse words have caused a division in their heart, and they have a continual battle with walking in a straight path with the Lord. When these word curses are broken over their lives, these brokenhearted people are healed.

A wholesome tongue gives life to others and to us. A wholesome tongue is a tongue that has the law of kindness upon it. We are to speak blessings, not curses, to others. Today make it your goal to only allow words that edify to come out of your mouth. Use your tongue today to glorify, extol and praise the Lord and to praise and edify others. Let the words you speak be words to build up, not to tear down; to unify, not to divide. Don't allow the devil to walk on the red carpet of your tongue today and use your tongue against yourself and others.

Lord, help me to speak only those things that will bring life to others. You have the words of life, and let me speak them boldly today.

May 13

READ: 1 Samuel 14:1–52; John 7:31–53; Psalm 109:1–31; Proverbs 15:5–7

Treasures in the House
Proverbs 15:5–7

Is your house filled with treasures? I remember visiting a home in New Jersey and our host showing us all the treasures he had collected from his travels all over the world. There were paintings, statues and every kind of bric-a-brac, each representing a country he visited. I thought to myself, *This man's life is wrapped up in his treasures and travels.*

Jesus exhorted us not to lay up treasures on earth where moth and rust can corrupt them and thieves can steal them. He said instead we should lay up for ourselves treasures in heaven.

There are many ways we can add to our treasures in heaven, but one of the greatest ways is to witness and share God's Word and love with people. People are precious to God, and they are God's treasures. We are God's inheritance, and whenever we invest in people, we are adding to our inheritance and God's inheritance. One of my favorite scriptures is Proverbs 24:3–4: "Through wisdom a house is built, and by understanding it is established; by knowledge the rooms are filled with all precious and pleasant riches."

Our home is not filled with treasures from our travels around the world, but we have had life, the Lord, our love and our home with a dear girl from China who spent five years with us. We also have a Russian son. Both are like a daughter and son to us.

One morning as I was sipping my coffee I realized how rich we were. Our home was filled with treasures—my husband, our three sons, our Russian son and our Chinese daughter. I gave thanks to the Lord for entrusting me for a season with such valuable treasures.

> *Help me to see every person in my life today as Your special treasure. Use me as Your instrument to care for and share Your love and Word with these precious treasures You have allowed me to be steward of on earth.*

135

God Looks at the Heart
1 Samuel 15:1–16:23

Prejudice is simply prejudging a person before we even get to know that person. We often make up our minds that we are not going to like a person simply because of his outward appearance. God warned Samuel when he went to anoint a new king of Israel not to look at the outer appearance of the man. He instructed Samuel to anoint one of the sons of Jesse. As each of Jesse's sons passed by, Samuel knew the Lord had not chosen any of those seven sons. He asked Jesse if all the sons were present, and Jesse told him that the youngest was tending the sheep. His name was David. When David appeared on the scene, he was very good looking and had a beautiful countenance. God, however, did not choose David because of his outward appearance. He chose him because He knew David's heart. David had a heart after God.

Psalm 113 tells us that God humbles Himself to see the hearts of men. It is an awesome thought that God sees and knows what is in my heart. What is so amazing is that when He looks into my heart and sees the potential for sin that is there, He still loves me. I had a vision once of the face of Jesus, and as I looked into the eyes of Jesus, I was overwhelmed with His compassion for me. First His eyes were like fiery laser beams that penetrated my whole being, and then His eyes were like dove's eyes— tender and full of compassion. Yes, He knows my heart, even the dark parts of it, but He still loves me. When He sees the dark parts of my heart, He longs to shine the light of His love into those dark areas and grace my heart with His love. He wants me to confess my sins to Him so He can forgive me and cleanse me from all unrighteousness.

Jesus also warns us not to look on the outer appearance of people. He tells us that the scribes and Pharisees looked good on the outside, but on the inside they were rotting and decaying. He calls them whitewashed sepulchers full of dead men's bones. God is not interested in the outer physical appearance. He is interested in the inner person of our souls. However, in the Law no priest could come into God's presence that had a deformity of any kind. He was to be faultless in appearance. Thank God we now have Jesus, our High Priest, who is perfect inside and out. We now stand in His righteousness before the Father, not our own.

When David was anointed to be king of Israel, God knew even though David might sin, he would always repent and turn his heart to the Lord. A perfect heart in God's sight is one that desires to go God's way every day. David wrote this: "I will behave wisely in a perfect way. Oh, when will you come to me? I will walk within my house with a perfect heart" (Ps. 101:2).

Let this be your prayer today.

May 15

Doing What Pleases the Father
John 8:21–30

Jesus said to the Jews, "I do always those things that please Him." Jesus had just shared that He only spoke those things that the Father taught Him. Jesus' life on earth was spent pleasing the Father. He was not sent to earth to please Himself or even others. He came to speak the Word the Father spoke to Him and to do the works He saw the Father do. Jesus' life on earth reveals how we are to walk daily.

We wake up every morning with three choices: We can choose to please ourselves, others or God. If we make the right choice, God will cause our day to be filled with peace and joy. If we choose to please ourselves, we will be miserable. I have yet to see a happy selfish person. If we choose to please others, we will be bound by what others think of us. There will be no lasting satisfaction, and we will always be manipulating situations and people in such a way that everyone seems to be happy. We will always be under pressure to receive the approval of others. People pleasing is rooted in the fear of man and is directly opposed to the fear of God. True fulfillment comes when we know we are living to please God, not man or ourselves.

Now you may ask, "What pleases God?" The answer is given in Jesus' own words to His disciples: "Do not fear, little flock for it is your Father's good pleasure to give you the kingdom" (Luke 12:32). "The kingdom of God is not eating and drinking, but righteousness and peace and joy in the Holy Spirit" (Rom. 14:17). When we give the kingdom to others through our words and deeds, we are pleasing the Father.

My life scripture is Philippians 2:13: "For it is God who works in you both to will and to do for His good pleasure."

Let this be your prayer this morning:

> *Lord, I want to think, do and say only those things that please You today. I trust You to enable me by the power of Your Holy Spirit to only do Your good pleasure this day. I choose to please You in all I do and say.*

May 16

Continuing in God's Word
John 8:31–59

I was speaking at a ladies' retreat, and a woman came to me after the meeting to ask my counsel about some things in her life. I asked her if she had looked into God's Word for her answers. She replied, "Oh, I've already read the Bible through years ago." This lady did not have the concept that the Word of God is our daily spiritual bread. When we pray "Give us this day our daily bread," we are not just praying for physical bread. We are also praying for the Father to give us fresh spiritual bread or manna, a fresh word from Him that will sustain us throughout the day.

The children of Israel were instructed to gather fresh manna every morning except for the Sabbath, which was a day of rest. If they took more than they needed, the manna rotted. They had to digest what they gathered, and they each were assigned a portion. We should treat God's Word like manna and be careful to daily receive our portion. Some people make the mistake of trying to digest too much of the Word daily, and they get indigestion. The Word is like vitamin C because it needs to be absorbed into our system daily to have the proper effect on our spiritual health. Paul tells Timothy that the Word of God is given to us for instruction, correction, reproof and doctrine.

The Holy Spirit has a fresh word for you daily, but you must ask Him for that word. It may only be one verse, but that verse will sustain you throughout the day. At the same time, reading the Bible through along with seeking a special word is of great value. I love reading the Bible through in a year because each day I receive portions of spiritual bread from the Old Testament, New Testament, Psalms and Proverbs. I know that I am daily receiving the full counsel of God's Word.

In this passage Jesus shares the qualifications of a true disciple. He said, "If you abide in My word, then you are My disciples indeed. And you shall know the truth, and the truth shall make you free" (John 8:31–32).

We love to quote the second verse, "You shall know the truth and the truth will make you free," but often we fail to meet the condition expressed just before this verse, "If you continue in My word." There are many Christians but few disciples who are willing to submit themselves daily for the instruction, reproof, correction and teaching of doctrine found in God's Word.

I asked the lady who said she read the Bible through years ago a question. I asked her if she looked in the mirror daily to check her makeup before she went out of her house. She replied, "Of course I do this." Then I exhorted her to daily look into the mirror of God's Word, and if she did this faithfully, each day she would grow in the beauty of the Lord.

May 17

READ: 1 Samuel 20:1–21:15; John 9:1–41; Psalm 113:1–114:8; Proverbs 15:15–17

A Joyful Mother
Psalm 113:1–114:8

It was Monday morning, May 17, 1999, when I received a call from the nursing home where mother resided for four years after her severe stroke. I was told she had passed away early that morning. It was my joy to visit mother at least four times a week and spend time with her.

She was eighty-nine when she died and was healthy except for a heart problem that required open heart surgery. She opted not to have this at her age, and the result was a massive stroke that paralyzed her whole right side. She did have her speech, however, and the words she shared with everyone were always so uplifting. My mother was the epitome of a joyful mother.

That morning the physician's assistant shared with me how special Mother was. She said Mother was always so cheerful, and all the aides loved going in her room because she was the bright spot on the fourth floor. I shared with her that I never remember my mother ever saying anything negative about anyone or ever complaining about anything. The physician's assistant replied, "Oh, I wished my daughters could say the same thing of me." I told all my friends to visit my mother if they were having a low day. She had a way of making you feel as if you were the most special thing in the entire world. Every time I visited her, she told me I was beautiful and precious! She told everyone this.

The morning she died I asked the Lord to give me some scriptures I could share when we had her memorial service. I heard Him gently speak to my spirit, "Look at Psalm 113." In this passage I found the perfect description of my mother. Verse 9 tells us, "He grants the barren woman a home, like a joyful mother of children. Praise the LORD."

It was not until later that morning when I was reading the portion of my daily Bible reading that I discovered Psalm 113 was the Psalm portion for May 17. As I read about the joyful mother the second time that morning, my mind flashed back to my childhood when I heard my mother singing and whistling in the kitchen. Sometimes she would go to visit neighbors in the evening, and I would wait to hear her whistle in the driveway upon her return before I could drift off to sleep. Today she is whistling and singing in heaven with my dad and others who have gone before her. I ended my devotional time this morning by singing the words to that great gospel song "What a Day That Will Be." This is truly the day the Lord has made; I will rejoice and be glad in it, and I will be a joyful mother.

Lord, help me to pass Your joy to others today.

May 18

READ: 1 Samuel 22:1–23:29; John 10:1–21; Psalm 115:1–18; Proverbs 15:18–19

Idol Worship
Psalm 115:1–18

When we spent three weeks in India in 1980, we agreed with our pastor and his wife that we would not visit any of the Hindu temples. We did not want to expose ourselves to the spirits that dwelled in these temples. We knew that even though man had made the idols in these temples, demonic spirits were all around them.

While we were in Madras, a man came up to us and asked us if we wanted to see a museum that had bronzes that dated back to the eleventh century. We agreed to follow him, and later wished we had not. As we entered the museum we felt the heaviness of demonic spirits and soon realized that all the bronzes were idols the Hindus worshiped. Some were so grotesque in appearance we wondered how anyone could worship such an image. Our pastor quickly made a beeline for the door and said, "We've seen your gods, but personally I prefer Jehovah God."

Today's reading in Psalm 115 tells us all about idols. Idols have mouths, but they cannot speak; eyes, but they cannot see; ears, but they cannot hear; noses, but they cannot smell; hands, but they cannot handle; feet, but they cannot walk. This psalm goes on to say, "Those that make them are like to them; so is everyone who trusts in them" (v. 8).

I found myself thanking God that I was not an idol worshiper. Then I realized that idols are just images in people's minds. God created us with a divine imagination to worship Him and Him only. However, we often crowd Him out with the other images in our minds. A good definition of an idol is anything you think about more than you think about God. With this definition, we have to be honest with ourselves and realize we do have idols in our lives. As the psalm says, we can become just like those idols—paralyzed in our effectiveness to share the gospel with others by speaking His word. When we have idols in our lives, we are unable to see others as God sees them; we are unable to hear others with understanding ears; we are unable to smell the sweet aroma of His presence; we are unable to touch others with His embrace; and we are unable to walk in His ways.

Whatever I put before God, no matter how good it may be, can become an idol in my life. God desires our first fruits, and He wants us to worship Him in spirit and truth. The highest form of worship is to do His will. We are hindered in doing His will if we allow other people and things to be first in our lives. Jesus said, "Seek first the kingdom of God and His righteousness, and all these things shall be added to you" (Matt. 6:33). Just prior to this admonition Jesus tells us to take no thought about what we are going to wear or eat, or even about what tomorrow will bring. When we concern ourselves with these things and allow our minds to be absorbed in thinking about such things, we become ineffective in His kingdom.

READ: 1 Samuel 24:1–25:44; John 10:22–42; Psalm 116:1–19; Proverbs 15:20–21

Precious Is the Death of Saints
Psalm 116:1–19

Psalm 116:15 is used in many funeral services, and the message conveyed is that God is blessed by the death of His saints. What a wrong interpretation of this scripture! Death is an enemy of God and has been since the Fall. God is the God of life, and death is the result of sin. God desired for us to live with Him in fellowship with Him forever when Adam and Eve were created. In His foreknowledge, however, He knew we would choose death over life. This is why Jesus had to come and die and be resurrected so that death would no longer be the conqueror. Jesus tells us in John 10:10 who is the author of death and who is the author of life. "The thief [Satan] does not come except to steal, and to kill, and to destroy. I have come that they may have life, and that they may have it more abundantly."

When Jesus died and was resurrected, death was swallowed up in victory. Jesus was given the keys to death and hell. The Bible tells us clearly, "It is appointed for men to die once" (Heb. 9:27). I believe every person has an appointment with death, and the time he is to die is written in the book of life. I always pray for people to make their appointment right on time, not a moment under or over what is written in their book of life. We can shorten our days by not being prudent in our care for our bodies. We also can shorten our days by living a life of sin because sin always leads to death. We must get our theology straight. Sin and death are inseparably linked, and sin never blesses God.

Then what does this passage mean when it says, "Precious in the sight of the LORD is the death of His saints"? The word *precious* in Hebrew means "costly." It is so costly for God to lose a living witness on earth through death. God does not need us in heaven. He needs us to be living witnesses on earth. When a saint dies, a light has gone out on earth. We are saints of light.

When my mother died, God rejoiced when He had the opportunity to greet her in heaven, but He also felt the same loss that everyone on earth who knew her felt. A shining light was snuffed out by the darkness of death. The good news is, however, that she is with Jesus in the spirit now. One day she will have a resurrected body to shine once again as a light on earth for Him. From the time of her birth, she was designed to be a living witness to shine with God's glory.

> *Lord, teach me to number my days that I might apply my heart unto wisdom. Help me to be wise in the way I take care of my body, which is the temple of the Holy Spirit. I want to live out my days according to what is written in my book of life, and I want always to be a shining light for You while I have breath on this earth.*

May 20

Seasoned Speech
Proverbs 15:22–23

I pray almost every morning, "Lord, put me in the right place at the right time." As I read this proverb, I now want to add to that prayer, "Lord, help me to speak the right thing at the right time." There is a time to speak and a time to keep silent.

Often the enemy gives us critical, judgmental thoughts about our mates and other people. Satan would love nothing better than for us to speak those thoughts out loud. Over my forty years of married life I have learned the voice of the enemy. When he gives me negative thoughts about my husband or about anyone, I always say, "Satan, if you think I'm going to give voice to your thoughts, you have got another think coming." I often share with people that if I had spoken all the thoughts the enemy planted in my mind to say to my mate, I would not be married today.

You have heard the expression, "You need to speak your mind." If we spoke our minds all the time, we would probably have a miserable life with no friends. Before I speak, I give what I want to say the "Think Test." The "Think Test" is found in Philippians 4:8, where Paul lists the things we are to think about:

Whatever things are true
Whatever things are honest
Whatever things are just
Whatever things are pure
Whatever things are lovely
Whatever things are of a good report
Whatever things are praiseworthy
Whatever things are virtuous

Before I speak I ask myself if what I am about to speak true, honest, just, pure, lovely, of a good report, praiseworthy and virtuous. If the words I am about to speak do not pass the "Think Test," then I do not say those words. You have heard the expression, "You need to count to ten before you speak." There are eight things listed in the "Think Test," and we can add two more—whatever things will edify and whatever things are gracious. Now we have our ten things to think about as we count to ten before we speak. You will find if you do this faithfully, you will be a person of few words, but the words you speak will have an impact on people that could change their lives. After all, we do have the words of life. Why should we waste our time speaking the words of death that Satan wants us to speak?

Lord, help my speech today to be seasoned with the things that are true, honest, just, pure, lovely, of good report, praiseworthy, virtuous, edifying and gracious.

142

Encouraging Ourselves in the Lord
1 Samuel 29:1–31:13

It looked as if David had lost everything, His city had been burned, His wives were missing, and all those who followed him turned against him and were ready to stone him. He was in great distress, but he made a choice. He made the choice to encourage himself in the Lord instead of giving up. I've often wondered how he encouraged himself in the Lord. When I meditated on this, I received a mental picture of exactly what David did that day when all seemed to be lost.

David was a psalmist, and he used his songs to encourage himself. I believe he always traveled with his small harp near his side, and on that day when all seemed lost, he took his harp from his belongings and began to play and sing. If you go to Israel, you will see the David harps being made today. This same harp was designed specifically for the musicians in the temple. David sang songs like: "Unto Thee, O Lord, do I lift up my soul" (Ps. 25), "The earth is the Lord's, and the fullness thereof; the world and they that dwell therein" (Ps. 24), "The Lord is my shepherd, I shall not want" (Ps. 23), "I will love thee, O Lord, my strength. The Lord is my rock, and my fortress, and my deliverer; my God, my strength, in whom I will trust; my buckler, and the horn of my salvation and my high tower. I will call upon the Lord, who is worthy to be praised: so shall I be saved from mine enemies" (Ps. 18) and many other of his psalms.

We can also learn to encourage ourselves in the Lord. Ephesians 5:18–21 tells us how we are to stay filled with the Spirit, and much of those instructions have to do with singing: "And do not be drunk with wine, in which is dissipation; but be filled with the Spirit; speaking to one another in psalms and hymns and spiritual songs, singing and making melody in your heart to the Lord, giving thanks always for all things to God the Father in the name of our Lord Jesus Christ, submitting to one another in the fear of God."

When we do the things listed above, we will keep our spiritual tanks full. The rest of this story is that all David thought he had lost was restored. Today if your circumstances seem overwhelming, overwhelm the discouragement by singing and making melody in your heart. Soon encouragement by the Holy Spirit will envelop you, and you will see how God is doing something even in the midst of difficult times.

Lord, help me to keep my spiritual tank full today. When I think I am about to run out of fuel, help me remember to encourage myself by singing songs, spiritual songs, hymns and psalms.

READ: 2 Samuel 1:1–2:11; John 12:20–50; Psalm 118:19–29; Proverbs 15:27–28

This Is the Day to Rejoice
Psalm 118:19–29

As I looked through my mother's things after her death, I found a beautiful writing she clipped from a church paper. I do not know who wrote it, but I made copies of it and passed it out at Mother's memorial service. The title of it is "The Gift of a Day." I have included it on the back page of this month's devotionals. It expresses what this psalm says: "This is the day the LORD has made; We will rejoice and be glad in it" (v. 24). The following poem is included in the reading:

> Build a little fence of trust, just around today;
> Fill the space with loving work, and therein stay.
> Look not through the sheltering bars upon tomorrow.
> God will help thee bear whatever comes of joy or sorrow.

As we arise in the morning we never know what will be facing us during the day. The good news is that God knows, and I believe if we will take time in His presence every morning He will prepare us to bear whatever we face, whether it be joy or sorrow. I especially remember the Lord preparing me in the morning for the day I hit a little eight-year-old boy with my car. It was an accident, and thanks to much prayer, the boy was spared. I even had the opportunity later to lead him to the Lord. On the morning of this accident, however, the Lord kept drawing me to spend more time with Him. As I was praying, there was a bird singing the most beautiful song just outside the window. It seemed as if the joy of the Lord came from that bird's song right into my soul and I was strengthened. I needed that extra measure of strength for what I faced that day. Each day is truly a gift from God, and whether it be joy or sorrow that we face, we can trust the Lord to see us through the day. One of my favorite phrases in the Bible is, "It came to pass." Whatever we are enduring on this earth, it too will pass.

The author of "The Gift of the Day" writes, "The gift of a day being what it is, surely we cannot maintain an indifferent attitude toward the Giver of it." What we receive each morning indeed is a sacred and solemn trust. How base were it then to abase it and abuse it, to spend any part of our day in ways from which He who gives it must avert His face! Let's ask Him to help us to use it as He wills.

It has been my custom to give the day to the Lord the first thing in the morning. I pray the following prayer; maybe you would like to join me this morning:

> *Father, I thank You for this day. It is truly a gift, so I give it into Your hands. Use me in any way You see fit today, and put me in the right place at the right time. I commit my words to You so that You may establish my thoughts. I commit myself and all I have planned for the day to You. Order it Your way.*

May 23

READ: 2 Samuel 2:12–3:39; John 13:1–30; Psalm 119:1–16; Proverbs 15:29–30

Happiness Comes From Serving Others
John 13:1–30

We talked yesterday about rejoicing and being glad every day of our lives. True joy is not conditional. We may be going through distress and trials, but in the midst of this we can rejoice and be glad. One might ask, "How can I be happy when so much is going wrong in my life?" The answer to this question is given in our New Testament reading in John.

Jesus taught His disciples a great lesson. Although He was master, He became a servant and washed His disciples' feet. After He finished He said, "The servant is not greater than his Lord, neither he that is sent greater than he that sent him." Earlier Jesus told them that He came to earth to serve. After He washed their feet Jesus said, "If you know these things, happy are you if you do them." He was saying the way to true happiness was the way of serving others. I just had a tour of a wonderful senior citizens' center, and the one leading the tour told us how she became a volunteer. She said she and her husband came to the center to sign up for computer classes, and they have worked there every day since as volunteers. She leads the tours and her husband helps in the kitchen. She was a very joyful person. I have yet to see a happy selfish person.

When we are going through a period of affliction, trials, or testings, this is the time we need to turn our focus off of ourselves and onto the Lord and serving others. We need to ask the Lord, "Is there something I can do to help someone now?" There is always someone in worse circumstances than we are, and just by praying for such people, we will begin to feel we have a purpose in the trial we are experiencing. The Bible tells us we are to comfort others with the same comfort we have received. Our preacher just preached a wonderful sermon on "Without suffering or pain, we would never know joy." If we have never experienced God's comfort and mercy, we could never expect to give it to someone else.

Today ask the Lord if there is someone you can comfort with God's comfort. As you focus on others and serve others, a lasting happiness will invade your life.

Lord, is there someone I can cheer and comfort today? Is there something I can do for another that will make their burden lighter? If nothing else, I can pray for that one in need, and then my own situation seems less overwhelming. Thank You, Lord, for showing me the way to true happiness.

Many Mansions
John 13:31–14:14

Jesus shared with His disciples that He was going away. They did not understand Him. He told them to not be troubled in their hearts because He was going to prepare a place for them.

When someone we love tells us they are leaving, there is always that fear that we may never see them again. Think of a little child crying when his mother drops him at the church nursery. There is the fear that once mother is out of sight, she may never come back. This fear of permanent separation overwhelmed the disciples, and Jesus knew their hearts were very troubled. The fear of abandonment, the fear of loss, the fear of the unknown, the fear of the future and all kinds of fear tormented them.

It is important to understand that God's goal is always to guard our hearts with His love, peace, joy, mercy and grace. The enemy's goal is to attack our hearts through fear or to break our hearts through rejection. Jesus said, "Let not your heart be troubled." Just prior to this admonition, the Lord had shared with Peter that he would deny Him three times before the cock crowed. Knowing their many fears, Jesus tried to comfort them with these words: "You believe in God, believe also in Me. In My Father's house are many mansions; if it were not so, I would have told you. I go to prepare a place for you. And if I go and prepare a place for you, I will come again and receive you to Myself; that where I am, there you may be also" (John 13:1–3).

It was the custom in the ancient Jewish culture for the bridegroom to build a home for his future bride. There was usually a year in which the couple was espoused to one another, and during that time the father of the groom kept a careful watch over his son's construction of a home. Only when the father felt the house met all of the specifications exactly did he then tell his son he could go and fetch his bride. Jesus said that only the Father in heaven knows the day or the hour when He will return to earth. The Father is watching carefully, and when all the living stones (those who have entered His kingdom) are gathered and placed in position, then He will tell Jesus to return for us (His bride).

Jesus was telling His disciples that the earth was not their home. We are all just passing through this earth; our final destination is our home in heaven. I heard the testimony of Betty Maltz, who had a vision of heaven, and she said that Jesus oversees all the building of the mansions. He is the master builder or the foreman of heaven. It was my privilege to lead a homosexual young man to the Lord just three months before he died. He was a talented decorator, and I often feel that he is helping decorate my mansion. No matter how my mansion looks, I know I will be eternally satisfied with my home in heaven because Jesus will be there. He is with me now in the spirit, but the day will come when I will see His resurrected body and look into His face. What a day that will be when my Jesus I will see! Even so, come quickly, Lord!

Seeking and Seeing His Face
John 14:15–31

Jesus just told the disciples He was going away, but He would not leave them comfortless. He promised them He would send them the Comforter, the Spirit of truth, but He made another promise that we often miss. Many of the promises in the Bible are conditional, and it is important we fulfill the conditions before we claim the promise. In this passage Jesus makes a conditional promise. He said "He who has My commandments and keeps them, it is he who loves Me. And he who loves Me will be loved by My Father, and I will love him and will manifest Myself to him" (v. 21).

What a promise this is. The word *manifest* means to show, reveal or make an appearance.

Many years ago I heard a lady share an interesting testimony. She and her husband had been standing on this promise for several years. Almost weekly they would remind God of His promise to manifest Himself to those who keep His commandments. This couple was careful to love God with all of their hearts and to share God's love with their neighbors, thus fulfilling the commandments. One night as they were in a deep sleep, they were awakened by a bright light in the room. Their eyes finally were able to focus, and they saw Jesus standing at the foot of their bed. He said nothing, but looked lovingly at them.

After hearing this testimony, I too began to stand on this promise. God has no pets, and if we fulfill the conditions of His promises, He will deliver what He has spoken in His Word. After six months of diligently seeking His face, I was awakened from a deep sleep after a Sunday nap. I saw a light in the distance, and as it drew closer to me, I saw the face of Jesus in that light. The love, joy and peace radiating from that face were beyond human expression. My spirit jumped inside of me, and I wanted to run and embrace Jesus. "Lord," I said, "I want to share Your face with the world because I know if they see Your face, everyone will come to You instantly. Your love is so compelling." Then I heard Him speak these words to my spirit: "I have not chosen to reveal Myself in this way to the world. Instead I have chosen to show my face to others through your face and the faces of all who believe in Me."

Perhaps you may never see the face of Jesus on this side of heaven, but you have the awesome privilege of letting others see His face through your own. Second Corinthians 4:6–7 says, "For God, who commanded the light to shine out of darkness, has shined in our hearts, to give the light of the knowledge of the glory of God in the face of Jesus Christ. But we have this treasure in earthen vessels, that the excellency of the power may be of God, and not of us" (KJV).

Divine Love
John 15:1–27

Most of us are familiar with the love chapter in 1 Corinthians 13, but did you know there is another love chapter in the Bible that is just as important? John 15 is that chapter. Here Jesus tells us that He is the vine and we are the branches. The word *divine* has "vine" in it, and the "di" is short for deity. One could say divine love is God's dependent love. So many of us, including me, try to have the qualities of love listed in 1 Corinthians 13, but we fail miserably. Love is the fruit of the spirit, and the nine fruit of the spirit all radiate from divine love. It is impossible to love as Jesus loved when He walked on earth over two thousand years ago. We can, however, demonstrate His love to others if we are totally dependent upon His Spirit. Jesus tells us to do three things to radiate His love daily:

1. Abide in Him (without Him we can do nothing).
2. Abide in His Word (faith operates through love and is based on God's Word).
3. Keep His commandments (love God with all of our hearts and love others)

Every day I pray, "Lord, help me to love as You love." I have to realize, however, that I have a part to play in continuing in His love. When someone abides with another, he lives in the same dwelling place. Where is your abode? Where is your dwelling place? Our dwelling place must be in the presence of the Lord. I have to remain in His presence through a conscious act of submission and a total act of surrender throughout the day. How do I submit and surrender? My part is to hear, hide and heed the Word of God.

1. Hearing His Word means I must have fellowship with Him (abide in Him).
2. Hiding His Word means I must let the Word have affect on my soul to change me.
3. Heeding His Word means I must obey what I have heard and what I have hidden.

Jesus is with us wherever we go, and He wants to manifest His love through us to the world. The mark of a Christian is His love, which is both compelling and compassionate. There is a passion in God's love for us that can only be conveyed through Jesus Christ His Son. God so loved the world that He gave His Son. Greater love has no man than he lay his life down for another. Jesus laid His life down willingly for the whole world, but if you were the only person existing in the world, He would have done the same. In response to such a great sacrifice, I can only spend time in His presence hearing His Word, hiding His Word and heeding His Word.

Lord, help me to abide in Your presence all this day long. With Your help I will do my part to continue in Your love.

READ: 2 Samuel 12:1–31; John 16:1–33; Psalm 119:71–80; Proverbs 16:4–5

Be of Good Cheer
John 16:1–33

The words Jesus spoke to His disciples seemed hard words to them. He was telling them He was going to go away and that they would forsake Him for a season. These were troubling words, yet Jesus ended His conversation with them by saying, "These things I have spoken to you, that in Me you may have peace. In the world you will have tribulation; but be of good cheer, I have overcome the world" (v. 33).

We live in troubled times, and it seems the condition of the world is worsening daily. There are wars, rumors of wars, famines and earthquakes just as Jesus said there would be in the end times. I feel we are in what Jesus called "the beginning of sorrows." The early labor pains have begun before His Second Coming is birthed, and according to the Scriptures, the labor will be most intense just before Jesus comes again. In the midst of all the tribulation and suffering promised us in the last days, we can be of good cheer. Jesus reveals the secret to peace in the middle of the storm and joy in the midst of tumultuous times.

Later, just before Jesus departed this earth, He gave us a great inheritance—His peace. He said this peace was not like the world offers. The world offers a temporary peace. Peace treaties are signed and broken. There are all kinds of peace movements, and many of the New Age teachings are about finding peace. Jesus' peace is different from the peace the world gives; Jesus' peace is permanent and eternal. The peace Jesus offers is not a feeling of well-being. It is not even peace of mind. The peace Jesus offers is a peace that passes our understanding. It is a peace that guards not only our minds, but also our hearts. The peace Jesus offers is Himself. He is our peace. He is the Prince of Peace, and it is His indwelling presence that brings peace to us in the midst of a world at war.

Jesus is able to keep our minds in perfect peace only as we willingly stay our minds upon Him.

How do we stay our minds upon Jesus? The answer is simple: We pray about everything and worry about nothing because we cast our every care upon Jesus. When we pray, the world will have no power to depress or discourage us, or even to make us fearful.

Peace in troubled times was promised to us by Jesus, and the fruit of peace is joy. The greatest joy robber in our lives is anything that disturbs our peace. Our peace is disturbed only when we are walking in the flesh instead of the spirit. We become frustrated, agitated, irritated. The moment we find ourselves in what I call "a wad," we must pray. I have yet to see a joyful frustrated, agitated, irritated person. When our minds are stayed upon Jesus, we can be of good cheer because we know the rest of the story. He has overcome the devil that seeks to rob our peace through oppression, depression, confusion and deception. Jesus has overcome the world with all of its distractions. Because He has overcome we can be of good cheer.

149

Where Is God's Glory?
John 17:1–26

So many in these last days are seeking God's glory even as Moses sought to see His glory. We, however, are living in the days after the cross and God has chosen to reveal His glory to others through us. We are the body of Christ, and if we believe and heed His Word, He is glorified in us. To think that we as flesh beings can shine radiantly with God's glory even as Moses did after his encounter with God on the mountain is amazing. In this passage Jesus makes it clear that He will not glorify us in the future, but He has already glorified those who believe in Him. Yes, there will be a day when the fullness of His glory will be revealed to the whole earth, but until that time, we have been appointed to be His glory on earth. Listen to Jesus' words: "Neither pray I for these alone, but for them also which shall believe on me through their word; that they all may be one; as thou, Father, art in me, and I in thee, that they also may be one in us: that the world may believe that thou hast sent me. And the glory which thou gavest me I have given them; that they may be one, even as we are one: I in them, and thou in me, that they may be made perfect in one; and that the world may know that thou hast sent me, and hast loved them, as thou has loved me" (vv. 20–23, KJV).

Where is His glory? His glory abides in every one who believes. Paul knew this secret and wrote, "Christ in you, the hope of glory." He also wrote, "For God, who commanded the light to shine out of darkness, hath shined in our hearts, to give the light of the knowledge of the glory of God in the face of Jesus Christ. But we have this treasure in earthen vessels, that the excellency of the power may be of God, and not of us" (2 Cor. 4:6–7, KJV).

Today don't seek His glory; release His glory. You are the container of a treasure beyond description—the glory of God. I like to think of it this way. You are an earthen vessel that contains liquid gold that has the potential of covering every person you encounter to make them shiny and glorious to behold. Remember everything precious in the tabernacle was covered with gold. I guess this is why I love gold so much. As a container of this liquid gold (God's glory), you must empty yourself in order for the gold to have an affect upon others. The purpose of this gold (the glory of God) is to cover the earth. Today you can cover all those you meet and see with His glory. As soon as you empty yourself by sharing His glory with others, you will receive a fresh supply of liquid gold (His glory) to give away. We were created to be His praise and His glory. GLORY! GLORY!

READ: 2 Samuel 14:1–15:22; John 18:1–24; Psalm 119:96–112; Proverbs 16:8–9

How to Let My Light Shine
Psalm 119:96–112

What a privilege to be the container of God's glory. However, for His glory to shine out of our lives, we have to fulfill two conditions— to hear and heed God's word. In Psalm 119, the longest chapter in the Bible, David declares what the Word of God means to Him. He says, "You word is a lamp to my feet and a light to my path" (v. 105).

For God's glory light to keep shining through us, we must continue in God's Word and abide in His Word daily. As we hear and heed His Word, He lights our path.

I remember being on a camping trip, and the bathroom was a good distance from our cabin. The only way I could find my way was to carry a flashlight. As I shone the light on my path, I could avoid the roots and rocks that might trip me up. The Word of God is our flashlight, and only His Word can save us from the roots of bitterness and the rocks of deception along the path of life. If the flashlight I planned to use on the camping trip had no batteries, I would have been in a mess. Just as a flashlight without batteries is useless, the Word without the Holy Spirit energizing and enlightening it to us is not useful. The Holy Spirit is the One who relays God's Word to us in an understandable, practical way. It is true that the Word of God never returns void and it always accomplishes what it is sent to do, but our receptivity of the Word of God depends upon our heart condition. Do we have a willing heart to learn and to apply God's Word in our lives? David said, "I have inclined my heart to perform Your statutes forever, to the very end" (v. 112).

We must hear God's Word with not just our physical ears, but also with an obedient heart. When we do this, the batteries in our spiritual flashlights will always be charged and ready to shine a light on our path. There are things that can block God's glory light from shining from our lives. The main block is unbelief and unforgiveness. I remember Corrie ten Boom giving a demonstration with a flashlight. She picked up a flashlight, turned it on and nothing happened. In her heavy Dutch accent she exclaimed, "What on earth is wrong with this flashlight? I keep turning the switch and nothing happens." Then she looked inside the flashlight and pulled out two dirty rags. "No wonder this light would not shine!" she exclaimed. Then she shared all of our own righteousness is as dirty rags. We must have the righteousness of Jesus Christ, and we must walk in that righteousness. The only way to do this is to confess our sins to Him and receive His forgiveness and cleansing. Even clean rags, however, in a flashlight will block it from shining. Those dirty rags (the sin in our lives of unbelief and unforgiveness) may become clean, but they must be replaced by the Holy Spirit's love. To cause this flashlight to operate, we need to put the batteries of God's love inside the flashlight. The love of God and also the glory of God is shed abroad in our hearts by the Holy Spirit.

May 30

Illumination
Psalm 119: 113–131

The Word of God is a light to our path, as we learned yesterday. Through the Word of God we can receive instruction, correction, reproof and doctrine that will keep us moving forward in our spiritual walk and also prevent our stumbling along the way. The Word of God not only shines a light on our path as we walk through this life, but it also shines a light into our hearts.

The Word of God is a two-edged sword that is able to divide the joints and marrow and discern the very thoughts and intents of our hearts. Think of a physical open-heart surgery when a skillful surgeon must open the sternum and cut through bone and muscle to reach the heart. Once the heart is exposed to the light, the surgeon then continues to use his delicate surgical tool that is a double-edged knife to do the repair work needed on the heart. Replacement of damaged valves or arteries takes place, the heart is knitted or sewn together, and then the blood to the heart after surgery is able to flow freely, taking needed oxygen to the brain and other parts of the body.

The Word of God is like the surgeon's double-edged knife. It cuts through and divides and discerns what is flesh (joint and marrow) and what is spirit in our lives. Thoughts come from three different sources, and only the Word of God can discern where our thoughts originate. The three origins of thoughts are from our flesh (our own desires or lusts located in our soul—mind, will and emotions); from Satan, who cannot read our minds but who does have the power to give us thoughts; or God. Our intents usually originate in our spirit. The Holy Spirit gives gentle impressions to our spirit. It is very easy for us to ignore such impressions and promptings of the Holy Spirit if we are not staying in God's Word daily. If we are faithful to daily receive our spiritual feeding through the Word of God, chances are that Word hidden in our heart will be able to help us discern which voice is speaking to us—the voice of our own flesh, the voice of the enemy or the voice of God. Of course, these voices are not audible, but nevertheless they influence our souls (mind, will and emotions) throughout the day.

Once the Word of God finds entrance into our souls, our broken hearts can be healed and knitted together, and the life-giving flow of His blood that avails all for us can cause our souls to be whole again. David said, "The entrance of Your word gives light" (v. 130). When the light of God's Word penetrates our soul, exposure of flaws takes place and the surgery and healing can begin.

Lord, help me to allow Your Word to enter deeply into my heart today to do the surgery needed to make my soul whole and well. Thank You.

May 31

READ: 2 Samuel 17:1–29; John 19:23–42; Psalm 119:132–155; Proverbs 16:12–13

Holy Order
Psalm 119:132–155

Order is something we all want in our lives. I never knew how much I appreciated order until I visited India, a country where confusion reigns instead of order. I asked the Lord why there is such confusion in India, and He reminded me that He was not the author of confusion. Satan is the author of confusion. Confusion reigns in India because there is so much idol worship. There are over three million gods worshiped in India. The whole atmosphere is charged with demonic oppression, and this oppression affects people's mental faculties.

God is a God of holy order. If we desire to live orderly lives, one of the ways to do this is to allow God's Word to bring order into our days. David prayed, "Direct my steps by Your word" (v. 133). This is an excellent prayer we can pray daily. His Word is not only a lamp to our feet and a light to our path, but it is also a road map to life that brings order into each moment we live. David also prayed in this psalm, "Redeem me from the oppression of man, that I may keep Your precepts" (v. 134). Deliverance from oppression both from men and demons happens when we keep God's precepts. The Bible speaks of "line upon line, precept upon precept," and this is the way we build order into our lives.

We live in a world of constant change, motion and noise. You've heard the expression, "Stop the world, I want to get off." We sometimes have days like that where instead of building order through His Word, we subject ourselves to many distractions (TV, radio, all kinds of entertainment) that draw us away from the presence of God.

There is a confidence and strength that comes into our lives when we keep our days quiet. The Bible says, "In quietness and confidence will be your strength." Of course, noise management is near impossible when we are in our work place or having a meal at a restaurant. This is why I love to steal myself away early in the morning while it is still dark; here I find my quiet place in the presence of the Lord that sustains me all the day long when the rush and bustle of the world begins. In this quiet place, I commit my works to Him for Him to establish my thoughts. There is always much to do each day, but the order in which these things are done is up to God. He desires to order my days in such a way that I am able to keep the main thing the main thing. The main thing is abiding in His love and His Word all the day long and sharing His kingdom with others.

Lord, help me to quiet myself in the morning before everything gets crazy. I commit my works to You so that You can bring order into my day. Put me in the right place at the right time, and help me to submit to Your will, not my own today. There are divine appointments You have for me today. Help me not to miss any of these appointments or anything You may have planned for me today. Help me to be led by Your Spirit.

READ: 2 Samuel 18:1–19:10; John 20:1–31; Psalm 119:156–176; Proverbs 16:14–15

I Will Not Return to This Place
John 20:1–31

This passage in John was always a mystery to me. Why did Peter and John believe Jesus was raised from the dead when they saw the linen napkin? Part of the burial clothing of a person in that day was a linen napkin that was wrapped around the head of the deceased. This part of Jesus' burial clothing was lying neatly folded in a place by itself. Listen carefully as John describes that event: "Peter therefore went out and the other disciple, were going to the tomb. So they both ran together, and the other disciple outran Peter and came to the tomb first. And he, stooping down and looking in, saw the linen cloths lying there; yet he did not go in. Then Simon Peter came, following him, and went into the tomb; and he saw linen cloths lying there, And the handkerchief that had been around His head, not lying with the linen cloths, but folded together in a place by itself. Then the other disciple, who came to the tomb first, went in also; and he saw and believed" (vv. 3–8).

The moment John saw the napkin wrapped neatly in a place separate from the linen clothing, he knew instantly Jesus was risen from the dead. I have heard so many theories about this, and one I found was very amusing. A teacher said Jesus was a neat person, and He was careful to fold the napkin neatly; this is why John knew it was Jesus who was risen and not someone else who had taken His body away. That explanation never satisfied me.

Finally, I discovered the full meaning of this scripture when I went to a conference on Jewish roots. At this conference we learned a lot about Jewish customs, and one in particular related to this incident recorded in John. In Jesus' day people ate with their fingers at low tables, so the host always supplied his guests with large linen napkins. If the guest enjoyed his meal and the dinner conversation, he let it be known to his host without a word. He crumpled his napkin and left it in the place where he ate. However, if the guest did not enjoy the evening, he also let it be known to his host without a word. He neatly folded his napkin just as it was at the beginning of the meal and left it beside his place. With this action, he was telling his host that he would never return to his home again. The moment John saw the napkin neatly folded in another place, he knew Jesus was saying, "I will not return to this grave ever again." John immediately recognized the message encoded in the piece of rolled-up fabric.

How much richer the Scriptures become when we understand the Jewish customs of Jesus' day. Reading the Bible is like searching for hidden treasure, and I am so thankful I finally struck gold with this passage after being taught about Jewish customs. We all would benefit if we knew more about our Jewish roots. Dig a little deeper today as you study the Word.

What Do You Love the Most?
John 21:1–25

The water gently washed over the heart-shaped rocks that were formerly pillars to an ancient temple. We looked in the distance across the Sea of Galilee and relived the story written in John 21. We were standing in one of my favorite spots on the shore of the Galilee. The place is called Peter's Primacy, and it is the place where Jesus cooked a meal for His disciples after He was resurrected. It was at this place that Peter had the opportunity to confirm his love to the Master three times after denying Him three times. This was Jesus' last meal with His disciples before He ascended, and something essential for their future happened here during their dinner conversation. Jesus told them of their future occupation in the kingdom.

The disciples had gone fishing and had caught nothing. They heard a voice on shore calling, "Children, have you any meat?" Still not recognizing Jesus, they responded, "No." Then Jesus instructed, "Cast the net on the right side of the ship, and you shall find." Peter then realized it was the Lord, and he girded himself and swam to shore to meet Jesus. The other disciples did as Jesus told them, and they followed Peter to shore, dragging a great catch with them. When they arrived, Jesus already had bread waiting and a fire going to cook the fish. Then Jesus asked Peter a very important question. "Simon, son of Jonas, do you love Me more than these?" Peter responded, "Yes, Lord; You know I do." Jesus said, "Feed My lambs." Then Jesus asked him again, Simon, son of Jonas, do you love Me?" Peter responded, "Yes, Lord, You know I love You." Jesus instructed, "Feed My sheep." Then Jesus asked the third time, "Simon, son of Jonas, do you love Me?" Peter responded, "Lord, You know all things. You know I love you." Jesus again instructed, "Feed My sheep."

When Jesus first asked Peter if he loved Him more than these, I believe Jesus was not pointing at the disciples; instead, He was pointing to the great catch of fish they had just brought to shore. Peter's livelihood was fishing, and it was something he loved to do. Every day his goal as a fisherman was to have a great catch. What Jesus was asking Peter was, "Do you love Me more than what you love to do the most?" What Peter loved the most was fishing. What do you love the most? It may be your job, your family or even yourself. It is easy for us to say "I love you" to Jesus and to others, but love demands action. Jesus knew Peter loved Him, but He gave Peter a specific way he could demonstrate his love to Jesus. Jesus told him first to feed His lambs (the little children). Then Jesus told him twice to feed His sheep. Children are so important to Jesus. Remember Jesus called the disciples "children." He sees us as children and He loves us, but He also sees us as those who can feed His Word to those both younger and older than us in the spirit and most of all to the unbeliever. Do you love Jesus? Feed His lambs then.

The Keeper
Psalm 121:1–8

What a comfort to know I have a keeper. We all need a keeper—a protector, provider and problem solver. Those who are blessed with good parents had the experience of the safety of a peaceful, loving home. I can remember the secure feeling I had when my dad came home from work and everyone was settled in our home for the night. I knew if we had any problems, Dad could handle them. I can remember my mother tucking me in at night. She used two giant safety pins to pin my covers down so I would not kick them off in the night. I went to sleep knowing the safety of a warm bed that would stay warm all night. My parents were good keepers, and they saw to my every need. I also have been blessed with a wise husband who keeps our checkbook balanced and sees to the financial, physical and spiritual needs of our home. He has been a wonderful keeper of me for over forty years, and I really need a keeper.

There are those, however, who have not had the blessing of good keepers in their lives. Some may have experienced a childhood of abuse or neglect. Some may have married unwisely a person who does not honor and cherish them. The good news is there is a place of safety for those who have had a lack or provision and protection. There is a keeper who will keep them and who in reality has kept them all of their lives.

We all have a keeper who is able to not only protect, provide and preserve us in this life, but also in the life to come and for all eternity. His name is Jesus. He is the keeper of our souls. The Bible tells us He is the bishop of our souls. Jesus will anchor your soul (mind, will and emotions) securely in hope even in the stormiest times of your life. As bishop of our souls, He is not so far above us that He cannot identify with us. He was tempted in all points even as we are, and He was touched with the feelings of all of our weaknesses. The Bible tells us He knows our every weakness; therefore, He is able to succor us (rescue us) when we go through temptations, trials and testings (Heb. 2:18). He is always there to provide a way of escape when things get overwhelming. He is our door of hope. He is our door to safety. David writes, "My help comes from the LORD, who made heaven and earth. He will not allow your foot to be moved: he who keeps you will not slumber. Behold, He who keeps Israel shall neither slumber nor sleep. The LORD is your keeper: the LORD is your shade at your right hand" (vv. 2–5).

He goes on in this psalm to describe the preserving and protecting power of the Lord. He is able to protect us from the sun, preserve us from evil and preserve our going and coming. He preserves our soul not only now, but forever more. Sometimes when we go through rough times, we think no one cares, especially if we live alone. Jesus cares, and He will keep you.

Who Is Like the Lord?
2 Samuel 22:21–23:23

One of my joys in life is to rise before dawn and praise the Lord with all of His creatures at sunrise. There is a verse in Psalms that says, "You make the outgoings of the morning and evening to rejoice" (Ps. 65:8). Have you ever noticed how the birds sing the loudest at dawn and sunset? I try not to miss this morning and evening symphony of worship, and I love joining my voice to it. I also love to see the morning star in the sky, and I recall Jesus' description of Himself: "I, Jesus, have sent My angel to testify to you these things in the churches. I am the Root and the Offspring of David, and the Bright and Morning Star" (Rev. 22:16).

In our reading today in 2 Samuel the last words of David are recorded. People's last words are always very important, and David's last words describe the Lord in many ways. His last words share how much the Lord meant to him throughout his lifetime. He says the Lord is the lamp who lights his darkness. He says the Lord is his buckler, rock, tower of salvation and his strength and power. The Lord is his teacher and meek instructor. David says the Lord's gentleness has made him great. The Lord is his security who helped him not to slip and is his deliverer from all adversaries, both physical and spiritual. David gives this beautiful description of the Lord that complements the Lord's words about Himself in Revelation 22:16: "And he shall be like the light of the morning when the sun rises, a morning without clouds, like the tender grass springing out of the earth, by clear shining after rain" (v. 4).

What a description of our Lord! Have you awakened to a cloudless sky after a stormy night and seen the tender grass shining after the rain? David is expressing descriptively the Lord's illuminating power, the clarity and brightness of His countenance, and the refreshing satiating personality of the Lord. He is the dawning of every day, the refreshing rain for my tender soul and the clarity of heart and mind I need for this day.

Who is like the Lord? There is no one exactly like the Lord. It is astonishing, however, that He has chosen to conform us to His very image.

Lord, today I want to be more like You than I was yesterday. I want to shine a light and move the clouds away for those who are oppressed today. I want to provide the refreshing rain of Your Holy Spirit to the one who is in a dry place. Only You can satiate and satisfy the souls of men, but use me today as Your instrument to deliver Your liberating power and sustaining power to others. Amen.

READ: 2 Samuel 23:24–24:25; Acts 3:1–26; Psalm 123:1–4; Proverbs 16:21–23

No Silver and Gold to Offer
Acts 3:1–26

It was about three in the afternoon when Peter and John encountered a lame man begging at the Gate Beautiful as they entered the temple courtyard. Peter looked into the man's eyes and said, "Silver and gold I do not have but what I do have I give to you: In the name of Jesus Christ of Nazareth, rise up and walk" (v. 6).

Peter then took the right hand of the man and pulled him up. Instantly strength came into his ankles and feet, and he entered the temple with them walking, leaping and praising God.

Peter gave all he had to give, and it was more than enough. He had the name of Jesus and the ability through the Holy Spirit to deliver and heal people. We have the same to give to others.

The name of Jesus and the power of the Holy Spirit are much more precious than silver or gold. We cannot take silver or gold with us to heaven, but we can take two very precious treasures to heaven with us— people with whom we have shared Jesus on earth and the Word of God we have hidden in our hearts. Peter delivered to this lame man the words of life that are eternal. Every day we have that same opportunity through phone calls, personal conversations, letters, writings and now even e-mail and chat rooms. Proverbs 25:11 says, "A word fitly spoken is like apples of gold in settings of silver."

When I read this proverb I visualize a beautiful painting of golden apples framed in silver, and the title is WORDS OF LIFE. Peter said, "In the name of Jesus Christ of Nazareth, rise up and walk." There are many spiritual cripples on this earth who need the words of life you have within you to deliver. Be on the lookout today for such people, and let your words be led, anointed and empowered by the Holy Spirit.

> *Lord, thank You for the words of life that are hidden in my heart. I know I can take them to heaven with me, but I want somehow to dispense some of these words to others today. Help me to do this if someone calls me on the phone or perhaps You have someone I need to call. Help me to share Your words through my writings and letters. The world is full of words that bring death and discouragement to people. Help my conversations today be seasoned with grace and my words to be life giving and life changing. Amen.*

June 6

Show and Tell
Acts 4:1–37

Most of us remember the days in grammar school when we would have "Show and Tell." Our homework assignment was to bring to school something we wanted to show the class, and then we were to share with the class all we wanted to about whatever we brought to school. The items often included a baby sister or brother, a favorite pet, a special rock, etc. There is something about the combination of seeing and hearing that makes an indelible imprint upon the brain. In this passage in Acts we see how it was now show and tell time for the disciples.

The disciples had experienced many visible demonstrations of the power of God during their walk with Jesus on earth. They were full of stories to tell about the things they had seen and heard. They were just beginning their journey without the physical presence of Jesus, but the power of His Spirit was evident. While they walked with Jesus they were given the power to heal the sick and cast out demons, and now they had the awesome responsibility of carrying the gospel to every nation. Miracles and signs were already happening. The religious leaders of that day believed the fire of the followers of Jesus was put out when Jesus died on the cross, but to their amazement they now had to contend with the roaring blaze of the Holy Spirit. Yes, the Spirit of God had been given, and the fire of the Holy Spirit was spreading uncontrollably. The disciples were asked to keep silent about Jesus, and their response was, "We cannot but speak the things that we have seen and heard." They could not keep silent about the changes that had occurred in their own lives and the lives of others.

If we are true disciples of Jesus, we also should not be able to remain silent about the things we have seen and heard about Jesus. There is no such thing as a silent witness. A witness always reports everything he has seen and heard. One of the major assignments of the Holy Spirit is to give God's Word voice on this earth. The Holy Spirit, however, does not have vocal cords. We are the ones who must supply the voice for the Holy Spirit. He tells us what we are to say, but if we remain silent, the message will not be conveyed through us, and we are the ones who will miss the blessing. I'll never forget a young man in our church who worked his way through Georgia Tech and who had a definite call to China. He worked a night shift as a security guard and then went to school during the day. Every Sunday he was faithful not to miss church or Sunday school, but some Sundays he was so tired he could hardly hold up his head. One Sunday he felt the Holy Spirit's gentle nudge to get up to the pulpit and give a word for the congregation. He battled with submitting to this nudge and said, "Lord, I'm just too exhausted even to go up to the front." Then he heard the still quiet voice of the Holy Spirit say, "That's all right, son; I'll use another." He bolted to his feet and delivered the word God had for us that day, and it was anointed. He did not want to miss his blessing. The Holy Spirit wants to use your voice to bless another today. Don't miss your blessing.

159

The Lord Is Round About You
Psalm 125:1–5

As the mountains surround Jerusalem, so the LORD surrounds His people" (v. 2). This psalm has great meaning to me since I have had the opportunity to see the mountains surrounding Jerusalem. Jerusalem is a city set on a hill, but there are mountains round about it. The way Jerusalem is positioned gives it a natural security system.

We too have a natural security system. Even as the mountains surround Jerusalem, the Lord is round about us. If we could have our spiritual eyes opened to glimpse into the spirit realm, we would see a mighty host of angels around us. We would never be fearful. A verse I like to speak aloud whenever I am in a frightening situation is, "The angel of the LORD encamps all around those who fear Him, and delivers them" (Ps. 34:7). Sometimes I am led to speak this Word in the morning during my quiet time with the Lord. When I remember to do this, I can almost feel an invisible shield of protection surrounding me.

I was so glad I prayed that the morning my car hydroplaned in a rainstorm on our return from our middle son's wedding. The whole weekend of the wedding we contended with tornado warnings all around. We and our niece had accidents because of the stormy weather. Thank God no one was hurt severely in either accident. I prayed for the safety of all those who would be returning home from the wedding that evening and Sunday. I used this verse of Scripture as a covering for all those who would be traveling in the storm.

As we left early Sunday morning to return to Atlanta in time for church, suddenly I lost control of the car and it spun into the woods. The car did several turns, and then the back of the car hit three trees. All I had time to say was "Jesus." The car was totaled. The police later shared with us that if our car had hit forward, my husband and I would have been killed. Truly I felt the angels of the Lord spin our car around to hit the trees with the rear of our car instead of the front. A friend later shared with me that she always prays for a chain link of angels to be placed around the vehicles of her loved ones as they travel each day. I have also added this to my morning prayers. What a comfort it is to know the angels are round about me and all those I pray for daily. Join me this morning as I pray for this protection.

Lord, thank You for Your angels who are round about me and all those who fear You. Thank You for the chain link of angels You place around every vehicle my loved ones and I will travel in today.

READ: 1 Kings 3:3–4:34; Acts 6:1–15; Psalm 126:1–6; Proverbs 16:26–27

Reaping Joy
Psalm 126:1–6

One of the fruit of the Spirit is joy, and whenever we sow love into the lives of others, we can expect to reap joy. There is nothing in this life that brings more joy to me than to see my children blessed and serving the Lord with faithfulness. If this brings joy to my heart, can you imagine the joy God experiences when He sees His children walking in love with others?

This psalm is one of the SONGS OF DEGREES. The songs of degrees were sung by the men and their families as they went up to worship the Lord three times a year. As they climbed upward to Jerusalem, a city set on a hill, they sang these songs. They remembered the great things the Lord had done for them, and this made them rejoice and be glad. Even though there were tearful memories, they knew their tears would reap joy one day. "Those who sow in tears shall reap in joy. He who continually goes forth weeping, bearing seed for sowing, shall doubtless come again with rejoicing, bringing his sheaves with him" (vv. 5–6).

We all have precious seed to bear that brings forth sheaves even if we have no natural children.

Those who have children have the opportunity to sow the seed of God's Word into their children and then enjoy seeing the results of their planting as their children reach adulthood. Those who do not have natural children also can sow the precious seed of God's Word into the lives of others, and they can experience the joy of many spiritual children. Any parent will tell you that their years of parenting included many tears, but what they see now is worth all the tears. Whenever anyone cries over a lost soul in intercession, that person also is sowing tears that will reap much joy later.

We can daily add to God's joy simply by walking in His ways and keeping His command to love Him with all of our hearts and our neighbors as ourselves. The thought of being able to sow joy into the heart of God as we sow love into the hearts of men is something to meditate on daily. If our motivation every morning is to love with the love of Jesus, the Holy Spirit will give us the power and grace to do just that. We will then have the joy of seeing many in heaven upon whom our tears of intercession and our touch of love had an eternal effect. There is a great harvest of souls waiting. Are you willing to spend some time reaping this harvest through weeping intercession? The joy that awaits you when you sow with tears is beyond expression.

Lord, forgive me for not sowing more into the lives of others by declaring Your Word to them and praying for them. Give me the grace and power to love like Jesus today, and I know this will undoubtedly include shedding tears that will later reap great joy.

Building a House for God
Psalm 127:1–5

One of the seminars I teach is called "BUILDING A FAMILY FOR GOD." I wrote a short book about this, and many of the principles I share in this book and seminar are presented in this psalm.

The first step in building a family for God is surrender. We have to realize that our children are lent to us by the Lord, and we are only stewards of them during their lifetime. They are God's inheritance and His special treasures, so we have to handle them with care. We also have to understand that God loves our children even more than we do and that we can trust Him to take care of them even when we are not on the scene.

The reality of God's ownership of my children sank in when I thought I might die young and leave my small children without my guidance in their lives. This thought struck fear in my heart, and I was tormented with it for weeks. One morning after battling with this fear all night long, I finally asked the Lord about the thought. I asked the Lord, "Is this thought of dying young from You, from me or from the devil?" The answer I received in my spirit was not at all what I expected. The Lord spoke to my heart the following: "So what if you did die young? Don't you believe that I would be able to keep your children in the center of My will all of their days on earth and I could fulfill through them all I desire without your being present?"

My heart was overwhelmed as I meditated on the question the Lord was asking me. He was asking me if I trusted Him with my children. I had to repent of my controlling ways and ask God to forgive me for not trusting Him with my children. Whenever we are controlling, this is a sure sign that we are not trusting the Lord. Whenever we are in fear, we also know that we are not trusting Him. That morning I gave my three sons to God, and on that morning I died. No, I did not die physically, but I died to my possessiveness of my children. I died to the control and manipulation I often demonstrated in the rearing of my children. I died to all my plans for my children and desired only God's plans for them. I died to the pride within me that said, "I have to parent them all of their lives so they can turn out the right way." Kingdom work was done that day, and from that day forward I knew God would be a much better parent than I ever could and He would be faithful to see my children through every trial. Much of my attempts to build a house for God was just vanity until I surrendered totally to the Lord. All three boys are serving the Lord faithfully and teaching their children to do the same. My husband and I give all the glory to God. "Unless the Lord builds the house, they labor in vain who build it."

Lord, help me to always hold lightly all You have given me on this earth and to faithfully hold tightly to You. Amen.

June 10

READ: 1 Kings 7:1–51; Acts 7:30–50; Psalm 128:1–6; Proverbs 16:31–33

The Blessings of Those Who Fear the Lord
Psalm 128:1–6

Throughout the Word of God there are many blessings listed that come to those who fear the Lord. We fear the Lord when we stand in awe of Him and desire to obey Him because we know His great love. When we fear the Lord, we desire to be obedient and walk in His ways. Some of the blessings that will overtake us as we fear and obey Him are listed in this psalm.

1. Happiness
2. Well-being
3. Fruitfulness
5. Seeing the peace of Jerusalem

First He promises happiness. This happiness is not the "ha-ha" kind of happiness, but it is a deep inner contentment no matter what the outward circumstances we encounter. Another blessing is that things will go well with us. This does not mean we will experience no troubles in this life. We all have one promise in common, and that is we are all promised tribulation.

Jesus said, "In the world you will have tribulation; but be of good cheer, I have overcome the world" (John 16:33). We have the promise that things will always work for the good no matter what we experience in this life if we love the Lord and are fulfilling His calling. Another blessing that comes when we fear the Lord is fruitfulness. Does this mean that barren women do not fear the Lord? We forget that we can have spiritual children if we never have our own natural children. Our table can always be filled with tender olive plants that need to be discipled and spiritually parented.

The last promise in this passage to those who fear the Lord is that they will have a long life and also will see the peace of Jerusalem. When we fear the Lord, we can expect to live eternally and to live in New Jerusalem where there will be continual peace. How blessed are those who fear the Lord.

Lord, I pray as David prayed: Keep me in the fear of the Lord all this day long. Amen.

June 11

Count It Not Against Them
Acts 7:51–8:13

As Stephen was being stoned he prayed. "And he kneeled down, and cried with a loud voice, Lord, lay not this sin to their charge. And when he had said this, he fell asleep" (Acts 7:60, KJV).

I never understood the importance of Stephen's prayer that day until I attended a seminar on forgiveness. This seminar opened my eyes to the importance of remitting the sins of others. Jesus gave this power to His disciples and to all those who would believe after them. John 20:21–23 records this vital impartation of power: "Peace be unto you: as my Father has sent me, even so I send you. And when he had said this, he breathed on them, and saith unto them, Receive ye the Holy Ghost: Whose soever sins you remit, they are remitted unto them; and whose soever sins you retain, they are retained" (KJV).

In this passage in Acts Stephen remitted the sins of those who stoned him. He prayed, "Lord, lay not this sin to their charge." Saul was present at the stoning of Stephen. The Scriptures say, "And the witnesses laid down their clothes at the feet of a young man named Saul" (Acts 7:58). Later we are told by Scripture that "Saul was consenting unto his death." It was through this prayer of Stephen's that Saul was open to hear from God on the Damascus Road. Stephen's prayer paved the way for Saul's conversion. We can do the same through praying for others in this way. First John 5:16 tells us how to pray for those we see sin. "If anyone sees his brother sinning a sin which does not lead to death, he will ask, and He will give him life for those who commit sin not leading to death. There is a sin leading to death. I do not say that he should pray about that."

Instead of criticizing and judging a brother when we see him sin, we should pray for him. We should cry out as Stephen did to the Lord, "Count it not against him." What happens when we remit the sin of another? We first must confess if we have committed a similar sin. We first most remove the beam from our own eye before we can pray effectively for the one that we see sin. When we remit a person's sins, that person is then able to hear the convicting voice of the Holy Spirit, and that person can then come to repentance. We are also praying for the protection of that person until that day when he repents and is cleansed from that sin. What a privilege we have as priests to remit the sins of others so Satan will not take advantage of them in their sinful state.

June 12

God Keeps Short Accounts
Psalm 130:1–8

Have you ever been offended? Most of the offenses I experience are those that I take up for others. The Bible is clear, however, that love is not easily provoked or offended. I have come to ask God's forgiveness for not walking in His path of love, and then to ask Him for the power to get back on that path. When we are personally offended, it is always because our pride has been hurt. Knowing this has helped me to stay on the path of love. The moment I am offended, I confess pride because I know it was my pride in some way that was hurt.

It is so important to quickly confess our own sin of pride and then to release the offense to the Lord instead of holding on to it. Satan loves nothing better than to have us keep mulling over the offense. He will put all kinds of accusations in our mind against the brother or sister who offended us, and all of those accusations are usually not founded on the truth. We know who is the accuser of the brethren, and he also is the father of lies.

We can learn a lot from David's prayer in this psalm: "If You, LORD, should mark iniquities, O Lord, who could stand?" (v. 3).

This scripture shows us clearly what God's character is. He is merciful and He does keep short accounts. He does not mark our iniquities. In Him we always find forgiveness. We are exhorted in the Bible to forgive as Jesus forgave. He said on the cross, "Father, forgive them, for they know not what they do." God forgives us for Christ's sake. He not only forgives us, but He also reconciles us to Himself.

If we sincerely want to grow to be more like Jesus every day, then we too must keep short accounts. The moment a person offends us, we must quickly forgive and reach out to him and be reconciled to him. If a person is offended by us, and we quickly ask his forgiveness and then express our desire for reconciliation, we are walking in love. That person, however, may not respond to our forgiveness because he may choose to carry a grudge or an offense for a long time. If this is the case, we must continue to reach out to this person in love until that day reconciliation occurs. Also pray for that person to be healed of all of his hurts because a person who remains in hurt also remains in unforgiveness and holds on to an offense.

Lord, forgive me for the times I have been offended. I confess my sin of pride and ask You to help me walk in love. Thank You, for not marking my iniquities, and help me not to mark others' sins against me, but instead forgive them quickly and seek reconciliation with them. Amen.

READ: 1 Kings 11:1–12:19; Acts 9:1–25; Psalm 131:1–3; Proverbs 17:4–5

God's View of the Poor
Proverbs 17:4–5

This proverb shares how God looks at the poor. Anyone who mocks the poor reproaches God. "He who mocks the poor reproaches his Maker; he who is glad at calamity will not go unpunished" (v. 5).

God sees the poor as His treasures. Whenever we speak against anyone on this earth, we are speaking against God. You've heard the expression, "God does not make any junk." I cannot stand when I hear derogatory words spoken against people who are of lesser means than others. You've probably heard the expression "white trash." I hate that expression because people are not trash; they are God's priceless treasures.

In our travels throughout the world, some of the happiest and most blessed people I ever met would be considered by our standards to be dirt poor. I'll never forget giving a pair of shoes to an evangelist in India. It was the first pair of shoes he ever owned. He put his new shoes on and danced round and round in them. He was forty years old. When we were in Mexico I recall the beautiful humility and love of these Mexican people who often were without even water to drink. They were so grateful for everything we gave them, and they always asked if they could do something for us in return. We gave a blanket to one man, and he in turn gave it to his daughter.

It was the only blanket the entire family had ever owned. Some of the Mexican people in the remote villages never took a shower because of the lack of water, but daily they experienced the showers of God's blessings. His blessings did not come to them as material things, but as eternal things like joy, love, peace and fulfillment.

In contrast, some of the saddest people I ever met were men and women of great wealth. I recall visiting a home where our host took great pride in all of the priceless treasures he and his wife had purchased in their travels all over the world. I never heard him mention any of his family members or speak of the people he met on these travels. Things seemed to be much more important to him than people. There was such an emptiness in this house even though it was filled with priceless treasures. As I left this man's home I thought, *All the treasures he possessed will one day be ashes, but the poor people we met in India and Mexico will last forever.* Those who know the Lord will live forever. Even though their bodies will turn to dust or ashes, their soul and spirit will live eternally, and one day they will receive a resurrected body.

I trust you fill your life with God's priceless treasures daily. Handle them with care and love.

Lord, forgive me if I have ever looked down on the poor. You never look down on people, but instead You humble yourself to see the hearts of men whether rich or poor. Help me to see the hidden treasure in the hearts of all those I meet today. Amen.

READ: 1 Kings 12:20–13:34; Acts 9:26–43; Psalm 132:1–18; Proverbs 17:6

Grand Children Are Crowns
Proverbs 17:6

As I am reading this proverb, I am also watching my husband walk his first grandchild. He is smiling from ear to ear as he strolls this crown princess. Children's children are the crowns of old men. I know my husband would prefer his grandchildren over ten thousand crowns. Each of our grandchildren is a crown of glory to my husband. Also as a father to three fine sons, he is the glory of his three sons. Glory! Glory!

We waited a long time to be grandparents as our oldest son was thirty-five when he married. We now are the proud grandparents of beautiful grandchildren, and we have an understanding of the word *grandchildren*. They are all grand, and we trust they think that their grandparents are grand. My mind can't help but flash back to the time when Adam's son Seth had a child. I guess Adam and Eve were the first proud "grandparents."

One can't help but see the family resemblance and personality traits in these little grandchildren.

Think about the joy our heavenly Father has when He see His character traits in His grandchildren. Wait a minute—I thought God had no grandchildren. Because of Jesus Christ, we have all become God's *grand children*. We now all can have the same personality and character traits of Jesus, and this is what makes us grand children. God sees all of His children through rose-colored glasses tinted with the blood of Jesus. Because of Jesus, He does not see our imperfections and shortcomings. He sees the priceless treasure all those who believe in His Son have in their hearts. He sees Jesus in our hearts, and He rejoices because daily we are becoming more like His Son. I know my prayer as my sons had their own children was that if they had sons, they would be just like their fathers. I'm sure God prayed a similar prayer, "Let My children be the spitting image of My dear Son."

We are the glory and praise of our heavenly Father. He rejoices every time that He sees more of His Son's character and glory shining through our lives. As God's grand children, we are also a crown of glory to our heavenly Father. Even if you are still single and are past the childbearing age, you can have grand children. Every person with whom you share Christ has the potential of becoming one of your grand children who will grow daily more and more like Jesus.

Thank You, Father, for seeing Your children as grand children. You look beyond our faults to see our needs, and You rejoice over us with singing. Father, may I have many crowns (people I have witnessed to about You) to lay before Your throne. Amen.

June 15

READ: 1 Kings 14:1–15:24; Acts 10:1–23; Psalm 133:1–3; Proverbs 17:7–8

Prejudice
Acts 10:1–23

We sat in the amphitheater under a cloudless sky. We were seated in an amphitheater built by Herod in Caesarea centuries ago. My husband read the account from Acts 10 to the people on our tour of Israel. As he read this story, I realized the great victory Peter had over prejudice in his life. We all need such a victory.

We are not born with prejudice, but our culture, environment, experiences and even parents often teach us prejudice. I never taught prejudice in my home, but I find myself late in life not completely free of this wicked sin. Where did I learn prejudice? It was through the media and the conversations others had with me. My first experience with prejudice happened when I was a little girl riding a bus in Atlanta. I went to sit in the back, and my mother stopped me and said, "You can't sit there." Later I learned the back of the bus was reserved for blacks only. This made no sense to me then and makes even less sense to me now.

Peter had a real problem with prejudice. He was careful not to associate with Gentiles. After all, the Gentiles were considered by many as "dogs." Paul reprimanded him for not eating with Gentiles. Knowing Peter's prejudice, God chose Peter to be the first to go to the Gentiles. It took a vision from God and a visitation by the Holy Spirit for Peter to consent to go with the men Cornelius sent to him. Cornelius was a man who feared God, but he had never heard the entire gospel. He was a Roman centurion, a Gentile. God chose Peter to be the messenger of the gospel to the home of Cornelius. Peter was told by the Lord to go with the three men who were sent to him because God sent them. He told Peter to go with them doubting nothing. Peter obeyed even though I am sure he had quite a struggle.

Is there a prejudice in your life? It may not be a prejudice against a certain race or culture. You may often prejudge people before you even get to know them. This is prejudice. The only way to pull down the stronghold of prejudice is to renew your mind. The truth of God's Word will shatter strongholds of prejudice. Remember God is no respecter of persons.

Lord, forgive me for the times I have looked on the outer appearance and behavior of people I first meet and quickly have made a judgment of them. You have shown me often that my quick judgments of others are not based on Your view of them. I recognize whenever I look down on someone, I am guilty of pride. Forgive me, Lord.

June 16

When to Cover Up
Proverbs 17:9–11

It is the nature of man to cover for himself when he has done something wrong. When Adam and Eve sinned, the first thing they noticed was that they were naked, and they were ashamed. They were vulnerable. They dressed themselves in fig leaves to cover their nakedness. Before this time Adam and Eve wore glory clothes. God's glory light shone around them and protected them from being vulnerable. We are created in God's image to show forth His glory, but since the Fall, Satan has used shame as a false covering for those who sin. The good news is that Jesus bore our shame on the cross. He became vulnerable and naked for our sakes so that we might be covered with His blood and robe of righteousness and thereby be protected from shame.

God killed an animal to make clothes for Adam and Eve. The covering of fig leaves was not sufficient to cover their shame. Blood had to be shed to cover their shame, because without the shedding of blood there is no remission of sin. Before sin entered the earth, there was no need to cover anything. Everything on earth was covered and protected by the glory of God.

Sin always brings shame into our lives if our hearts have not been hardened to sin. The Bible tells us that if a man hides iniquity in his heart, he will not prosper. We are not the ones appointed to cover our own sins. Jesus wants us to be honest with Him and confess our sins to Him so He can forgive us our sins and cleanse and cover us with His blood. There is nothing that feels better than coming clean with God through the confession of our sins. After confessing our sins, the enemy no longer has a foothold to cause us to be ashamed or condemned.

This proverb tells us there is a proper time for us to cover sin, however. That time presents itself when we see another person sin: "He who covers a transgression seeks love, but he who repeats a matter separates friends" (v. 9).

Whenever we tell a person about the sins of another, we are passing on a bad report, which is gossip. We also cause the person we told to be prejudiced against the one who sinned. When we discern sin in another person's life, we are to pray and never repeat what we discern to another. Sometimes, however, the Lord may call upon us to confront that person with the sin, but this is always done in private one on one with that person. On rare occasions the sin may be presented to the church if the person is unrepentant, but in most cases God wants us to seek love, pray for that person and cover their transgression by not sharing it.

Lord, forgive me for the times I have told a person's sin to another. Help me never to do this again.

READ: 1 Kings 18:1–46; Acts 11:1–30; Psalm 135:1–21; Proverbs 17:12–13

The Devil Can't Swim
Psalm 135:1–21

When I read this passage about the vapors ascending from the ends of the earth, I recall one of the funniest yet most penetrating sermons I ever heard. The psalmist writes, "He causes the vapors to ascend from the ends of the earth; He makes lightnings for the rain; He brings the wind out of His treasures" (v. 7).

The sermon I heard included this verse about the vapors ascending from the ends of the earth. The sermon was entitled "The Devil Can't Swim." It was preached by a young evangelist who was on fire for the Lord. His major point was that the devil hates water (especially the water of the Word of God and the River of Life of the Holy Spirit). He used as his text the account of Jesus casting the demons out of the man called "Legion." The demons cried out to Jesus and asked Him not to send them to a far country. Jesus sent them into a herd (over 2,000) of swine, and the swine ran down a steep hill into the sea and drowned (Mark 5). He said that demons don't like water because they always go to the dry places when they are cast out.

He based this on Luke 11:24, which says, "When the unclean spirit goes out of a man, he goes through dry places, seeking rest; and finding none, he says, 'I will return to my house from which I came.'"

This evangelist then proceeded to tell us how we can drown demons just as Jesus did. He said that when we praise and worship the Lord with all of our hearts, vapors are sent from earth into the heavens, and glory clouds form. God dwells in the midst of our praise. When these glory clouds are filled with the vapors from our praise, they begin to release the showers of blessings from the Lord—the former and latter rain, the refreshing rain of the Holy Spirit. Remember the old hymn "Showers of Blessings." One verse says that "mercy drops flow from His throne," and this literally is what happens in the spirit realm when we praise the Lord. As the rain of the Holy Spirit falls, the demons have to flee because they hate that kind of water. If you want to drown the devil, keep praising God all the day long.

Lord, help me to drown all the demonic forces that may try to come against me today. I will praise You all the day long.

June 18

READ: 1 Kings 19:1–21; Acts 12:1–23; Psalm 136:1–26; Proverbs 17:14–15

Water Works
Proverbs 17:14–15

We talked yesterday about the holy rain that descends when we praise the Lord. Today's proverb talks about strife and compares it to the letting out of water. We have a dam close by us, and on certain days the dam is opened to let out the water into the river. Before this happens, an alarm sounds to warn all those on the river to go to shore to avoid the rushing current that is about to be released. If anyone ignores that warning alarm and does not reach shore, he runs the risk of having his boat capsized by the raging currents, and he could drown.

When we get into strife, it is like the letting out of water. First the current of anger is at a low level, but if we continue in strife, the anger level raises to such a raging current that we run the risk of capsizing ourselves and the ones we are coming against in strife. The advice in this proverb is to leave off contention. Do you know that the source of all contention is pride? We want to prove our point, so we argue until we supposedly win. There are, however, no winners when strife continues. Another source of strife is jealousy that left uncontrolled can lead to murder. The first murder was rooted in jealousy. Cain killed Abel because he felt God favored Abel over himself. He was jealous. James tells us that where there is envy, there is also strife that leads to confusion and every evil work (James 3:16).

If you don't want a flood of evil work in your life, then leave off contention. Avoid strife at any cost.

> *Lord, forgive me for when I have allowed strife to take control of my life. I have hurt others with my words, and I am so sorry. Help me with the power of Your Holy Spirit to avoid strife in the future. Thank You, Lord.*

Multiplication
Acts 12:24–13:15

This passage in Acts reveals some of the secrets of multiplying the church through the spread of the gospel. The first verse says, "But the word of God grew and multiplied."

One of the secrets to causing an increase in the spreading of God's Word and multiplying the members of the body of Christ was fasting and praying. We see this in Acts 13:2–3. "As they ministered to the Lord and fasted, the Holy Spirit said, 'Now separate to Me Barnabas and Saul for the work to which I have called them.' Then having fasted and prayed, and laid hands on them, they sent them away."

To be effective in spreading the gospel, we have to recognize that our first ministry is to the Lord, not our own ministry. We minister to the Lord through fasting and prayer, and it is at those times that we receive clear direction about what to do and when to go. This is exactly what happened in the early church. Several men gathered together and began to fast and pray, and they received clear direction from the Holy Spirit. The church today is just now coming into the understanding of how fasting affects the spread of the gospel and the coming of revival. The last revival in the United States occurred because men met together to pray and fast. We now are seeing a new interest in prayer and fasting, and many in the body of Christ are fasting and praying for revival in the United States. Jesus gave us a command to pray for laborers for the harvest. As we participate in praying for laborers for the harvest, we also become laborers because prayer is labor. No new births ever occur without the labor of prayer preceding them.

Another secret of spreading the gospel is separation. Once a person is discipled, it is time for him to separate himself from that disciple and disciple someone else. This is what happened to Barnabas and Saul. Both had a similar call, and until this time of prayer and fasting, they always worked with the other men as a group in the spread of the gospel. The Holy Spirit spoke to those praying and told them it was time to send Barnabas and Saul out on their own. They would be a gospel team no longer attached except through prayer to those other men. Barnabas and Saul could have refused to separate themselves from this fine group of prophets and teachers because they enjoyed such wonderful fellowship with them. Don't we sometimes see that attitude today in some churches? People get satisfied with their little fellowship, and no one is being sent out with the gospel. We can become so attached to the church that we forget the purpose of the church—to disciple many nations. Jesus told Peter to feed His lambs and His sheep if he truly loved Him. We have the same commission. We run the risk of becoming spiritual gluttons by not fulfilling the Great Commission.

What Concerns You?
Psalm 138:1–8

Everyone alive has concerns, and it amazes me that God knows about each concern we have. More than that, He is able to perfect those things that are a concern to us. David writes, "Though I walk in the midst of trouble, You will revive me: You will stretch out Your hand against the wrath of my enemies, and Your right hand will save me. The LORD will perfect that which concerns me: Your mercy, O Lord endures forever; do not forsake the works of Your hands" (vv. 7–8).

These words are so comforting I am tempted to write them in bold print and put them on my refrigerator. The moment we have a concern about anything, we need to give it to the Lord. Peter exhorts us to cast our cares upon Jesus because He cares for us. He is the author and finisher of our faith, so He knows exactly how to see us through hard times. The promise is God will revive us in the midst of trouble, and not only that, but He will also cause us to triumph over every spiritual adversary.

Is there a concern in your life today that seems overwhelming? Give it to the Lord and He will perfect it. If you try to handle it yourself without prayer, God will not be able to do all for you He desires to do. Give Him complete liberty to perfect your concern today, and cease from your own works. God is able and wants to help.

Lord, forgive me for the times I have worried and fretted over those things that are a concern to me. Your Word says to cast every care upon You because You care for me. You are more concerned about the situation I am in than I am. You have a plan, and I know You will hold my hand through these difficult times. You know the beginning from the end, so I know You are better at figuring things out than I am. I cry out for wisdom today, and I cast every care upon You. You are sufficient to meet all of my needs and to perfect all of my cares.

God's Concern for Us
Psalm 139:1–24

Yesterday we talked about how God can perfect everything that is a concern to us. Today we see how God is concerned for us and knows us intimately. In fact, God knows my needs before I even share with Him these needs in prayer. David writes, "For there is not a word on my tongue, but behold, O LORD, You know it altogether" (v. 4).

David says God understands our thoughts from afar off. He has been watching and caring for us even from the time we were in our mother's womb. This psalm shares how God thinks about us continually. His thoughts toward us are numbered more than the sands on the seashore. We can do nothing but stand in awe of our God's infinite interest in us. The question we need to ask ourselves is, Are we half as interested in God as He is in us? We have entered a covenant relationship with God through our belief in His Son Jesus Christ. Our goal daily should be to get to know the true God more intimately. Wouldn't it be wonderful if we could all say our first thought upon waking in the morning is of the Lord and then we continue thinking about Him all the day long? He is constantly thinking about us.

God wants our mind to be centered upon Him continually, not just because He loves this, but He knows great peace will come to us if we will do this. Every day we have to deal with distractions and do battle to bring our thoughts captive to the obedience of Jesus Christ. There is a way, however, we can anchor ourselves in the Lord, and no matter what hell breaks out during the day, we will have peace. The way to do this is to take time to listen to God every morning. Jesus knew how to keep His thoughts directed toward the Father: "The LORD God has given Me the tongue of the learned, that I should know how to speak a word in season to him who is weary. He awakens Me morning by morning, He awakens My ear to hear as the learned. The Lord GOD has opened My ear, and I was not rebellious, nor did I turn away" (Isa. 50:4–5).

The first thought Jesus had in the morning was the Father. He was awakened by the Father's voice, and then He listened carefully to what the Father had to tell Him. Because He did this faithfully, the following stability was given to His day:

1. Words were given that would encourage others during the day.
2. Personal direction was given.
3. The ability to obey was imparted.
4. Strength for the day was infused into His body, soul and spirit.
5. The ability to endure and have a determined will to do God's will was received.

Don't you need all five today? Then take time this morning to listen to the Lord.

June 22

READ: 2 Kings 3:1–4:17; Acts 14:8–28; Psalm 140:1–13; Proverbs 17:22

A Merry Heart
Proverbs 17:22

In recent years some medical doctors have used "laugh therapy" with their patients. I heard a story about a lady who was healed through laughter. Her doctor prescribed a steady diet of "The Three Stooges." She was instructed to watch the videos of their old films as much as possible. It worked. She actually laughed her way to health. This secret was known by Solomon, who writes, "A merry heart does good, like medicine, but a broken spirit dries the bones."

Medical research has discovered that healing enzymes are sent throughout the body when we laugh. Over the years I have learned that God has a sense of humor. He loves to rejoice.

You've heard the expression, "An apple a day will keep the doctor away." I believe "a laugh a day will keep the doctor away." A great healing comes to us when we are able to laugh at ourselves. When we take ourselves too seriously, we are just no fun to be around. My pappy was a great storyteller, and he had a dry wit. He had lots of friends who always wanted to take him on fishing trips because they enjoyed his stories, humor and company. I believe the disciples felt the same way about Jesus. One of my favorite pictures of Jesus is the one that portrays Him laughing.

In contrast, a broken spirit causes dry bones. This condition in modern terms would be called osteoporosis. The bones naturally become more brittle with old age, but we can hasten this condition if we have a broken spirit. A broken spirit is usually caused by rejection. In counseling many brokenhearted people, I have seen the toll rejection has had on their bodies. It is hard to have a merry heart if we live with an abusive husband or a rebellious child. Yet it is a merry heart that will get us through even oppressive situations.

What can a person who is trapped in an oppressive situation do to maintain a merry heart?

I gave the answer to this question to a friend who called me today. Her husband emotionally abuses her with his critical, judgmental spirit. In his eyes she can do nothing right. I told her to fill her house with praise when he is at work. Keep praise music on all day and sing songs to her children. All the day long she can sing hymns, psalms, spiritual songs and make melody in her heart to the Lord.

God has given us the garment of praise that lifts the spirit of heaviness. I know if this dear lady will fill her house with praise, she will charge the atmosphere with the presence of the Lord, and her husband will be affected. So many that are oppressed or depressed seek to self-medicate themselves with alcohol, over-the-counter drugs or other drugs. We have God's medicine bottle, and the directions read: Take seven praise pills a day and rejoice in the Lord.

REJOICE IN THE LORD ALWAYS, AND AGAIN I SAY, REJOICE!

Watching Our Tongues
Psalm 141:1-10

David knew how important the words we speak are. Throughout the Psalms, he prays for God to help him control his tongue. He prays in this psalm, "Set a guard, O LORD, over my mouth; keep watch over the door of my lips" (v. 3).

What a great prayer to pray daily. We learn in James that no man can control his own tongue, nor can he tame it. Only the Holy Spirit is able to train and tame our tongues. Proverbs tells us that death and life are in the power of the tongue. James speaks of the tongue as an unruly small member of the body that has great power. "Even so the tongue is a little member, and boasteth great things. Behold, how great a matter a little fire kindleth! And the tongue is a fire, a world of iniquity: so is the tongue among our members, that it defileth the whole body, and setteth on fire the course of nature; and it is set on fire of hell. For every kind of beasts, and of birds, and of serpents, and of things in the sea, is tamed, and hath been tamed of mankind: But the tongue can no man tame: it is an unruly evil, full of deadly poison. Therewith bless we God, even the Father; and therewith curse we men, which are made after the similitude of God. Out of the same mouth proceedeth blessing and cursing. My brethren, these things ought not so to be (James 3:5–10, KJV).

Since no man can tame the tongue, we must submit this unruly member of our bodies to the Holy Spirit daily. If we have the desire to order our conversations aright all the day long, we must pray as David did: "Lord, set a guard over my tongue." When people speak unkindly about others, I am so tempted to say to them, "Watch out; your heart is showing." We speak what is in our hearts, and sometimes it is horrifying to discover how wicked our hearts can be.

One of the keys to ordering our conversation aright daily is to listen more than we talk. This is why the Lord gave us two ears and only one mouth. First we need to listen intently to the Holy Spirit as He seeks to direct our conversations. Have you ever been about to say something, and suddenly you hear the still quiet voice of the Holy Spirit within you say, "Don't say that." If we have prayed for Him to watch our conversations then we need to be listening carefully for His instructions during the day. Second, we need to listen with understanding to the person who is speaking to us. Their words will reveal their heart, and the Holy Spirit can reveal what is in their heart to you. Often people are critical and negative in their conversations because they are hurting or fearful. Pray quietly as you listen to others, and the Holy Spirit will then give you a healing edifying word to speak to that person you are listening to. You have the words of life to share with someone today. Let the Holy Spirit order your conversations today.

The Complaint Department
Psalm 142:1–7

In the old days stores had complaint departments. These departments are now called Customer Service, but the name change has not changed the function of these departments. Customer service usually handles disgruntled people who have purchased something they are not satisfied with and have brought it back to the store for an exchange or for their money back. Those who stand behind the desks of customer service think they have a tough job, but their job does not compare to the job Moses had. He had over 600,000 complaining, murmuring Israelites at his throat day and night. At one point in the travels through the wilderness Moses asked the Lord to show him favor by just killing him. He had had it with their complaints, and he knew God was weary of it also.

God, however, does not mind when we pour out our complaints to Him directly. David knew this, and he wrote, "I cry out to the Lord with my voice; with my voice to the Lord I make my supplication. I pour out my complaint before Him; I declare before Him my trouble (vv. 1–2).

God is the Divine Complaint Department. He does mind it when we murmur and complain to others, however. He knows by our negative comments we stir up others to be unhappy with their situation. Have you ever been around a negative person and at the end of the day you are totally worn out? I had a Russian Jewish friend to whom I ministered on a regular basis, but when I did, I was exhausted at the end of the day. All she did was murmur and complain. Nothing I or anyone else did seemed to satisfy her. The last time I saw her alive was on her birthday. I wanted to be sure of her salvation so I asked her if she knew for sure she would go to heaven and did she love Jesus. She said yes to both questions, and then I said, "Well, Sophie, in heaven you will have no complaints."

God's wrath was kindled when the people of Israel murmured and complained to one another. His mercy, however, was extended to David when David poured out his complaint to the Lord. David said, "God will deal bountifully with me." He knew that whatever was wrong at that time in his life, only God had the ultimate power to change it, and He was full of grace and mercy. I believe the fact that David knew where to pour out his complaint was one of the reasons he was called a man after God's own heart.

Have you ever had people complain to you, and the whole time they are complaining you are thinking, *Well, what on earth do they think I can do about this?* God alone has the only power to work eternal change in our own lives and the situations we encounter. He does not give us our money back either, nor does He let us return our situations and circumstances to Him. Instead, He gives us the grace to get through our circumstances. He deals bountifully with us.

The Power of Praise
Acts 16:16–40

Picture Paul and Silas in stocks in prison. They should have been so discouraged and depressed, but this was not their state at all. They had been beaten, and I am sure the stocks were irritating their fresh wounds, yet they made a quality decision. They decided to praise the Lord anyhow. They began to sing praises to God. Suddenly there was a great earthquake, and the foundations of the whole prison were shaken, causing the doors of their cell to fling open. The guard of the prison awakened and was in great fear. This guard was about to kill himself because he knew he would be killed if Paul and Silas escaped. Paul cried out, "Do not harm yourself, for we are here." Then this prisoner fell at their feet and asked, "What must I do to be saved?" Paul answered, "Believe on the Lord Jesus Christ, and you and your house will be saved." The guard took them to his house, where Paul and Silas explained to the whole household about the Lord. The guard washed their wounds and then everyone in his household was baptized.

What a story, and it all began with the decision Paul and Silas made to praise the Lord in spite of their circumstances. I heard someone say that they believed the earthquake occurred because God was tapping His toes in rhythm with their praises.

Perhaps we are not in stocks as Paul and Silas were, but there are days that we feel we are bound by oppression and tied up with doubt and unbelief. Sometimes life can be overwhelming, but we can overwhelm whatever circumstance we are experiencing if we will make the decision to praise God anyhow. No matter what we are experiencing in this life, we can praise the Lord for His goodness, mercy, longsuffering, delivering power and on and on. As we get our focus off the circumstances and onto our mighty God, suddenly we too experience an earthquake. The chains that were binding us begin to fall off, the prison door swings open and we are free. We should not, however, take our freedom for granted. We are set free for a purpose, and that purpose is to set others free. Remember the guard took Paul and Silas to his home where his whole family heard the gospel and was saved.

Has God set you free from oppression and depression through praise? The garment of praise always lifts the spirit of heaviness. Then tell somebody. The same liberating power you experienced is available to all those who are oppressed. The joy of salvation awaits all those you will tell of God's liberating power. Tell someone today how Jesus set you free.

Lord, I have experienced the liberating power of praise many times in my life. Help me to be faithful to testify about these times to others. They too can be set free, but they need someone to tell them how. May I be that person who shares the power of praise with them.

Hold Your Peace
Proverbs 17:27–28

This proverb basically says, "If you have any sense at all, keep your mouth shut." Solomon puts it more eloquently when he writes, "He who has knowledge spares his words, and a man of understanding is of a calm spirit. Even a fool is counted wise when he holds his peace: when he shuts his lips, he is considered perceptive."

When we have an understanding heart, we have an excellent spirit, and we will listen more than we speak. We would save our souls from many troubles if we learned to be a people of few words. Whenever we speak anything aloud, demon spirits are listening, and they will use the very words we speak against us.

Satan cannot read our minds, but he hears our minds if we speak them out. I heard someone say that if we are always giving others a piece of our mind, we run the risk of becoming half-witted.

We are exhorted in this proverb to hold our peace. I have always prayed for my sons to have the same excellent spirit Daniel had. Daniel was a young man who was exalted to high positions because he knew what to say, when to say it, how to say it and also when to be quiet.

When we hold our peace, we make even our enemies to be at peace with us. Daniel had adversaries, but these adversaries eventually saw the evidence of the mighty God Daniel served when he was thrown into the fire and into the lions' den. Daniel never said a word against his nation, but instead he prayed diligently for his nation, and he even confessed the sins of his nation as if they were his own. A person has an excellent spirit when he uses his voice to pray for the leaders of his nation rather than murmur and complain and criticize those in authority. I flinch every time I hear a joke about our president, because I know how such talk is strictly against what we have been taught in the Word. The Word teaches us we are to speak evil of no man and to honor those in authority. We are exhorted in the Bible to use our tongues to edify, not to tear down. I know many times I have failed in this area. You may want to join me as I confess this to the Lord.

> *Lord, forgive me for the times I have used my tongue to tear down rather than to edify. Forgive me for the times I have criticized my leaders instead of praying for them. Help me to be a person of understanding who has an excellent spirit. Help me to listen more than I speak, and may the words I speak always be pleasing in Your sight.*

179

Many in the City
Acts 18:1–21

The red and yellow poppies shook gently in the breeze under a postcard blue sky as we looked upon the ruins of Corinth. Once a great city where Paul spent over a year and a half, it now was covered with a field of poppies. We were spending some time in Greece just after our tour to Israel. As I looked at what was left of Corinth, I understood why Paul spent so much time there. It must have been a beautiful city. We actually saw the judgment seat area where Gallio drove the Jews from his presence.

Even though Paul met with much opposition from some of the religious Jews in the city, God had His people on the scene. The Lord told Paul that He had many who believed in Him in that city. I am sure this encouraged Paul.

Do you know the condition of your city? Are there many believers in your city? My heart was strengthened when I saw the leaders of my city testify to their belief in Jesus at a memorial service for a policeman killed in the line of duty. I heard the mayor of the city and the sheriff of the county tell of their love for Jesus. I wanted to shout. In our city people are meeting to pray for our city on a regular basis, and we are beginning to see the fruits of these prayers. There were probably people meeting in the city of Corinth to pray, and Paul had not even met them yet.

This morning as you pray, remember to pray for the leaders of your city and for its citizens. Pray for revival in your city. God hears these prayers, and He will increase the number of believers in your city if you will faithfully pray for it. Join me this morning as I pray:

> Lord, forgive me for when I have failed to pray for my city. You want this city to be a city set on a hill, a city filled with believers. I pray for every laborer in my city who is ministering in some way to the needy, down-trodden, and even to those in high positions politically and economically. May the believers increase in this city and send revival to those who already believe.

Fervent in Spirit
Acts 18:22-19:12

When my children were little I would find Bible heroes, and then I would pray for my sons to be just like them. One of these Bible heroes was Daniel, who had an excellent spirit. Today we see another Bible hero whom we would like our children to emulate. His name was Apollos.

Luke describes him in this eighteenth chapter of Acts: "Now a certain Jew named Apollos, born at Alexandria, an eloquent man and mighty in the Scriptures, came to Ephesus. This man had been instructed in the way of the Lord; and being fervent in spirit, he spoke and taught accurately the things of the Lord, though he knew only the baptism of John" (vv. 24–25).

This Jew named Apollos must have truly made an impression on all he met. He was fervent in spirit even though he had not yet received the baptism in the Holy Spirit as the disciples did in the upper room during Pentecost. Even without this additional empowerment of the Holy Spirit, Apollos had great fervor. Aquilla and Priscilla took him aside and explained to him about the baptism in the Holy Spirit. Apollos was described as follows:

1. An eloquent man
2. A mighty man in the Scriptures
3. A man instructed in the ways of the Lord
4. A man with a fervent spirit
5. A man who accurately taught the Word of God
6. A bold man

We could pray a prayer for all of our children and ourselves to be just like Apollos. The prayer would be like the one below:

Lord, mold me into a person of excellence who is eloquent in speech. Cause me to be mighty in the Scriptures and instruct me daily in Your ways. Keep me fervent in spirit. Use me in teaching Your Word to others, and give me the boldness I need to be an effective witness today.

Are You Confused?
Acts 19:13–14

God is not the author of confusion. Satan is. We learn this in this chapter in Acts. Wherever idols are worshiped or participation in the occult is present, there is confusion because the author of confusion is on the scene.

Several Jews in Ephesus who were not sincere believers in Jesus Christ took it upon themselves to try to deliver a man vexed with an evil spirit. The demon in the man recognized that these seven men did not have the authority of Jesus Christ or the power of the Holy Spirit. The evil spirit spoke through the man saying, "Jesus I know, and Paul I know, but who are you?" The man under the influence of this demon then became violent and attacked the seven men, who fled naked from the scene. The news of this encounter spread throughout the city of Ephesus, and many became believers because of the very testimony of an evil spirit. That evil spirit acknowledged that he knew Jesus. This is a great example of how often the weapons the enemy sends against us do not prosper and are turned back upon him. Many were led to confess their involvement with Satan through certain practices, and they came forward and burned their curious books and other occult items.

The whole city became stirred, and many were confused. The confusion came because so many in the city were in idolatry. They worshiped the goddess Diana, and this opened the door for many evil spirits to influence and confuse the people. My youngest son was in confusion for a period of time in his life, and it was because he had opened the door to Satan through listening to rock music, which led to doing drugs. Later, however, my son recognized his sin and confessed and renounced these practices, and the door to Satan was shut. The confusion left him, and he was delivered from drugs. He now is a missionary to Hungary.

Are you confused today? Ask the Lord if you have opened the door to the author of confusion through dabbling in the occult. Maybe you used to read the horoscope daily or played with a Ouija board. Perhaps you went to a fortuneteller just in fun. These practices need to be confessed as sin and renounced, and when you do this, you will no longer have a door open to confusion. You can look forward to clarity of mind and peace of mind and heart.

Lord, show me if I have opened the door to Satan through things I did in the past. I want to confess and renounce these things and close the door to Satan and his demonic spirits of confusion.

June 30

READ: 2 Kings 17:1–18:12; Acts 20:1–38; Psalm 148:1–14; Proverbs 18:6–7

Not Counting Our Life Dear
Acts 20:1–38

Fear is one of the greatest enemies of every Christian. Satan seeks to paralyze us with fear. Fear is Satan's anesthesia that causes us to be frozen on his operating table where he can perform wicked surgery on our souls. One of the secrets of the early church's success in the spread of the gospel is that those early believers loved not their lives to the death. When we read Revelation 12:11, we often skip over the last part. This verse reads, "And they overcame him [Satan] by the blood of the Lamb, and by the word of their testimony, and they did not love their lives to the death."

When we overcome the fear of losing our lives for the sake of the gospel, we become as bold as Paul was. Many had warned Paul that he would face much persecution and even death, but his response was as follows: "But none of these things move me, nor do I count my life dear to myself, so that I may finish my race with joy, and the ministry which I received from the Lord Jesus, to testify to the gospel of the grace of God" (Acts 20:24).

Recently I read a poem written by E. H. Hamilton. This poem was found among the belongings of Betty Stem, who was martyred along with her husband in China many years ago. This poem expressed Betty's total lack of fear. She did not count her life dear to herself. Here are a few of the thoughts expressed in this poem:

> Afraid? Afraid of what?
> To feel the spirit's glad release?
> To pass from pain to perfect peace?
> The strife and strain of life to cease?
> Afraid? Afraid of that?
> Afraid? Afraid of what?
> Afraid to see the Savior's face?
> To hear His welcome into grace?
> The glory gleam from wounds of grace?
> Afraid? Afraid of that?

This favorite poem of Betty's expressed so eloquently her lack of the fear of death. She loved not her life to the death. Would you have such courage?

Lord, forgive me for ever being fearful of persecution or death for the sake of the gospel. May I overcome the devil because I love not my life to the death.

READ: 2 Kings 18:13–19:37; Acts 21:1–17; Psalm 149:1–9; Proverbs 18:8

Warfare Through the Dance
Psalm 149:1–9

Most of us are familiar with the Indian war dances, which always occurred before they entered warfare with their enemies. Dancing and rejoicing before the Lord is also an effective weapon before we go to war against Satan. We have the scriptural example of this when Jehoshaphat sent the singers ahead of his army and ambushments against their enemies were established. "And when he had consulted with the people, he appointed singers unto the Lord, and that should praise the beauty of holiness, as they went out before the army, and to say, Praise the Lord; for his mercy endureth for ever" (2 Chron. 20:21, KJV).

We learned the importance of rejoicing before the Lord with singing and dancing through attending a fellowship in Jerusalem. The Zion Fellowship is a unique fellowship that spends a lot of time in praising the Lord with the dance. Ruth Heflin, who heads this fellowship, has written a book called *Glory* in which she expresses the importance of the dance in spiritual warfare. She relates in her book *Glory* the following: "I believe that dancing brings an anointing for the nations. I never let a day go by without dancing. I have danced in the toilets of 707s, 747s and DC-10s. How do I do it? Straight up and down."

Ruth urges her readers not to let a day go by that they don't dance before the Lord. I am just now catching on to the power and anointing in rejoicing before the Lord in the dance. David made this discovery years ago when he wrote, "Let them praise His name in the dance; let them sing praises to Him with the timbrel and harp" (v. 3).

If you have not tried rejoicing before the Lord in the dance, you can start today. Put on some praise music and dance before the Lord. The Lord loves to see you dance before Him, because after all, He rejoices over you with singing. David was a man after God's own heart because he often danced before the Lord with all of his heart. We are exhorted to praise the Lord with our whole being. Dancing is a good way to do this. Have a good day and a good dance.

Lord, I want to be free in my worship and praise to You. Help me to get rid of all self-consciousness and just have my eyes on You as I praise and worship You. Set my feet to dancing, Lord.

July 2

READ: 2 Kings 20:1–22:2; Acts 21:18–36; Psalm 150:1–6; Proverbs 18:9–10

Turning the Clock Back
2 Kings 20:1–22:2

How many times have you thought, *I wish I could turn the clock back to the good old days of my youth when there were solid values and virtues?* I know I have thought many times of my high school years when drugs were only done by what we considered the "weirdos" and sex outside of marriage was taboo. What happened to those days of innocence?

There are many reasons we might want to turn the clock back. Maybe we want to relive the good times or redo some mistakes we have made. In the passage today we see how God was able to turn the clock forward and also backward. There is something we forget about God, and that is there is no time or space with Him. He is infinite, eternal and omnipresent. As human beings we often become servants of time, but God never intended man to live this way. He created us to be eternal beings, but after the Fall we became time conscious and time bound.

Hezekiah asked God for more time, and God granted his petition. Isaiah had just given Hezekiah the news that he would soon die. In response to this prophetic word, Hezekiah began to weep and pray to the Lord. He beseeched the Lord to remember how he walked before Him in truth and with a perfect heart and had done that which was good. Isaiah was on his way out of Hezekiah's presence when the Lord instructed him to go back and tell Hezekiah that He had heard his prayer. He told Isaiah to tell Hezekiah that He had seen his tears and that He would heal him and grant him fifteen more years of life.

Hezekiah wanted a sign to confirm this word, so he asked the Lord to turn the sundial backward ten degrees as the shadow passed before it. God also granted this request, and this affected time forever. The whole earth lost ten degrees of time. This story tells us the power of effective intercession because God heard Hezekiah's prayer and changed His original plan for Hezekiah. He even changed time for Hezekiah. Fasting and prayer can change nations and can withhold God's judgment against those nations.

During this fifteen-year period Manasseh, Hezekiah's son, was conceived. He turned out to be one of Israel's most evil kings. Sometimes God grants our request to add years to our lives, but in reality we might be better off being content with the years He has given us. We can shorten our days by not being wise in the way we treat our bodies. A good prayer to pray is:

> Lord, I leave my days in Your hands. I want to make my appointment with death not a day late or a day early according to what is written in my book of life in heaven. Teach me to number my days that I might apply my heart to wisdom and learn the best ways to treat my body while I still have breath on this earth.

185

Dealing Faithfully
2 Kings 22:3–23:30

Josiah was king and began his reign at the young age of eight years old. The Scriptures tell us he did that which was right in the sight of the Lord and walked in all the ways of David his forefather. He turned not aside to the right hand or to the left. Wouldn't we all love to have such words said about us when our life reaches its end here on earth?

Psalm 23 tells us that God leads us in paths of righteousness for His name's sake. I used to pray for my three boys to not veer off that righteous path. Two sons, however, did veer off the path for a short season, but they returned, and now they are serving the Lord with all their hearts. The great thing about our Lord is that He is not only the one who leads us in paths of righteousness, but He can also restore us when we veer off that path. His desire, of course, is that we always walk close to Him because our very lives represent His name on earth. He wants us to stay on the righteous path, because when we do, we bring glory to His name. We cannot destroy the reputation of God, but often when we veer off the path of righteousness, others see this and say God was not able to keep us. Others may think less of God than they did before if our lives do not speak of God's faithfulness to keep us. In fact, Moses appealed to God to not destroy the children of Israel because others were looking and would conclude that God was not strong enough to keep His people.

God is looking for faithful people who will keep on track by staying on that path of righteousness. In today's reading we see such faithful men. Josiah set about to restore the temple and hired carpenters, builders and masons to buy timber and other supplies to repair the house. None of these workmen were required to give an accounting of the monies they spent because they dealt faithfully.

No king was ever like Josiah, who turned to the Lord with all his heart, soul, and might. As soon as Josiah discovered the law, he had it read to all the people, and then went about obeying the law by destroying all idolatry and occult worship in the land.

God is looking for Josiahs in this day. Will you be one?

Lord, I desire to be found faithful when You return. Help me not to turn to the right or to the left. May I serve you with all my heart, soul and might all my days.

Making Snap Judgments
Proverbs 18:13

Today's proverb warns against making a decision before you have all the facts. So often we hear what we want to hear and then make decisions accordingly. We need to hear all the facts before we move ahead. Remember the phrase, "Just give me the facts, man."

Besides hearing all the facts before we make a decision, there is something else we must always do. We need to inquire of the Lord. Our Bible heroes made so many mistakes when they failed to inquire of the Lord before making decisions. We always get into trouble when we make snap judgments and move in haste.

One of our Bible heroes made such a mistake. His name was Joshua. Joshua was given instruction by the Lord to destroy his enemies completely and this included all the neighboring countries. He was not to make any alliances or leagues with them. Gibeon was a neighbor of Israel who heard of the might of Israel and was afraid. The Gibeonites got together and designed a conspiracy in which they would try to get Joshua to make a league with them. They were very clever in this attempt, and it worked. They sent several men in tattered clothing and worn shoes. These men also carried moldy bread to give the appearance they had traveled a long way. When they presented themselves before Joshua, they were so convincing that Joshua made a league with them. He forgot one very important thing. He forgot to inquire of the Lord. The league was made and could not be broken even after Joshua discovered the Gibeonites' deception. The Gibeonites became servants to Israel and could not be destroyed. Later they gave Israel a lot of trouble. All of this could have been prevented if Joshua had inquired of the Lord before making such an alliance. (See Joshua 9:3–26.)

Before making any big decision it might be prudent to do the following:

1. Hear all the facts
2. Hear what God thinks about it through researching the Word on the matter.
3. Hear what others we trust think about the matter. There is safety in many counselors.

Today we celebrate the signing of the Declaration of Independence. I am sure our forefathers diligently inquired of the Lord before writing such an extraordinary document.

Lord, forgive me for moving in haste so many times without waiting to inquire of You. I need Your guidance and wisdom. Help me never to move ahead again on a decision of importance without inquiring of You and seeking counsel from Your Word and others.

The Glory and The Lifter of My Head
Psalm 3:1–8

"**B**ut thou, O LORD, art a shield for me; my glory, and the lifter up of my head" (v. 3, KJV). We sing a chorus taken from this psalm often in our church, and every time I sing it I feel strength rise up within me. The proverb reading today asks who can bear a broken spirit. There are so many today with broken spirits who need the Lord to be the glory and the lifter of their heads. The Lord came to heal the brokenhearted, and only He has the power to do this. When we feel lower than a snake's belly, the Lord comes and lifts our heads up.

There is a lady in our church who never smiles. She never raises her hands in praise to the Lord, and often she just sits and stares into space. She has a broken spirit, and she needs Jesus who can be the glory and the lifter of her head. In ministering to this lady I discovered she also has much unforgiveness in her heart. Until her unforgiveness is dealt with, the chances of her having an emotional breakthrough to enable her to receive the healing of her heart are slim.

The Lord longs to lift up our heads, and He loves being a shield about us, but we can block his help by hanging on to bitterness and resentment because of unforgiveness. The Lord desires to sustain us, but if we continue in unforgiveness we cannot receive His sustaining power—the very power that can heal our hearts.

Lord, don't allow me to ever remain in unforgiveness. Show me quickly if there is someone I need to forgive, and then give me the grace to do it. Thank You for being the glory and the lifter of my head.

A Good Conscience
Acts 24:1–27

God created man to be directed by the Spirit. When He breathed into Adam, he became a living soul. The image of God was indelibly imprinted in Adam's being. The breath of God was the very Spirit of God infusing into the flesh body of Adam. That spirit sometimes is referred to as the core of our being. The soul part of man is his mind, will and emotions.

Conscience was not formed until Adam and Eve partook of the tree of the knowledge of good and evil. Until the Fall, man had total oneness with God and unbroken fellowship with Him. There was no need of conscience before the Fall because man was totally led by the Spirit of God within him. When Adam and Eve sinned, they died spiritually and could no longer be led by the Spirit of God. They then had to be led by their consciences.

Every person born since the Fall is born with a conscience (something inside of them that tells them what is good and what is evil). As I observe one of my grandchildren, who is just a toddler, I am intrigued with the fact she seems to instinctively know when she has done something wrong. Conscience is a good thing because the whole world would be without restraint if people did not have a conscience.

God's desire is that we all have good, clear consciences free from guilt and shame. He provided that possibility for us all when Jesus bore our shame and guilt on the cross. People lose sleep at night because they have a guilty conscience. They know they have done something wrong, but they are not willing to reveal it and confess it to others and to God.

Paul makes a statement in today's reading that should be the goal of every Christian. He says, "This being so, I myself always strive to have a conscience without offense toward God and men" (v. 16).

The only way to reach this goal is to confess our sins one to another and to God. If we offend anyone in word or deed, we must ask their forgiveness. Being honest about our sin with God and man is the only way to have a clear conscience void of offense. Those who have been born again by the Spirit of God can now be led by the Spirit of God once again, and they can enjoy eternal fellowship with God through His Son Jesus Christ. The Holy Spirit can show us if we need to confess anything that is blocking our fellowship with God and causing us to feel guilty.

Lord, is there a sin I need to confess? I want my conscience to always remain clear without guilt or shame. Thank You, Lord, for making that possible for me by Your death on the cross. Help me to live a life void of offense to God or to man.

The Morning Hour
Psalm 5:1–12

Some people are morning people, and others are not. We have a Russian son whom I know not to talk to until he has had his first cup of coffee. People who are not morning people are usually a little resistant when they hear testimonies of people who spend their first waking hour with the Lord. To such people I share that they also can spend their first hour of the morning with the Lord because morning begins at midnight. Both the midnight hour and the later morning hours are precious to God.

David tells us in the psalm, "My voice shall You hear in the morning, O LORD; in the morning I will direct it to You, and will I look up" (v. 3).

If you are a night owl instead of a morning dove, you can be one of the first voices God hears in the morning if you begin your prayer time at one minute past twelve. Some people are just more keen and productive at night than in the early morning hours. Whether it be at midnight or six in the morning, God is intently listening for the sound of your voice. He can't wait to hear your praises, worship and prayer requests. If you miss talking with God for a whole day, He misses your voice.

We forget sometimes that prayer is simply conversing with God. There are some people I just love to talk to. I've thought about why I enjoy my conversations with these people so much. Here are a few reasons I discovered.

1. They listen carefully to what I am saying.
2. They make comments about what I am saying.
3. They have interesting things to share with me.
4. The level of our conversation is always edifying.

After coming up with this list, I realized God's conversations with me are even more edifying and rewarding than the people with whom I love to converse. So why do I put off my conversations with God? You might ask yourself the same question.

Lord, sometimes I feel I have to do battle daily to find that quiet time when I can converse with You. Forgive me for my busyness. Help me faithfully to direct my prayer to You in the morning while the house is quiet and I can hear Your voice more clearly. Help me not to miss out on these precious times with You.

July 8

READ: 1 Chronicles 5:18–6:81; Acts 26:1–32; Psalm 6:1–10; Proverb 18:20–21

The Fruit of Our Mouths
Proverbs 18:20–21

One of my most hated tasks as a homemaker is cleaning out the refrigerator. I always dread it because I come up with some pretty nasty-looking and smelling items. Some fruits have turned into penicillin. There is nothing more smelly or nasty than rotten fruit. Bugs and flies are attracted to rotting fruit. Today's proverb tells us, "A man's stomach shall be satisfied from the fruit of his mouth; from the produce of his lips he shall be filled. Death and life are in the power of the tongue, and those who love it will eat its fruit."

Have you ever bitten into an apple and discovered it was rotting around the core? Many times I have looked forward to eating a banana, but when I peel it, it is all dark and mushy on the inside. Whatever words we speak, we often will have to eat them. We eat the fruit of our lips, and too often the fruit of our lips is rotten fruit. Whenever we speak a negative, critical word, we will have to eat the rotten fruit of our lips. Recently my husband and I have been teaching a marriage enrichment course, and these sessions have been very revealing. So far we have only had one couple to come, and we are grateful for this since this couple is all we can handle. When we gather, the husband and wife do nothing but pour out accusations against one another. The room is filled with negative, critical, hurtful words, and I can almost smell the rotting fruit.

Jesus tells us that living water should flow out of our bellies, not rotten fruit. James compares the mouth to a fountain: "But the tongue can no man tame; it is an unruly evil, full of deadly poison. Therewith bless we God, even the Father; and therewith curse we men, which are made after the similitude of God. Out of the same mouth proceedeth blessing and cursing. My brethren, these things ought not so to be. Doth a fountain send forth at the same place sweet water and bitter? Can a fig tree, my brethren, bear olive berries? either a vine, figs? so can no fountain both yield salt water and fresh. Who is a wise man and endued with knowledge among you? let him shew out of a good conversation his works with meekness of wisdom" (James 3:8–13, KJV).

Rotten fruit from our lips results from rotten unforgiveness, resentment, anger, pride and bitterness within us. When we speak unkindly to one another we are poisoning our own bellies and the bellies of others. Negative words cause the person delivering them to have indigestion, and also the one who hears them to have an upset stomach. Just as bugs and flies are attracted to rotten fruit, demon spirits are attracted to rotten words. Think about this today.

READ: 1 Chronicles 7:1–8:40; Acts 27:1–20; Psalm 7:1–17; Proverbs 18:22

Finding a Good Thing
Proverbs 18:22

Wives are good things. Some women may object to being called a "thing," but it is a good thing when a man finds a wife and enters married life. Not everyone will marry, and I was beginning to think none of my boys would ever get married. From the time they were small boys I prayed for godly mates for them. Now they are all married to godly wives, and we have grandchildren. All three were married in a span of nine months. I share this with singles that are looking for a mate to illustrate how fast things can change in their lives.

A wife is a good thing because she is a helpmate for her husband, and believe me, my boys needed all the help they could get. They are all fine young men, but they are still under construction, as we all are. It thrills me to see how their wives have exhorted and encouraged them to be the best Christians, lovers, partners, businessmen, sons and fathers they could be. These precious "things" have undergirded and supported my sons, and they have also polished many of their rough edges. They have comforted them when they were down and cheered them to reach heights they never could have achieved without their constant affirmations and appreciation for the potential latent within each of them.

As I thought of the role of a wife as helpmate, my mind was drawn to the Holy Spirit. He is our helper, and His function in our lives is very similar to the function of a wife. He exhorts, encourages, supports, guides, undergirds, teaches and challenges us to reach our greatest potential in the Lord. He also polishes our rough edges as He conforms us to the image of Jesus Christ. For those that are not married, the good news is that you have a helpmate (the Holy Spirit) who is your helper through life. We all have found a good thing by allowing the Holy Spirit to be our helper.

> Lord, thank You for sending Your Holy Spirit to be my helper through this life. He is always available to help me if I will just turn to Him daily whenever I need help.

The Message of Angels
Acts 27:21–44

Something I've noticed in reading through the Bible every year are the things angels say when they visit us on earth. Over and over again they greet those on earth with the words, "Fear not." We remember the words of the heavenly hosts as they announced the birth of Jesus: "Fear not; for behold, unto you is born in the city of David a Savior..." The words of Gabriel to Joseph and Mary were "Fear not." In today's reading in Acts we see the angel appearing to Paul as he is being transported to prison on a boat that was encountering heavy seas. The angel said, "Fear not, Paul; thou must be brought before Caesar; and, lo, God hath given thee all them that sail with thee" (v. 24, KJV).

Paul was able to pass this message on to those aboard the ship. There were 276 souls on board the ship. Paul advised that they not abandon ship, but instead remain on board and lighten the ship by throwing as much as they could overboard so the ship would be more manageable. First he exhorted them to eat as much as possible since they had been fasting for fourteen days and needed sustenance to give them strength for the journey ahead. Several times in this passage Paul tells them to "be of good cheer." Do those words sound familiar to you? Jesus told us all to "be of good cheer, for I have overcome the world." He also said many times while He walked on earth, "Fear not."

Have there been times in the past when you wanted to abandon the ship of life? Trials and testings came upon you in rapid succession and you felt you would drown in a sea of troubles. Then you cried out to the Lord and He heard you. His message to you at that time was the same message of the angels: "Fear not, for I bring you good tidings of great joy. Be of good cheer, for I have overcome the world." He also said, "I will never leave you or forsake you. I will be with you always even until the ends of the earth."

In this world we will have times of tribulation, but it gives me great comfort to know I am not alone. Jesus is with me always, and as long as I do not allow my heart to be troubled by troubles, I will get through whatever trials may face me. Not only is Jesus holding my hand through every trouble, but I also believe I have two angels who never leave my side. Why do I believe this? There were two angels present at the grave of Jesus. They also said, "Fear not." I believe our Lord, who is the captain of the hosts of heaven, has assigned at least two angels to every believer, and these angels will not only be with us through our life on earth, but they will also accompany us as we travel to heaven after our death.

Today take great comfort in the knowledge that no matter what you are going through you are not alone. Present with you through the angry sea of trials is the Trinity (Father, Son and Holy Ghost) and at least two angels who are watching over you. The message God and His angels have for you today is, "Fear not; be of good cheer because Jesus has overcome the world."

July 11

Snake Bit

Acts 28:1–31

We saw yesterday how 276 souls aboard Paul's ship were spared. In today's reading we see how Paul's life was spared. All those on board the ship swam to the island of Malta, where they were well received by the natives there. There was a chill in the air, and when Paul gathered sticks for a fire, a snake bit him. No harm came to Paul, and this was a great witness to all present.

Most people have a natural fear of snakes. I believe this fear is part of our nature because Satan appeared as a snake to Eve. That wicked serpent is still tempting people, and many are bitten by him. Satan is able to send his venom in to us if we give in to temptation. The bite of a poisonous snake can lead to death if an antivenom serum is not administered quickly. Another way to avoid death if a poisonous snake bites you is to cut out the flesh and all tissue that is around that bite before the poison has a chance to flow into your blood stream. You have heard stories of how people have been spared by quickly taking a knife to cut out the area in the flesh of the snakebite.

Removing the snakebite of sin in our lives follows this same pattern. We have two choices. We can recognize the bite of sin quickly in our lives and confess it quickly, thereby receiving the antivenom serum of the blood of Jesus, which purifies and protects our lives from the death sin can cause in our lives.

The other choice is for us to take action and cut out the flesh part of our lives that has been bitten by sin. This action is called denying yourself. Satan is no dummy, and he knows your weak areas. He knows just the place to send his poison into your flesh because he sees that area of your flesh is very vulnerable. For example, if the weak area in your life is lusting after the opposite sex, Satan will see to it that you will have opportunity to give into that lust by putting things continually before your eyes or thoughts in your mind that begin to poison your system. The only way to overcome this satanic attack is to cut out the infected flesh. David made a covenant with God not to put any evil thing before his eyes. We can quickly deal with the area of sin by cutting out any activity that would lead to further infection of sin in our lives. To some this may mean no longer watching worldly television programs or reading worldly magazines.

No harm came to Paul when the snake bit him because he was filled with God's Spirit and covered by the blood of Jesus. I would not suggest that you handle snakes to find out if you have the same protection. But you can rest assured that you do have the same protection against the snakebite of sin. When that wicked serpent bites you, you now know what to do— confess your sin, repent and receive the cleansing of the blood of Jesus or cut out any activity in your life that will give Satan an advantage over you through temptation. No harm will come to you if you will be faithful to do your part. God is always faithful to do His part. Jesus has overcome in every area you are tempted so that you may overcome every temptation.

To the Jew First
Romans 1:1–17

Jesus made it clear while He ministered near the Galilee and in Jerusalem that He came to minister first to the house of Israel. This was His first charge by the Father. He carried the message of the kingdom of God to the Jew first. We have the same commission Jesus had, but many of us have forgotten to go to the Jew with the liberating message of the gospel. Paul in this passage reminds us of our commission to the Jew first (v. 16).

Over the years I have seen many Jewish people completed in their faith when they have heard the good news of the kingdom. It seems that Jewish people who come to know Jesus as their Messiah are more zealous than the Gentiles who have known Jesus for years.

When we were in Russia at a festival designed to reach out with the message of the gospel to Jewish people, I heard the testimonies of many completed Jews. They all searched for a relationship with God deeper than they had in their Judaism. In Judaism they knew God as the King of the universe, but now through their belief in Yeshua, they received the spirit of adoption whereby they now could call God "Abba," which means "daddy" in Hebrew.

Jesus came to preach the gospel of the kingdom of God, which is something everyone who exists on earth desires. The gospel of the kingdom of God is simply the good news that on earth if we accept the King of this kingdom by faith, we can enter into His domain or dominion of peace, joy and right standing with God the Father. I have not met anyone who did not desire to have peace of mind and heart, joy and a feeling of rightness about themselves. I believe that preaching the kingdom of God is the way to reach the Jewish people today. We need to ask them if they want continual peace and joy in their lives, and the response will always be yes. Then we need to share with them that we know about a kingdom they can live in here on earth where they will always experience peace and joy no matter what circumstances they are encountering. This should peak their curiosity, and then we can share about not only the King of the universe, but also the King of this kingdom. Jesus said, "The law and the prophets were until John. Since that time the kingdom of God has been preached, and everyone is pressing into it" (Luke 16:16).

Some Jewish people are familiar with the Law and the prophets, but now they need to know about the kingdom of God so they can press into it. Are you willing to reach out to God's chosen people with this message?

Lord, forgive me for keeping this good news to myself. I need to share it with Jewish people and with all those You place in my path. Open doors for me to share with Your chosen people. Amen.

The Cycle of Unbelief
Romans 1:18–32

This passage in Romans gives the cycle of unbelief. Unbelief is the root of all sin, and we see the progressive degradation of sin that befalls a person who does not believe in Jesus. The first step in unbelief is the denial that God exists. People often ask me if God is merciful, how could He send anyone to hell who has never heard the gospel? My response is always that even nature reveals there is a God; no one will go to hell unless they choose to. Originally hell was reserved for the devil and his angels, but because of the Fall there will be people in hell now who have chosen not to believe. Paul concludes that such people are without excuse because the invisible things of God from the creation of the world are clearly seen. Paul then shares the cycle of unbelief and how it always leads to eternal death instead of eternal life. People who remain in unbelief do the following:

1. They do not glorify God.
2. They are ungrateful.
3. They become vain in their imaginations.
4. They enter into idolatry.
5. They dishonor their bodies between themselves.
6. They enter into unnatural affections—homosexuality and lesbianism.
7. They develop a reprobate mind.
8. They enter into all kinds of unrighteous acts such as fornication, wickedness, covetousness, maliciousness, envy, murder, debate, deceit, malignity, whispering, backbiting, hatred of God, pride, boasting, disobedience to parents, breaking covenants.
9. They become unmerciful, implacable and spiteful.

We believers can make our own list based on the opposite of this list. The believer in Jesus Christ glorifies God. He is grateful, pulls down vain imaginations, does not enter into idolatry, honors his body and the bodies of others, and does not enter into unnatural affections. He has the mind of Christ and is full of righteousness, which manifests as faithfulness, sexual purity, kindness, unselfishness, speaking the truth in love and refraining from gossip, backbiting and maligning others. He imparts life to others, humbles himself and is obedient to parents. He is merciful, cooperative, loving, faithful and full of understanding. He keeps covenant with God and his fellowman.

Which list appeals to you? One can see clearly that the life of a believer is pleasant, filled with grace, love and blessings and light. The life of an unbeliever is filled with wickedness, curses and darkness. This should challenge us all to share the good news with others that they can be translated from this kingdom of darkness rooted in unbelief to the kingdom of light rooted in the belief in the Lord Jesus Christ.

July 14

READ: 1 Chronicles 16:37–18:17; Romans 2:1–23; Psalm 10:16–18; Proverbs 19:8–9

Judging Righteously
Romans 2:1–23

There are only a few things we are permitted to judge according to the Scriptures. We are permitted to judge ourselves, to judge or know others by their fruits and to judge the times. We are warned by Paul and Jesus of the danger of judging others. The reason it is so dangerous to judge another is because if we misjudge or accuse another, we open ourselves up to the very same things we are judging in another person. We can judge a person's actions, but we cannot judge their motivations. Only God can know the hearts of men. Sometimes the Lord may give us discernment about what is in another person's heart, but this knowledge is not to cause us to judge, but instead to cause us to pray for that person.

We have a righteous Judge who judges all things. He judges us and gives to every man according to his deeds. That righteous judge is Jesus. If we are saved, our salvation will not be judged, but our works on earth will be judged, and we will be rewarded accordingly. As the Lord judges our works, He also sees the motivations in our hearts when we did those works. Sometimes we fall into the trap of doing good deeds for others because it is expected of us or because we want the praise of men. Our works on earth that will last forever are those works we do in love and obedience to God's will and the leading of His Spirit.

Several years ago I was visiting regularly a troubled girl in a mental institution. It seemed my visits were availing nothing, and I was burdened down with the obligation to visit this girl. My pastor had asked me to do this, so I did. One day a prayer warrior asked me, "Linda, did the Lord ask you to visit this girl?" I thought for a moment, and then I realized He never led me to do this, but instead I was visiting this girl out of obligation, not obedience to the Lord. I learned a great lesson that day. People can ask us to do many things, and we can do many good deeds, not out of love and obedience to the Lord, but out of obligation to men.

There are works created from the foundation of the earth that we are to walk in. I believe when we die the works that will last forever and not be burned will be those that are written already in our book of life. We also need to be careful to obey God not out of duty, but out of love for Him. When I think about how I need to get my own act together and be busy about the Father's will, I will not have time to sit in judgment of others. I daily pray that the Lord will cleanse my heart of every wrong motivation and cause my actions in obedience to Him and in reaching out to others always to be rooted in love. Jesus came to do the will of the Father, and every action He displayed on earth was rooted in His love for the Father. I want to be like Jesus in His desire always to please the Father rather than men.

Lord, forgive me for the times I have done works simply out of obligation to others. Purify my heart and cause me to always be motivated by love, not duty.

READ: 1 Chronicles 19:1–21:30; Romans 2:24–3:8; Psalm 11:1–7; Proverbs 19:10–12

When the Righteous Can Do Little
Psalm 11:1–7

The Scriptures are full of the blessings that come to those who live righteously. There are many promises in the Word like, "The fervent prayer of a righteous man avails much." Other passages say that righteousness exalts cities and nations. Sodom would have been spared if God had found ten righteous men residing there. Without righteous men, our nation also would not exist. It is because there are still righteous people left in this nation that the United States has not experienced the full measure of God's judgment. The righteous can do much, but when the foundations are destroyed, the righteous are unable to do much to save a nation, city or family.

Today's reading says, "If the foundations are destroyed, what can the righteous do?" (v. 3). Our founding fathers established this nation upon godly principles that are now forbidden in our state school systems. You have heard it said, "As the family goes, so goes a nation." We are faced with a great threat in this nation because the foundations of family life are beginning to crumble. The government is researching what makes a family unit when the Bible clearly defines the family unit. There is still hope for this nation, however, because many righteous men and women are praying and fasting for this nation.

I have a friend who is a great prayer warrior. She is confined to a wheelchair, but she travels the world to pray for the foundations of nations. She goes wherever the Lord leads her to go, and usually shortly after her visits to these nations dramatic changes take place in the government and the church in those nations. She desired greatly to go to Mongolia to pray for that nation, but she could not physically go there because she learned they had no wheelchair provisions in hotels, etc. This did not stop her from going to Mongolia through her prayers, and her prayers availed much. I was just at a meeting where a Mongolian told of the awakening occurring in Mongolia. My friend specifically prays that the foundations of these nations would remain in place and not be destroyed so the righteous will be able to do the work needed in these last days.

Even though you might not be able to travel the world as my friend has, your prayers for your own neighborhood, city, state and nation will avail much. Perhaps you would like to join me today in praying for the foundations to be secured so the righteous can continue their work in this last great harvest.

> Lord, I pray for the foundations of our nation not to be destroyed. Restore the family and turn the hearts of the fathers to the children and the children to the fathers so a curse will not come upon us. Return our nation to the godly principles it was founded upon.

July 16

Who Is Righteous?
Romans 3:9–31

Yesterday we talked about what righteous people can do to save a city and nation. In today's reading we hear Paul's dramatic statements "There is none righteous, no, not one" (v. 10). "For all have sinned and fall short of the glory of God" (v. 23).

Paul is setting the backdrop for the rest of his letter to the believers in Rome. He is making it clear that righteousness is not based upon what we do, but upon who we are. If any of us seek to establish our own righteousness by doing righteous deeds, we will always be a failure. True righteousness is only possible through belief in Jesus Christ. He alone is the only righteous One, and only when He abides within us by the Holy Spirit are we able to be righteous men and women. In another letter Paul reveals how we can obtain such righteousness. He says, "Not by works of righteousness which we have done, but according to his mercy he saved us, by the washing of regeneration, and renewing of the Holy Ghost; which he shed on us abundantly through Jesus Christ our Saviour; that being justified by his grace, we should be made heirs to the hope of eternal life" (Titus 3:5–7, KJV).

We can only obtain true righteousness when we believe and receive Jesus Christ as our Lord and Savior. He is the only One who can cleanse us of all unrighteousness. There truly is none righteous, except for those who believe in Jesus Christ. Once we have received Jesus Christ, our lives are translated from the kingdom of darkness into the kingdom of light that is ruled by Jesus Christ. We become the salt of the earth, able to preserve neighborhoods, cities and nations. We also can add flavor to the life of others when we introduce them to Jesus Christ. We are lights shining in the midst of darkness, and we are commanded to continually let our lights shine that men may see our good works and glorify God in heaven. Good works will follow us when we believe in Jesus because He does these works through us. The moment I strive to do a righteous work, I am not believing or trusting in Jesus. We are to surrender ourselves to Jesus, and He then can work righteousness in us and through us. He can even cause us to be instruments of righteousness that can lead others to enter into His righteousness.

What a privilege to be a partaker of the divine nature of Jesus Christ. He has a righteous nature, and as we abide in Him, we will continually be conformed to His righteousness. We can be transformed by the renewing of our minds, and as we surrender our bodies to Him, we can walk daily in His righteousness. It is His righteousness that draws men to Himself, not our own. Today let your light shine by walking in the spirit all the day long. When you do this, good works will always be manifested in your life, and others will notice.

READ: 1 Chronicles 24:1–26:11; Romans 4:1–13; Psalm 13:1–6; Proverbs 19:15–16

The Work of God
Romans 4:1–13

In one of the Gospels Jesus was asked the question, "What must we do to do the works of God?" His reply was, "Believe on Him." Paul makes it clear in this passage that we are justified by faith, not by works. He used Abraham as an illustration. If his works justified Abraham, then he would take the glory himself. God considered Abraham a righteous man simply because he believed. Paul also speaks of David and how he writes in a psalm about the blessedness of the man who is counted righteous not because of his works, but because of his belief and trust in God. If we consider ourselves as working for the Lord, then we are working out of debt, not out of grace.

For so long in my own life I was working (doing all the right things a Christian should do) to please God. In essence I was trying to earn points with God by what I did. I was a Christian, but I was bound in my effectiveness because I was not allowing God to work through me. All of this changed when I was twenty-six. I was attending a retreat, and we were asked to go by the lakeside and find a quiet spot. Then we were instructed to ask God questions and wait for an answer. This was new to me since all my conversations with God until that time were one way conversations. I simply gave my prayer requests and then said "Amen." I never realized God had many things to share with me, and I never stopped to listen. The question I asked God was simply, "What was wrong with my life?" I noticed other Christians seemed to have more joy than I did, and I wanted to know why. Then I heard the Lord speak the following to me not in an audible voice, but in His still quiet voice within me. He said "Linda, what is wrong with your life is that you have been trying to earn my love. My love is free. I gave it to you two thousand years ago on the cross. Receive My love today, rest in My love and quit trying to earn My love. Quit working for Me and allow My Spirit to work through you. If you did nothing but sit on that log by this lake the rest of your life I would still love you."

It was almost too good to be true. I understood for the first time that God's love for me did not depend upon what I did, but upon what He did on the cross two thousand years ago. On that day I resigned as an employee of God and became a co-laborer with Him and a joint heir with Him. I stopped trying to keep up with Jesus by following Him, but instead let Him begin to live His life through me. When we believe and trust God, then God does His work through us and He receives all the glory. My life scripture is, "For it is God who works in you both to will and to do for His good pleasure" (Phil. 2:13). God gives me daily the desire to do His will, and then He enables me to do His work that day by empowering me with His Spirit. What then is my part? My part is to believe and trust Him, and then to obey Him as He leads me through the day by His Spirit. "Lord, lead me today by Your Spirit and help me to obey."

July 18

Investing in the Kingdom of God
Proverbs 19:17

Two of the treasures we can take to heaven when we die are people we have witnessed to and the Word of God we have hidden in our hearts. There is another way we can invest in God's kingdom here on earth and at the same time add to our heavenly bank account. Today's reading reveals this way. It says, "He who has pity on the poor lends to the LORD; and He will pay back what he is given."

The thought that we can lend to God seems odd since God owns everything. He owns the cattle on a thousand hills. What need does He have for us to lend to Him? Most banks are happy to loan money to people. They know they will be paid back more than the amount of the loan because they add interest to the payments. Wouldn't you love to find a bank that was willing for you to lend to it, and in return this bank would pay you back the amount you loaned and even more than you loaned? God is the corporate president of such a bank.

When we lend to God, we do not charge interest, but He pays us back abundantly with interest. We give directly to God when we offer sacrifices of worship, praise, our bodies for His use daily, our time and finances. We loan to God when we give to the poor. What we give to the poor, it is a loan to God because we become the instrument to bless someone who can never pay us back. Our loan is not to the person, because he cannot pay us back. But our loan is to God, and He pays us back. The treasure God receives when we lend to Him by giving to the poor is pure delight and joy when He sees how this poor person has been blessed by our generosity. Nothing makes God happier than to see the poor being fed and clothed by those who care in the body of Christ.

God was delighted on the day we gave pair of shoes to an Indian pastor who for his forty years on earth had gone barefoot. The moment this pastor put these shoes on, he ran and jumped and praised the Lord. I believe God was running and jumping right along with Him. God was rejoicing over that scene with singing and dancing. Today you may have an opportunity to lend to God by giving to the poor. The rewards of such a loan are beyond expression.

Lord, help me to lend to You by giving to the poor. I realize some people are poor spiritually because they have never known Your love. No one has invested the time it takes to share with them the gospel. Don't allow me to miss out on any opportunities You may present to me today to lend to You by giving to those who are physically poor or spiritually poor. Amen.

How Love Is Dispersed
Romans 5:3–21

Most Christians I know want to grow more like Jesus daily. They want to be able to love as Jesus loved. The school of love, however, could be called the school of hard knocks. If all is going well in our lives, those who watch our lives will say, "It's easy for them to be loving because they have never had the problems I have experienced." It is when we go through hard knocks—tribulations, trials, testings and temptations—that the love of God is shed abroad in our hearts. It is when our own human love has reached its limit that God steps in and disperses His love within our hearts to equip us to dispense His love to others. Experiencing the love of God is only possible for us when we become totally dependent upon Him. When we recognize that without Him we can do nothing, then we recognize also that without His love in our hearts we have no quality love to give to others.

When we were without strength, Christ died for us. And now when we are without strength to love another, Christ lives through us to dispense His love from our weak vessels to others. This passage in Romans shares the sequence that occurs that causes God's love to be manifested in and through us. First we go through one of these terrible "T's"—trials, tribulations, testings, temptations. How we respond during such times depends alone upon our dependency upon God in troubled times. If we respond with patience at such times, then experience is added to our lives and hope is birthed. People around cannot see the love God has shed abroad in our hearts, but they can see the patience and hope we display in troubled times. They may even ask us to share with them the reason we are at peace and have such hope.

The experience we gain through troubled times is invaluable because we then can look back at the hard-knock times in our lives and see how God revealed His love to us and gave us hope. We can share with others that God has no pets. He was able to get us through a time of trouble, and He is also able to deliver them through their hard knocks. Through their hard times, God will give them a personal love story to tell. I guess this is why James tells us to rejoice when we experience all kinds of trials. During these times God is dispersing His sustaining love to us in our own hearts so we in return can dispense that sustaining love to others. Whatever you are going through today, I can say with all assurance after my fifty years as a Christian, that God's love will see you through this. He is faithful. God's love never fails.

Lord, I am human, and I hate pain and troubles, but one of your promises to me as a Christian is that I will experience suffering. Who wants it, and who needs it? The answer to this question I understand today. Others need to see You show Yourself strong on my behalf when I am at my weakest. Others need to see that Your grace and love are sufficient to carry me through whatever suffering I experience on this earth.

July 20

READ: 2 Chronicles 1:1–3:17; Romans 6:1–23; Psalm 16:1–11; Proverbs 19:20–21

You've Got to Serve Somebody
Romans 6:1–23

One of the things men rebel against is serving a master. Many rebel against serving God because they feel they will not be able to do their own thing. What rebellious people do not realize is that even though they are not serving God, they are serving another master when they do their own thing. When we resist God, we submit to Satan. When we submit to God, we are able to resist Satan.

In this passage in Romans Paul makes it quite clear that we are all servants. We are either servants of sin or servants of righteousness. The fruit of sin is death. The fruit of righteousness is peace, joy and life. We have to decide which fruit we want our lives to produce. If we honestly look at this choice, it truly is a "no brainer." Who on earth would choose death over life, peace and joy? Yet many make such a choice daily when they seek to do their own thing rather than God's thing.

Paul exhorts us to offer the members of our bodies as an instrument of righteousness unto God. If we do not offer the members of our bodies to God, then we have by our own neglect or apathy submitted the members of our bodies to Satan through giving into our own lusts. If we do not reckon ourselves dead daily to sin, then the members of our bodies will be alive to lusts and to Satan's plan, not God's plan for our lives. A daily prayer I pray is:

Lord, I offer the members of my body today to You to be used as instruments of Your love, righteousness, peace and joy.

When I pray this prayer, I know I have submitted to God, and I also know He will give me the strength to resist the devil and give me the power to say no to my own lusts. If I sincerely want to do God's thing today instead of my own thing, He will move heaven and earth to see that I have the power and ability to do His will. In fact, He has already moved heaven and earth to empower me to do His thing instead of my thing. The earth quaked when Jesus died on the cross for me, and the heavens were opened when Jesus ascended victorious over sin and death.

God only wants one thing from us today. He wants us. We can offer our bodies as a living sacrifice to Him today by offering the members of our bodies to be used as instruments of His love, righteousness, peace and joy. If we will do this, the power of heaven and earth are at our disposal. His name is Jesus. He is all power and has defeated every other power in rebellion against Him. He has defeated Satan and provided a way for us to escape from our own fleshly lusts. Hallelujah!!!

July 21

READ: 2 Chronicles 4:1–6:13; Romans 7:1–14; Psalm 17:1–15; Proverbs 19:22–23

True Satisfaction
Proverbs 19:22–23

This proverb speaks of something that will cause us to be continually satisfied. That special satisfying something is called "the fear of the Lord." When we fear the Lord, which means to love Him and to keep His Word, we will abide satisfied.

Most men and women seek satisfaction in life. Some seek it through pleasure, some through material things, some through food, but only the fear of the Lord will cause continual satisfaction in our lives. The fear of the Lord will give us a satisfaction that causes us to want more. The best way to explain it is when you eat a good meal, you are satisfied, but this does not mean you won't be hungry again. The continual satisfaction of the fear of the Lord in our lives causes us to continually seek to draw even closer to Jesus. We have tasted some of the good things of walking with Jesus daily, but we want to walk even closer to Him. We know our walk of drawing closer to Him will last eternally, so the possibility of His satisfying and satiating our souls moment by moment both in this life and the next is a reality.

Continual satisfaction is one of the promises to those who fear the Lord listed in this proverb. Two other promises are given in this passage to those who fear the Lord. The promise of life and the deliverance from evil are promised to those who fear the Lord. No evil will befall those who fear the Lord. Does this mean a person who fears the Lord will be exempt from troubles? Of course it doesn't. It means that whatever evil Satan has planned for us will ultimately work for our good if we fear the Lord daily. No weapon he throws our way will prosper, and only God's good plan for us in the end will prevail.

Why do bad things happen to good people? Nothing bad in God's sight is going to happen to us if we daily walk in the fear of the Lord. Oh yes, it may seem bad to us at the time we are experiencing suffering or trouble, but in the end whatever seems bad will work for our good because God is a good God. His goodness is everlasting, and His mercy endures forever.

In the midst of whatever we consider a bad thing happening to us, there is a good God who is working out His eternal purposes in that situation. I saw a bumper sticker that said, "Good God, bad devil." God cannot be tempted with evil, neither does he tempt any man with evil. God only allows Satan to tempt us with evil because God plans to have us overcome the temptation, trouble or trial by depending upon His goodness.

Lord, I am challenged today to walk in the fear of You by obeying Your Word and loving You with all my heart. I have the confidence now if I am faithful to do this You will never allow evil to overcome me. Thank You.

July 22

READ: 2 Chronicles 6:14–8:10; Romans 7:15–8:8; Psalm 18:1–15; Proverbs 19:24–25

Our Only Hope
Romans 7:15–8:8

How on earth can we be like Jesus? To be like Jesus and to glorify Him on earth is one of the main purposes God has for us in this life. How often do I fall short of demonstrating His love, mercy and forgiveness to others? When I fail in my daily witness, there is but one hope. This hope is Jesus Christ. I have to abandon my flesh to Him and allow Him to conform me to His image. I cannot do it, and the more I try the more I fail.

Paul talks about this dilemma in this passage from Romans. He finds himself doing those things he does not want to do and saying those things he does not want to say. He recognizes that it is sin in him doing these things. Sin always leads to death and he cries out to God, "Who shall deliver me from the body of this death?" Then he says, "I thank God through Jesus our Lord." Only when we are completely dependent upon Jesus can we have any hope of being like Him. Daily I pray the following prayer:

Lord, I offer myself to You today. I offer my body, soul and spirit to You. I ask for Your anointing to be upon me. Let Your Spirit of wisdom and understanding, counsel and might, knowledge and the fear of the Lord be operative in my life today. Help me to walk in Your Spirit and to stay filled with Your Spirit all the day long. You are my only hope of glorifying the Father today in my life. Be glorified today in me. Amen.

You might want to join me in this prayer today. I know if you pray this with your heart as well as say it with your words, the Lord will use you today to glorify Him.

READ: 2 Chronicles 8:11–10:19; Romans 8:9–23; Psalm 18:16–34; Proverbs 19:26

The Way, the Word, the Work
Psalm 18:16–34

In Psalm 18, there is one verse that says it all: "As for God, His way is perfect; the word of the Lord is proven; He is a shield to all who trust in Him" (v. 30). To walk through this life with God's success, we must walk in His ways, live by His Word and trust in Him. A successful person in God's view is one who walks daily in God's Spirit and obeys His Word. The only work we do on this earth that will remain eternally are those things done not by our own self-effort but by the guidance of the Holy Spirit and the grace of God. Paul says it well when he declares it is grace that labors through him.

The key to walking daily in the Spirit is to trust God with all of our hearts and lean not on our own understanding. As we trust God with all of our hearts, He will prove His Word to be true in this life. Who tries the Word of the Lord? We do. Every day we trust what we are hearing from the Lord through His Word and through the promptings of the Holy Spirit. When we act in faith upon His Word and His guidance, God will then work through us both to will and to do of His good pleasure. We believe and trust, and He accomplishes His will through our lives.

The perfect illustration of this was an experience Arthur Burt had when he was on a bus in England. Arthur is an evangelist from Wales, and God uses him mightily even now when he is in his eighties. He shares about riding a bus when it was pouring down rain outside. Suddenly he heard the following instruction: "Get off the bus at the next stop." He argued with this still quiet voice and said, "But it is pouring down rain outside, and I have not arrived at my destination." Thus ensued a battle Arthur describes as a battle between "the fanatic in the attic" and "the fellow in the cellar." Sometimes the Holy Spirit asks us to do things that are not reasonable in the natural. The Holy Spirit was asking Arthur to do something past his human logic. The fellow in the cellar that was Arthur's flesh was saying, "It's pouring outside, and besides, the next stop is not my stop." The fanatic in the attic won the war, and Arthur got off the bus.

As he ran for shelter he saw a car approaching him. Then the car stopped right in front of him, and he recognized a lady he had met at some of his meetings. She yelled past the rolling thunder, "Arthur Burt, is that you?" He replied, "Yes," and then she offered him a lift.

He gladly got in her car, and then she asked, "If you don't have anything to do in the next two hours, would you like to accompany me to a prayer meeting?" He didn't have anything pressing, so he answered in the affirmative. That prayer meeting where he ended up sharing from the Scriptures turned out to be one of the most powerful meetings Arthur had ever led. Since that experience Arthur tries to obey quickly that still quiet voice of the Holy Spirit who often asks him to do things that seem illogical in the natural. God's ways are higher than ours. We must trust him and lean not to our own understanding.

Hope Is a Part of Faith
Romans 8:24–39

Without faith it is impossible to please God. By grace are we saved through faith, and this faith is not of ourselves. Instead it is a gift of God. Therefore none of us can boast. This passage in Romans says that we are saved by hope. Paul writes, "For we are saved in this hope, but hope that is seen is not hope, for why does one hope for what he sees?" (v. 24). Another passage in Hebrews gives the definition of faith: "Now faith is the substance of things hoped for, the evidence of things not seen" (Heb. 11:1).

When we put Romans 8:24 alongside Hebrews 11:1, we have a clearer understanding of how saving faith works. For anyone to enter into salvation, they must believe that God exists and that He is the rewarder of those who diligently seek Him. They must believe in something they cannot see. They must believe that Jesus Christ lived, died and was resurrected from the dead and now lives to make intercession for us.

We believe, not because we have seen things with our own eyes, but because we have heard them from God's Word. Faith comes by hearing and hearing by the Word of God. Faith is believing and receiving something in the now. When I believe, I receive what I believe by confessing my belief with my mouth. The Scriptures say, "The word of faith is in thee, even in your mouth." When we confess with our mouths and believe in our hearts that Jesus Christ is Lord, we are saved. Hope is then born in our hearts. Once I am saved, I have the hope of eternal life, and this hope is also something I cannot see now, but I believe by faith it is true now. Faith is in the now, and hope is in the future.

Hope is the very substance faith is based upon, and that substance is God's Word, His promises to us that are in the future. Faith in the now always births hope in us for the future. As believers we share the blessed hope that one day we will live with Jesus forever. Praise the Lord!

July 25

A Treasure More Precious Than Gold
Psalm 19:1–14

I go on a treasure hunt every day. As I read the Bible through each year, I always find a new nugget I missed in the years past. The Bible is a treasure chest filled with gold and jewels. The gold and jewels found in the Word of God are His promises and principles. The principles are the statutes and commandments of the Lord, and they keep us from evil. The promises are given to those who fear the Lord. The fear of the Lord is clean and endures forever.

As I look into God's Word, I find the treasures of hidden wisdom that are all in Christ Jesus, the living Word. The Holy Spirit is narrator as I read the Word, and I can hear His gentle voice teach me daily. I try not to miss His classroom ever because I know He has many surprises for me each day.

This psalm has been put to music, and as I sing it today, I am reminded once again about the precious treasure many are missing in their lives.

> The law of the LORD is perfect, converting the soul:
> The testimony of the LORD is sure, making wise the simple.
> The statutes of the Lord are right, rejoicing the heart:
> The commandment of the Lord is pure, enlightening the eyes.
> The fear of the Lord is clean, enduring for ever,
> The judgments of the Lord are true and righteous altogether.
> More to be desired are they than gold, yea, than much fine gold:
> Sweeter also than honey and the honeycomb.

Don't miss your treasure hunt today.

The Word of Faith
Romans 9:25–10:12

As I read this passage I see in my mind's eye the religious Jews in Israel as they bobbed back and forth, their prayer shawls waving gently with their movements while they prayed earnestly at the Western Wall. I just returned from Israel and saw this same scene, which always brings tears to my eyes. They are praying for Messiah—when Messiah has already come. These Jews have great zeal in their religious activity, but they are without knowledge. Paul recognized this. He says about them, "For I bear them witness that they have a zeal for God, but not according to knowledge. For they being ignorant of God's righteousness, and seeking to establish their own righteousness, have not submitted to the righteousness of God" (Rom. 10:2–3).

These religious Jews in Paul's day and in our day sincerely want to do what pleases God, but in all their works they have missed doing the one work that is required—to believe. Without faith it is impossible to please God, and every work we do that is not based upon our faith in Jesus Christ is not pleasing in God's sight. No one on earth can establish his own righteousness because there is none righteous, no, not one. Jesus tried to make this clear to His Jewish brethren in His teaching and preaching here on earth. He told them that if they sinned in one part of the Law, they were guilty of breaking the whole law.

Whenever I pray at the Western Wall in Israel, I pray for all Israel to be saved. There will be a remnant in Israel saved as Paul declares. God's requirement for salvation is spelled out in this passage when Paul says, "The word is near you in your mouth and in your heart (that is, the word of faith, which we preach): That if you confess with your mouth the Lord Jesus and shall believe in your heart that God has raised Him from the dead, you will be saved. For with the heart one believes unto righteousness, and with the mouth confession is made unto salvation" (Rom. 10:8–10).

Join with me today as I pray for both Jewish and Gentile unbelievers who have not yet made the above confession of faith with their mouths or believed in their hearts.

Lord, I pull down the strongholds of unbelief, doubt and pride in the minds of those who need salvation. Give them the gift of faith to believe and unveil their eyes so that they might have understanding.

READ: 2 Chronicles 19:1–20:37; Romans 10:13–11:12; Psalm 21:1–13; Proverbs 20:4–6

How Will They Hear?
Romans 10:13–11:12

Paul continues his discussion about what it takes to be saved. He says, "For whoever calls upon the name of the LORD shall be saved" (Rom. 10:13). Then Paul shares how it will be impossible for people to call upon the name of the Lord if they have never heard the gospel. "How then shall they call on Him in whom they have not believed? And how shall they believe in Him of whom they have not heard? And how shall they hear without a preacher? And how shall they preach unless they are sent? As it is written: How beautiful are the feet of those who preach the gospel of peace, who bring glad tidings of good things!" (vv. 14–15).

Every time my husband reads these verses he begins to weep. So many have not heard, and so many will never hear unless we go and tell or pray and send others to tell. We are exhorted to pray for laborers for the harvest. From the time my boys were toddlers, I prayed God would use them as laborers in this last final harvest. We just visited our youngest son in Budapest, Hungary, where he and his wife are reaching out to both Jews and Gentiles there with the good news. My middle son, with his wife and two babies, teaches and shares in China. Our son in Atlanta is active as a laborer locally as he shares on his job and on his many business trips.

How beautiful are the feet of them who bring good news. Your feet do not have to travel across the sea to share the glad tidings. Today the Lord might just have you walk across the street to share with your neighbor. At my age my feet are no longer physically beautiful because I have two hammer-toes and two huge bunions, but God sees them as beautiful if I will not hesitate to share the good news of our Savior with others.

Lord, help me to be alert today for opportunities to share the glad tidings with others. Direct me to those whose hearts are ready to receive.

Jesus on the Cross
Psalm 22:1–18

The psalms David wrote were directed by the Holy Spirit, who knows the future. David was inspired by the Holy Spirit in this psalm to prophetically write about Jesus' death and His mission on earth. We know that as Jesus was dying on the cross, He cried out, "My God, My God, why have You forsaken me?" Jesus was quoting from this psalm. David writes in this psalm about the piercing of His hands and feet. We know this did not happen to David, but it did happen to Jesus Christ. David in the spirit saw the scene of the cross, and he recorded what he saw and heard.

David continues to describe this dramatic scene in verses 14–18: "I am poured out like water, and all my bones are out of joint: my heart is like wax; it is melted in the midst of my bowels. My strength is dried up like a potsherd; and my tongue cleaveth to my jaws; and thou hast brought me into the dust of death. For dogs have compassed me: the assembly of the wicked have enclosed me: they pierced my hands and my feet. I may tell all my bones: they look and stare upon me. They part my garments among them, and cast lots upon my vesture" (KJV).

None of these things happened to David, so we know he was speaking of Jesus Christ. Why did God forsake Jesus? He had purer eyes than to behold evil, and when Jesus became sin for us, the Father had to turn away from Jesus. As Jesus was poured out like water, He drank from the cup He asked the Father to remove from Him when He agonized in the garden. This cup was the cup of God's wrath, and He drank this for all of us so that we would not be appointed to wrath. Jesus became the perfect drink offering as well as the perfect Lamb of God slain for us from the foundation of the earth.

Lord, I can only bow my knees in thanksgiving for what You did for me on the cross. Because You became sin for me, I will never have to face God's wrath. Thank You! Thank You! Thank You!

The Rest of the Story
Psalm 22:19–31

Almost everyone in the United States is familiar with the famous sign-off of the commentator Paul Harvey as he finishes his news report. He says, "Now you know the rest of the story." In yesterday's reading we left the account of Jesus on the cross with the soldiers parting His garments. Today's reading tells the rest of the story and also shares how this wondrous story will be told to the whole world.

Although Jesus for a moment in time experienced separation from the Father because of our sin, we see in the remainder of this psalm the glorious restoration and redemption story. When Jesus turned unto the Father and cried out, God heard His cry, and even though the Father had to turn away for a moment, He did not forsake Jesus forever. We know the grave could not hold Jesus and that Satan and death were defeated when Jesus died and later was resurrected. Now the whole earth will remember and one day turn and acknowledge Jesus Christ as Lord. This psalm tells us that all the kindred of the nations shall worship before Him. His kingdom will come on earth, and all those who believe will rule and reign with Him.

Paul unveils his great burden in the Book of Romans for his Jewish brethren. He earnestly desires that they all be saved. He makes the bold statement in Romans 10:13 that all who call upon the name of the Lord shall be saved. When Jesus sets His feet on the Mount of Olives, the mountain will split in half and the Jews who remain in Israel will look upon the one they pierced. The veil over their eyes will be dropped even as the veil over the eyes of Joseph's brothers was dropped when he revealed himself to them. On that day the Jewish remnant will look at Jesus' hands and feet, and they will see the nail prints. They will mourn as families for days. Until this day occurs we have a great responsibility to God's chosen people. They may not be there on that day, so today is their day of salvation. They need to know the whole gospel story, and it is recorded right here in one of their psalms. The psalm concludes, "A posterity shall serve Him. It will be recounted of the Lord to the next generation. They will come and will declare His righteousness to a people who will be born, that He has done this."

I love to tell others the rest of the story. Pray for opportunities today to share these glad tidings with others.

July 30

READ: 2 Chronicles 26:1–28:27; Romans 13:1–14; Psalm 23:1–6; Proverbs 20:11

The Only Thing We Need to Owe
Romans 13:1–14

Each day our national debt and the debts of many citizens are rising. The convenience of the credit card is sending many to a debtor's prison. I heard recently that the average credit card debt for the American household is $20,000. Can you imagine the interest that will accumulate if this debt is not paid off in a year's time? It is a terrible thing to be in bondage to financial debt. We all need to follow Paul's admonition in this passage "Owe no one anything except to love one another, for he who loves another has fulfilled the law" (v. 8).

We all are in debt. We have a debt we could never pay, and it is the debt of sin in our lives. Jesus, however has paid this debt.

Through His death on the cross and His resurrection, Christ Jesus has washed clean the debt of sin I owed. When we see Him face to face, He will say our debt has been canceled. We do have one debt, however, and we must pay off this debt daily. We must show our love to others by sharing how they too can be debt free.

He Is Lord Whether You Believe It or Not
Romans 14:1–23

The lordship of Jesus Christ is clearly stated in two of our readings today. Psalm 24 declares the earth is the Lord's and the fullness thereof. Many, however, will never acknowledge the lordship of Jesus Christ. Paul tells us in our Romans passage that there will be a day when every knee will bow and every tongue will confess that Jesus Christ is Lord. There will be a day of judgment in which everyone will have to give an account of how they lived their lives on earth. On that day Jesus, the just judge, will reveal the hearts of men. Who am I then to judge my brother today? This is the question Paul addresses in this passage. He says, "Therefore let us not judge one another anymore, but rather resolve this, not to put a stumbling block or a cause to fail in our brother's way" (v. 13).

I always am reminded of this verse when I am tempted to judge another person. When we resist the temptation to judge another, we not only spare that person much hurt, but we also spare ourselves a lot of trouble. Jesus said, "Judge not, that ye be not judged. For with what judgment ye judge, ye shall be judged, and with what measure ye mete, it shall be measured to you again" (Matt. 7:1–2, KJV).

Instead of judging others, I have learned the hard way to release all judgment to the Lord. Jesus alone is the only righteous judge, as we see in Psalm 9:7–8: "But the LORD shall endure forever; He has prepared His throne for judgment. He shall judge the world in righteousness, and He shall administer judgment for the peoples in uprightness."

What a relief it is to me not to have to sit on the judgment seat. The next time you are tempted to judge another, picture that judgment throne with a sign on it, "Reserved for the Only Righteous Judge."

How to Pray for Others
2 Chronicles 30:1–31:21

God has made us kings and priests unto God (Rev. 1:6). Because we are kings and priests, it is helpful to look into the Old Testament to see what the early priests did. We need to know how they ministered to the people and exactly what their office as priest required. The good news is that we can be even more effective as priests than the priests of the early days. We now have a high priest, Jesus Christ, who through His blood shed on the cross has given us boldness to enter into the holy of holies to find grace whenever we have a need.

With the office of priest come both great privileges and great responsibilities. One of the greatest privileges the priest had in the early days was to pray for and bless others. We also have that same privilege. In this passage we learn several ways in which the priests fulfilled their function as intercessors for the people:

1. The priests had to sanctify themselves (30:15).
2. The priests sanctified the people by sprinkling the blood (30:16–17).
3. The priests pardoned the people (30:18).
4. The priests each had a special task to fulfill in the temple (31:2).

As priests who intercede for God's people we fulfill the function of priest when we:

1. Sanctify ourselves through God's Word (John 17:17).
2. Sanctify the people by sharing God's Word with them (John 17:8, 16–21).
3. Pardon the people by remitting their sins (John 20:21–23).
4. Fulfill our office faithfully in the body of Christ.

Our major responsibility as priests is to abide in Christ's love and His Word. It is the Word of God that causes us to be sanctified (set apart from the world to do service for God). We also have the responsibility to pray for those that we see who are in sin. Listen carefully to these words in 1 John 5:16: "If any man see his brother sin a sin which is not unto death, he shall ask, and he shall give him life for them that sin not unto death. There is a sin unto death: I do not say that he shall pray for it" (KJV).

The only sin we cannot remit in another person's life is the sin of rejection of Jesus Christ. We cannot absolve another person from this sin. If we had that power, a person's free will to choose Christ would be dissolved. We can, however, fervently pray for that person's salvation.

Lord, give me the grace to faithfully fulfill the office of priest You have given me. Help me to continually abide in Your Word and Your love.

More With Us Than With Them
2 Chronicles 32:1–33:13

For years my husband and I did not have daily prayer together. In fact, we had been married twenty-five years before we started praying together daily. Of course, we did pray for things as they came up, but usually we had our own quiet time with God individually. During those years, however, I had a very special prayer partner. Her name was Zira, our precious little dog. Every morning she would crawl up in my lap and sit quietly as I prayed to the Lord. I often opened my eyes slightly to see what she was doing. Every time I did this, I saw Zira looking up to heaven. I believe Zira could see my angels watching over me. I am convinced that small infants and animals are able to see into the spirit realm. God gives a few of His saints this ability, but in His mercy He usually chooses not to reveal to us what is all around us in the spirit realm. We probably would be frightened if we had this ability.

In our passage today, Assyrians far outnumbered Judah and surrounded Hezekiah. Hezekiah was not afraid, however, and made the following statement to his army: "Be strong and courageous; be not afraid nor dismayed for the king of Assyria, nor for all the multitude that is with him, for there be more with us than with him: With him is an arm of flesh; but with us is the LORD our God to help us, and to fight our battles. And the people rested themselves upon the words of Hezekiah king of Judah" (32:7–8, KJV).

Hezekiah was given the supernatural revelation of the mighty army of angels who were on his side. This is why he could say there were more with his army than with Sennacherib, king of Assyria. The Lord truly is on our side, and He is ready to fight every battle for us. Even though we cannot see them, angels surround us. In the Book of Psalms we learn that the angels of the Lord are encamped round about those who fear the Lord.

Later in this passage we see where the Lord sent an angel to cut off all the mighty men of valor and the leaders and captains in the camp of the king of Assyria (33:21). It only took one angel to put to flight the mighty army of Assyrians.

During the Six-Day War in Israel, Egypt suddenly retreated. An Egyptian soldier was asked why Egypt ceased their progress, and he shared, "Our armies saw mighty armies all dressed in white and we were afraid." God's arm is always stronger than the arm of flesh, and He is ready to do battle for us. At His disposal are two-thirds of all the angels in heaven. Satan only gained one-third of the angels when he fell. Our angels far outnumber his.

We too can be strong and courageous and not dismayed every day if we will only remember, there are more with us than with our enemy. If God be for us, who can win against us?

Flattery and Gossip
Proverbs 20:19

Tattletell! Tattletell!" Remember yelling this phrase at your sisters or brothers when they told your parents about something you did? It is sad to say, but many of us have never outgrown the tattletell stage. We are still telling on people to others.

Do you know what gossip is? Gossip is sharing a bad report whether true or not with another person. How often have you heard a brother or sister in the Lord pass a bad report about someone? I always feel very awkward when this happens.

How should we respond to gossip? It is best not to listen to bad reports at all, but sometimes that is impossible when someone just blurts a report to you before you have a chance to gather your wits about you. The way I respond now is to say, "What you have shared may or may not be true about this person, but I choose to believe the best about him/her. Why don't we pray for this person right now." This usually will keep gossips away from you if you will consistently respond in this manner.

When we hear a bad report about someone, it is then very hard to erase that negative image of them from our minds. We are cautioned in the Bible not to speak evil of anyone, even if a person is truly evil. We are exhorted to speak only those things that edify and to only think of those things that are of good report, pure, virtuous, true and beautiful.

This proverb also warns us about flattery. I try to stay away from people who flatter. Now I love compliments, but some people are too profuse in their compliments, and this is flattery. Flattery occurs when we compliment others with the impure motive of gaining something from them or manipulating them in some way.

I must admit I have flattered my husband many times to build him up before I make a request of him. This is manipulative, and I confess this as sin, for truly it is. Lord, forgive me.

> *Lord, forgive me for the times I have listened to negative reports about others. I recognize now that when I do this I am entertaining gossip. Forgive me also for the times I have flattered others with the impure motive of manipulating them. Help me to speak only those things that edify, to listen only to those things that minister grace to me and to refrain from manipulation through flattery. Purify my heart, O Lord, and my lips.*

A Blameless Life
1 Corinthians 1:1–17

Is it possible to live a blameless life? As I meditated on our New Testament reading today, the verse that gave me great hope was, "Who will also confirm you to the end, that you may be blameless in the day of our Lord Jesus Christ" (v. 8).

We all have sinned and come short of the glory of God, but as we confess those sins, Jesus cleanses us from all unrighteousness. It would be impossible for us to live a sinless life because the Bible tells us that our hearts are despitefully wicked. John also tells us that if we say that we have not sinned, we are a liar. (See 1 John 1:8.)

When two of my boys were into the things of this world, I cried out often to the Lord in prayer for them. One day as I was praying for them I said, "Lord, I do not want my boys to be ashamed of anything they have said or done on this earth when they see You face to face." My heart was comforted when I heard the Lord speak these words to my spirit, "Your boys will be fine when they see me face to face. I bore their shame on the cross, and all the sins they have confessed I have forgotten. I see your boys now as fine, even though they are not completely walking with me daily. They are fine as gold. I see them as my three golden vessels."

Could it be true? It's too good to be true!! It is true!! It is true!! Jesus Himself will present us all before the Father, and we will be blameless before Him, without spot or wrinkle. When we accepted Jesus as our Lord and Savior, we received His righteousness, not our own, and it is His righteousness within us that will enable us to be blameless before the Father. Whatever we have confessed to Him as sin and repented of has been dropped into God's mighty ocean of love. Jesus has put up a sign in that ocean, and it says, "No fishing." We would all sink quickly if we reviewed our past failures and sins without knowing the Lord's forgiveness. God's Word is true. "If we confess our sins, He is faithful and just to forgive us our sins and to cleanse us from all unrighteousness" (1 John 1:9).

Can we live a blameless life? The answer is yes. The condition, however, is that our hearts are turned toward Jesus and we honestly confess our sins to Him.

Lord, help me to confess those sins Your Holy Spirit convicts me of today.

The Jew Seek a Sign
1 Corinthians 1:18–2:5

When we went to Russia to be intercessors for a music festival in St. Petersburg, we heard many testimonies of Jewish people. As they shared how their lives had been changed when they received Yeshua (Jesus), these testimonies all had a common theme. I do not recall hearing one testimony that did not include some type of sign that God used to reveal His Son Jesus to them as their Messiah. In our reading today we see Paul's insight into those with whom he was sharing the good news. He says, "For Jews request a sign, and Greeks seek after wisdom; but we preach Christ crucified, to the Jews a stumbling block and to the Greeks foolishness, but to who are called, both Jews and Greeks, Christ the power of God and the wisdom of God" (1 Cor. 1:22–24).

Paul knew how to reach the Romans, Greeks and Jews. God gave him great wisdom and discernment about people as he preached in different cultures. The way to reach a Jewish person with the gospel is entirely different from the way to reach an intellectual. Paul was able to do both in an effective way because I believe he asked God for wisdom before he preached to different cultures. We need to do the same.

As we toured Israel, our Jewish guide shared an example of a dramatic testimony of a Jewish person and how God used signs to reveal Himself to him. His name was Dror, and our entire tour group was touched when he shared God's supernatural sign to him. He had received a four-year scholarship to study music in Germany. He came from generations of fishermen and carpenters who lived on the Galilee. His grandfather and grandmother were some of the earliest pioneers from Russia who came to Israel to ready the land for future generations. While he was studying in Germany, the Lord appeared to him in a vision. He saw the face of Jesus framed by the Sea of Galilee, which is shaped like a harp. He heard the words, "Why are you here? My presence is more at the Galilee than here. Return to the Galilee." He was not a believer, but this vision began his search for the Lord. Dror obeyed the voice, quit school and returned to the Galilee. Each day he rode his bike out to the sea from his kibbutz to seek the Lord. On one of these days he saw several people by the sea who were pulling an old boat out of the water. His cousin was among those who had been digging for months to recover a boat that dated back to the time of Jesus. You can see this boat now on display in a museum by the Galilee. As soon as the boat was lifted out of the water, a rainbow stretched from one side of the sea to the other side. It was midsummer, a time when there is usually no rain. This was Dror's dramatic sign that Jesus was real, and even the Jewish people on the dig confessed that the rainbow was a sign that this boat was very special.

I believe it was one of the boats Jesus used many times to cross the Galilee.

What God Has Prepared
1 Corinthians 2:6–3:4

One of my most favorite times of the year is Christmas. The preparations for this time give me great excitement. I usually begin early during the spring sales to buy winter clothes as gifts for our family that includes three sons and their wives, our grandchildren, a Russian son and Chinese daughter, and now another daughter named Misha. I diligently search for gifts they will enjoy, and I can't wait until Christmas day when they open their gifts. Sometimes we give trips to the children, and they love this.

Think of the joy our heavenly Father had as He prepared things for us from the foundation of the earth. He has prepared special gifts we can use throughout our lives that will help us as we share His love and kingdom with others. He also has prepared trips for us to take, people to see and many works to do. Before we were born, God had a specific plan for our lives that unveils to us as we hear and obey His voice. It would boggle our minds to see what God has in His mind and heart for each of us. Paul expresses this so well in this scripture: "But as it is written: 'Eye has not seen, nor ear heard, nor have entered into the heart of man the things which God has prepared for those who love him. But God has revealed them to us through His Spirit. For the Spirit searches all things, yes, the deep things of God'" (1 Cor. 2:9–10).

I would be a terrible mother if on Christmas day I told all my family, "I have wrapped some very special gifts for each one of you, but I will not tell you where to find them." God wants us to know all about all the things He has prepared for us, and He has given His Holy Spirit to reveal these things to us.

When I was a little girl, my parents never wrapped our presents. Instead, on Christmas Eve they laid all of our gifts under the tree. Often I would with great expectation slip out of my bed and crack the living room door open so I could get a sneak peak of what gifts were awaiting me.

Today God wants you to take a sneak peak at all the things He has lovingly prepared for you. Ask the Holy Spirit to show you some of the works God has in mind for you to do, some the gifts He wants you to use and some of the places He wants you to go. If you will be quiet and still and wait upon the Lord after you have asked this question, you will be amazed at what the Holy Spirit will tell you. He may not reveal everything to you now, but He will be careful to reveal just what you need to know today.

Father, thank You so much for all the things You have prepared for me. Thank You for giving me the Holy Spirit who can reveal these things to me. I would love to take a sneak peak today to see some of these things.

READ: Ezra 5:1–6:22; 1 Corinthians 3:5–23; Psalm 29:1–11; Proverbs 20:26–27

How Is Your Building?
1 Corinthians 3:5–23

My husband and I have only built one house in our lifetime. We lived in an apartment close by to the sight of the home we were building, and one of our joys was to check almost daily on the progress of our new home. We had the privilege of choosing the carpet, the other flooring, paint, wallpaper, lighting fixtures and many other things for our new home.

This passage in 1 Corinthians gives three images of those who follow Jesus. We are called laborers, God's husbandry or garden, and God's building. God has chosen us to be co-laborers with Him in His vineyard, and at the same time He looks upon us as His own special garden. We are often called the plantings of the Lord in the scriptures. We talk about a great harvest of souls in this last day and spreading the seed of God's Word. God also has called us to be co-laborers as we build up His kingdom here on earth, and at the same time He looks upon us as His own valuable building. Each believer is the temple of the Holy Spirit.

Paul emphasizes in this passage the importance of laying the foundation of our own temple carefully and exhorts us to build with the right materials. He says, "According to the grace of God which was given to me, as a wise master builder I have laid the foundation, and another builds on it. But let each one take heed how he builds on it. For no other foundation can lay than that which is laid, which is Jesus Christ. Now if anyone builds on this foundation with gold, silver, precious stones, wood, hay, straw, each one's work will become clear; for the Day will declare it, because it will be revealed by fire; and the fire will test each one's work, of what sort it is. If anyone's work which he has built on it endures, he will receive a reward" (vv. 10–14).

I recall reading this passage to my boys when they were young. I drew pictures of a house made of gold, one made of silver and precious stones, one made of wood, one made of hay and one made of stubble. Then I asked them which house would burn down first. They answered, "The house made of stubble." Then I shared that each of their bodies was a building designed to be a home for God. I asked, "If you were building a home for God, which material would you use to build such a home?" They responded, "I would build a home for God with gold and silver and precious stones." How is your building progressing, and what materials are you using to build your own personal home for God? You are the temple of the Holy Spirit.

Lord, help me to build my personal home for You with the finest materials.

August 8

Judge Nothing Before the Time
1 Corinthians 4:1–21

Whenever we judge others we are exalting ourselves into a position reserved only for Jesus Christ. Jesus is the author and finisher of our faith, and only He knows the rest of the story of any person's life. Paul says he cannot without flaw even judge himself. Paul clearly states that the One who judges him is the Lord.

We would be much better off if we released all judgment into the hands of the Lord Jesus Christ, who truly is the only righteous judge. He alone has the ability to see into the hearts of men, and He alone knows the rest of the story. Jesus knows the secret motivations of every heart. We can judge men's actions, but we can never judge their motivations because only Jesus knows what makes a man do something. The day will come when Jesus will judge the secret counsels of the hearts of men. At that time He will bring to light the hidden things of darkness, and every man will receive his just reward.

A time of judgment is coming, and if we busy ourselves with getting our own act together, we will not have time to be criticizing or judging others. We are all still under construction, and God is not finished with any of us yet. We are being conformed daily to the image of Christ Jesus, and we often fall short of the glory of God. We need to learn to be patient with one another because the author and finisher of our faith is not finished with our lives yet.

Often I see things I do not like in others. One of my greatest weaknesses is judging those who judge others. I have a hard time loving critical, judgmental people, yet I know God loves them as much as He loves me.

Just recently we had an experience that taught me a good lesson. We were traveling with a couple to Florida, and suddenly our discussion centered upon one man in our church. Several negative things were said about this man when the wife of the other couple stopped this conversation in its tracks. She asked, "What do you like about So-and-So? Are there any qualities you see in him that are Christlike?" We began to meet this challenge, and each of us came up with many good characteristics and qualities of this person whom we shortly before were criticizing.

Since this conversation, I have learned when I begin to think negatively about someone to stop immediately and begin to think about the good things I see in this person. Suddenly my negative, critical thoughts dissolve as I begin to praise the Lord for knowing this person. Each of us is of great value in the kingdom because, after all, Jesus bought us with His very own blood.

> *Lord, help me to see others as You see them. You saw each person born on this earth as a person worth dying for. Who am I to criticize someone whom You esteemed so highly? Help me to esteem others higher than myself.*

Judging the Sin
1 Corinthians 5:1–13

Yesterday we talked about judging nothing before the time. However, we see in this passage that Paul definitely makes a judgment. Remember we said we could judge people's actions, but we do not have the ability to judge their motivations. Only God knows the hearts of men. The judgment Paul makes in this passage is against the sin of fornication. This is the only sin that is a sin against one's own body. Listen to what Paul says about this. "I wrote unto you in an epistle not to company with fornicators: yet not altogether the fornicators of this world, or with the covetous, or extortioners, or with idolaters; for then must ye needs go out of the world. But now I have written unto you not to keep company, if any man that is called a brother be a fornicator, or covetous, or an idolater, or a railer, or a drunkard, or an extortioner; with such an one no not to eat. For what have I to do to judge them also that are without? do not ye judge them that are within? But them that are without God judgeth. Therefore put away from among yourselves that wicked person" (vv. 9–13, KJV).

This seems to be a contradiction to what Paul just said about not judging others. Paul, however, gives us permission to break fellowship with those who are fornicators, covetous, idolaters, railers, drunkards and extortioners. What would happen in your church if the pastor said, "Will all those who are having sex outside of marriage, those who are wanting to possess what others have, those who are putting other things and people ahead of God, those who get drunk and rail, and those who cheat on their taxes please stand up?" How many do you think would stand up? The truth is we have no way of knowing who has entered such sinful activity unless we actually have talked to such a person and they have admitted their sin, yet are unrepentant. Such was the case in Corinth. The body of Christ knew for a fact that this man had entered into a sexual relationship with his father's wife. Fellowship with this person, therefore, had to be broken until this man became repentant. Paul advised that the body break fellowship with him and deliver him into the hands of Satan until he did repent. Paul's judgment seems harsh, yet Paul's ultimate motive in such a judgment was restoration of this man to the fellowship when the man repented, which we read later did happen.

Lord, first purify my own heart and purify all those who are my brothers and sisters in the Lord.

Who Can Judge?
1 Corinthians 6:1–20

We continue to meditate on judging others. First we learned not to judge anything before the time. Yesterday we saw where Paul judged the sin of a fornicator in the body and exhorted the body at Corinth to break fellowship with him until he repented. Today's passage states an amazing fact about our ability to judge: "Do you not that we shall judge angels? How much more, things that pertain to this life?" (v. 3).

In this portion of his letter to the Corinthians, Paul exhorts the church to settle disputes between themselves rather than taking them to a court of law. When we enter courts of law we are dealing with people who are not submitted to the Lord Jesus Christ. They often are not godly counselors. God has given gifts of wisdom and discernment to certain people in the body who can give godly counsel and help settle disputes within the church.

We are at fault when we go to law against a brother or sister in Christ. Even as I am writing this, I know of a Christian man who is suing his wife for divorce. As of yet, only depositions have been given, and the wife and I are praying this will not go to court. This should never be in the body of Christ. I am reminded of how Pastor Cho in Korea settles disputes between wives and husbands in his church. He requires the couple to go to Prayer Mountain and fast and pray there for three days. He shares that when a couple is willing to do this, the great counselor, the Holy Spirit, is able to bring peace and restoration in the marriage. Once a case gets into the court system, there is the possibility of great damage to the souls involved. No one wins if things are settled without godly counsel.

Paul in this passage also gives a list of sins that are committed by the unrighteous. He lists fornicators, idolaters, adulterers, effeminate, abusers of themselves with mankind, thieves, covetous, drunkards, revilers, extortioners—and he declares those who do such things will not inherit the kingdom of God. Then he quickly adds, "And such were some of you. But you were washed, but you were sanctified, but you were justified in the name of the Lord Jesus and by the Spirit of our God" (v. 11).

We as believers were in the world and did worldly things, but now we are in the kingdom of God, and these unrighteous acts should not be a part of our lives any longer. Fornication, Paul states, is the only one of these sins that is a sin against your own body. Since we are the body of Christ, we should not join the members of our body that belong to Christ to someone other than our marriage partner. Jesus is able to cleanse any of the above sins if we come to Him in true repentance and ask for His forgiveness. This is the good news. Through Jesus Christ we can become unworldly and filled with the kingdom of God—peace, righteousness and joy in the Holy Spirit. There is no unforgivable sin except the rejection of Jesus Christ who forgives.

The Pavilion of God
Psalm 31:19–24

Nothing can wound more than the accusations of others, especially if a friend accuses you. David had this experience. What causes a critical, judgmental spirit? The root cause is pride. When we are hurt by others, it is a sign that we have pride in our hearts. When we hurt and wound others with our words, we are also guilty of pride.

The best definition I ever heard of *humility* is "seeing others as Christ sees them and also seeing yourself as Christ sees you." Think about it. If we walked in such humility, we would not see the negative in others because we would see them as Christ sees them. Jesus values each person the same. We all were considered worthy of His great sacrifice on the cross. God so loved the world that He gave His only begotten Son. God gave His Son for the whole world, but the whole world sadly will not receive or believe in such a great sacrifice. If we saw ourselves as Christ sees us, we would not be easily hurt because we also would see ourselves as someone who has value and worth. No matter what others think of us, we are assured of the fact that there is One who loved us enough to die for us. This thought will be a pavilion to shield us when others come against us with accusations.

David learned how to overcome when others accused him. He knew there was a safe pavilion he could run to that protected him from the strife of tongues. That safe place was the presence of the Lord where he was comforted and restored. David says, "You shall hide them in the secret place of Your presence from the plots of man; You shall keep them secretly in a pavilion from the strife of tongues" (v. 20).

Who is the "them" referred to in such a great promise? The "them" is all those who fear the Lord and put their trust in Him rather than in men. When I read this passage, I picture myself in a beautiful white pavilion or gazebo set in a field of wild flowers beside a peaceful lake. Inside that pavilion are soft, white satin pillows that protect my ears from hearing the accuser of the brethren (Satan). All sounds of strife cease, and I can only hear the voice of the Lord. Here I recognize who my true enemy is—not people, but the principalities and powers that operate through people. Here my perspective is restored and I can do warfare against the enemy instead of justifying myself to others when I am accused. Here I find peace and rest for my soul, and here the accuser is silenced and I can respond in love to my accusers. Here I can love the Lord and am empowered to transmit that love to others.

Lord, help me to run to this pavilion whenever others accuse me.

August 12

READ: Nehemiah 3:15–5:13; 1 Corinthians 7:20–40; Psalm 32:1–11; Proverbs 21:5–7

Why Are We So Blessed?
Psalm 32:1–11

Each day I live I come to appreciate the cross and what happened on that dreadful, but victorious day over two thousand years ago. I am a blessed person for no other reason than the blood of Jesus that was poured out for me to cover my sins. David had not yet seen the crucified and resurrected Lord in the flesh, but I believe he saw Him in the spirit. David understood the power of forgiveness of transgressions, the covering of sins and the pardoning of iniquity. He says, "Blessed is he whose transgression is forgiven, whose sin is covered. Blessed is the man to whom the LORD does not impute iniquity, and in whose spirit there is no deceit" (vv. 1–2).

David knew the power of confession, and he says, "I acknowledged my sin to You and my iniquity I have not hidden. I said, 'I will confess my transgression unto the LORD,' and You forgave the iniquity of my sin. Selah" (v. 5).

David mentions three things we need to confess to God—our sins, our transgressions and our iniquities. Sin is falling short of the glory of God, transgression is sinning against another, and iniquity is the bent to sin or the want to sin. Sin is a thought or action. Transgression is an action against another person or against God's law. Iniquity is the attitude of our hearts.

David saw in the spirit how there would be One to come who would forgive all of our transgressions, who would cover our sins and who would cleanse our hearts. This One is spoken of by Isaiah 53: "But He was wounded for our transgressions, He was bruised for our iniquities: the chastisement for our peace was upon Him, and by His stripes we are healed" (Isa. 53:5). "Yet it pleased the LORD to bruise Him; He has put Him to grief. When You make His soul an offering for sin, He shall see His seed. He shall prolong His days, and the pleasure of the LORD shall prosper in His hand" (v. 10).

It is beyond our human comprehension that it pleased God to bruise Jesus for our sakes. Such love seems beyond expression, yet it was expressed fully on the cross when Jesus died for our sins, was bruised for our iniquities and was wounded for our transgressions. Amazing love! Such love demands my life, my all!

What Stands Forever?
Psalm 33:1–11

In a world that is falling apart, we need a place of security. Earlier we spoke of such a place—the pavilion in the presence of the Lord where we can hide from the strife of tongues. If you have ever experienced an earthquake or a tornado, you have an understanding of how your life depends upon where you place yourself. If you are in an earthquake, you are to brace yourself in a doorway. If you are in a tornado, you are to go to your basement or storm cellar.

The Scriptures predict that everything that can be shaken will be shaken in the last days. We just got through an unpredictable time when some feared many things in our lives would temporarily be shaken or changed because of Y2K. Thank God, no major interruptions to our lives occurred, but many people, even Christians, were in a panic-survival mode. There is a place of security in which we can place ourselves, and this place will withstand every storm, every earthquake and every economic disaster. It is a place that will not be shaken today no matter what our circumstances are, and it will not be shaken in the future. This place will stand forever.

This place is the Father's heart. We can only reach this place if we surrender all to Him. When we trust in the Lord with all of our heart and refuse to lean on this world's system or any arm of flesh, we have completed our journey to the safe place—the Father's heart.

God's heart is ever turned to us, but unless we seek Him with all of our hearts, we will not experience the safe place of His presence. In His presence is fullness of joy even in the midst of grievous times. In His presence is peace that passes our understanding even when confusion seems to be reigning in the world. In His presence is comfort as well as victory in troubled times. This psalm clearly tells us what will stand forever: "The counsel of the LORD stands forever, the plans of His heart to all generations" (v. 11).

God's Word and the plans (or thoughts) of His heart will stand forever. Do you know that the Word tells us that His thoughts toward us outnumber the sands on the seashore? God is not surprised by anything we may face in the future. He has already gone ahead of us and provided a way of escape; a safe place in the midst of troubled times. After all, as this psalm says, "He spoke, and it was done; He commanded, and it stood fast" (v. 9). As we stand fast on His Word and are still in His presence, the earth can tremble, the storms can come, but we also will be able to stand forever.

Lord, help me not to fear evil tidings. Help me instead to place myself daily in Your presence. In Your Presence is where I belong for the rest of my days here on earth and also into eternity. Thank You for this safe place.

227

Spring Up, O Well!
Nehemiah 7:61–9:21

In today's passage we learn the importance of the joy of the Lord. Nehemiah says, "For the joy of the LORD is your strength" (Neh. 8:10). We saw this fact demonstrated in a dramatic way when we attended the first Jewish festival that was held in St. Petersburg, Russia. This festival was designed to reach out to the Jewish people. The music artists shared not only their music, but also their personal testimonies of how they came to know Jesus as their Messiah. The first evening as people gathered into the auditorium, I studied each face. The people seemed expressionless, almost without any emotion, and I did not see one smile. Then the music began.

At the end of the performance these dear Russians were out of their seats dancing joyously before the Lord. What happened? The well of the living water that seemed dry within them was primed, and they were able to drink from the wells of salvation with joy. Many were saved that night, and for the first time living water began to bubble within them, and then it overflowed.

On that night I understood the assignment that was given to me as we traveled throughout Russia. The Lord had spoken to my heart, and He told me to speak aloud in the metro and on the streets of Russia these words, "Spring up, O well!"

Russia had just been delivered out of seventy years of Communism's oppression. God desired to dress the Russian people with the garment of praise that would lift their heaviness. So many in Russia have a serious drinking problem and we learn in Scripture that it is the spirit of heaviness that often causes dependency upon alcohol. People self-medicate to lift their spirits with the wrong kind of spirit (alcoholic beverages) when only the Lord can lift our spirits permanently. On this night, those attending the concert were ignited by the joy of the Lord. They all would need this joy to strengthen them for the troubled days ahead.

All believers have a well within them that they can daily draw from to sustain them and give them strength. They draw from this well with buckets of joy. Sometimes we do not feel joyful, but if we will prime our well by praising the Lord anyway, suddenly the joy of our salvation is restored. Don't fail today to let your well of salvation spring up and overflow. Say to your soul today, "Spring up, O well!"

> Lord, I need strength to face this day, and I know Your joy is my strength. By faith, even though at first I feel nothing, I choose to praise You. Spring up, O well, and let Your joy overflow from my soul.

Daily Positioning Ourselves to Receive Blessing
Psalm 34:1–10

What a thrill it is for us to watch our grandchildren as they begin to crawl first, and then pull themselves up to a standing position. Shortly thereafter they begin to take their first steps. Sometimes, however, in their efforts to pull themselves up to the standing position, their legs get tangled and they cannot move. Someone has to come to their rescue and position them once again so they can hold on and stand up.

God, our heavenly Father, also delights as He sees us pulling ourselves up spiritually to a standing position. He knows that once we are in a standing position, we are ready to walk in the Spirit as our spiritual legs are strengthened. It grieves Him when we get tangled with sin and the world because then we are paralyzed and unable to walk in the spirit. In His mercy He often comes to our rescue and reveals our sin to us so we can confess, repent and become untangled with sin and all its consequences.

Today's psalm gives us several ways we can position ourselves to receive the strength of the Lord to walk in the Spirit. Walking in the Spirit always results in great blessing. Let's look at some of these ways to position ourselves to constantly walk in the Spirit:

1. Have a grateful heart. Bless the Lord and praise Him (v. 1).
2. Brag on the Lord. Tell others what He has done for you (v. 2).
3. Make the Lord the most important person in your life (v. 3).
4. Seek the Lord daily and fellowship with Him (v. 4).
5. Pray and cry out to the Lord for deliverance from all your troubles (v. 6).
6. Fear Him. Stand in awe of His goodness and worship Him (v. 7).
7. Enjoy the Lord. Delight yourself in Him and taste His goodness (v. 8).
8. Trust in Him with all of your heart (v. 8).

When we do the above things, we are in a position to walk in the Spirit all the day long. We can position ourselves this morning in our prayer time as we enter into His gates with thanksgiving. Rehearse all of His works and wonders; seek Him and fellowship with Him. Fear and stand in awe of Him as you worship Him. Make your petitions known to Him, enjoy His presence and trust Him with your day today. Now you are ready to walk today in the Spirit, and you have positioned yourself to receive every blessing God has designed for you this day.

Lord, I enter your presence this morning through prayer, and I look forward to walking with You all day. Thank You for the blessings that await me.

READ: Nehemiah 11:1–12:26; 1 Corinthians 10:15–11:2; Psalm 34:11–22; Proverbs 24:14–16

What Would Jesus Do?
1 Corinthians 10:15–11:2

Many today are wearing a bracelet with the initials *W.W.J.D*? This stands for, "What would Jesus do?" My older sister was impressed with a family who counseled their children to ask "What would Jesus do?" when they were wrestling with whether to do something or not. The answer to the question "What would Jesus do?" is always the same. The answer is, "Jesus would always do what would bring glory to His heavenly Father."

In this passage Paul gives the right answer also to this question. He says simply, "Whether you eat or drink, or whatever you do, do all to the glory of God" (1 Cor. 10:31).

The above statement is a great measuring rod we can use to determine if we should do something or not. We need to ask ourselves the question, "Is what I am about to say or do going to glorify my heavenly Father?" If it will not glorify Him, then we should not say or do it.

Sin is simply falling short of the glory of God. We will not fall short of the glory of God if we are constantly seeking to glorify Him. A prayer I try to pray every morning is the one below. You might want to join me in praying it this morning.

Father, help me today to say and do only those things that will bring glory to You. I offer the members of my body—my mind to think Your thoughts, my tongue to extol You and to speak edifying things to others, my hands to do Your works and my feet to walk in Your ways and Your will today.

READ: Nehemiah 12:27–13:31; 1 Corinthians 11:3–16; Psalm 35:1–16; Proverbs 21:17–18

Cleansing the Chambers
Nehemiah 12:27–13:31

Have you ever been in a home where the garbage has not been emptied for days, the dishes are stacked a mile high, and bed sheets have not been changed for months? When my son was on drugs and living with two other boys in a rental house, I went to visit him. No one answered the door, but the door was opened, so I thought maybe Ray was sleeping. I opened the door, and what faced me was unbelievable. It was just like the home I described above. When I discovered no one was home, I set about to straighten things out as best as I could. After two hours of work and a spray of room deodorizer, the house was in much better order.

We may never neglect our own home this way, but we can neglect our own temple. Our bodies are the home of the Holy Spirit, and often we need to cleanse the chambers of this home. The garbage of unconfessed sin and the wrong attitudes that keep us from serving God with our whole heart can cause quite a stench in the our personal temples. Confusion can clutter the chambers of our mind, and doubt and unbelief can soon gain a foothold.

In our reading today we see where Nehemiah had to cleanse the chambers where Tobiah lived. Tobiah had taken the things that belonged to the priests and had hidden them in his chambers. Tobiah was an enemy of Israel and Nehemiah. He had scorned Nehemiah as he set about to rebuild the walls of the city. Eliashib prepared a chamber in the house of the Lord for this enemy of Israel to live. When Nehemiah found out about this, he said, "And it grieved me sore: therefore I cast forth all the household stuff of Tobiah out of the chamber. Then I commanded, and they cleansed the chambers: and thither brought I again the vessels of the house of God, with the meat offering and the frankincense" (Neh. 13:8–9, KJV).

Tobiah, an enemy of God, had been enjoying all the things that belonged to the priests. We too have an enemy who loves to rob us of the things of God that belong to us as priests. Jesus calls Satan a thief and a liar who is out to destroy us. If we allow Satan to house himself in one of the chambers of our temple (our mind, soul or body, which is the temple of the Holy Spirit), we will begin to stink with sin. Make no mistake. Satan wants to take over not just one chamber in your holy temple, but he wants to take over your entire body and use it for his dirty work. If we fail to cleanse the chambers of our home where the Holy Spirit lives, then before you know it, the dirt and filth of Satan will spread into more chambers. We will find ourselves far away from the sweet aroma of the presence of the Lord Jesus Christ. We are holy vessels that contain the Holy Spirit. I am challenged by this reading, and I hope you are challenged also to do a house cleaning daily through confession and repentance of sins.

READ: Esther 1:1–3:15; 1 Corinthians 11:17–34; Psalm 35:17–28; Proverbs 21:19–20

The Righteous Tongue
Psalm 35:17–28

Many years ago I did a study on the tongue of the righteous and the tongue of the wicked. This study revealed to me the power of the tongue and led me to write a book called *The Tongue—a Mighty Weapon.* Whenever I give talks to others, I like to speak about the power of our words and what God created our tongues to do. There is a psalm that says, "He that orders his conversation aright glorifies the Lord." (See Psalm 50:23.) Our tongues were made to glorify the Lord, to praise Him, to worship Him, to encourage and edify others, and to share the gospel with them.

Satan, however, wants to use our tongues to wound and hurt others and ourselves. In Mexico when I was teaching young children, I asked them this question, "How many of you would like to totally disarm the devil today?" They all eagerly raised their hands. Then I instructed them to stick out their tongues. "Now pull your tongue out," I shared, and of course they laughed because no one could pull their tongue out. Then I said, "If we could pull our tongues out we would disarm the devil." Another proverb says, "He that keeps his lips is wise and he keeps his soul from trouble." (See Proverbs 21:23.)

In this psalm David says, "And my tongue shall speak of Your righteousness and of Your praise all the day long" (v. 28).

If we made our goal daily to speak of His righteousness and to give the Lord praise, our tongues would not be available to the devil to do his dirty work for him. Today let your tongue glorify and extol the Lord in praise as you share with others all of His wonders and works.

Lord, help me to order my conversation aright today so that I glorify You always with my tongue.

READ: Esther 4:1–7:10; 1 Corinthians 12:1–26; Psalm 36:1–12; Proverbs 21:21–22

God's Character
Psalm 36:1–12

The reason people do not trust God is because they do not have a complete view of His character. To trust anyone we must know that this person speaks truthfully, has no guile and has our best interest at heart. The Psalm and Proverb readings today express so beautifully God's character. In Psalm 36:1–12 we see these attributes of God's character listed:

1. God is merciful—His mercy extends to us from heaven (v. 5).
2. God is faithful—His faithfulness reaches the clouds (v. 5).
3. God is righteous—His righteousness is like the great mountains (v. 6).
4. God is just—His judgments are great and deep (v. 6).
5. God is loving and kind—His loving-kindness is excellent (v. 7).
6. God is provider, protector and preserver (vv. 6–8).
7. God is a life giver—in Him is the fountain of life (v. 9).

After listing all of these wonderful character traits of God, David speaks of the one thing that keeps us from trusting God: pride. David says, "Let not the foot of pride come against me" (v. 11).

The pride of life is trusting ourselves and our own resources more than we trust in God. We fail to trust God because we have an idol we worship more than we worship God. That idol is self.

In our Proverb reading we see how we can pull down the idol of self in our own lives. Solomon writes, "He that follows after righteousness and mercy finds life, righteousness and honor." We all want to be significant, but in God's kingdom we must lose our life to find our life. When we stop trusting in ourselves more than we trust in God, we will really begin living because His life becomes our life. Remember, He is the fountain of life. As long as we take control of our own lives rather than surrendering them to God, we are on a road that will lead to death. We are on a dead-end street. Jesus came that we might have life and have it more abundantly, but we have to walk in His ways and allow Him to take over our wills for us to experience the abundant blessings promised to us.

Father, when I meditate on Your character, I gain confidence to put my trust completely in You. You know what is best for me; often I do not have a clue. Help me to always pull down the stronghold of pride in my life. The moment I feel I have everything under control, help me recognize quickly that I am headed for a fall. Pride always leads to a fall. Help me to stop trusting in myself and my own ability and surrender my will to You.

Why Faith, Hope and Love Last Forever
1 Corinthians 12:27–13:13

Most people are familiar with this passage of Scripture. It is often used in wedding ceremonies and often referred to as the "Love Chapter." Chapter 13 of 1 Corinthians has much to say about love, but because of its familiarity we often miss the rich depth of this passage. After reading this passage one day, I asked the Lord a simple question that I have always wondered about. I asked Him why faith, hope and love last forever. In response to my question, I heard with my spiritual ears the following: "Faith, hope and love last forever because they are the eternal soul of Jesus Christ. Your soul consists of mind, emotion and will. Jesus also had a soul, but His soul was without sin. He had no lusts, even though He felt what it was like for you to be tempted. He was touched with the feelings of all of your weaknesses. His mind, however, was filled with faith; His emotions were anchored by hope, and His will was controlled by love."

As I meditated on what I heard in my spirit that day, I began to recall scriptures that confirmed this Word to me. I thought about the times Jesus was moved with compassion upon the people. His will was always to do the will of the Father, and God is love. His will was always controlled by love. Jesus felt all the emotions we feel, but He never lost hope. His hope was firmly anchored in the purpose for which He had come. He knew He would provide the way when He died on the cross and was resurrected to secure permanent hope for all mankind. The moment the veil of the temple was rent, God threw out the anchor of hope from His throne room, and now we all have the hope of eternal life and fellowship with the Father always. Jesus never doubted His destiny. He had faith always that the will of the Father would be accomplished in His life. His destiny was to become sin for us. Yes, the one who knew no sin at all would become sin for our sakes that we might be delivered from the power of sin in our lives.

Daily we are being conformed to the image of Christ as we cooperate with the Holy Spirit in this process. Our destiny is to have a soul like that of Jesus. The Holy Spirit is transforming us by the renewal of our minds as we read, hear and obey God's Word. Faith is ever growing in our minds and hearts. The Holy Spirit is constantly reminding us that our hope should always be placed in Jesus. It is our hope of eternal life that provides the anchor for our emotions when the seas of life get rough. The Holy Spirit prompts us to humble ourselves and surrender our wills by casting every care upon Jesus. When we do this, the Holy Spirit is able to shed abroad in our hearts the very love of Jesus Christ. Is it well with your soul today? Are you cooperating with this marvelous transforming power of the Holy Spirit? Today is a good day to pray:

Lord, mold me and melt me. Make me after Thy will while I am waiting, yielded and still. AMEN.

234

August 21

READ: Job 1:1–3:26; 1 Corinthians 14:1–17; Psalm 37:12–28; Proverbs 21:25–26

The Blessings of the Righteous
Psalm 37:12–28

We have talked a lot about the blessings that come to those who have been made righteous through Jesus Christ and who abide daily in Him and His Word. I did a study once on the multitude of blessings that actually overtake those who fear the Lord and who walk uprightly with Him. Of course, the blessings to the righteous do not guarantee they will not experience troubles. In fact, the Word of God says we will be persecuted for righteousness' sake, and yet even with this will come a blessing. The Word also says many are the afflictions of the righteous, but the Lord Himself delivers them out of them all. We have to remember that the end of every trial in a righteous person's life will develop something better in our lives than before. Our readings for the rest of this month in Job certainly prove this to be true.

The afflictions a righteous person suffers will develop character traits that are Christlike in him. The only way the fruit of patience can develop in our lives is through experiencing trials and temptations. You have heard people probably exhort you not to pray for patience because only tribulation works patience in our lives. Even though we will experience many troubles in our lives, we have a sure promise that if we walk uprightly, God will deliver us either in or out of these troubles.

David lists some of the blessings of righteous people in this psalm.

1. The righteous person has provision.
2. The righteous person is upheld by the Lord.
3. The righteous person has an eternal inheritance.
4. The righteous man is never put to shame.
5. The righteous person will be satisfied by the Lord even in hard times.
6. The righteous person obtains mercy because he is merciful.
7. The righteous person inherits the earth.
8. The righteous person has direction because his steps are ordered by the Lord.
9. The righteous person is never forsaken.
10. The righteous person will never be utterly cast down.
11. The righteous person will have direction because the Lord will order his steps.
12. The righteous person is preserved forever.

You have heard of the many twelve step programs offered today. There is only one step you need to take to receive all twelve of these blessings. That step is to receive Jesus Christ as your Savior and Lord.

Let All Things Be Done to Edify
1 Corinthians 14:18–40

As Paul was giving instructions to the church about how their services were to be conducted, he exhorted the church to let everything be done to edify. How different our lives would be if the motivation of our relationships with others was always to edify them— to build up one another in love. Our conversations would be seasoned with grace, and we would never be condescending, judgmental or critical in our words to others. We would esteem one another higher than ourselves, and we would ever be on the alert to serve and support one another in love.

I try to ask myself the following questions before I say anything:

1. Will what I have to say build up or tear down?
2. Will what I have to say add or subtract from the kingdom of God, which is righteousness, peace and joy in the Holy Spirit?
3. Will what I have to say bless or burden the person I am talking to?
4. Is what I say pure, lovely, virtuous and of good report?

If we all stopped to ask ourselves these questions before we speak, we would be men and women of few words. We would also be blessed men and women because we would be a blessing to others. We would save ourselves from many troubles if we spoke only those things that edify. Proverbs 21:23 says, "Whoever guards his mouth and tongue keeps his soul from troubles."

Join me as I pray for the Lord to let the law of kindness always be upon my lips.

Lord, I have blown it so many times by saying things that were unwise. I humbly ask for Your forgiveness, and now I ask for Your supernatural ability, Your grace, to season my tongue with kindness and enable me to speak only those things that edify. Thank You.

Who Is Our Daysman?
Job 8:1–11:20

Job in this passage cries out for a daysman to stand between him and God. He was crying out for a mediator between God and himself. Job did not know that God's plan from the beginning of the earth was to provide such a daysman. Jesus Christ, who would be our intercessor and our redeemer, is now our daysman or mediator who stands on our behalf before God. Later as we read the Book of Job, we see how God revealed His plan to Job, and Job finally knew he had a redeemer—one who could buy back everything he had lost, one who could redeem his very own soul from destruction.

We are all familiar with Handel's *Messiah* and the part that declares, "I know that my redeemer liveth, and He will stand in the latter day." This is based on what Job finally knew in the Spirit. Job knew one day he would stand before God justified and made righteous because of his faith in this redeemer. Job also believed in the resurrection because he says later that his flesh would see God.

Job knew Jesus by the revelation of the Holy Spirit even as David knew Him. Even though Jesus had not been born as a babe in Bethlehem, He was seated next to the Father making intercession for Job and for David. Jesus was with God in the beginning of Creation, and by and through Jesus was everything made. He is the living Word who flung the universe into being, and later He was the Word made flesh.

Thank God we can know our redeemer personally. We have an advantage over David and Job. We can read about our redeemer's life on earth, the people He touched, the conversations He had with the Father and others, the experience He had on the cross, and His death, burial, resurrection and ascension to His former place—the right hand of the Father.

Join me as I praise Jesus, my redeemer, my daysman, who enables me to stand before the Father because of His righteousness. The Father through the Son has redeemed me from a life of darkness in sin and has translated me into His kingdom of light, which is filled with His righteousness, peace and joy. I can say with Job, "I know my redeemer lives, and one day my flesh will see Him face to face." What a day it will be when I see my daysman face to face. Hallelujah!!

The Gift of Helplessness
Job 12:1–15:35

Throughout our lives there is one goal God has for us. His goal is that we become totally dependent upon Him. There is also one goal Satan has for us as we live our lives on earth. His goal is that we become totally independent. Interdependency is God's heart for us. Independence is Satan's plan for us.

Here in this passage from Job we see how Job knew he could do nothing without God. He had to trust God in everything simply because everything that exists came from God. Job says with God is strength and wisdom. He has the power to make the weak strong and the strong weak. He is in charge of nations. Our days are determined by Him.

Because Job knew the power and greatness of God, his only choice in this life was to trust Him with His life, possessions and everything. Job says, "Though He slay me, yet will I trust Him" (Job 13:15).

Knowing God's power and wisdom caused Job to acknowledge that his own ways were ever before the Lord. He was completely dependent upon the Lord. He says, "The hand of the Lord has wrought everything and the soul of every man and every living thing is in His hands. He gives breath to every living thing." (See Job 12:9–10.)

Job was able to get through his trials because he knew his life was in God's hands. He had to depend upon Him and Him alone. This is called the gift of helplessness. God gave Job the gift of helplessness that opened the door for him to have the revelation of the Lord of lords, King of kings, his redeemer and his restorer. Job had nowhere to go but the Lord. His friends offered little comfort, and his wife exhorted him to curse God and die. Job had no where to look but up. His circumstances were so traumatic that if he dwelled on them, he would be swallowed up with cares. Because of God's beautiful gift of helplessness, he had no other choice but to release all of his cares to his redeemer. The rest of Job's story reveals God's love and care for Job.

Catherine Marshall, the author of many books and wife of Peter Marshall, a well-known Presbyterian pastor and one time chaplain of the Senate, tells the story of when she contracted TB. She could do nothing but lie in the bed for several years. Then one day she recognized that she was closer to God than she had ever been in her life, and she thanked God for the gift of helplessness. She told the Lord if she had to be bed bound the rest of her life, she was willing to be if she could continue to know His presence as she did. Shortly after this declaration to the Lord, Catherine was healed and raised up off her sick bed. Helplessness brings total release.

Let Everything Be Done With Love
1 Corinthians 16:1–24

Paul exhorts in his letter to the Corinthians that everything we do be done in love. What a great idea! Actually this is not an idea at all. It is a commandment. Jesus summed up the whole law in two commandments—love the Lord your God with all your heart, and love your neighbor as yourself. If love were our motivation in everything we did, our lives would be blessed.

I often say to my husband, "Life would be so easy if people would just love one another." Most of the difficulties we have in our relationships with others are because we have pride or a selfish attitude. We are easily offended because we are not walking in love. We become bitter in trials instead of better because we are not walking in love.

One of my dearest prayer partners always spoke on love whenever she was called to speak at a meeting. She said love never fails. I do not believe the body of Christ needs more teaching. I believe they simply need to focus on these two commandments. If they did this, the world would take note. The mark of a Christian, Frances Schaeffer said, is love. "See how they love one another" was a statement made about the early church. I pray it is a statement that can be made about the church today. Church splits always happen for one reason. Pride raises its ugly head, and no one is willing to humble himself and ask forgiveness. What a testimony it would be if those who have left the local bodies came back and said, "I want to ask your forgiveness. I was wrong to cause division in this church."

When the world sees churches splitting and leaders in moral sin, the world can say with grounds, "The church is filled with hypocrites." When there are differences between husband and wives, the root of the problem is always pride. Pride is the great enemy of love, and we need to constantly pull down any stronghold of pride in our own lives. Love covers a multitude of sins also. The nit-picking that goes on in churches would cease if we walked in love. Listen carefully to Paul's exhortation to the church: "Watch, stand fast in the faith, be brave, be strong. Let all that you do be done with love" (vv. 13–14).

I believe Paul was saying, "Quit acting childish, and act with maturity." A young child is selfish in nature and cries when he can't have his way. It is time for the church to rise up like men and be willing to even lay our lives down for one another if needed—what a revolutionary idea. Once again, this is not an idea. Jesus said the man who is willing to lose his life would gain his life. Are you willing to lose for the sake of love?

Lord, forgive me for the times I have allowed my selfish pride to stand in the way of love. Help me to constantly pull this stronghold down in my life and give me the grace (Your supernatural ability) to walk in love always.

The Benefits of Humility
Proverbs 22:2–4

Yesterday we shared how the major thing that stands in the way of our doing all things with love is pride. Today we look at the benefits of humility. Jesus was the perfect example of humility. We are told in the Scriptures that He humbled Himself and became a servant. He emptied Himself of everything but love. God is love. He issues the invitation to every one to come to Him and learn meekness and lowliness of heart. Truly I believe Jesus is the only one who can help us learn all about humility. There have been many wonderful books written on humility. But none of those books will change us unless we are willing to sit at the feet of the Great Teacher who can instruct us perfectly in meekness and lowliness of heart.

The benefits of humility are many. Three of these benefits are listed in this proverb: "By humility and the fear of the LORD are riches and honor and life."

The riches spoken of here are not necessarily material wealth. Some of the poorest people on earth are the meekest people. In our travels to Mexico and India we saw some of the poorest people on earth. Their humility put me to shame. I remember a camp meeting in Mexico when these poor Mexicans were flat on their faces before the Lord worshiping Him with all of their hearts. I didn't want to get on the floor because it was dirty. Lord, forgive me. These people were poor financially, but they were rich spiritually. They knew the joy of the Lord and His peace, and they expressed it boldly.

We are exhorted by Peter to humble ourselves by casting every care upon the Lord. This is another great benefit of humility. Humble people do not have one care on this earth. They have given every care into the hands of Jesus. Whenever we become anxious about anything, we are in pride. We are not trusting the Lord, and we have not released our cares to Him. He truly cares for us. We will only find rest for our souls when we humble ourselves and cast every care upon Him.

Another benefit of humility is that we can see ourselves as Jesus sees us. People who are always down on themselves and feel rejected are in just as much pride as those who think too highly of themselves. Jesus sees you as a person worth dying for. Who are you to be down on yourself? You are His priceless treasure.

Exaltation is another benefit of humility. Every one on this earth longs for riches, honor and life, and all of this is found in the kingdom of God. To enter this kingdom we must humble ourselves and say, "I need You, Jesus." When we say those words, Jesus hears, and we begin the lifelong process of learning meekness and lowliness of heart from Him. When we enter this kingdom, we are exalted to the high position of kings and priests.

READ: Job 23:1–27:23; 2 Corinthians 1:12–2:8; Psalm 41:1–13; Proverbs 22:5–6

The Word of God Esteemed Higher Than Food
Job 23:1–27:23

As a mother of three growing boys and a husband who all love to eat, I spent most of my time in the kitchen cooking for this hungry brood. One of my favorite scriptures in the Bible is found in Psalm 86, where a verse reads, "He delivered my hands from the pots." I have been standing on this promise for years, but I find myself still cooking.

Another promise the Lord gave me is in this passage of Job. One day after sweating in the kitchen putting together one more meal for these meat-and-potato men, I heard the Lord speak to my heart: "The day will come when your family will count My Word as more important than their necessary food." When I heard this word I did not know it was in the Scriptures, but later I found it in Job 23:12: "I have not departed from the commandment of His lips; I have treasured the words of His mouth more than my necessary food."

It was almost too good to be true. Could it be that the day would come when the first thing the boys did before they ate breakfast was to read God's Word? Could it be that one day some of my men would even miss a meal in order to fast and seek God? Could it be that one day my hands truly would be delivered from the pots? Yes, it could be!! Hallelujah!! I have seen this promise fulfilled in the lives of my men. They still love to eat, but they now eat to live instead of living to eat. Their lives are sold out to Jesus, and they esteem His Word highly. His Word is the daily bread we need. Don't miss any meals feasting with God in His Word this week.

Savor the Flavor
2 Corinthians 2:9–17

One of my favorite things to do when I was a child was to lick the bowl after my mother made homemade fudge or lace cookies. I savored the flavor as I first used a spoon to scoop the leftover batter, and then I would use my tongue to make sure I had not missed one morsel. I savored the flavor.

Paul, in his letter to the Corinthians, speaks of every Christian as the sweet savor of Christ to God. He says, "Now thanks be unto God, which always causeth us to triumph in Christ and maketh manifest the savour of his knowledge by us in every place. For we are unto God a sweet savour of Christ, in them that are saved, and in them that perish. To the one we are the savour of death unto death; and to the other the savour of life unto life. And who is sufficient for these things?" (vv. 14–16, KJV).

Webster's defines *savor* as "that quality of something which acts on our sense of taste or smell." As representatives of Jesus Christ in the world we should transmit to others both a sweet smell and a good taste. We are the salt of the earth, and if you have ever tasted a dish with no salt added, you know how important salt is. Salt enhances the flavor of things and also preserves them. As the salt of the earth we need to enhance the flavor of this world. People around us, whether saved or not saved, should be attracted to our flavor. There should be such a contagious joy and peace in our lives that people want to hang around us and savor the flavor of Christ in our lives. Some may even ask such questions as, "Why are you so joyful?" "Why do you have such peace when every thing is this world seems to be falling apart?" "What is the reason for your hope?"

When we enter a room of people, we should bring the sweet odor of the presence of the Lord with us. I'll never forget the time I took my mother to a women's retreat. Her favorite perfume was Tea Rose. One morning as we took our seats for the morning talk, a lady in front of us said, "The presence of the Lord truly is here, and He smells just like roses." We did not say a word because we did not want to burst her bubble. People, however, should be able to smell the presence of the Lord wherever we go, and they should be able to taste and see that the Lord is good as we share the good things He has done in our lives.

> Lord, may those I see today savor the flavor of the life of Christ within me. May others desire to taste every morsel of Your Word as I share with them.

Looking in the Mirror
2 Corinthians 3:1-18

When I look in the mirror daily I notice I am aging. Each day there seem to be more wrinkles and brown spots. There is nothing I can do to stop the aging process. I cannot stop the clock from ticking. There is a mirror, however, I can look into, and I can be changed. I will not become more beautiful on the outside, but I will be more beautiful on the inside. This mirror is God's Word. As I look into this mirror I behold the glory of God, and that glory is contagious.

The image I behold in the mirror of God's Word is what I am destined to look like. The day will come when I will look like Jesus. No, I will not become Jesus. I will still be a woman, but the Scriptures promise that when I see Him I will be like Him. When I went to India I met a young man who I had a very hard time loving. He was manipulative, and this is something I hate. One day I told the Lord, "I'm looking forward to heaven, but if this young pastor is in heaven, I'd rather not see him." Then I heard with my spiritual ears these words: "Oh, you will love being with this young man because he will be just like Me." I knew this was the Lord, and I knew what He said was true. If there are people you have a hard time loving here on earth, you can look forward to seeing them in heaven because they will be just like Jesus.

Remember the witch in the fairy tale who said, "Mirror, mirror on the wall. Tell me who is the fairest of all." We know who is the fairest of all. Jesus Christ is the fairest of ten thousand. He is the Lily of the Valley and the Bright and Morning Star. The good news is I don't have to wait till I get to heaven to be more like Jesus. Each day I live and walk in the Spirit I am being conformed to His very image. As Christians we are all predestined to be conformed to the image of Jesus Christ. As we look daily into the mirror of His Word, we are changed from glory to glory. Paul says, "But we all, with unveiled face, beholding as in a mirror the glory of the Lord, are being transformed into the same image from glory to glory, just as by the Spirit of the Lord" (v. 18).

All that remains to be said is GLORY!

Thank You, Lord, for the promise that when I see You I will be like You. Help me to daily cooperate with the Holy Spirit as He changes me from glory to glory.

What Makes You Shine?
2 Corinthians 4:1–12

When our middle son was in China as a teacher of English for two years, one of his students asked Ron what made him shine. This student recognized the light of the Lord's countenance upon Ron. Paul tells us in this letter to the Corinthians that Jesus is the light who has shone into the darkness of our hearts. He says, "For God, who commanded the light to shine out of darkness, hath shined in our hearts, to give the light of the knowledge of the glory of God in the face of Jesus Christ. But we have this treasure in earthen vessels, that the excellency of the power may be of God, and not of us" (vv. 6–7, KJV).

Jesus is the light of the world that lights every man who is born into this world. Jesus calls us the light of the world, and He exhorts us to let our lights shine before men that they might see our good works and glorify the Father in heaven.

A candle shines the brightest in a very dark place. China is a country where much darkness exists. This is why the light of Jesus through Ron's face shone so brightly. We are all lights shining the midst of a very dark world.

I had the privilege of seeing the face of Jesus in a vision as I was waking from a Sunday nap. His face was encircled in light, and the expression on His face was one of exuberant joy, exhaustless love and empowering peace. When I saw His face, I asked the Father why He did not choose to show the face of Jesus to the whole world. I remember praying:

> Father, if I could just have a video of Jesus' face and could show it to all my lost friends, they would instantly repent. I know, Father, the love in that face would compel the worst sinner to turn from his ways to follow Jesus.

My request was answered with words that changed my life: "I have not chosen to reveal my Son's face to the world in such a way. Instead I have chosen all those in the body of Christ to reveal the face of Jesus to others through their faces."

Is the light of the glory of God in the face of Jesus Christ shining through your face today?

244

August 31

READ: Job 37:1–39:30; 2 Corinthians 4:13–5:11; Psalm 44:8–26; Proverbs 22:13

Faith Is Never Silent
2 Corinthians 4:13–5:11

The spirit of faith always causes us to speak. Faith is active, and faith is never silent. When faith is operative in our lives, we will speak about our faith to others. Paul says the following about the spirit of faith: "We having the same spirit of faith, according as it is written, I believed, and therefore have I spoken; we also believe, and therefore speak, knowing that he which raised up the Lord Jesus shall raise up us also by Jesus, and shall present us with you" (2 Cor. 4:13–14, KJV).

In his letter to the Romans, Paul quotes again a scripture from the writings of David. Paul writes, "But what saith it? The word is nigh thee, even in thy mouth, and in thy heart: that is, the word of faith, which we preach: That if thou shalt confess with thy mouth the Lord Jesus, and shalt believe in thine heart that God hath raised him from the dead, thou shalt be saved" (Rom. 10:8–9, KJV).

The scripture Paul referred to in both of these passages is found in Psalm 116:10. David says, "I believed, therefore I spoke."

The word of faith we all need to speak is that Jesus Christ is Lord. He lived; He died; He took away our sins; He was raised from the dead and now lives forever. This is the gospel in a nutshell. Every believer possesses these words of faith. The question is, Will we be diligent to release these words of faith to others?

If we believe that our faith is personal and something we do not want to share with others, I would question the faith we are claiming. True faith demands a verbal expression, "Go and tell!"

Who will you tell today?

September 1

The Great Exchange
2 Corinthians 5:12–21

My middle son, Ron, was in Bogota, Colombia on a mission journey. He went with a team into a drug dealing area called the Cartuge. His team visited a drug rehabilitation center there where criminals were learning about Jesus and being born again. When Ron entered the center he felt impressed by the Holy Spirit to offer to wash the feet of these men. Many of them did not know the story of Jesus' washing the feet of His disciples, so Ron read it to them. After the reading of the Scripture, the foot washing began.

Each team member knelt with a bowl of water and towel to minister to the man they felt the Holy Spirit wanted them to minister to on that day. One on the team members named Dave had just put on a brand-new pair of socks that morning. When Dave removed the socks from the man he was ministering to, he heard the Holy Spirit say, "Give him your socks." As soon as he finished praying for this man, Dave took off his socks and said, "I want you to have these. They are a gift to you." The man picked up his filthy socks and handed them to Dave. He said, "I want you to have my socks. They are a gift to you." Dave hesitated for a moment and then put this man's stinky socks on his feet and said, "Thank you."

What a great demonstration of exactly what happened on the cross. Our reading today says, "That is, that God was in Christ reconciling the world to Himself, not imputing their trespasses to them, and has committed to us the word of reconciliation. Now then, we are ambassadors for Christ, as though God were pleading through us; we implore you on Christ's behalf, be reconciled to God. For He made Him who knew no sin to be sin for us, that we might become the righteousness of God in Him" (vv. 19–21).

On the cross Jesus was willing to wear our filthy socks of sin so that we could have the clean socks of His righteousness. He dressed us in His robe of righteousness. He who knew no sin became sin for us that we might be made the righteousness of God in Him. Because of this divine exchange we can live a new, clean spotless life!! What an exchange!!

Lord, often I feel I have nothing to give You, and then You remind me I can always give You my own sins. When I do this by confessing my sins, You give me the gift of cleanness of heart and mind. Help me to never wear the dirty socks of sin by refusing to confess my sins so not only can You forgive me, but also cleanse me of all unrighteousness.

September 2

READ: Ecclesiastes 1:1–3:22; 2 Corinthians 6:1–13; Psalm 46:1–11; Proverbs 22:15

In His Time
Ecclesiastes 1:1–3:22

Solomon says, "He has made everything beautiful in its time" (Eccles. 3:11). God's timing is not our timing. We go through so much in this life, and often what we go through is not pleasant. We wonder at those times what good will come from such trying experiences. Over my fifty years as a Christian I have experienced many trials and tribulations. I can honestly say now, however, that all these difficult times have worked for the good in my life.

The good those trying times have worked in my life is the change of character I have experienced. My greatest desire is to grow more like Jesus every day I live. Even the most horrific trials have woven something of the character of Christ in me. Jesus learned obedience through the things He suffered. Is there any other way we can learn obedience? If there is, I have not found it yet.

I recall hearing a lady speak on suffering, and at that time I did not receive her message. I was young in spiritual things and felt that God would certainly see to it that I lived a blessed life without much suffering. Then I realized if I wanted to be like Jesus, I too must drink of His cup of suffering. Tough times always draw me nearer to Jesus. When things are going well in my life, sometimes I do not spend the time with the Lord I should, and soon I begin to sail through life without depending upon His daily guidance and presence. Each difficulty I experience sends me to the Word of God and to His throne room of grace. When I cry out to God in my distress, He hears me and lifts my soul to a higher place than before.

When I cling to Jesus and cry out to Him, I discover the secret of overcoming whatever crisis I face. I learn that obedience is an act of my will and has little to do with how I feel at the moment. In His presence when I approach His throne in time of need, I abandon my will to Him, and He sets the sail of my will to ride through whatever storm I am experiencing.

The reading in Psalms today says it all. "God is our refuge and strength, a very present help in trouble. Therefore we will not fear, even though the earth be removed, and though the mountains be carried into the midst of the sea; though its waters roar and be troubled, though its mountains shake with its swelling. Selah" (vv. 1–2).

Whatever you are going through today, God intends to make it beautiful in His time. He is the Creator, and He is creating you into His image through every trial you experience—and Jesus is beautiful.

Lord, help me to surrender daily to Your beautiful, creative will.

READ: Ecclesiastes 4:1–6:12; 2 Corinthians 6:14–7:7; Psalm 47:1–9; Proverbs 22:16

We Shall Return the Same Way We Came
Ecclesiastes 4:1–6:12

When Ron, our middle son, was about eight years old, he asked us this question: "When we meet Jesus in the air, will we have on any clothes?" My husband thought for a moment, and then said with an official scholarly voice, "Son, the Bible says naked we come into the world and naked we leave the world." Our son surprised us with his response when he said, "Streakers in the sky." The whole family laughed uncontrollably. The thought expressed, however, is true. We cannot take it with us. As some have said, "I have never seen a hearse pulling a U-Haul."

So many in this life spend years accumulating material things that will not be translated to heaven with us. The Egyptians used to fill their tombs with riches in the hope that those treasures would go with them into the next life.

When my mother died I was made acutely aware of how our earthly possessions can be quickly dispersed or dissolved. When my mother was first widowed we were faced with closing up the house she had lived in for over thirty years. The attic and basement were bulging with things she had saved over the years. My sister and her husband gave most of this away and only kept the essentials she would need in her new apartment. All of her earthly belongings at that time were reduced to fit into a two-bedroom apartment. When she had her stroke and had to live in a nursing home, we had to reduce her belongings to fit into one room because we knew she would never return to her apartment. After her death, I gathered up her things in her room in the nursing home; they all fit into three plastic trash bags.

My favorite definition of heaven is, "Heaven is where there will be no stuff." We should all be challenged by the goal to accumulate in our lifetime those things that will be translated with us to heaven. What can we take with us? There are only four things we can take with us to heaven: the people we have witnessed to, the Word of God we have hidden in our hearts and sown into others, the prayers we have prayed and all the times we have spoken about the Lord to others. In fact, a book of remembrance is in heaven, and each time we remember the Lord and His mighty works and talk about Him to others, we add to our book of remembrance. These are the treasures we can take from earth to heaven.

Lord, help me to invest more in people than I do in things. I don't need more stuff, and there are so many who need You. Lead me to someone today with whom I can share the greatest treasure of all—Jesus Christ and His kingdom.

READ: Ecclesiastes 7:1–9:18; 2 Corinthians 7:8–16; Psalm 48:1–14; Proverbs 22:17–19

Repentance
2 Corinthians 7:8–16

Repentance is a necessary step to salvation. Salvation, however, is a free gift that requires nothing but faith to receive it. The Bible tells us, "For by grace you have been saved through faith, and that not of yourselves; it is the gift of God, not of works, lest anyone should boast" (Eph. 2:8–9).

Isn't repentance a work that we do? The repentance necessary for salvation is the repentance from our unbelief to faith. We turn away from our unbelief, and we receive the gift of faith to believe that Jesus died for our sins, was buried, was raised from the dead and now sits on the right hand of God to make intercession for us.

Paul writes, "For godly sorrow produces repentance leading to salvation, not to be regretted; but the sorrow of the world produce death" (v. 10).

God gives us sorrow for our sinful life through conviction of our own sin and through convincing us of our desperate need for a Savior. This sorrow brings us to a place where we cry out to God for forgiveness, and He gives us the gift of faith then to believe. Only after salvation do we have the power to overcome the sin in our lives and to turn completely away from it. When we examine the process of salvation in our lives, we suddenly realize it is all a grace work of God. Our part is simply to receive His gift of faith and believe. Belief is truly the only work of God that is required for salvation. Jesus made this clear in the passage below. "What shall we do, that we might work the works of God? Jesus answered and said unto them, This is the work of God, that ye believe on him whom he hath sent" (John 6:28–29, KJV).

We see in the Scriptures how the exhortation to repent is usually followed with the exhortation to believe. Unless we repent of our unbelief, we cannot receive the gift of faith unto salvation. When we stand before God's throne, we will have nothing to boast about. We will bow before our Lord with thanksgiving because He alone has made salvation possible for us. God purchased us with the shed blood of Jesus so Jesus can present us before the Father spotless, shameless and faultless. Glory! How can anyone reject so great a salvation?

September 5

READ: Ecclesiastes 10:1–12:14; 2 Corinthians 8:1–15; Psalm 49:1–20; Proverbs 22:20–21

To Sum It Up!
Ecclesiastes 10:1–12:14

Ecclesiastes is a rather negative book written by one of the wisest men who ever lived. Solomon, however, saves his wisest words for the conclusion of Ecclesiastes. After sharing that all of life is vanity, Solomon does give the major priority of life. If we lived our lives on earth with what he shares as our first priority, the conclusion of our lives would not be vanity. The conclusion of our lives would be lives lived to the glory, honor and praise of God.

What is this priority? Solomon speaks these words of wisdom: "Let us hear the conclusion of the whole matter: Fear God and keep His commandments, for this is man's all" (Eccles. 12:13).

This admonition sounds very much like the statement made by the One who is all wisdom, Jesus Christ. Jesus replied to the question, "What is the greatest commandment?" with these wise words: "Thou shalt love the Lord thy God with all thy heart, and with all thy soul, and with all thy mind. This is the first and great commandment. And the second is like unto it, Thou shalt love thy neighbour as thyself" (Matt. 22:37–39, KJV).

Each day I live I am reminded to keep the main thing the main thing. Both Solomon and Jesus shared with us what the main thing is. To sum it all up: The main thing is to love God and love your neighbor. Why is it so hard to do this? Love benefits all concerned. Love benefits the one who gives love and the one who receives love. I often tell my husband, "Life would be so easy if people would just love one another." This is another "sum it all up" statement that is true. This does not mean life will be without difficulties and trials, but love will carry us through every trouble. The reason people find it so hard to love one another is simple. Love never fails. Satan knows this, so he works tirelessly to cause division and strife, bitterness, jealousy, pride and anger in our lives. The price to love another is the same. It means laying down our pride. Pride causes selfishness, strife and jealousy. Another reason it is so hard for us to love God and others is because we cannot do it in our own strength. We must depend upon God to shed the love of God abroad from our hearts, and often we do not daily submit ourselves to Him for that wonderful work to be accomplished in us. Perhaps you will want to join me this morning in a prayer that sums it all up:

Lord, I love You. Help me to love today as Jesus loves. Amen.

250

September 6

Conversations
Psalm 50:1–23

With the introduction of TV and the computer, we have become a generation of listeners and receivers, not speakers and givers. In the advancement of technology we have lost one of the greatest arts—the art of conversation. I heard recently that a father spends on the average one-half an hour weekly speaking to his children.

When God created us, He created us for His pleasure. An important part of His pleasure was to hear our voice praising and worshiping Him. Our psalm reading today tells us whoever offers praise glorifies God, and God will show His salvation to the person who orders his conversation aright. The word *salvation* means wholeness in every way. This psalm is saying the person who has a wholesome tongue will lead a wholesome life (a life of salvation filled with wholeness in every area).

God loves to hear our voice, and if we do not fellowship with Him daily, He misses the sound of our voice. He also loves to hear us talk to others about Him, and He loves to hear our voice whenever we declare His Word.

One of our sons spent two years in China. During this period, I remember what a joy it was when we talked long distance. I loved hearing the sound of his voice and catching up on all of his news. During those conversations, there seemed to be no distance separating us. Whenever we take time to fellowship with the Lord, the distance between heaven and earth is dissolved. We experience His kingdom here on earth every time we talk with Him. Remember, prayer is simply talking to God, and it involves all the elements of conversation we use with our loved ones. Such conversations involve praise, information, requests, affirmation, etc. and listening to the one who is talking with us.

Does God seem distant from you today? Perhaps you have lost the art of conversing with Him in prayer. Prayer involves both speaking and listening to God. Prayer involves both giving and receiving. Remember, there is no time or space with God. He is as near to you as your next breath.

Start today by ordering your conversation aright by first talking to your first love, the Lord. He is waiting eagerly to hear your voice. Remember that He promises salvation (wholeness) to all those who order their conversations aright. Offer Him praise and glorify Him today.

Lord, forgive me for the many times I have missed fellowshiping with You. I know You love for me to talk with You daily. Help me not miss out on any conversations with You.

READ: Song of Solomon 5:1–8:14; 2 Corinthians 9:1–15; Psalm 51:1–19; Proverbs 22:24–25

The Power of Confession
Psalm 51:1–19

David was called a man after God's own heart. Yet, he was also a man who committed adultery. He was a man after God's own heart because he realized he sinned against God and confessed his sin before God and repented of it. God heard David's cry, and when the life of David was mentioned in Chronicles, his sin of adultery was not mentioned. God not only forgives, but He also forgets. He not only blots out our transgressions, but He also cleanses us. John writes about God's complete act of forgiveness in 1 John 1:9: "If we confess our sins, He is faithful and just to forgive us our sins and to cleanse us from all unrighteousness."

If we turn to God in humbleness of heart after we have sinned and confess our sin with a heart that seeks not to commit that sin again, God cleanses us and empowers us to overcome the next time we are tempted in that area.

God does not stop at forgiving and cleansing. He also empowers us to overcome temptation, and He restores the joy of our salvation. It never ceases to amaze me when I think of God's extravagant love. Paul writes of his desire that all know the height, the depth, the length and the width of God's love. The height of God's love is His grace that enables us to overcome whatever we need to overcome, especially sin. The depth of His love is His forgiveness that reaches into the deepest recesses of our heart to both forgive and cleanse. The length of His love is His mercy that endures forever to all generations. The width of His love is His truth that causes us to live free from bondage. Whenever we speak His truth, walk in His truth and are truthful about our own sin, we experience the boundless width of the freedom of His love.

David experienced the height, the depth, the length and the breadth of the love of God. He made himself available to experience God's extravagant love the moment he confessed and repented of his sin. The power of confession is that it provides the open door for us to receive the power of God's love.

Lord, reveal to me today if there is anything I need to confess to You. Help me to always have a heart toward You as I daily am honest with You about my own sin. I want to experience Your extravagant love today.

The Benefits of Obedience
Isaiah 1:1–2:22

Yesterday's devotion shared how complete God's forgiveness through Jesus Christ is. Jesus not only forgives us, but He also cleanses us, restores us and empowers us when we confess our sins to Him. The Book of Isaiah that we begin today reveals the heart of the Father so beautifully. Throughout your readings in Isaiah you will see the longing of God's heart to gather His little ones to Himself and to once again be in fellowship with them. He thirsted for fellowship with Israel, but their stiff-necked pride and rebellion separated them from the very One who always sought to do them good.

Israel was unwilling to obey God. The only thing God requires of us is a willingness to obey. He then supplies the power to obey. We will never enter into the attitude of an obedient heart unless we have faith and trust in God. Even our own relationships here tell us it is nearly impossible to obey someone in whom you have no faith or trust. The first step to obedience is trust. We must trust and rely on God more than we trust and rely on our own resources, our own strength or intellect. We must also have faith. This faith is more than just believing He exists. The kind of faith that works an obedient attitude into our hearts is the faith that believes God is a good God and that He is the rewarder of those who diligently seek Him.

Whenever you have a thought that God is mean or uncaring or that He has forgotten and abandoned you, reject that thought immediately. Those thoughts are lies from the enemy. Satan knows that if he can get us to doubt God's goodness, then we will be vulnerable to the temptation to rebel against what God has commanded. Satan pulled this trick in the Garden of Eden, and he was successful. He put doubt into the mind of Eve by getting her to think God was withholding something good from her. In reality God was withholding the tree of the knowledge of good and evil from her because He knew once she partook of its fruit, she was destined to sin and death. The Ten Commandments are all for our good. They were not given to withhold us from anything but that which would cause harm and destruction in our lives.

An obedient heart is a heart that is grateful for God's goodness. I have never seen a thankful rebellious person. Paul tells us in Romans 1 that one of the first things that opens the door to rebellion in our hearts is being ungrateful. Listen to Isaiah's words: "'If you are willing and obedient, you shall eat the good of the land; but if you refuse and rebel, you shall be devoured by the sword'; for the mouth of the LORD has spoken it" (Isa. 1:19–20).

The benefit of obedience is to taste daily the goodness of the Lord, which leads to blessing upon blessing.

Lord, I want to obey You. Give me a willing, grateful heart always.

Who Is a Fool?
Psalm 53:1–6

Throughout our lives we may do things that seem foolish to others. Paul said, "We are fools for Christ." I'll never forget hosting a dentist and his wife who were full time in the ministry of the Lord. They traveled wherever the Lord told them to go. The dentist had a successful dental practice and gave up the security of this business to obey the Lord's call on his life.

When we first met this couple, nothing in their manner or outward appearance was impressive. What was outstanding in their lives, however, were a love and zeal for the Lord that few have. To the world, these two would be considered foolish. They, however, were fools for Christ.

The guest room where we housed them was right next to our bedroom. Only a thin wall separated us from them when we slept. As I was drifting off to sleep one night I heard the Lord say, "You are housing two of my precious fools who have laid their lives down for My sake."

God is always pleased when we do things that appear foolish in the eyes of the world for His sake. I would rather be a fool for Christ than a fool who says in his heart, "There is no God" (Ps. 53:1).

The world is filled with brilliant fools who deny the existence of God. Their intellect blocks them from the childlike faith needed to enter into the kingdom of God. The truly wise are those who not only believe there is a God, but who are willing to sacrifice all for Him. The two fools for Christ in our guest bedroom were actually two of the wisest people I have ever met.

Lord, help me to be willing to appear foolish to the eyes of the world. I want to do Your will more than I want to please men. Your opinion of me is much more important than the world's opinion of me. By the way, I don't mind it at all if you call me one of Your fools.

READ: Isaiah 6:1–7:25; 2 Corinthians 11:16–33; Psalm 54:1–7; Proverbs 23:1–3

His Train Fills the Temple
Isaiah 6:1–7:25

We are entering the High Holy Days for our Jewish brothers and sisters. This is the season of their New Year and their ten days of awe, which end with the Day of Atonement. The timing varies according to their calendar, but this season usually occurs during September. We will be speaking more of these days of awe, which is a time set aside for the Jewish people to examine their hearts in preparation for the Day of Atonement. They review the last year and confess anything they did or said that they feel did not please God. They cry out for God's mercy for another year of life so they might be written in the book of the righteous. The Jewish people believe there is a book of the righteous, a book for those who have not been too sinful and a book for the wicked. Join me the rest of this month as I too join our Jewish brothers in examining my own life. Also, this would be a meaningful time to lift our Jewish brothers and sisters before the Lord by praying for the veil that is over their eyes to drop so they may see Jesus as their Messiah. He is their hope of glory.

Isaiah, a good Jewish prophet, had a magnificent encounter with God. Listen to his words. "In the year that King Uzziah died, I saw the Lord sitting upon a throne, high and lifted up, and the train of His robe filled the temple" (Isa. 6:1).

When Adam and Eve were created, they were dressed with God's glory. There was radiance that covered their nakedness. God has similar glory garments. One time I learned that as we praise the Lord, the radiance of His presence in heaven and on earth intensifies. He has given us the garments of praise that lift the spirit of heaviness. Every time we praise Him, His glory garments intensify. Our praises do more in the heavenlies than we think. What a privilege it is to dress God with our praise every morning. God is a Spirit, and you can see His form only because of the glory garments He wears. Isaiah saw Him sitting upon a throne, high and lifted up, and His train filled the temple. His glory garments did not just fill the temple, but they also filled the whole earth. The whole earth was filled with His glory.

Recently I heard a message by a man who had an encounter with God. He said God visited the church where he was a guest speaker and the glory of the Lord just kept coming in waves upon the people. It was at that moment he remembered this Isaiah passage. He also remembered the scene of the wedding of Princess Diane and Prince Charles. Princess Diane wore a wedding dress with a train that extended beyond the aisle of the cathedral and out the door. God's presence came and just kept coming because His train filled that church. The response to His presence was repentance. Everyone prostrated themselves on the floor and wept. This too was Isaiah's response. Isaiah wrote, "Woe is me; for I am undone! Because I am a man of unclean lips, and I dwell in the midst of a people of unclean lips: for my eyes have seen the King, the LORD of hosts" (v. 5). Pray for us all, including our Jewish brothers and sisters, to see His glory.

Awake—the Light Has Come
Isaiah 8:1–9:21

As we continue to think of our Jewish brethren during these High Holy Days, we only have to wonder how they have missed seeing the Messiah clearly presented in their prophets, the psalms and even the Pentateuch. The only explanation is what Paul speaks clearly about in Romans. The Jewish people have a veil over their eyes that has been placed there by God. Should we pray for this veil to be dropped if this is God's will? The answer to this is a resounding yes. We have the hope and promise of God that this veil will be dropped, and the day will come when the Jewish people will recognize Jesus as their Messiah. Until that day we can be diligent in prayer for the Jewish people. Today many Jewish people are accepting Jesus as their Messiah. Our recent trip to Israel revealed much more openness on the part of secular Jews to discuss faith with others. I believe this is a direct result of the prayers of many Christians for Israel and the Jewish people.

In this passage Isaiah prophesies so eloquently the birth of Jesus: "The people that walked in darkness have seen a great light: they that dwell in the land of the shadow of death, upon them hath the light shined... For unto us a child is born, unto us a son is given: and the government shall be upon his shoulder, and his name shall be called Wonderful, Counsellor, The mighty God, The everlasting Father, The Prince of Peace. Of the increase of his government and peace there shall be no end, upon the throne of David, and upon his kingdom, to order it, and to establish it with judgment and with justice from henceforth even for ever. The zeal of the LORD of hosts will perform this" (Isa. 9:2, 6–7, KJV).

This prophecy also goes on to say, "And all the people shall know..." Here is the promise to claim for the Jews as we pray for them. Jesus truly is the light that lights every man who comes into the world. John speaks of this as He shares that John the Baptist was not the light. He says, "He was not that Light, but was sent to bear witness of that Light. That was the true Light which gives light to every man coming into the world. He was in the world, and the world was made through him, and the world did not know him. He came to His own, and His own did not receive Him" (John 1:8–11).

Pray today for the Jewish people to recognize and accept Jesus, the Light of the world.

The Rod and Stem
Isaiah 10:1–11:16

We continue to think of the Jewish people during their High Holy Days. In Isaiah we see another prophetic scripture about their Messiah: "And there shall come forth a rod out of the stem of Jesse, and a Branch shall grow out of his roots: And the spirit of the Lord shall rest upon him, the spirit of wisdom and understanding, the spirit of counsel and might, the spirit of knowledge and of the fear of the Lord" (Isa. 11:1–2, kjv).

The rod spoken of in this passage is Jesus, and the stem is His heritage in the house of David. Jesse was the father of David, and God promised that the throne of Jerusalem would always be in the line of David. We had a dear Jewish friend who came to know Jesus as his Messiah simply because he read the first chapter of Matthew. As you know, the orthodox Jews are forbidden to read the New Testament. My friend Abraham had a Christian guitar teacher who gave him the whole Bible as a gift when he finished his lessons for the year. Being a good orthodox Jew, Abraham threw the Bible in the garbage without reading it. Later when the teacher asked Abraham how he liked the gift he gave him, Abraham replied, "I lost it." "Well, we can fix that," the teacher replied as he handed Abraham another Bible. This time as Abraham was walking home with another Bible in hand, he decided to sit down and read the first few pages of the New Testament. He read the genealogy of Jesus, and that was enough to convince him that Jesus was truly his Messiah. When he saw how the lineage of Jesus is from the house of David, he knew Jesus was the chosen One. He kept his Bible and hid it so he could read more.

The day will come when Jesus, the rod out of the stem of Jesse, will rule over all nations. His headquarters will be Jerusalem, and the government will be upon His shoulders. Jesus read this very scripture in the temple. He spoke of the special anointing that rested upon Him: the spirit of wisdom and understanding, counsel and might, knowledge and the fear of the Lord. This same anointing is available to all those who have received Jesus as Lord and Savior. Thank God we have this same anointing Jesus had, and this anointing will equip us for anything we face today.

Father, thank You for giving me the same anointing Jesus had when He walked on earth. Help me today to yield to this anointing so that Your will and work will be accomplished in me today.

READ: Isaiah 12:1–14:32; 2 Corinthians 13:1–14; Psalm 57:1–11; Proverbs 23:9–11

In That Day
Isaiah 12:1–14:32

We are still in the days of awe. I hope you are praying for your Jewish friends during this holy season for them. Pray for that veil to be dropped over their eyes and for the eyes of their understanding to be opened. This passage in Isaiah speaks about a special day that will happen in Israel. That day will be filled with praise because God's chosen people will at last know Jesus as their Messiah. They will know the God of their salvation, and with joy they will draw water from the wells of salvation. They will see all the excellent things God has done, and God will be their strength and song.

The days of awe will no longer be observed because His chosen will know that their names are written in the Lamb's Book of Life. No longer will they have to ask God for another year of life with the hope that in that year their names would be removed from the Book of the In-Between and placed in the Book of the Righteous.

What a glorious day that will be when Jew and Gentile will worship together in Jerusalem. In that day they will actually speak the things Isaiah wrote: "And in that day thou shalt say, O LORD, I will praise thee: though thou wast angry with me, thine anger is turned away, and thou comfortedst me. Behold, God is my salvation; I will trust, and not be afraid: for the LORD Jehovah is my strength and my song; he also is become my salvation. Therefore with joy shall ye draw water out of the wells of salvation. And in that day shall ye say, Praise the LORD, call upon his name, declare his doings among the people, make mention that his name is exalted. Sing unto the LORD; for he hath done excellent things: this is known in all the earth. Cry out and shout, thou inhabitant of Zion: for great is the Holy One of Israel in the midst of thee" (Isa. 12:1–6, KJV).

What a great day that will be for all of Israel. You can have a part in ushering that day in by praying now for Israel and all the Jewish people.

September 14

READ: Isaiah 51:1–18:7; Galatians 1:1–24; Psalm 58:1–11; Proverbs 23:12

What True Wisdom Is
Proverbs 23:12

We leave our study of Isaiah and prophetic scriptures about the Messiah and look briefly into Proverbs. This proverb gives the secret to effective Bible study: Apply your heart to instruction and your ears to the words of knowledge.

The Bible is the manual for life, and it gives the instructions for living a blessed, meaningful life, a life that glorifies God. If you are like me, I often read instructions, and then I try to short-cut the instructions. I get myself into a real mess when I do this. There is no short-cut to effective Bible reading. First, we must listen carefully to what the passage says, and then we need to do what it says. Faith without works is dead. The words of life are in the Scriptures, but it is up to us to ignite that seed of life so that it blossoms into a mature tree of righteousness. We are the plantings of the Lord. Unless we allow the water of the Holy Spirit to satiate our souls daily as we read God's Word, we will miss out on the transforming and renewing of our minds by the Word of God, and our hearts will not be changed. We must also listen to the Lord and come to know Him intimately.

We live in an age where knowledge has increased dramatically. God has been gracious to my husband and me. He has given us the opportunity to be mother and father-like ones to four very brilliant young people—Christina, our Chinese daughter; Vladimir, our Russian son; Misha, who lives in our apartment (at the age of nineteen Misha was a full professor in a college, and now at age 23 she has two masters degrees); and Daniel, who is living temporarily with us while he awaits entering Emory University as a junior. He entered college at fifteen and has already worked two years on Wall Street. Vladimir graduated with highest honors from Georgia Tech, and now is working with Price Waterhouse. We were sitting at the table with Misha and Daniel the other night, and my husband and I were overwhelmed with the knowledge of these two brilliant young people. All my husband and I could add to the conversation was to nod our heads and say "Wow!" We were impressed with the fact that knowledge has increased in these last days and most people know a lot more than we do. This keeps us humble. I kidded with our house guests and said, "Now I know the plan of the Lord. It is to send as many brilliant people as possible into this home to help us get our own act together. We need all the mental assistance we can get at this age."

This proverb exhorts us to apply our ears to the words of knowledge. There are a lot of intellectual fools who know many facts, but they have not come into the knowledge of the one fact that will affect them eternally. That fact is that Jesus Christ is Lord of all. We know a professor who has so much knowledge, but in God's sight he is a fool because he does not believe God exists. The Bible says that it is a fool who does not believe in God. When we read the Bible we must understand that we are not just gaining more knowledge about God. The goal is to know Him intimately, not just know about Him. I trust you have experienced this.

The Power of Singing
Psalm 59:1–17

David says, "I will sing of Your power; yes, I will sing aloud of Your mercy in the morning" (v. 16). David speaks of singing about God's power and mercy because he knew the power of singing. David was a psalmist, and it was his custom to sing continually.

In my fifty years as a Christian I have discovered nothing draws me into the presence of the Lord more than singing. One of the key ways Paul tells us to stay filled with the Spirit is to sing hymns and spiritual songs, and to make melody in our hearts. Paul says in his letter to the Ephesians, "And do not be drunk with wine, in which is dissipation; but be filled with the Spirit, speaking to one another in psalms and hymns and spiritual songs, singing and making melody in your heart to the Lord, giving thanks always for all things to God the Father in the name of our Lord Jesus Christ, submitting to one another in the fear of God" (Eph. 18–21).

Most of my morning times with the Lord are spent singing to Him, and when I wait for a moment after I sing to Him, often I will hear a song in the my spirit from the Lord. My mother was a soloist who sang all over Atlanta in many churches. One of my happiest memories of my childhood was hearing her singing in the kitchen. She sang hymns while she cooked. Throughout her whole life she always seemed to be full of the joy of the Lord, and His love always radiated from her to others. I think she had learned the secret to staying filled with the Spirit.

As you read this you may say to yourself, "But I can't sing," or "I work all day, so how could I sing all day?" Paul gives the answer to this when he tells the Ephesians to speak to themselves in hymns, psalms and spiritual songs and make melody in their hearts. If you lack the ability to make melody when others cannot hear you, rest assured the Lord will hear you as you make melody in your heart to Him. He loves the sound of your heart as well as the sound of your voice. It is a melody of love.

Let his melody of love ring out in your heart today.

READ: Isaiah 22:1–24:23; Galatians 2:17–3:7; Psalm 60:1–12; Proverbs 23:15–16

Looking Forward to the Fall
Isaiah 22:1–24:23

Summer is my least favorite season, so I always search for reasons I can be thankful for this time. I hate to sweat, and Georgia in the summer is no place someone who hates to sweat.

The other evening, as I was watching the sunset, I began to think of reasons to thank the Lord for the summer. I came up with this list: the sights of lightening flies, sparkling skies on warm summer nights, the tastes of lemonade and ice tea, the warmth of sun bathing by the beach, and the sounds of katydids, July flies, June bugs and crickets in the night. I used to be so thankful for summers, because it meant being home from school, sleeping in late and just plain vegging out. I always looked forward, however, to that first crisp coolness in the air that comes to Georgia about mid-September. I look forward now to the trees being dressed in their coat of many colors and the crunch of leaves under foot as I walk with my husband by the river. As I look forward to the radiant foliage and then later to the snow-covered pines in the winter, I think of this scripture in Isaiah: "Though your sins are like scarlet, they shall be as white as snow" (Isa. 1:18).

Then as I see the leaves fall to the earth and thick clouds gather to usher in winter rains and an occasional snow, this verse comes to mind: "I have blotted out, like a thick cloud, your transgressions, and like a cloud, your sins. Return to me; for I have redeemed you" (Isa. 44:22).

Fall is always the season when the High Holy Days are celebrated by the Jews, and the days of awe, which are the days of inward reflection, culminate in the Day of Atonement. The sad part of the Jewish faith is that they have no *kippur* (covering for their sin). Only God can open their hearts to understand the truth that Jesus died to provide the covering for their sin. His shed blood is their covering as well as ours for all sin, but they do not understand this. Today's scripture tell us also that Jesus holds the keys of David: "The key of the house of David I will lay upon his shoulder; so he shall open, and no one shall shut; and he shall shut, and no one shall open" (Isa. 22:22).

Only Jesus has the key that will turn the hearts of our Jewish friends to know Him as their personal Messiah and Savior. Jesus holds this key; we do not. Pray that He will open the hearts of your Jewish friends and unveil their eyes to behold Him and know Him as their Messiah.

> *Lord, I pray You will open the hearts of the many Jews who need to know You. Just as Joseph finally revealed himself to his brothers who sought to kill him, please reveal Yourself to Your Jewish brethren. They are Your brothers.*

READ: Isaiah 25:1–28:13; Galatians 3:8–22; Psalm 61:1–8; Proverbs 23:17–18

Look What the Lord Has Done and Who He Is
Isaiah 25:1–28:13

I will praise Your name, for You have done wonderful things," Isaiah writes. Praise and worship always exalt the Lord. When we praise the Lord, we exalt Him as we speak of the wonderful things He has done. Such praise will naturally lead us into worship, where our focus shifts from what God has done to who God is. This reading in Isaiah is a beautiful blend of worship and praise. Listen as Isaiah declares the many wondrous works the Lord has done. Listen to a few of them:

1. He defeats the enemy and defends the righteous.
2. He swallows up death in victory.
3. He wipes away our tears.
4. He takes the veil off the eyes of His chosen.
5. He brings down the pride of our enemies.
6. He keeps us in perfect peace as we keep our minds on Him.
7. He ordains peace and His works through us.
8. He causes Israel to blossom and bud and to fill the face of the world with fruit.
9. He gathers the outcasts of Israel.

A person's actions always reveal his character. The works we do on earth that will stand the test of time and will not be burned on judgment day are those works that stem from abiding in the Vine, Jesus Christ, and showing forth the fruit of the Spirit (Gal. 5:22–23). All the works done outside of the Spirit will be burned. As we look at the characteristics of God and the marvelous works that result from these characteristics, let's turn our hearts to worship:

1. He is mighty, strong and our advocate because He defends the righteous and defeats the enemy.
2. He is our redeemer because He has swallowed up death in victory.
3. He is our comforter because He wipes our tears away.
4. He is all truth because He reveals who He is.
5. He is meek and temperate because only He can bring down pride.
6. He is faithful and longsuffering because He keeps us at peace through trials.
7. He is creator because He ordained and created works for us to do.
8. He is the vine because only as we abide in Him can we blossom and bear fruit.
9. He is love because He draws us to Himself with His bands of love.

Today praise Him for what He does and worship Him for who He is.

No Schoolmaster
Galatians 3:23–4:31

Didn't you just love to have substitute teachers when you were in school? When you walked into the classroom and you saw another teacher, you breathed a sigh of relief and probably thought to yourself, *Oh boy, this means no pop quiz, and we'll probably have a free study period!* Often some of the rascals in my class would give the substitute teacher a hard time. Substitute teachers earn every penny of their pay.

This never happened to me in school, but what if you entered your classroom and there was no teacher at all? You looked on the board, and written on the board in bold letters were these instructions: "Do whatever your heart tells you to do during this class period. I trust you." What would your response be to such an instruction? Would you want to be as bad as you could be and misbehave, maybe throw spit balls at your classmates? I know what my reaction to such an instruction would be. I would want to live up to the trust that teacher had placed in me. I would feel that the teacher really thinks I am mature enough to behave myself in her absence, and I want to prove to her I can do this. In fact, I think I would encourage all my classmates to demonstrate their capability of being mature and responsible by behaving themselves also.

Such a day may never come in the classroom of a school, but such a day has come spiritually. Paul makes the following bold statements: "But before faith came, we were kept under the law, shut up unto the faith which should afterwards be revealed. Wherefore the law was our schoolmaster to bring us unto Christ, that we might be justified by faith. But after that faith is come, we are no longer under a schoolmaster. For ye are all children of God by faith in Christ Jesus" (Gal. 3:23–26, KJV).

The fullness of time has come when Jesus Christ came and was made under the Law, but now has redeemed all those who were under the Law and has given us the spirit of adoption that makes us His children and makes God our daddy. The law now is written on our hearts, and we no longer have to have a schoolmaster. Jesus has become our life, and we now live by the faith of the Son of God who loved us and gave Himself for us. Jesus, the obedient One, has fulfilled the Law so that now we are under grace (God's unmerited favor), which enables us to walk in the Spirit and thereby keep the law, which is to love God and love our neighbors as ourselves.

School is not out because we are ever learning in the school of life. Our teacher is now the Holy Spirit who lives within us, and He is the One who obeys through us.

READ: Isaiah 30:12–33:12; Galatians 5:1–12; Psalm 63:1–11; Proverbs 23:22

Rejoicing in Trials
Psalm 63:1–11

We talked earlier about giving thanks for trials because ultimately they work for our good; also, proven character is developed in us. This thought does not appeal to our natural mind, especially when we are in the midst of a heavy-duty trial. David sometimes buckled under his trials, but even at those times he spoke to his soul and told his soul to hope in God. Focus is the main issue in trials, and as we see in our psalm reading today, David had his focus exactly where it should be. We all can learn how to focus on the Lord in troubled times. Thank God for a psalmist like David who writes beautiful, but also very practical psalms.

In this psalm David first declares His need for the Lord. He is going through a dry time and feels like there is no water (v. 1). He thirsts to see God's power and glory in the sanctuary (v. 2). Then David turns his focus from his need onto God and begins to praise Him. He shares the fact that God's loving-kindness supercedes every trial and is better than life itself. David's lips begin to praise the Lord (v. 3). He continues steadfastly focusing on the Lord by blessing the Lord and lifting up his hands to the Lord.

Then David makes a faith statement in the midst of a dry time in his life. He says, "My soul shall be satisfied as with marrow and fatness, and my mouth shall praise You with joyful lips." The feeling of joy is normally absent when we are in a desert place, but David makes a decision with his will to praise the Lord with joyful lips (v. 5). He also remembers the Lord and meditates in the night watches (v. 6). Often when we are going through a trial, it is hard to sleep, but we can use these waking hours to meditate upon the Lord. David remembers how God has helped him in the past (v. 7). We can always gain proper focus in a trial when we remember how God hid us in the shadow of His wings in the other trials (v. 7).

David makes a determination of his will not to give up because he knows God is upholding him with His right hand (v. 8). He then declares the defeat of his enemies. Sometimes it is good in the midst of a trial to declare aloud the ultimate defeat of the enemy. This is spiritual warfare. Remember, God is allowing Satan to come against you for only one reason. He believes in you and knows if you depend upon Him in the trial, you will be victorious.

David ends his psalm with this beautiful statement: "The king shall rejoice in God." I have a little saying that helps me focus on Jesus in trying times: God will always turn the gory into glory if I trust in Him and keep my mind stayed upon Him.

READ: Isaiah 33:13–36:22; Galatians 5:13–26; Psalm 64:1–10; Proverbs 23:23

Silencing the Accuser
Isaiah 33:13–36:22

Have you ever been falsely accused? I can remember several times in my life when people have accused me falsely. Nothing hurts worse. You know in your heart that you did nothing wrong. Yet if you try to justify yourself to your accuser, he usually refuses to accept what is true about the situation. Every day of our lives we deal with a false accuser. His name is Satan. He continually accuses us, and unless we are on the alert, we can easily fall into condemnation.

In our reading today we see how Rabshakeh was sent by the king of Assyria to accuse Hezekiah. Rabshakeh tells Hezekiah he is barking up the wrong tree if he is putting his trust in God. He actually is mocking God's power. He speaks all of this in the Hebrew tongue in earshot of all those who are on the wall. Eliakim, Shebna and Joah ask Rabshakeh to speak in the Syrian language instead of the language of the Jews because they did not want those on the wall to hear his accusations. This did not bother Rabshakeh at all; he wants all of those on the wall to hear what he has to say. He downgrades Hezekiah to his own people and says Hezekiah is trying to deceive them. He says that Hezekiah lied to them when he told them they would defeat the Assyrians. King Hezekiah told all who heard these accusations not to answer them, so they held their peace.

We can learn a lot from this little story. When others accuse us falsely, we can rest assured that Satan has inspired the accusation. Because we know we are not fighting against flesh and blood, but against principalities, powers, rulers of darkness and wickedness in high places, we do not have to reply to the accusation by defending ourselves. The Lord is our defender, and it is better for us to remain silent. We can silence our enemies in the most effective way when we remain silent. This is what Jesus did when He was accused. The moment we begin to defend or justify ourselves, we are not allowing the Lord to fight our battle. Instead we are trying to fight it ourselves. If we keep silent when accused, this really annoys our accuser because he has no more material to accuse us even more.

I had the experience one time of being accused of being a false teacher. I later found out that the person accusing me had accused almost every speaker of being a false teacher when they shared at the group she attended. This person sent me a blazing letter, so I wrote one back. Then another letter came that accused me of even more, based on some of the things I wrote in my last letter. Finally, I heard in my spirit, "Keep silent. Do not write her again." This finally silenced her judgmental, critical, accusing spirit. The accuser always wants us to defend ourselves, but we need to allow the Lord to be our defense. He will justify us if we will let Him, and the enemy will be put to flight. Remember, in quietness and confidence will be your strength.

What to Do When You Feel God Has Forsaken You
Isaiah 37:1-38:22

This passage records two prayers of Hezekiah. One prayer asks God for his healing and deliverance from his enemies. The other prayer expresses a vivid word picture of how Hezekiah felt before he knew the Lord would restore him to health and deliver him from his enemies. He says, "Like a crane or a swallow, so I chattered; I mourned like a dove; my eyes fail from looking upward" (Isa. 38:14). He speaks of his age departing from him and how he believed he would not see the Lord in the land of the living.

This descriptive prayer of Hezekiah has great meaning to me because my son who served in China as a teacher of English had the same feelings Hezekiah did. When he shared his testimony about his first few months in China, he included this verse of Scripture because it expressed so well exactly what he was feeling. God heard Hezekiah's cry, and He also heard Ron's cry. What seemed to Ron at the time as a disastrous decision to go to China became a decisive victory for him and for the Lord. Until his departure to China, Ron had experienced relatively little obstacles or trials. Remember, it is trials that develop character in us. More character was developed in Ron during his two years in China than I thought possible. When he returned, he had developed a grateful heart, an appreciation for life, patience and longsuffering, gentleness and kindness, and most of all, love. Ron had always been gracious, but there was a depth of thankfulness in his heart that developed because of God's faithfulness to him through hard times. He appreciated life and people because God turned his thoughts to others rather than to himself. He grew in patience and longsuffering as he stood in line for hours and sometimes almost a day to get train tickets. Just the huge population in China makes travel very difficult. He tells the story of the time when he just decided to climb over the shoulders of people to get to the front of the line because he had to get on the train. The Chinese laughed and cheered him as he made his valiant effort to get to the front of the line. He learned his lesson, however, when he saw the police waiting for him when he reached the ticket office. His heart was in his throat, especially when he saw the bamboo stick that awaited him. To his surprise the police ushered him to another ticket booth without a word and with the bamboo stick pointed to the sign that said "Foreigners only." He learned gentleness and kindness from the Chinese people who, for the most part, are a gentle people, and he learned love. When he had to say good-bye to his Chinese friends, he wept bitterly because God had placed such a love in his heart for these dear people.

God heard Hezekiah's cry, healed his body and delivered him from his enemies. In the process of these trials, however, Hezekiah, I am sure, grew in character also. We cry out to God when troubles come, but maybe we should thank Him first for allowing such troubles that will develop character within us that could not be accomplished any other way.

The One Thing We Can Count On
Isaiah 39:1-41:16

So many in this life are looking for something to hang their hats on—a solid something, an unmovable something, something that they can count on that will never change and will always be. This passage in Isaiah tells us that the Word of God shall stand forever. The Word of God spans time and eternity and gives us something that is established and unshakable to hold on to through this life. Everything we see now on this earth will one day be ashes. Isaiah tells us, "The grass withers, the flower fades, but the word of our God stands forever" (Isa. 40:8).

My husband loves to give me flowers for no reason at all. It is his way of saying "I love and appreciate you." The moment I receive flowers, I cut their stems while they are in water, and I add a packet of preservative to the water so the flowers will last a little longer. Soon, however, the vibrant colors begin to fade; the leaves begin to shrivel, and if left too long, they begin to rot. Nothing smells worse than water that contains rotting flowers. God has given us a bouquet of flowers, however, with infinite variety that will never fade or decay. This bouquet is the Word of God that lasts forever. Flowers are given to people to congratulate them, to celebrate a special occasion, to applaud them, or just to say "I love you." I will always remember the lovely flower arrangements sent to us when my mother passed away. These gifts of flowers were expressions of the love people had for my mother.

In Russia we noticed that all during the performance of the singers at this musical festival we attended, people walked down the aisle and placed flowers on the stage. This was their way of applauding the individuals who were performing. God is daily placing a bouquet of flowers especially for us on the stage of our life because He applauds us. He wants our lives to have the smell of freshness that newly cut flowers have, and He wants our lives to always be brilliant with the light of His glory. This bouquet is the Word of God, and we cannot smell the freshness of it each day if we fail to pick His Word up and read it. We have to remember also that it is not the Word itself that has power. It is God, His Holy Spirit and the living Word Jesus (the Holy Trinity) that give the written Word the power to renew and transform our lives.

God is pleased with us, and He loves and adores us. Today He has placed a bouquet on the stage of our lives. Pick it up, and when you do, if you listen carefully, you may hear God's applause and the applause of the angels. During the Russian musical festival, I never saw a performer leave their flowers on the stage. They always picked them up and took them with them as they left the stage. When we leave the stage of this life, we also can take God's bouquet (His Word) with us into eternity. Have you smelled His fresh bouquet to you today? Have you read the card He placed on it? The card says, "To You with Love."

Precious in His Sight
Isaiah 41:17–43:13

This passage in Isaiah is a powerful prophetic chapter about the Messiah, Jesus, the Holy One of Israel, and what He will do for Israel. It speaks about Him healing the brokenhearted, setting free those who are in prison, holding their hand, taking them through the fire and through the river to safety. Then God tells Isaiah the reason for the protection and deliverance of His people. The Holy One of Israel says, "Since you were precious in my sight, you have been honored, and I have loved you" (Isa. 43:4).

The whole world longs to hear these words spoken by someone to them. Does it build you up and comfort you when someone calls you precious? When my mother was bedridden because of a stroke, I loved to go and visit her at the nursing home. She could only speak a few words at a time, but the words she spoke were so edifying. She always told me I was beautiful and so precious to her. I told all my friends to visit Mother if they wanted a real lift for their day. In fact, during the course of my mother's life I do not recall any negative words she ever spoke about anyone. What a legacy she left to my two sisters and me! We have a lot to live up to. During her illness that lasted four years, she must have said that I was precious close to a thousand times.

Do you know today that you are precious in the sight of the Lord Jesus? He sees you as valuable, and He loves you. If you do not know this or feel this is true, I pray you will have eyes and ears today open to see His beauty and to hear Him say, "You are precious in My sight."

Often at funerals ministers quote Psalm 115:16, which says "Precious in the sight of the LORD is the death of his saints." Some even say that God called this person home because he was needed in heaven. I always have a little shiver when I hear this because it is such a wrong interpretation of this scripture.

The word *precious* in Hebrew means costly. It is costly to God for a saint to die because a light has gone out on earth. A living witness who glorifies God on earth has left earth, and it is very costly to God. He does not need us in heaven, but He needs us on earth to be His witnesses. It was costly to God to have my mother leave this earth because He lost one of the most beautiful voices on earth who was able to sing solos for many and who was able to give His Word voice on earth. She was a shining light who always edified others and glorified God. Today tell your family and friends how precious they are to you while they are still with you on earth.

A New Thing
Isaiah 43:14–45:10

always looked forward to Christmas because I knew I would receive a whole new outfit that even included new underwear. As soon as the opening of presents was completed, I ran and got into a hot tub and then dressed in my new outfit. I wanted to be squeaky clean before I put on my new clothes. When I came out in my new outfit, my daddy always said, "You look beautiful."

The longing in every heart is not only to have new things, but also to feel fresh and clean. Perhaps you did not have the loving childhood I experienced, but God can make all things new for you. You may have even experienced some type of abuse that has made you feel unclean and dirty even today as an adult. Maybe your memories of your childhood are not pleasant at all, and you would like to take a giant eraser and just wipe out every bad memory. The good news is that God has a new beginning for you even today.

Today is your day of salvation (wholeness). Today you can begin again with a new slate, a new life. Today you can be born again, and no matter what your past is, you can become as clean and sweet as a freshly bathed infant. The moment you accept Jesus Christ as your Lord and Savior, He has a bath for you that cleanses you from all sin. His blood shed on the cross for you can wash every sin away. He has a fresh set of clothes for you also. It is His robe of righteousness.

You may already be saved, but there is still a residue of your past that you just can't wipe from your memory. The memories of abuse, rejection and failure often cling to us like the leaves of an oak tree that fail to drop until new leaves pop out in the spring. Isaiah 43:18–19 tells us what to do with the past: "Do not remember the former things, nor consider the things of old. Behold, I will do a new thing, now it shall spring forth; shall you not know it? I will even make a way in the wilderness and rivers in the desert."

Maybe your life was like a wilderness, and you thirsted for love as a man in the desert thirsts for water. Here is a promise to stand on; rest assured God's will is to perform this in your life. He desires to make a way for you today in the wilderness of your life. Your part is to focus upon Jesus and not the past. "Do not remember the former things." God desires to satiate your soul with the living water of His Holy Spirit. Your part again is to not dwell on the past or consider the things of old. Your part is to forgive all those who wronged or hurt you, and also to forgive yourself for past failures. A new thing is coming your way today. Pray this prayer with me:

Lord, I choose to forget the past and look for the new today. Heal my heart, O Lord!

How to Build a House
Proverbs 24:3–4

We have only built one house in our lifetime, and it was interesting to watch the structure being formed day by day. First, the foundation was laid carefully. Some of the plumbing even went into the foundation area before the cement was poured on top. Then the wood frame went up, and the rooms in the house were carefully measured and framed. Finally the roof trusses were placed, and the roof was laid. Perhaps you have never built a house to live in, but we all are building spiritual houses. This Proverbs reading talks about how we should build our spiritual house: "Through wisdom a house is built, and by understanding it is established; by knowledge the rooms are filled with all precious and pleasant riches."

The house we built in Savannah will not last forever, but the spiritual house we are building will go with us into eternity. The spiritual house that will last forever is a house built through wisdom and established by knowledge. Then we can fill the rooms of this home with priceless, precious and pleasant riches—our children. We have had the privilege of not only filling our home with our own children, but we have also housed a Chinese daughter for five years and a Russian son for seven years; now we are housing another daughter and son for a season. One day when I was in the kitchen I suddenly realized how rich we are. God has filled the chambers of our home over the years with three precious natural children and has added to our riches with three more.

Some people, however, are single or are married and have no children. Can these people still fill the rooms of their spiritual home with precious and pleasant riches? The answer to this question is yes. People are God's treasures and His inheritance. Whenever we invest in people with our time, prayers or money, we are filling the rooms of our spiritual home with God's riches. Whenever we share the gospel with others, we are adding to those riches stored in the rooms of our spiritual home. One day we will be amazed at how the rooms in our mansions in heaven are filled with treasures—people our lives have touched.

When we retired, we thought we were through having children, and we got ready for the empty-nest time. God has never allowed us to have an empty nest, and I am grateful that He has trusted us to house some of His most priceless treasures. Is your spiritual house full of priceless riches? Each day you live you can add to those treasures in heaven by investing your own life into the lives of others.

Lord, I want to add to my treasures in heaven today.

September 26

READ: Isaiah 48:12–50:11; Ephesians 4:17–32; Psalm 69:1–14; Proverbs 24:5

A Great God
Isaiah 48:12–50:11

This passage in Isaiah speaks of God's greatness and His infinite interest in mankind. This very morning I enjoyed a lesson on the "Fear of the Lord" that gave documented facts about the great expanse of our universe. The teacher shared how many light-years it would take for us to travel to a far galaxy, and it was mind boggling. We are just now coming to the understanding of the vastness of our universe. Yet, God says He spans the heavens with His right hand. The span of my own hand is about five inches or less. Think of how big God is who can span the whole universe with His right hand.

God is big, and there is no debating this fact, but He is not so big that He overlooks the finite needs of mankind. He knows even the number of hairs on our heads. "[God] teaches you to profit, [God] leads you by the way you should go" (Isa. 48:17).

It is by His mercy that God positioned the earth so perfectly that we do not fear being burned up by the sun or overwhelmed by the waters of the sea. At the rebuke of the Lord the sea is dried up, and He is able to make rivers in the wilderness. What a great God we serve. Remember, however, that everything that concerns you is a concern to Him.

There was an incident in my life that proved He is interested and hears our prayers even over the smallest details. My neighbor who lent me her napkins for a dinner party called me in distress because she was missing one of the napkins. I thought I had returned all of them to her. I began to search diligently for the lost napkin, and she even called another friend to pray I found it because she was having a dinner party that evening. The friend's mother heard the conversation and said, "I wouldn't bother God by praying for a silly napkin." These napkins, however, were precious to my neighbor, and they were a special wedding gift to her. Because we all prayed, I was led to look behind my washing machine. There behind my washing machine was the missing napkin, and I rejoiced. So did all of the prayer warriors involved.

God is big, but He is not so big that He cannot hear your prayers over the smallest matters. He perfects everything that is a concern to you, and those napkins were a great concern to me and my neighbor also. God is faithful.

Lord, thank You for caring about the smallest details of my life.
I am encouraged now to pray for anything that I am concerned
about. You truly care about whatever I am concerned about.

The Life of Jesus
Isaiah 51:1–53:12

One would think it would be impossible to read all about the life of Jesus in the Old Testament. There are, however, many prophetic scriptures in the Old Testament about the life and death of Jesus. Our reading in Isaiah today has one of the most famous ones. I have a friend who is a rabbi in a Messianic congregation, and he always tells his Jewish friends who do not believe in Jesus to read Isaiah 53. This is an amazing prophetic chapter that tells all about the rejection of Jesus and how He bore our sins, griefs, transgressions, iniquities and punishments in His death. It speaks of how God made His soul the offering for sin.

God revealed to Isaiah the whole story of Jesus, and Isaiah recorded it hundreds of years before the birth of Jesus. I weep when I read how Jesus was brought as a lamb to slaughter and He spoke not a word. I have been told that sheep are always silent just before they are slaughtered. They allow the one who is to kill them to do this job without any resistance on their part. Jesus was the perfect lamb of God who takes away the sin of the world. What a joy to be on the other side of the cross, to experience the full salvation. Isaiah writes about this in chapter 51: "Lift up your eyes to the heavens, and look on the earth beneath. For the heavens will vanish away like smoke, the earth will grow old like a garment, and those who dwell in it will die in like manner; but My salvation will be forever, and My righteousness will not be abolished" (v. 6).

How can anyone neglect to receive such a great salvation?

Lord, help me to witness to my Jewish friends by asking them to read Isaiah 53 and other prophetic scriptures in Isaiah. Then open their eyes and ears to see and hear the truth about the great salvation that awaits them.

Restoration of the Rejected
Isaiah 54:1–57:14

rejected person is always vulnerable to the enemy's weapons. This passage in Isaiah lists the ten weapons the enemy tries to use against rejected people.

1. Fear
2. Confusion
3. Shame
4. Abandonment
5. Affliction
6. Restlessness
8. Oppression
9. Grief
10. Condemnation

The good news, however, is that God promises us that none of these weapons shall prosper and that we will have the power to condemn every word of judgment; this is our inheritance as servants of the Lord (v. 17). The enemy may fire every weapon against us, but we will not be vulnerable if we recognize our maker, God, as our husband. We are accepted in the Beloved. Jesus Christ is the Beloved of God, and when we are in Him, we have a husband who will protect us from all the weapons of the enemy. He will be our sun and our shield against every fiery dart of the enemy.

Thank You, Lord, for being my husband who shields and protects me from the weapons of the enemy. Heal any former wounds I may have received in my early years because I was vulnerable to rejection.

God's Chosen Fast
Isaiah 57:15–59:21

It has been my custom over the years to have seasons of fasting. Fasting has many benefits, but the goal of fasting is not to get God to do something for you. When we fast, it is our time to intercede for others and also to have our own hearts changed. This passage in Isaiah lists several ways we can pray for others during a season of fasting. I must add there are different ways of fasting. Perhaps because of medical reasons you are not able to do without food. Many people do a Daniel fast, which is simply eating vegetables only. Other people fast on fruit juices. Some fast from watching TV.

How do we intercede for others in our seasons of prayer and fasting? We can pray prayers that will do the following:

1. Loosen the bands of wickedness of others
2. Undo heavy burdens people are carrying
3. Set free those who are oppressed
4. Break all kinds of bondages in others lives

I used to keep a list of men in our church who never attended church with their wives. During my season of prayer and fasting I always prayed for these men to be saved and set free from all bondage and that they would accompany their wives to church. I had the privilege of seeing one of those men saved and set free, and he now attends church regularly with his wife.

Besides praying when we fast, we can also do acts of kindness toward others. We can feed those who are hungry and bring the outcast into our homes. I have a friend who fasts regularly, and she has brought many a homeless man into her home for dinner. She also has been able to see the spiritual progress of one of these men over a period of more than three years in which he has lived in their home. We also can give clothes to those who need them. These are just some of the ways we can reach out to others as well as pray for them.

One of the main ways we can cooperate with God in changing our own hearts during a fasting time is to not hide ourselves from our own flesh. This means we are to be available to be reconciled to those who are closest to us, our own families. Perhaps there is someone you need to forgive in your own family. Don't run from this. Instead, run to this person and humble yourself and ask their forgiveness.

The promise of God when we do these things in prayer and fasting is that He will reward us by hearing our cry. His presence will be with us, and also our health will spring forth. The primary agenda in fasting is to love one another through prayers of intercession and service to them. When we put others first, then our own needs and hearts are changed.

READ: Isaiah 60:1–62:5; Philippians 1:27–2:18; Psalm 72:1–20; Proverbs 24:11–12

Majestic Ministry
Isaiah 60:1–62:5

So many Christians spend their lives looking forward to when their ministry will be released in power. While they are waiting, they miss so many opportunities. The great ministry they hope to have one day may never develop. Many years ago when I almost died, the Lord taught me about the ministry of the moment. As I felt my spirit leaving my body as I was hemorrhaging after a miscarriage, I realized I might not have another minute to live. At that time I learned how precious every minute is. True ministry is seeing every moment as an opportunity to minister to another person or to the Lord.

This passage in Isaiah shares the ministry of Jesus; that is the ministry we are to allow to flow freely from us as we are empowered by the Spirit. Jesus said the Spirit of the Lord was upon Him to anoint Him to do seven things:

1. To preach good tidings to the meek (preach the gospel)
2. To proclaim liberty to the captives (deliverance)
3. To open the prison doors for those who are bound (deliverance)
4. To proclaim the acceptable year of the Lord and His day of judgment
5. To comfort those who mourn
6. To give them beauty for ashes, the oil of joy for mourning and the garment of praise for the spirit of heaviness (healing the brokenhearted)
7. To cause us to be planted as trees of righteousness (discipleship)

The above is the ministry of Jesus. It also is your ministry today. Be watching today for opportunities to reach out to the rejected, preach the gospel, to tell people of the liberating power of Jesus, to disciple someone or to speak of the Lord's coming to another person. The person you are face to face with right now is your ministry.

Lord, help me to be diligent to look for the opportunities to have You minister through me today. Help me never to miss the ministry of the moment.

When We Doubt God, What Happens?
Psalm 73:1–28

All of us from time to time in our lives have been besieged with doubt. In this psalm David was saying to God, "What is the use of living a righteous life? All the wicked are prospering, and here I am suffering." He felt this way until he went into the sanctuary and sought the Lord. As he quieted his spirit, he began to hear the voice of the Lord, and he understood the end of the wicked. He understood that the wicked ultimately would be judged and destroyed, but he would be accepted by God and not destroyed. Then David makes this wonderful statement: "Nevertheless, I am continually with You; You hold me by my right hand. You will guide me with Your counsel, and afterward receive me to glory" (vv. 23–24).

What a statement! From doubt to total security. The thought of God holding me by my right hand through whatever storm I am facing overwhelms my soul with comfort. I can remember as a little girl how safe and secure I felt when my father reached for my right hand to assist me across the street. As we first started to cross the street, a little fear and doubt would assail me, but I knew I would make it safely across because Daddy was always on the alert to watch out for any traffic that was coming toward us. We cross many streets in this life, and God, our heavenly Father, knows what is coming our way. He will always see us across safely whatever trial or test we might be facing.

What is facing us on the other side of the street? When we cross the last street in this life, glory awaits us. Think of it. I like what my pastor's wife says about the death of His saints. She shares that the saints at death say "Halle-" on this side and "-lujah" on the other side. David said, "You will guide me with Your counsel, and afterward receive me to glory." What have we to fear? We do not even have to fear death because Jesus has taken away the sting of death, and the grave no longer holds any victory.

How did David reach a place of such security and safety after having such doubt and fear? He quieted his spirit and began to remember the times God had held his right hand through other horrific troubles and trials.

Today you may be going through a deep struggle with your faith. The fiery darts of doubt are coming toward you like rushing traffic. You are in the middle of the street of this trying circumstance. Remember, God has not abandoned you. He is holding your right hand, and He will see you safely across this difficult time and all the trials you may face in the future.

Lord, thank You for holding my right hand and for giving me Your counsel.

The Wicked and the Just

Proverbs 24:15–16

Yesterday's reading spoke of the ultimate destruction of the wicked. The proverb for today speaks of what will happen to the wicked and the just. The wicked man falls into mischief. The just man may fall even seven times, but he will get up each time. The just man always rises again. The wicked, however, falls forever.

We thought yesterday about our heavenly Father holding our right hand as we cross the streets of this life. The reason why the just always keep getting up even though they may fall is simply because God is holding their right hand. The moment they fall, His strong right hand pulls them back up again.

One of my favorite scriptures is Psalm 37:23–24: "The steps of a good man are ordered by the LORD and He delights in his way. Though he fall, he shall not be utterly cast down; for the LORD upholds him with His hand."

Two images come to my mind as I read these verses. First, I see the Lord as the Good Shepherd. One of His sheep has rolled over on his back and cannot right himself because his wool is too heavy. The Good Shepherd comes and sets the little sheep on his feet again.

Another image was given to me by a speaker who shared a vision she had of the Lord. She shared that she had always pictured Jesus with His back turned toward her as she followed Him. One morning in prayer the Lord corrected her view, and she saw the Lord face to face with her. He was walking backwards with His arms outstretched as a loving father does when he is coaxing his one-year-old to take his first step. Jesus was ready to instantly catch her when she started to fall because His eyes were trained on her always. His strong arms were always outstretched to catch her.

Today you may feel flat on your back. Jesus your Good Shepherd is near you to set you on your feet again. You may feel you cannot take one more step because your burden is so heavy. Jesus is face to face with you, and the moment you feel so weak that you begin to stumble, He reaches out to you and lifts you up. He is the glory and the lifter of your head.

Lord, You know what I am going through right now. Forgive me for not trusting You with my burdens. I come to You this morning, and I know now You will lift my heavy burden and set me on solid ground.

October 3

READ: Jeremiah 1:1–2:30; Philippians 4:1–23; Psalm 75:1–10; Proverbs 24:17–20

Pray About Everything; Worry About Nothing
Philippians 4:1–23

Most of us are familiar with the phrase that is "batted about" so casually today: "Don't worry, be happy." There is a way you can not worry and be happy no matter what you are facing in this life—*pray*. The phrase should be revised to say, "Don't worry, PRAY!" If we followed this admonition, our lives would be filled with joy (not just a happy "ha-ha" joy, but an inner joy that will strengthen us in all circumstances).

Worry is a sin. Worry is negative meditation. When we meditate, we roll over and over again in our minds the same thing. When we worry, we keep thinking over and over again the same negative thought. Both my mother and mother-in-law were worriers. I think since they both went through the Great Depression a little worry bug was implanted deep within them, and it was hard to shake it off. Most of the things they worried about never came to pass.

Worry usually comes when we play the "what-if" game. This is one of Satan's favorite games, and he loves it when we begin to play it with him. When we are always thinking about the things that could happen in the future, we are in a fantasy land of deception. Satan has deceived us, and once again he has gotten our hearts and minds off the now into the never-never land of future events that may never come to pass. Two of Satan's main tactics are to get our minds off the now by getting us to wallow in the past and worry about the future. Faith can only operate in the now; that is why Satan always wants to direct our thoughts away from the now.

We pay a great price when we worry. Satan has robbed us of the faith that can only operate in the now, and often he finds entrance into our lives to do further damage through fear of the future. Worry and fear are bedfellows; we must not allow them to climb into bed with us. If we do, we will be robbed of our peace, subject to mental and emotional torment, and even subject to physical illness and affliction. Worry is not worth the price we have to pay.

This passage in Philippians gives the cure-all to worry. It says, "Don't worry about anything. Instead, pray about everything." The moment a worry thought comes our way, we need to say, "Thank you, Satan, for giving me that thought, because that very thought causes me to get on my knees to pray." James tells us to submit ourselves to God and resist the devil. Prayer is one of the key ways we submit ourselves to God. A worrying person can never be successful in resisting Satan, but a praying person will always have the victory over "old slewfoot."

Have you tormented the devil today? Every time you pray when worry thoughts come your way, Satan is tormented. He will be tormented, and you will receive the peace that passes your own understanding and God will set a guard around your heart and mind. DON'T WORRY, PRAY!

Lord, forgive me for the times I have worried instead of praying.

October 4

READ: Jeremiah 2:31–4:18; Colossians 1:1–20; Psalm 76:1–12; Proverbs 24:21–22

A Prayer for Those Who Love
Colossians 1:1–20

When my children were young, I used to pray Scripture prayers for them aloud. Most of the Scripture prayers came from the letters Paul wrote to the different churches. Today's reading in Colossians has one of the prayers I prayed regularly for my three sons. It is an excellent prayer that you can pray for anyone you love. Paul said, "I do not cease to pray for you." These were the things he prayed: "That you may be filled with the knowledge of His will in all wisdom and spiritual understanding; that you may walk worthy of the Lord, fully pleasing Him, being fruitful in every good work and increasing in the knowledge of God; strengthened with all might, according to His glorious power, for all patience and longsuffering with joy" (vv. 9–11).

These are prayers you can torment the devil with when he gives you thoughts of worry about your loved ones. When we pray God's Word instead of just our own thoughts, we give Satan a double whammy. We submit ourselves to God through prayer, which causes us to humble ourselves under the mighty hand of God by casting our every care upon Him. Remember our admonition yesterday, "Be anxious for nothing, but in everything by prayer and supplication, with thanksgiving, let your requests be made known to God" (Phil. 4:6). When we cast our cares about our loved ones on Jesus, we can no longer keep whirling in the worry state about our loved ones and Satan is defeated. Humility is one of our strongest weapons against Satan. When we pray God's Word we are always praying according to God's will. Satan is wounded greatly by the fiery darts we send him when we speak God's Word aloud in prayer against him.

Are you concerned today about your family and loved ones? Then use the scriptures above to pray for your loved ones right now. Also remind Satan that God has promised to perfect everything that is a concern to you. Give slewfoot a double whammy today, and peace will flood your soul.

Lord, I humble myself before You and cast all of my cares and concerns for my loved ones into Your loving arms. I pray that my children, husband and all my loved ones might be filled with the knowledge of Your will in all wisdom and spiritual understanding. I pray that they might walk worthy of You and please You and be fruitful in every good work. I pray that they daily will increase in the knowledge of You and will suffer long and be always patient and longsuffering because You fill them with Your glory and joy.

October 5

READ: Jeremiah 4:19–6:14; Colossians 1:21–2:7; Psalm 77:1–20; Proverbs 24:23–25

The Great Mystery
Colossians 1:21–2:7

For so long in my own life I did not understand the mystery Paul speaks of in his letter to the Colossians. I received Jesus as my Lord and Savior at nine years of age, and from nine to twenty-six years of age I struggled to walk in the ways of the Lord. I would do well for a season, and then I would find myself drifting. Finally the day came when I was twenty-six and that mystery began to be unveiled to me.

I was at a retreat, and the leader told all attending to find a quiet spot around the lake. Our instructions were to be still and quiet and ask the Lord questions and then wait for answers. This was new to me because my prayer life before this time was always a one-way conversation with the Lord. I came to Him with my needs and requests, and then hung the prayer line up in His face. I couldn't wait to sit down with the Lord because there was a big question I wanted to ask Him, and I hoped He would give me a straight answer. The big question was, "Lord, what is wrong with my life?"

When I asked Him this question, I sat on a log by the lake and waited for the answer. After waiting only a few moments I heard this answer spoken not in an audible voice but spoken to my spiritual ears. "Linda, what is wrong with your life is that you have been trying to earn My love. I gave My love to you freely two thousand years ago when I died on the cross for you. You need to receive My love today and quit trying to work for Me. Instead, let Me work through you. Rest, relax and receive My love today. If you did nothing but sit on that log the rest of your life, I would still love you."

On that day the mystery (Christ in you the hope of glory) became a reality in my life. I realized that day that it was God who worked within me both to will and to do of His good pleasure. No longer would I be working for Him, but He would be working through me. On that special day I became rooted in His love and established in His faith instead. I understood that His love within me could love anyone through me. No longer did I have to struggle to love others. I understood that it was His faith within me that would enable me to be steadfast in faith throughout my life. What joy flooded my soul on that special day.

Is Christ in you today? Do you realize what this means? Within you dwells the One by whom and to whom all that is created was created. Within you dwells the miracle worker, the lover of every soul, the giver of life abundant, the forgiver of sins, the restorer of the broken heart, the healer of sickness and disease, the Prince of Peace, the breaker of every yoke of bondage. Within you dwells the One most glorious. Christ in you, the hope of glory.

He Has Won the Victory
Colossians 2:8–23

It was the custom in the days of Paul for a conquering nation to parade down the streets in triumph with their spoil and their prisoners of war in chains behind them. Triumph is the celebration of victory. This scripture speaks of King Jesus having spoiled principalities and powers. He made a show of them openly, triumphing over them. What a comfort to know that every demon has been spoiled. They have been made a show of openly.

Then you may ask, Why do we still wrestle with demonic oppression? When demonic spirits try to oppress us, we need to say aloud, "The Lord Jesus has already made a show of you openly, and He has triumphed over you." The enemy wants us to believe that Jesus has not already dealt with him and his demons. Jesus said, "It is finished," on the cross, and He meant just that. Demonic spirits need never win the victory over us because Jesus has already won the victory over them. Satan and his demons will only have success in our lives if we give into them through fear because we have been deceived and believe they have power over us. Jesus clearly said He has given us all power over all the power of the enemy. That means ALL. We, however, must believe this and take our stand against the enemy by using the blood of Jesus and the word of our testimony. We need to testify to those demonic spirits that seek to bring us low that because of the blood of Jesus they are defeated foes.

The moment depression, oppression, heaviness, discouragement or any other down feeling comes upon us, we need to first submit ourselves to God and then resist the devil. We first dress ourselves in the full armor and the garment of praise that can lift all oppressive spirits. Then we need to speak aloud to those demons that try to harass us. We can remind them of this scripture, and we can say, "Jesus has won the victory over you. You were defeated on the cross because of the blood of Jesus. I bind you in the name of Jesus and by the power of the blood of Jesus, and I tell you to leave me now and do not return." Have you ever tried this when you know the devil is tormenting you with fear or discouragement? Give it a try. You will be surprised what will happen. Often by just saying the name "Jesus" aloud we can put the enemy to flight.

The next time you are harassed by Satan and his demons, picture in your mind the triumphant march of Jesus with every demon bound by His blood marching in total defeat behind Him. You will then feel a surge of power within you, and you can exercise all power over all the power of the enemy. We never have to put up with the devil because he has already been put out.

Lord, forgive me for not taking the authority that is mine in Your name and by Your blood to bind the enemy. Help me to always remember that You have already defeated Satan and all of his demons. Thanks be to God for the victory that is always ours and who always causes us to triumph through Jesus Christ.

Dressing Ourselves
Colossians 3:1–17

Not a day goes by that we don't have to dress ourselves. I love to have what I call "robe days." These are days when I go nowhere and just stay in my nightgown all day. Even on those days, however, I have to put a robe on just in case someone comes to the door. Often I find myself thinking ahead about what I am going to wear the next day. Jesus, however, tells us not to think ahead about what we will wear or even what we will eat. Granted, we do need to make some preparations ahead of time, but we should never be absorbed with thoughts of what we will wear or eat. It is interesting that when I get together with other ladies we often are talking about clothes and sharing recipes. I believe our times together would better be used if we talked about the Lord together. After all, without Him we would have neither clothes nor food. When we are absorbed with what we wear and eat, we are declaring we do not trust God to provide these things.

Paying too much attention to my appearance and what I wear is a stronghold I am still battling. Satan knows clothes are my weakness. It amazes me that I will be worshiping the Lord in church and suddenly the thought comes, "What are you going to wear tomorrow?" Guess where that came from! One of the ways I can counter those thoughts is to think immediately about the outfit God wants me to dress myself in every day. What is this outfit?

This outfit is very special because it is fresh and new, and it makes us look like Jesus. This outfit is called "the new man." Paul says in this passage, "And have put on the new man who is renewed in knowledge according to the image of Him who created him…"(vs.10). "Put on therefore, as the elect of God, holy and beloved, bowels of mercies, kindness, humbleness of mind, meekness, longsuffering; forbearing one another, and forgiving one another, if any man have a quarrel against any: even as Christ forgave you, so also do ye" (vs. 12–13, KJV).

Jesus does not want to see us wearing the old dirty and worn outfit of the old man. This outfit included anger, wrath, malice, blasphemy and filthy communication. Now when I start thinking about what I am going to wear tomorrow, I pray the following prayer:

> *Lord, there I go again thinking about what I am going to wear. Right now I put on Your garment of praise and I dress myself in the "New Man." Thank You for this beautiful outfit that makes me look just like You.*

October 8

READ: Jeremiah 10:1–11:23; Colossians 3:18–4:18; Psalm 78:59–72; Proverbs 24:28–29

God Expects Respect
Colossians 3:18–4:18

One of the major problems with youth in our culture today is their lack of respect for parents and teachers. Our son Ron wanted to be a teacher of chemistry in high school. He finished his degree at Georgia Tech and then began his practice teaching at a high school in an exclusive neighborhood. He experienced such a great lack of respect from his students that he decided not to finish his practice teaching. Later Ron had the opportunity to teach in China, and the students respected and honored him. He loved teaching in China, and he plans to return.

The trouble with our nation today is the lack of the fear of the Lord. God has been reduced to a Santa Claus-type image who never would chasten us if we are bad. Some people say "the fear of the Lord" is simply honoring and standing in awe of God. The fear of the Lord is much more than this. God has not changed. He deals with us with judgment and mercy. He still judges nations, and if a nation falls completely from their belief in Him, such nations will be reduced in their power and influence in the world. We should be fearful of disobeying God because disobedience will always bring consequences that are not pleasant.

We will be judged according to the works we did on earth. If we are saved, we will not be disqualified from eternal life, but we may be disqualified from many of the rewards in heaven. We should tremble at the Word of God instead of looking at the Word as a name-it-claim-it book of promises. God's Word is filled with promises, but most of these promises have conditions we must fulfill. One of the main conditions we must fulfill before we can claim the promises of God is to honor and obey God. Just as students will learn nothing in the classroom if they are rebellious and disobedient, we will learn nothing in the school of life if we are rebellious and disobedient. In the end we will fail at life and no one wants to fail.

Our passage in Colossians exhorts us to do the following: "And whatsoever you do, do it heartily, as to the Lord, and not to men, knowing that from the Lord you will receive the reward of the inheritance; for you serve the Lord Christ. But he who does wrong will be repaid for what he has done, and there is no partiality" (Col. 3:23–25).

Because God is no respecter of persons, we should respect and honor Him daily in both our words and deeds. God expects respect, and we should teach our children to respect and honor Him with their actions and words. The fear of the Lord is taught, not caught. I am afraid many of us have failed to teach the fear of the Lord to our children, and we are reaping what we have sown.

Lord, help me to live daily in the fear of You.

Spiritual Nursing
1 Thessalonians 1:1–2:8

I was at a time in my life when I felt I needed to get more education and go to work. My sons were facing college later, and I wanted to do my part in paying for their education. One morning as I was having my quiet time, I read 1 Thessalonians 2:7: "But we were gentle among you, just as a nursing mother cherishes her own children."

That's it, I thought to myself as soon as I read this passage. *God wants me to be a nurse.* The next week I found myself down at my old college. I prayed for favor with the admissions to count all my former credits. They informed me I could finish a nursing course in two years, and in fact, this was the last two-year R.N. course they would offer at this school. In the future you would have to go for four years to receive your R.N. I was delighted. This had to be God because it was the seventh day of the seventh month in 1977. I bounced out of the admissions and came home to report to the children that their mother was going to be a full-time college student.

Two quarters into nursing I realized I might have missed God. I attended a course called "Introduction to Nursing," and the professor only talked about when she retired how great it would be when she could do her needlepoint and garden. I thought to myself, *I can do this now. Nursing must not be all it is cracked up to be if she is looking so forward to retirement.* When I hit Chemistry 101, I knew I could not go on, so I left college and returned to cook my boys' dinner that evening. I had not been able to do that for six months. The boys and my husband asked, "What happened? Did you flunk out?" "No," I replied. "I copped out before I flunked out."

The following week I asked the Lord, "What on earth was all that about? After all, I thought You were telling me to be a nurse." The answer I received was so comforting. I heard the following with my spiritual ears: "I do want you to be a nurse, but not in the physical. You are called to be a spiritual nurse—to bind up the brokenhearted and to set at liberty those who are bruised."

The mistake I made is one many of us make in the course of our lives. I had interpreted a spiritual instruction with my natural mind, and I moved in haste on my own understanding rather than inquiring more of the Lord. That day in prayer I also was instructed not to worry about financing the boy's education. Instead I was just to pray for my husband to prosper in his job, and he did.

Today the Lord is giving you instructions. Will you listen with spiritual ears?

October 10

Gathering Unto the Lord
Jeremiah 14:11–16:15

We are living in the last days, and many of the prophecies in God's Word about Israel have been fulfilled. One of these main prophesies is in our reading in Jeremiah today. The prophet Jeremiah speaks of a time when Israel will no longer say, "'The LORD lives who brought up the children of Israel from the land of Egypt,' but 'The LORD lives who brought up the children of Israel from the land of the north and from all the lands where He had driven them.' I will bring them back into their land which I gave to their fathers" (Jer. 16:15).

We had the joy of hosting a couple who have had a ministry in Israel for fourteen years. They began a ministry in Jerusalem called "Friends of Israel." Friends of Israel has a distribution center for immigrants coming into Israel. Sharon, the wife of the couple, shared they are expecting triple the number of Jewish immigrants this year compared to other years. Recently the millionth Jewish immigrant entered Israel.

Alijah (the return to the land of Israel) is happening in mammoth proportions as the God of Israel gathers His chicks to the country that surrounds Jerusalem. What is God's plan? As we see this great ingathering, we understand the fulfillment of the prophecy in Zechariah 12. This prophecy will happen when the Lord returns. "And I will pour on the house of David and on the inhabitants of Jerusalem the Spirit of grace and supplication, then they shall look on Me whom they have pierced. Yes, they will mourn for Him as one mourns for his only son, and grieve for Him as one grieves for a firstborn" (Zech. 12:10).

God is gathering the children of Israel as a mother gathers her chickens, because all Israel will be saved in that great day when Jesus returns and sets His foot on the Mount of Olives. The Jewish people in Israel will see Him, and they will repent. God promises to open a fountain of cleansing for this holy remnant that will remain and believe.

Don't give up praying for your Jewish friends. Pray that God will reveal Jesus to them as their Messiah even today.

Father, I pray for the protection of the Jewish people left in Russia and for all those You have chosen to return to the land of Israel. As you gather Your chosen from the four corners of the earth, I ask humbly that You would gather those Jewish people I know into Your loving arms and introduce them to Jesus, Your Son and their Messiah. I ask this in the name of Jesus.

285

October 11

READ: Jeremiah 16:16–18:23; 1 Thessalonians 4:1–5:3; Psalm 81:1–16; Proverbs 25:6–7

The Repentance
1 Thessalonians 4:1–5:3

Anew series of books has just been produced that speaks of the last days. The series is called Left Behind. These fiction novels, which are based on Scripture, speak of the day of "the Rapture,"a day many believe the saints of the Lord will meet Jesus in the air. That day is described in detail in this series. Trains, planes and cars will crash suddenly, and those left behind will not know that something supernatural has happened. Some members of families will be taken in the Rapture, and others will be left behind.

Our New Testament reading in 1 Thessalonians tells us that the Lord will come as a thief in the night. Suddenly, without warning, the trumpet blast from heaven will usher in that great day. The graves of saints will be opened, and both the dead and living believers will meet the Lord in the air to receive their glorified bodies.

The thought of such a scene is mind-boggling. Scripture, however, is clear, and it is written to comfort us. This scripture is often read at Christian funerals. If this scripture does not bring you comfort, chances are you have not acknowledged Jesus as your Lord and Savior. The question is not, "Will this really happen?" The question to ask is, "When this happens, will I be ready?" Paul in his letters makes it clear that we are to live each day expecting the Lord's return. If you knew for sure that Jesus would return today, how on earth would you live out your day?

Meditate on what you would do if you knew today was your last day on earth. I have thought of this often, and here are some of the things I think I would do. I would call all of my loved ones and friends and tell them how much I love them. I would spend a lot of time with the Lord in prayer and listening to His Word. I would try to reach as many of the unsaved as I could to tell them the wonderful story of Jesus' love for them. I would make sure I had confessed and repented of all of my sins.

Our youngest son Ray used to stand in our carport and look up to the sky. When I asked him what he was doing, he said, "I'm looking for Jesus in the clouds. He may come today." Truly Jesus may come today. Are you ready?

Lord, how different my days would be if I lived each day as if it were my last day on earth. Forgive me for my procrastination, my waste of time, my apathy and my busyness. Help me today to take time with You, and also to share the good news of Your love with those I meet today. Today may not be my last day on earth, but it may be the last day on earth for those I meet today.

October 12

READ: Jeremiah 19:1–21:14; 1 Thessalonians 5:4–28; Psalm 82:1–8; Proverbs 25:8–10

I Can't Do It, Lord!
1 Thessalonians 5:4–28

Do you know what you are called to do on this earth? We all as believers have common callings such as being witnesses in this earth, lights shining in the midst of darkness, salt to give flavor and preserve the lives of others by introducing them to Christ and discipling them. I believe, however, that each believer has a specific calling from God on his life.

What is a calling? A calling is the point where your passion meets a place of great need. A calling is not a vocation. It is not an office in the church, or even one of the fivefold ministries (teacher, evangelist, preacher, apostle and prophet). A calling is a common thread that gathers the various seasons and events of your life into one beautiful garment tailor-made for you—a garment that displays God's glory in a unique way. Let me share with you how God revealed His calling to my family members and myself. Discovering your own personal calling involves asking, seeking and knocking in prayer and then listening for the answer.

When my boys were very young, I asked the Lord to show me their calling in life. As I sought the Lord in prayer, He shared the following with me: "I have called your oldest son, Russ, to be a bridge between races. I have called your middle son, Ron, to be a bridge between nations. I have called your youngest son, Ray, to be a bridge between families."

I shared this word from the Lord with each of the boys, and all three are fulfilling their God-given call. Later I discovered the Hebrew word for *priests* is bridge. One morning as I was waking from a deep sleep, I heard a whisper in my ear. I knew it was the Lord, and He was calling me "Jochabed." I heard, "Wake up, Jochabed." I didn't know who Jochabed was, but I knew the Lord was calling me by a new name. I looked Jochabed up in the Bible and found she was the mother of Aaron and Moses—the first priests. God had called me to be a mother of priests (bridges).

My husband discovered his calling while seeking the Lord alone on Stone Mountain. He heard the Lord call him Joseph. We looked up *Joseph* in Hebrew and found it means "provider." Then as we researched we discovered that three Josephs in the Bible were all providers: Joseph, Israel's son, provided food for his whole family and all of Egypt during a famine; Joseph, the guardian father of Jesus, provided a home and nurturing for Jesus in His childhood; and Joseph of Arimathea provided the tomb for Jesus. My husband's motivational gift is giving.

I discovered my own calling when I asked the Lord which part of the body I was. Was I a foot, eye, hand or what? I heard in my spirit He had called me to be a voice, and then I remembered this was the call of John the Baptist—a voice crying in the wilderness, "Prepare ye the way of the Lord." This call has taken many forms in my life—teaching, writing, singing, etc. Ask the Lord today what your call is. As you ask, seek and knock, you will discover your own calling.

READ: Jeremiah 22:1–23:20; 2 Thessalonians 1:1–12; Psalm 83:1–18; Proverbs 25:11–14

How Does Your Garden Grow?
2 Thessalonians 1:1–12

My husband and I were so excited about beautifying our backyard, so we went and bought some brightly colored azaleas and other plants. We labored to plant them. As we look today at our back garden, we see only dried-up bushes. We had such a drought this summer, and because of water restrictions, we could not water the plants. They all withered and died.

Such is the case in the life of many Christians. With great enthusiasm they receive Jesus and then begin to plant God's Word in their hearts. Often, however, the enthusiasm wains, and suddenly they find themselves in a spiritual drought. The only way out of a spiritual drought is to begin once again to refresh your spirit with the water of God's Spirit and His Word.

Our New Testament reading today speaks of three things we are to grow in daily—faith, love and patience. Paul says, "We are bound to thank God always for you, brethren, as it is fitting, because your faith grows exceedingly, and the love of every one of you all abounds toward each other" (v. 3).

What a compliment Paul paid to the church at Thessalonica. He said their faith was growing exceedingly and their love toward one another was abounding. He goes on to say that their patience also was great.

Wouldn't it be wonderful if others noticed we were growing daily in faith toward God, love toward one another and patience in all circumstances and tribulations? How is your garden growing today? It might be time to water faith, love and patience with the Word of God poured upon you by the Holy Spirit.

Paul ends this reading in Thessalonians with a wonderful prayer. I would like to pray a similar prayer for you this morning and also for myself:

Father, in Jesus' name I pray for the persons reading this devotional. I pray that they would be counted worthy of their calling and fulfill all the good pleasure of Your goodness and the work of faith with power. I pray that the name of our Lord Jesus Christ might be glorified in them according to the grace of our God and the Lord Jesus Christ.

Will We Go Through the Tribulation?
2 Thessalonians 2:1–17

The question "Will we go through the tribulation?" has been discussed in many books and by many teachers. People do not like the thought of going through any tribulation. In fact, when tribulation comes, they want an easy out. One of the promises of God we do not like to claim is, "In the world you will have tribulation, but be of good cheer, I have overcome the world." Jesus said this, and we will all suffer some tribulation in this life. There will be a day, however, when there will be tribulation as never before on this earth. This is a seven-year period at the end of this age when there will be horrific trials. All of us would like to escape this period of time, but the more I study Scripture, the only promise I can hold on to to comfort me about the last days on earth is, "We are not appointed to wrath." If one studies Revelation, he will discover that the last three and one-half years of the Great Tribulation will be a time on earth when all kinds of plagues are poured out on the earth. This is the time of God's wrath, and these various trials are called the bowls of wrath. I am convinced the church will not be on earth during this last three and one-half years because we are not appointed to God's wrath. The statement is made in Revelation that at this time no one left on earth will repent.

Personally I hold to the mid-trib theory, but I believe God wants us to not be absolutely sure. I heard someone say they believed in the pan-trib—it will all pan out in the end. God's main concern is that we be ready whenever He chooses to come again. The Bible tells us that not even Jesus knows the time. Only the Father knows, and when it is time for Jesus' return to earth, the Father will tell Him. If Jesus does not know, then I find it very presumptuous of me to try to figure it out and to be convinced that I have discovered exactly the time of our departure from this earth when Jesus comes to receive His own. We can, however, know the season, and all I can say is the season is very near.

Whether you are a mid-trib, post-trib or pre-trib really does not matter. Your opinion holds no effect on God and His plans. However, this passage in Thessalonians does tell us what matters to God. "Therefore, brethren, stand fast and hold the traditions which you were taught, whether by word or our epistle" (v. 15).

This exhortation causes me to bow my knee and pray. You may want to join me.

> *Lord, help me to stand fast in these last days. I do not want to be one of those who fall away. I trust You as the author and finisher of my faith, and I believe the good work You have begun will be finished.*

READ: Jeremiah 26:1–17:22; 2 Thessalonians 3:1–18; Psalm 85:1–13; Proverbs 25:16

How the Lord Greets Us
Psalm 85:1–13

Greetings are so important. The way we greet people always reveals how we feel about them. If we only greet with a handshake, those we greet are distant friends. If we greet with a kiss and a hug, we usually are greeting those we love and call near and dear to us.

How does God greet us? This psalm gives the answer. First God greets us with mercy and truth, and then He kisses us with righteousness and peace. With truth He springs out of the earth to greet us, and with righteousness He descends from heaven in the bodily form of Jesus to greet us with a holy kiss. The life of Jesus Christ is God's greeting to us. He greets us daily with His peace, His love, His righteousness, His truth, His comfort, His faithfulness and on and on. Jesus is God in the flesh, and how great it is to come to know the Father through Jesus. Sometimes when I picture Jesus He is kissing me first on the left cheek and then on the right cheek. Then He holds my face and looks into my eyes for a long long time. I feel such a surge of compassion within me that I want to jump, leap, shout and ascend to heaven where I can be with Him always.

Today I celebrate my birthday. I used to read a book to my boys about different animals and how they greet us. The chicken says, "Cock a doodle do," the bird sings a sweet song, but the bear gives us a great big bear hug. On every birthday of my loved ones I always say as I hug them, "This is a great big birthday bear hug from me."

Two thousand years ago God, our heavenly Father, gave us all a great big birthday bear hug when Jesus was born on this earth. He was Immanuel, God with us, and He is still giving us great big hugs and kisses. If you have never experienced His hugs and kisses in the spirit, today is your day. Be still for a moment and reach out to Him in praise and worship. Soon you will know His sweet embrace and kiss, and it will carry you through the rest of the day.

Thank You, Lord, for giving me Your kiss of truth, righteousness, mercy and grace through Jesus Christ. I love Him so much. What a joy it is to know His presence even though I cannot physically feel His hugs and kisses. What a day it will be when I will feel His physical arms around me and know the tender kisses on my cheeks. Thank You, Lord, for letting me experience this now on earth in the spirit.

October 16

READ: Jeremiah 28:1–29:32; 1 Timothy 1:1–20; Psalm 86:1–17; Proverbs 25:17

Teach Me Your Ways
Psalm 86:1–17

This is one of my favorite psalms. I pray this psalm almost every morning. I usually paraphrase several verses and pray, "For You are God. You do wondrous things. Teach me Your ways, Lord. I want to walk in Your truths. Unite my heart to fear Your name, and I will glorify You forevermore."

God has been faithful over the years to hear my prayer. My desire has always been to know the ways of the Lord, not just His works. The children of Israel knew the mighty works of the Lord, but only Moses knew His ways. What is the difference between His works and ways? The works of the Lord are always the outer manifestations of His power, but the ways of the Lord are His character traits and His heart. When we begin to know His ways, we can be secure in His love for us. We can be confident in His desire to grant us all we need to get through whatever circumstances in life we may face.

All we need is found in God's character. He is longsuffering, patient, merciful, loving, joyful, peaceful, kind, truthful and full of grace. The more intimately you know someone, the more you can trust Him. When I married my husband I thought I knew Him, but even after many years of marriage I am still learning his ways. My trust level in my husband has increased greatly because I know now how much he loves me. I never question this. However, when we were first married, I sometimes was not secure in his love for me. It was not because he didn't love me. It was because I was insecure in my ability to hold his love forever. This dilemma is one we will never face with God. His love for us is forever and for all eternity, and nothing we do or say will stop His love for us. Of course, many times we may not please Him, but His love is unconditional.

My husband and I have a great relationship now because we both are secure in our love for one another. We never have to prove our love to each other. When we get to know God's character through intimate fellowship with Him, we realize we never have to prove our love to Him. He loves us, and all we have to do is receive His love and walk in His love with others. God's ways truly are wondrous.

Lord, I want to know You in a deeper way than I did yesterday.

Will My Loved Ones Be Saved?
1 Timothy 2:1–15

All of us have people who are near and dear to us who are not saved. You may even have immediate family members who still have not received God's great gift of salvation.

Several years ago I was on an Evangelism Explosion team. This was a program designed to train Christians in sharing the gospel with others. We were coupled with a trainer who shared the gospel with others as we observed. After one of these sessions, my trainer shared with me that she didn't believe her son would ever be saved. She said he was rebellious and on drugs, and she wondered if it was God's will to save him. I shared with her this scripture: "For this is good and acceptable in the sight of God our Savior, who desires all men to be saved and to come to the knowledge of the truth" (v. 4).

Based on this scripture I showed her how it is God's will to save her son. Then I prayed with her in faith for the salvation of her son.

A year later I was teaching a Bible study when a young girl came up to me afterwards. She said she was visiting and that I did not know her, but I knew her mother-in-law. Then she asked, "Do you remember going on visits with a lady in Evangelism Explosion and you prayed with her about her son?" I answered, "Yes." She continued, "Her son was saved six months ago, and I am his wife. I wanted to thank you for praying for him." What a joy it was for me to know another precious soul was added to God's kingdom and to see such a speedy answer to prayer.

God desires that your loved ones not perish. Whenever you pray for the salvation of another, you can know for sure you are praying God's will in that situation. Maybe there are those you would like to pray for today. Pray with me now for these precious souls.

Father, in the name of Jesus, I humbly ask with faith for the salvation of ____, _____, _____ and _____. I know now that it is Your will to save them. You say in Your Word if we pray anything according to Your will, we have the petitions we desire of You. Thank You for saving these dear souls, and I eagerly await the manifestation on earth of these prayers.

October 18

READ: Jeremiah 31:27–32:44; 1 Timothy 3:1–16; Psalm 88:1–18; Proverbs 25:20–22

God Put On an Earth Suit
1 Timothy 3:1–16

The major belief that reveals whether or not a religion is true or not is the belief in the mystery of godliness Paul writes about to Timothy. He says, "And without controversy great is the mystery of godliness: God was manifested in the flesh, justified in the Spirit, seen by angels, preached among the Gentiles, believed on in the world, received up into glory" (v. 16).

The dividing line between Christianity and other faiths is the belief that Jesus Christ is God in the flesh. God put on an earth suit and came and lived among us. When I was a little girl one of the most popular toys was an ant farm. I remember watching for hours a colony of ants enclosed between two pieces of glass. I could watch these ants, but I could not totally identify with them. The only way I could totally identify with them was for me to become an ant, get myself inside those two panes of glass and begin to work alongside of them. This is exactly what God did when He became flesh. God is a Spirit, and for God to identify with us totally He had to become flesh and Spirit. He had to put on an earth suit and dwell among us. Jesus, the Son of man, Immanuel—God with us—was the earth suit God wore for thirty-three years on earth.

Because God was in Christ Jesus reconciling the world to Himself, He could identify with us completely. Jesus was touched with the feelings of our infirmities, and He experienced sorrow, grief, pain, weakness, weariness and all the feelings we experience in our bodies, because like us, He had a body. Jesus was also tempted in all points even as we are tempted, yet He was without sin. Jesus knew exactly what it felt like to be tempted by Satan because He was tempted by the devil in the wilderness. Jesus knew what it felt like to long to eat and fulfill His bodily needs when He was tempted to turn the stone into bread after fasting for forty days. Jesus knew what it felt like to be tempted to take a short-cut to glory when Satan tempted Him to throw Himself off the pinnacle of the temple. Jesus knew what it felt like to be tempted to possess the world (climb the ladder of success quickly by bowing down to Satan's way instead of God's way). Jesus did not give into any of these temptations, but instead He overcame by using the sword of the Spirit and saying, "It is written." He overcame so that we might overcome through Him, but this does not negate the fact that Jesus felt just as we do when we are tempted. He, however, was without lust or sin.

Because Jesus experienced all the points of temptation that we experience, He now can make perfect intercession for us. Jesus can quickly rescue us when we are tempted if we will just call on His name. Because Jesus felt every thing we feel except lust, He knows how to comfort us in our weakness. This is the mystery of godliness—Immanuel—God with us, and He still is. Jesus ever lives to make intercession for us, and He sits in His resurrected form on God's right hand. Jesus knows what you are facing today, and right now He is praying for you.

October 19

Seducing Spirits
1 Timothy 4:1–16

The Holy Spirit is the "great teacher." Jesus says He, the Holy Spirit, will lead us into all truth, and He will bring to our remembrance everything that Jesus spoke about while He taught on earth. Whether we like to admit it or not, we all have a teacher. Some people have deceived themselves into thinking they are their own boss and they don't have to learn anything from any man. The truth, however, is that every day of our lives we are learning something. Our teacher may be experience, environment, hard knocks, etc., but ultimately we are taught either by Satan and his demons or by God and His Holy Spirit. Jesus gave us a great invitation. He said "Come to Me, all you who labor and are heavy laden, and I will give you rest. Take My yoke upon you and learn from Me; for I am gentle and lowly in heart, and you will find rest for your souls. For My yoke is easy and My burden is light" (Matt. 11:28–30).

Jesus was yoked to the Father the whole time He was on earth. He only did those things He saw the Father do, and He only said those things the Father told Him to say. When Jesus died and was resurrected, He then sent the Holy Spirit to us. Now we can take the yoke of the Holy Spirit upon us and learn of Jesus every day. The Holy Spirit takes all the things of Christ and shows them to us. Thank God for such a great teacher to learn from every day. I do hope you will choose to come to Jesus daily and allow the Holy Spirit to teach you meekness and lowliness of heart. This, however, is your choice. God will not make you sit at His feet daily. Some people even choose to sit in Satan's classroom of life.

This passage in Timothy tells us about Satan's teachers and speaks about what they are teaching. Paul shares with Timothy that in the last days seducing spirits will speak lies in hypocrisy. They will forbid to marry and command us to abstain from meats. These seducing spirits will speak through men and teach these false doctrines. Many cults today exhort their people to be vegetarians, and some even tell you not to marry. Seducing spirits are also sent by Satan as a frontal attack to soften us for the kill. The kill is when we give into our own lusts and commit sin. First, however, we listen to the suggestions and teachings of seducing spirits. Have you ever heard a message like this: "Why don't you try this? It won't hurt anyone, and nobody will know." Guess where that suggestion came from? It came from a seducing spirit, so we need to learn to recognize quickly the whispering thoughts a seducing spirit tries to implant in our minds. You can easily overcome such suggestions from seducing spirits by saying aloud, "You will have to deal with Jesus because I am under His authority and He is my teacher. I can do nothing without His permission." That will torment seducing spirits, and you will spare yourself the torment that follows giving in to their suggestions through submitting to your own lusts instead of Jesus.

Who will be your teacher today? I hope you choose to learn from Jesus.

October 20

Whom Do You Rebuke?
1 Timothy 5:1–25

Later in 2 Timothy Paul writes Timothy and tells him to rebuke those who oppose themselves by going their own willful way even after they have walked for a season with Christ Jesus. We are to rebuke those who will not endure sound doctrine, but who instead walk after their own lusts. In today's reading we see a clear warning to Timothy about not rebuking certain people. Paul says, "Rebuke not an elder, but entreat him as a father; and the younger men as brethren" (v. 1, KJV).

Rebuke should always be done with a meek spirit. If we ever rebuke anyone, we should do it with the attitude that but for the grace of God we also might go our own willful way. The reason Paul tells Timothy not to rebuke an elder is because of the respect we should show toward our elders. Timothy should leave such rebuke to another elder. Whether Paul is speaking of not rebuking those in the office of eldership in the church, we do not know. The message, however, is clear. Timothy was exhorted not to rebuke those who were older than him either in the spirit or in the flesh. I believe the understanding was for Timothy to leave such rebuke in the hands of older people or more mature Christians. We know Timothy was very young.

Timothy is also exhorted not to rebuke younger men. I believe this exhortation to Timothy was to protect those who were young in the spirit from being crushed by such a rebuke. We have to constantly be reminded that reproof and rebuke are for only one purpose. We rebuke or reprove a brother or sister in Christ with meekness of heart and with the intent to soften the heart of such a brother of sister so that they will repent. Reproof and rebuke are always used to restore a brother, not to crush or embarrass a brother or sister in Christ.

Paul in this letter is challenging us all to tread lightly when we feel we should reprove or rebuke a fellow Christian. We always have to do this with a heart of love toward this person, not a heart filled with criticism and judgment. Remember, if we rebuke or reprove in any spirit other than the spirit of love, we open ourselves to fall into sin in the same way the one we have rebuked fell. Remember Jesus' words: "Judge not, that you be not judged. For with what judgment you judge, you will be judged; and with what measure you use, it will be measured back to you" (Matt. 7:1–2). What a sober thought to end this devotional with! I am challenged to tread lightly in reproving and rebuking. Frankly, if I am busy about my Father's business, I won't have time to judge the sins of others.

> *Lord, forgive me for looking at the sins of other more than I look at my own sins. We have all sinned and fallen short of the glory of God, and I confess to You the many times I have sat in judgment of others.*

295

The Fruits of Pride
1 Timothy 6:1–21

Yesterday we were exhorted not to judge others. One of the reasons we are critical and judgmental of others is because we are walking in pride instead of walking in love. There are two forms of pride—superiority and inferiority. We either think too highly of ourselves, or too lowly of ourselves. When we think too highly of ourselves, we delight in criticizing and putting down others. When we think too lowly of ourselves, we often try to elevate ourselves by putting others down. Whether we think too highly of ourselves or too lowly of ourselves, we are not seeing ourselves as God sees us. Humility is seeing ourselves as God sees us, and when He looks at us He says one thing, "You are worth the death of My own Son." This is the price that was paid for you, and therefore you are seen by God as a precious treasure—a treasure worth dying for, and He did just that.

Whenever we are in pride—superiority or inferiority—we are no longer in a position to resist Satan. In fact, we place ourselves in the position to be resisted by God. The Bible tells us that God resists the proud and gives grace to the humble.

Why does God resist the proud? God knows the rotten fruit pride will cause in our lives, and He resists us and will continue to resist us until we humble ourselves and confess our pride. Our heavenly Father knows we instantly remove ourselves from a position of victory to a position of defeat the moment we get into pride. He died to give us the victory over Satan.

This passage in 1 Timothy lists the rotten fruit of pride. They are:

1. Ignorance
2. Strife
3. Meaningless debate
4. Envy
5. Railings
6. Evil surmising
7. Perverseness
8. Disputes
9. Corruption of the mind
10. Living in error rather than truth
11. Covetousness
12. Greed

This list should convince us that we should humble ourselves before God daily and ask Him to help keep us from ever being prideful. True humility will come to us only as we see ourselves as God sees us. Today would be a good day to humble ourselves before our Lord. You might want to join me as I do this:

Lord, I humble myself before You by casting my every care upon You. You and You alone are able to get me through this day. I refuse to trust in my own strength or resources. Instead I place my trust in You. I refuse to be down on myself today. Instead I will continually praise You for giving Your Son on the cross to save me. Thank You for counting me worthy.

What Is the Origin of Fear?
2 Timothy 1:1–18

Today's New Testament reading is one of my favorite scriptures. I have memorized 2 Timothy 1:7, and I use it often against the enemy as an effective sword of the spirit to wound him when he tries to wound me through fear. Listen to this wonderful scripture: "For God has not given us the spirit of fear, but of power and of love and of a sound mind."

Fear will always come knocking at our door throughout our lives. We must, however, learn how to slam the door in its face when Satan uses this wicked weapon against us. If Satan can get us to be afraid, then we lose the ability to resist him, and he knows this.

I had an experience with fear that almost robbed me of a trip to Israel. My husband was thinking of taking our two oldest boys and me to Israel with a tour our church was sponsoring. I was enthusiastic about the trip until I received a call from my prayer partner. My prayer partner called me before we made our final decision on whether to take this trip or not. My prayer partner told me about a lovely vision she had of our whole family riding in a chariot in heaven. She said she saw us all dressed in white with crowns on our heads. She thought she was telling me something that would edify. However, all I could see was our whole family going down over the ocean in a Boeing 747. I hung up the phone, paralyzed with fear.

The next day I told my husband I decided not to go on the trip to Israel, but he could go and take the two oldest boys while I stayed behind with the youngest boy. He had no idea why I suddenly had a change of mind. Later that week I was traveling in my car, and my thoughts about all I had to do that day were interrupted by this thought: "Where does fear come from?" Immediately I remembered 2 Timothy 1:7, and I knew God never gives a spirit of fear to anyone. Then I heard in my spirit this thought: "Satan is trying to rob you of a great blessing." I knew these thoughts came from the Lord, and upon returning from a full day of errands, I told my husband I wanted to go to Israel.

That trip to Israel was my first, and since that time I have been seven times. My husband and I lead tours every two years to Israel. The blessing Satan was trying to rob me from was seeing my husband and two sons baptized in the Jordan River. What a joy to see my family affirm their faith this way, and this had been my desire for all of them for years.

We cannot allow a spirit of fear to ever dictate to us what we will do in the future because if we do, we will always be robbed of a blessing. Today you might want to make a resolve with me to send Jesus to answer the door for you if fear comes knocking at the door of your heart.

Lord, forgive me for the times I have allowed fear to rob me of blessings.

October 23

Passing the Torch

2 Timothy 2:1–21

It was 1996, and Atlanta was hosting the summer Olympics. Runners carried the Olympic torch from the West Coast to Atlanta. Different runners were chosen for the major cities to run several miles with the torch, and then it was passed to the next runner. Our neighborhood was excited because the runners were going to pass the torch just a couple of blocks from our neighborhood. We all turned out en masse to see this meaningful event. It was thrilling to see one runner hand the torch to another.

Paul talks in this passage about passing the torch of the gospel to faithful men. He says, "And the things that you have heard from me among many witnesses, commit these to faithful men who will be able to teach others also" (v. 2).

One of the joys we have as parents is now seeing our three sons serving the Lord and teaching others the truths of God's Word. John also had this joy and writes, "I have no greater joy than to hear that my children walk in truth" (3 John 4).

As we pass the torch of the truth of God's Word on to our spiritual and physical children, we must also pray they will walk in those truths. The impartation of truth is key in kingdom living, but walking in those truths is what pleases God most. We must walk our talk, not just talk the walk.

The moment the Olympic torch was passed from one runner to the next, the next runner began instantly to run with the torch. My prayer is today that whatever I have been able to teach others will inspire them not only to retain such truths, but to walk in these truths and live a life that glorifies our heavenly Father.

Lord, strengthen everyone I have shared Your truths with and help them to apply these truths and walk in these truths. Help them to run the race of life well and always glorify You in both word and deed.

Walking in Love
2 Timothy 2:22–3:17

Yesterday we prayed for those who receive the torch of God's truth from our hand to run the race of life in such a way that they glorify God. In this chapter of 2 Timothy, Paul gives Timothy specific instructions about how to run the race of life well. He says, "Flee also youthful lusts: but follow righteousness, faith, charity, peace, with them that call on the Lord out of a pure heart. But foolish and unlearned questions avoid, knowing that they do gender strifes. And the servant of the Lord must not strive; but be gentle unto all men, apt to teach, patient. In meekness instructing those that oppose themselves; if God preadventure will give them repentance to the acknowledging of the truth; and that they may recover themselves out of the snare of the devil, who are taken captive by him at his will" (2 Tim. 2:22–26, KJV).

What a great exhortation to Timothy and to us all. It is interesting how many aspects of the fruit of the Spirit that is love is included in this exhortation. Paul mentions faith (v. 22), love (v. 22), peace (v. 22), gentleness (v. 24), patience (longsuffering) (v. 24), meekness (v. 25), temperance (purity because we have fled our own lusts) (v. 22).

To run the race of life well we must walk not only in God's truths, but we must also walk in God's love. If a runner in competition in a field and track event bumps another runner in order to reach the finish line first, he may win the race, but he has lost in God's sight. When we walk in love, we must avoid strife and debate (foolish questions) because strife always opens the door to Satan and all of his demons. The root of strife is either pride or jealousy, and the fruit of pride is confusion and every evil work.

Lord, I want to win the race of life, and I now know the only way to do this is to walk in love. Help me to love today as You love.

Winning the Race
2 Timothy 4:1–22

Paul finishes his final instructions to Timothy, and we all would do well to heed those instructions. Timothy was a teacher and preacher of God's Word. He had the gift of evangelism. We are all preachers, teachers and evangelists if we are true believers. Even though we may not hold the office of teacher, preacher or evangelist in the church, our lives and speech daily preach and teach what we believe to others. Anytime we share the love of Christ with another, we are an evangelist. Paul gives specific instructions about how Timothy should preach and teach. He says:

1. Be instant in season (we all must be ready to give a reason for our hope).
2. Reprove (reproof is always done with a meek spirit with the goal is to restore).
3. Rebuke (rebuke is also done in meekness to help our brothers, not hurt them).
4. Exhort (both reproof and rebuke should be couched in exhortation).
5. Be longsuffering (reproof and rebuke with exhortation should be done with a willingness to suffer long and forbear [come alongside] a brother or sister in Christ to help them eventually be restored).
6. Teach sound doctrine (we must be careful to teach truths correctly).
7. Endure (we will never win the race if we do not learn to endure to the end).
8. Prove your ministry (we prove our ministry by walking in love and righteousness).

Paul finished the course of life and ran it well. The crown of righteousness was laid up for him because he looked forward to the coming of the Lord. We too will receive such a crown if we eagerly await the Lord's return. I am challenged by Paul's and Timothy's lives to run the race of life well.

> Lord, remind me daily to walk in love and in Your truth. Truth without love is cruel, and love without truth does not change lives. Help me to pass the torch of Your truths to others and to love as You love.

October 26

Make a Joyful Noise
Psalm 97:1–98:9

God loves silence, but He also loves songs of praise and joyful sounds. He created each bird with a special song. I love to be awakened by the song of a red bird, and this happens often since we live in woods that are swarming with red birds. When God created the heavens and the earth, He created them to declare His glory. Even the trees clap their hands in joy. The heavens rejoice and declare His glory. Every time I hear a clap of thunder, I am reminded of the awesome and glorious power of God.

We attend a church that spends the first thirty minutes of the service praising and worshiping the Lord in song. Sometimes visitors are put off by the length of time we spend in praise and worship, but I know God is pleased with it. He loves to hear our voices raised in adoration to Him, and I know the angels are joining us in every chorus we sing.

In Psalm 98 David writes about the joyful sounds creation makes: "O sing unto the LORD a new song; for he hath done marvellous things: his right hand, and his holy arm, hath gotten him the victory... Make a joyful noise unto the LORD, all the earth: make a loud noise, and rejoice, and sing praise. Sing to unto the LORD with the harp; with the harp, and the voice of a psalm. With trumpets and sound of cornet make a joyful noise before the LORD, the King. Let the sea roar, and the fulness thereof; the world, and they that dwell therein. Let the floods clap their hands: let the hills be joyful together" (vv. 1, 4–8, KJV).

One morning when I was singing to the Lord one of my favorite hymns, "O Worship the Lord," I meditated on the verse that says God is pavilioned in splendor and girded with praise. Suddenly I saw how praise impacts the heavenlies. We are instructed to put on the garment of praise, and when we do this the spirit of heaviness is lifted off of us. God is a spirit, and every time we praise Him we are dressing Him in garments of praise. God is a spirit, so no one can see a spirit unless there is some form or shape. When we praise God, the light of His glory intensifies and actually provides garments of light that clothe Him. Every time we praise God on earth, His manifest presence grows brighter and brighter not only in heaven, but also on earth. God's glory garments are our praise. What an awesome thought to know that as I praise the Lord this morning I am dressing God in glory garments. He dwells in the midst of our praises.

Thank You, Lord, for the great privilege of dressing You this morning in glory garments as I praise You. Help me always to take time to do this daily.

The Joys of Growing Old
Titus 2:1–15

I don't feel aged, but since I am celebrating fifty-plus years as a Christian as I write these devotionals, I guess I have to admit that the golden years have now overtaken me. When I entered the season of the golden years of my life, I rejoiced because it has been a great season of teaching for me. In this passage of Titus Paul tells Titus that older women should teach younger women. Then he lists those subjects that should be taught to younger women. He says older women should teach younger women to:

1. Be discreet
2. Be chaste (pure)
3. Be good keepers of their homes
4. Be obedient to their husbands

I have always wanted daughters, and I was thrilled to finally get some girls in the family. I constantly prayed for my future daughters-in-law:

Lord, may my future daughters-in-law first love You with all their hearts, and then may they simply adore their husbands.

God wonderfully answered this prayer, and all my sons are happily married. Their wives are such wonderful complements to them in every way. All three sons now are teamed with women who love the Lord with all of their heart. As I looked at this list of what older women are to teach younger women, I thought to myself that truly my daughters-in-law could teach me some of these things. All three daughters-in-law are discreet and pure. They have the desire always to walk in a way that will glorify the Lord. They all have such a desire to beautify their little nests, and they all have a great gift of hospitality. They always try their best to be obedient to their husbands as unto the Lord.

If you are an older woman, maybe the Lord is calling you to mentor and be a mother-like one to young women. You do not have to have daughters or daughters-in-law to do this. You can be the mother of many daughters in love. Before I was gifted with such precious daughters-in-law, I mentored several young women, and it has been my joy to see them grow in the Lord.

Today you might want to pray with me for more opportunities to mother God's spiritual children. Remember always that God will grant you the wisdom to do this, and His love far surpasses your own love for those you will teach.

Lord, help me always to be willing to teach others by example and speech.

Caught and Taught
Titus 3:1–15

Yesterday we learned what older women should teach younger women. Today we see a list of subjects to be taught to younger men. Younger men should be taught to develop the following:

1. Sobermindedness
2. A pattern of good works
3. Sincere, correct doctrine
4. Sound speech (speak evil of no man)
5. Obedience to employers and government leaders
6. Faithfulness
7. Denial of worldly lusts
8. Righteous living
9. Humility and meekness

The list for young men is much longer than the list for young women. I've always thought that women have an easier job than our men do because we only have to obey our husbands. Husbands, however, have the responsibility of provider, protector and priest in their homes. Both young men who are married and unmarried need to be taught all of the above.

It seems to be an impossible list, doesn't it? How could anyone attain these fine qualities? The answer to that question is that they cannot obtain such lofty goals, ideals and character qualities. These things need to be taught to younger men, but first they must be taught that they cannot develop in these areas if Jesus Christ is not Lord of their lives. Jesus is the obedient One and is the only One who can give them the supernatural grace (God-given ability) to accomplish such worthy goals. Young men need to first catch on fire for Christ before they can be lights shining in this world.

There is a slogan being battered around in revival circles, "Catch the fire." Paul tells us clearly in the rest of this chapter that it is the Holy Spirit who imparts these wonderful attributes to us. He says, "Not by works of righteousness which we have done, but according to His mercy He saved us, through the washing of regeneration and renewing of the Holy Spirit, whom He poured out on us abundantly through Jesus Christ our Savior" (v. 5).

If we were taught we had to attain these goals in our own strength, we would be extremely discouraged. Thank God, Paul makes it clear that the Holy Spirit is the One who helps us to not only receive such marvelous teaching, but also to live and walk in what we have been taught. The Holy Spirit imparts these character qualities to all of us. They are caught, not just taught.

October 29

READ: Lamentations 1:1–2:19; Philemon 1:1–25; Psalm 101:1–8; Proverbs 26:20

What Is a Perfect Heart?
Psalm 101:1–8

David speaks of walking within his house with a perfect heart. This has been a prayer of mine daily: "Lord, help me to walk in my house with a perfect heart." When I pray this prayer, I am also making a covenant with God:

1. I will set no wicked thing before my eyes.
2. I will hate wickedness and will never join myself to it.
3. I will not be rebellious, presumptuous or proud.
4. I will surround myself with righteous and godly friends.
5. I will not keep company with gossips, slanderers or the proud.
6. I will keep my eyes on those who are faithful to God.
7. I will not allow deceitful people to live with me.
8. I will not keep company with liars.

As you review this list, you may be thinking to yourself, *I've done all of the above.* You may think you have not allowed wickedness to enter your home, but I came to the understanding that if I have allowed unrighteous music, videos, magazines or TV or radio programs to be seen, read and heard in my home, I have joined myself to wickedness.

For most of the childhood of our sons we did not have a TV. It was glorious because we had more time to communicate with one another, more time to play games with one another and more time to be quiet before the Lord. We now have a TV, but we only watch the news and some sporting events. Sometimes we watch a good TV show or movie, but the time spent in front of the tube averages no more than four hours a week.

Having a quiet home without the TV or radio constantly sending messages into my home has helped me to hear more clearly the messages God wants to convey to me each day. There is a verse that says, "In quietness and confidence will be your strength." When the distractions of radio and TV are done away with, there is a pervading peace and joy that strengthen us for our daily tasks. I find that TV watching and constant noise in my ear drain me. We keep our TV upstairs and only watch it when we need to know the news, weather or want to watch an edifying movie or the video. You may want to try doing the same. I guarantee you will grow to love the quiet and relish the joy of the Lord.

> *Lord, forgive me for allowing worldly things to control me instead of my controlling them. I know in order to keep my mind stayed upon You each day, I need to get rid of some of these worldly distractions. Help me.*

October 30

READ: Lamentations 2:22–3:66; Hebrews 1:1–14; Psalm 102:1–28; Proverbs 26:21–22

His Mercies Are New Every Morning
Lamentations 2:20–3:66

In my yearly reading the Bible through, one of the books I breeze through quickly is Lamentations. This book is so negative, yet in the midst of the lamentations of Jeremiah are rich nuggets about God's faithfulness. Listen to just a few verses: "It is the Lord's mercies that we are not consumed, because his compassions fail not. They are new every morning: great is thy faithfulness. The Lord is my portion, saith my soul; therefore will I hope in Him. The Lord is good unto them that wait for him, to the soul that seeketh him. It is good that a man should both hope and quietly wait for the salvation of the Lord." (Lam. 3:22–26, KJV).

One of my favorite hymns is "Great Is Thy Faithfulness." I love the words to that great hymn that declares, "Morning by morning Your mercies are new." "Lord, have mercy" is a common expression in the South. The truth is the Lord does have mercy, and His mercies are new every morning.

If you wake up complaining and murmuring and dreading the day, you have bolted the door of your heart to God's great mercy. You can open the door by demonstrating a grateful, merciful heart. To obtain mercy, we must be merciful. I learned many years ago that when I choose to have a pity party, I have chosen counterfeit mercy. I want to pet myself and pamper myself and wallow in my discouragement. When I do this, I miss experiencing the real thing—God's mercy. Have you ever noticed that none of your friends want to attend your pity parties? Pity parties are usually experienced when we are alone, but don't fool yourself. There is an audience of demons watching and waiting for an open door to discourage you even more.

Let's close the door today to counterfeit mercy and open the door wide to God's mercy, which is new every morning. Pray this prayer with me:

Lord, forgive me for the many times I have felt sorry for myself. Help me never to have a pity party again because I want to experience Your new mercies every morning. Great is Your faithfulness.

Living for His Honor and Glory
Hebrews 2:1–18

We've talked much about winning the race of life and running it well by walking in truth and love. We talked about the crown that awaits all those who love the appearing of Christ. Most of us, however, go through life without the realization that we already are wearing a victor's crown. Listen to what the writer says in Hebrews: "Thou madest him [and all of us] a little lower than the angels: thou crownedst him with glory and honour, and didst set him over the works of thy hands. Thou hast put all things in subjection under him... he left nothing that is not put under him" (vv. 7–8).

We need to remind ourselves daily of the crown of glory and honor that rests upon our heads throughout our days on this earth. If we daily recognize this invisible crown, I believe we would live our lives differently. We were created to be a praise, honor and glory to God. This means our days on earth need to be spent in praise and lived in such a way that we glorify God in both word and deed.

The sad reality is that many lose this crown in their lives because they go their own way instead of living in the fear of the Lord. The crown tumbles off their head, and the only way they can once again wear this crown is to humble themselves by bowing their knee to God. As we humble ourselves and bow our knees in submission once again to God, He reaches for this crown and places it firmly once again upon our heads. God always humbles Himself to see a repentant heart. We all sin and fall short of the glory of God, but what we do when we sin has everything to do with wearing the victor's crown of glory and honor. If we confess our sins and repent of them, we can rest assured that this crown of glory will be upon our heads, because if we confess our sins, Jesus is faithful and just to forgive us of our sins and to cleanse us of all unrighteousness.

Is your crown of glory and honor fastened securely to your head today? If it is not, then bow before our Lord in sincerity and contriteness of heart and allow Him to once again fasten this glorious crown on your head. Continue after this to walk in truth and love, and you will be wearing this crown when you finish this race of this life.

Lord, I have been challenged by these readings in October, especially the letters to Timothy, to run the race of this life well. Thank You for giving me the strength and ability by Your Holy Spirit to do this. I am totally dependent upon Him to run the race of life well through me. Thank You.

READ: Ezekiel 1:1–3:15; Hebrews 3:1–19; Psalm 104:1–24; Proverbs 26:24–26

Exhibit Exhortation
Hebrews 3:1–19

We live in a day when many are falling away, and one of the main reasons is the severe lack of exhortation between brothers and sisters in Christ. The letter to the Hebrews could be subtitled "EXHORTING BELIEVERS TO EXHORT." We are urged to exhort one another daily while it is still today. If we are faithful to exhort one another, we will not be as likely to fall for the deceitfulness of sin.

The hardening of our hearts comes when we stop fellowshiping with others, and if no one calls to say they have missed us, we begin to think nobody cares. That is exactly what the devil wants us to believe. No one would fall away from the faith into unbelief if they were daily being prayed for, encouraged and exhorted by their fellow believers. If I knew that someone from my church would be calling me weekly just to encourage me and ask me how I was doing, I would not want to let this person down.

There was a lady in our church who took upon herself the ministry of notes. She continually wrote notes to those in the body of Christ, and all of her notes were so encouraging and uplifting. This lady is no longer in our church. Perhaps no one wrote notes of encouragement to her. I really miss this ministry.

In our readings in the letter to the Hebrews we will discover exactly how to encourage and exhort one another. I am convinced that most Christian counseling centers would be closed if the body of Christ was doing its job of exhortation. All of Paul's letters begin with an exhortation to the church he is writing to, and then he shares some of the things they need to improve upon in their service to the Lord. We do not know who the author of Hebrews is, but whoever he was, he understood the importance of the ministry of exhortation.

I am exhorted by the following scripture to take seriously the beautiful ministry of exhortation: "Beware, brethren, lest there be in any of you an evil heart of unbelief in departing from the living God; but exhort one another daily, while it is called 'Today'; lest any of you be hardened through the deceitfulness of sin" (vv. 12–13).

> Lord, forgive me for not exhorting my brothers and sisters in Christ daily. I pray You will help me establish this beautiful ministry of exhortation by giving me at least one name daily of someone who needs a call or a note of encouragement. Then help me, Holy Spirit, not to pass that opportunity by, but instead to act upon those gentle impressions You give me. Thank You.

Tempted in All Points
Hebrews 4:1–16

This passage in Hebrews speaks of Jesus as our High Priest who was tempted in all points even as we are tempted. He, however, never sinned. Jesus called himself the Son of man often because He was flesh, blood and bone just as we are. God tented Himself in flesh so He could experience all we experience except sin. As a man, Jesus was subject to temptation just as we all are. Jesus was led by the Spirit into the wilderness to be tempted of the devil. One thing we often forget is that God sometimes allows the devil to tempt us. God gave permission to the devil to tempt Job. God, however, is not the tempter, as James clearly teaches: "Let no one say when he is tempted, 'I am tempted by God'; for God cannot be tempted by evil, nor does He tempt anyone. But each one is tempted when he is drawn away by his own desires and enticed" (James 1:13–14).

The Holy Spirit led Jesus into the wilderness to be tempted of the devil. God knew Jesus would overcome, and He did just that. If our heart is toward God and we want to glorify Him in word and deed, we also may experience temptations that have been allowed into our lives for one reason. The temptations God allows are to strengthen us in our spiritual warfare abilities as we use the mighty weapons of our warfare to pull down strongholds in our mind. Satan has the ability to place images and thoughts in our minds, but we have been given the supernatural ability through our faith in Jesus Christ to resist such thoughts and images and to pull them down.

Because of the Fall, we have three lusts—the lust of the flesh (seeking to overindulge one or more of our five senses), the lust of the eye (vain imaginations and fantasies in our minds) and the pride of life (trusting in ourselves and our own resources more than we trust in God). We did not have these lusts before Eve and Adam sinned. Instead, we had three beautiful desires—the desire to enjoy God, the desire to worship God and the desire to glorify God. The desire to enjoy God was perverted into the lust of the flesh; the desire to worship God was perverted into the lust of the eye; and the desire to glorify God was perverted into the pride of life. All of these lusts are found in the soul (the mind, the emotions and the will).

Jesus was tempted in all points even as we are. Jesus had these beautiful desires, and since Satan was successful in perverting these desires in Adam and Eve, he knew he could do the same with Jesus. It did not work. Jesus was tempted to turn the stone into bread, and if He had given into this temptation, His desire to enjoy God would have been perverted. Jesus was tempted to bow down and worship Satan with Satan's promise that He would have all the kingdoms of this earth. Jesus resisted this temptation, and His desire to worship God was not perverted. Jesus was tempted to throw Himself off the pinnacle of the temple, but once again Jesus resisted this temptation with the Word of God, and His desire to glorify God was not perverted. Jesus overcame each temptation with the Word of God. We now can overcome through the power of the blood of Jesus and the Word of God.

Obedience
Hebrews 5:1–14

Obedience is a word that usually causes us to flinch. Something inside of us does not like that word. That something inside of us is called "the flesh." I recall the story of the little boy who was told over and over again by his mother to sit down and be still. Little Johnny finally obeyed, but he told his mother, "I'm sitting down on the outside, but I'm standing up on the inside." Obeying outside without having an obedient heart inside is still rebellion.

Ever since the Fall, we have been subject to our flesh, which is rebellious. One has only to observe an eighteen-month-old baby for a short time to discover the natural man in our sinful nature is rebellious. We were all born with the desire to have our way instead of God's way.

In this passage in Hebrews we see an interesting verse of scripture: "Though He was a Son, yet He learned obedience by the things which He suffered. And having been perfected, He became the author of eternal salvation to all them who obey Him" (v. 9).

None of us like to suffer. In fact, we usually dislike the word *suffer* more than the word *obedience*. Jesus, however, suffered. The apostles suffered. What Paul went through alone is enough to tell us he was not exempt from suffering. Listen to his words: "Are they ministers of Christ? (I speak as a fool) I am more; in labours more abundant, in stripes above measure, in prisons more frequent, in deaths oft. Of the Jews five times received I forty stripes save one. Thrice was I beaten with rods, once was I stoned, thrice I suffered shipwreck, a night and a day I have been in the deep; in journeyings often, in perils of waters, in perils of robbers, in perils by mine own countrymen, in perils by the heathen, in perils in the city, in perils in the wilderness, in perils in the sea, in perils among false brethren; in weariness and painfulness, in watchings often, in hunger and thirst, in fastings often, in cold and nakedness" (2 Cor. 11:23–27, KJV).

Can your list of suffering match Paul's? Jesus, however, not only suffered, but He tasted death for us all. Jesus was the suffering servant mentioned in Isaiah 53. He was wounded for our transgressions and bruised for our iniquities. The chastisement of our peace was upon Him, and by the stripes He bore, He purchased our healing. Jesus learned obedience through the things He suffered. Suffering in our lives will never result in the fruit of an obedient heart unless we submit our lives totally to God. Jesus said, "In this world you will have tribulation, but be of good cheer; I have overcome the world." No one is exempt from suffering. The question we need to ask ourselves, however, is, Will we learn obedience to God in the midst of our suffering?

Hearts Made of Stone
Ezekiel 10:1–11:25

There was a song in the late fifties called "Hearts Made of Stone." I'm sure the writer of this song had no idea he was quoting Scripture. The promise to Israel in Ezekiel 11:19 is, "Then I will give them one heart, and I will put a new spirit within them, and take the stony heart out of their flesh, and give them a heart of flesh.

When we were in Israel we walked along the shore in Natanya. As we were walking on the beach we noticed hundreds of smooth pebbles shaped like hearts. We collected as many as we could carry back with us to the States. Many in our tour put these hearts in baskets, and as they prayed for the peace of Jerusalem daily, they lifted up the basket to the Lord and proclaimed this Scripture promise: "I will take the stony heart out of their flesh, and will give them a heart of flesh." What a great promise to claim for all of our Jewish friends. God has already begun this wonderful transformation in His chosen people.

Every time we return to Israel, we see more openness to the gospel. Twenty years ago there were no Messianic congregations (Jewish believers in Jesus as their Messiah). Now there are over eighty congregations throughout Israel. The veil over God's chosen is slowly being pulled down.

Never give up praying for your Jewish friends. God has great plans for them. He desires to change their hearts. For a season their hearts have been hardened, but the Word of God is like a hammer. That Word can break in pieces the hardest stone. Pray that your Jewish friends will be pursued by God's Word. I often pray this way for the Jewish people I know. Maybe you would like to join me in this prayer, and when you do, mention by name the Jewish people you want God to touch.

Father, in Jesus' name I pray for _____. I ask You to pursue these people with Your good Word. When these Your chosen turn on the TV or radio, let them tune into a station that is speaking Your Word. Send laborers to them who will speak Your Word to them. I also ask for the gift of faith for these precious chosen people. Give them that gift so they might believe that Jesus, Your Son, is also their Messiah.

READ: Ezekiel 12:1–14:11; Hebrews 7:1–17; Psalm 105:39–45; Proverbs 27:3

The Time Is Now
Ezekiel 12:1–14:11

There are many prophetic scriptures in Ezekiel. In this passage God promises to no longer prolong His Word. He says, "For I am the LORD, I speak, and the word which I speak will come to pass; it will no more be postponed" (Ezek. 42:25).

God always performs the word He sends. The question we on earth often ask is, "When will this word be fulfilled?" Until it is fulfilled we wait expectantly with thanksgiving and with assurance that God will fulfill His promises and prophesies. Think of how long Abraham had to wait before the son of promise, Isaac, was born. He wearied of waiting and, at the urging of his wife, went ahead of God and fathered a child named Ishmael, who was born to Hagar. This impatience has cost Israel dearly. We would not have the Arab-Jewish problem today if Abraham had not become impatient. We can learn much from the father of our faith. We need to learn to wait upon God with the assurance that He will fulfill His promises at His appointed time, not ours. Finally Sarah conceived and gave birth to Isaac. God had said she would be visited at the appointed time. There was an appointed time for Sarah to give birth, and God saw to it that her time came right on time even though she was in her nineties.

Later as we read about Abraham we see how he was complimented on his faith because he hoped against hope when he was too old to be a father. He was one hundred years old, but he did not consider his body dead and believed God would fulfill His Word. He was fully persuaded that God was able to perform that which He had promised. When we receive a promise from God, we must trust His timing and resist the temptation to make things happen ourselves.

Let's face it. Abraham "blew it," but so do we. The good news is that God redeemed his mistake and did perform exactly the word He had given to Abraham. I believe the waiting time between the promise and the performance of God's Word is being shortened in this day. God promises to do a short work in the last days, and this is because the Lord is coming soon.

Be encouraged today. Whatever God has promised you, rest assured He will deliver. He is true to His Word. Ask the Holy Spirit to help you wait with patience for the appointed time God has ordained to perform that promise in your life. Remember, good things are worth waiting for; resist the temptation to go ahead of God. He is faithful to perform His promises in His time.

Lord, forgive me for sometimes going ahead of You. Help me to learn to wait upon You with the assurance that Your timing is much better than mine. Thank You, Lord.

Live!!!
Ezekiel 14:12–16:42

This passage in Ezekiel speaks of Israel and how God had mercy on Israel and gave Israel life. Ezekiel speaks of Israel's birth and how no man had pity upon her. Israel was like a newborn cast into an open field with no one even nearby to cut her umbilical cord. Then Ezekiel shares how God has pity on her: "And when I passed by you and saw you struggling in your own blood, I said to you in your blood, 'Live!' Yes, I said to you in your blood, 'Live!'" (Ezek. 16:6)

Israel was on the verge of hemorrhaging from her own sin if God did not have mercy upon her. The life is in the blood, and sin always brings death, the Bible tells us. I have experienced hemorrhaging, and my hemorrhaging was also connected with an aborted birth. I miscarried a child after my second son was born, and I felt my life draining out of me as the blood from my body flowed freely. When we sin, we also will feel the life draining out of us. If we do not repent, death will come into our body. The fruit of the seed of sin is always death if we let it grow in our lives by watering sin daily with our disobedience. God is a merciful God, however, and just as He had mercy on Israel, He has mercy on us.

At the moment of my hemorrhaging I was too weak to pray for myself. My husband, however, was with me as I was rushed to the hospital. He was praying for me. Not only was he praying for me, but many brothers and sisters in an African American church were praying for me. I had begun an interracial prayer group that met in an African American Baptist church. I was at this meeting when I began hemorrhaging, and one of the brothers there lifted me in his strong arms and drove me to my mother's home, where we called the doctor for help. In the ambulance I felt my spirit leaving my body, and I truly believe it was the prayers of others that saved my life.

When we sin, we need to call upon the help of our brothers and sisters in Christ. Sometimes we are too weak to resist the enemy if he tempts us again in the same area. Their prayers will keep you from hemorrhaging to death spiritually. We have the great privilege as intercessors to speak life into those we see sinning. As we remit the sins of others for them and ask for God to send a spirit of repentance upon them, we will see life come back to these people who were on the verge of dying. Listen to this verse of Scripture: "If any man see his brother sin a sin which is not unto death, he shall ask, and he shall give him life for them that sin not unto death. There is a sin unto death: I do not say that he shall pray for it" (1 John 5:16, KJV).

The only sin unto death we cannot remit for another is the sin of rejection of Jesus Christ. If a person has been presented the gospel and refuses to receive Christ, we cannot remit this sin.

The Law Written on Hearts
Hebrews 8:1–13

Earlier this month we saw God's promise to turn the hearts of stone of His chosen people into hearts of flesh. Israel was disobedient to God, and Jesus was rejected by His own. Yet, God has not rejected Israel. He promises to make a new covenant with them when He will write the law of God on their hearts and put the laws in their minds. Yesterday we shared the only sin we cannot remit for others is rejection of Jesus Christ. Even though many of our Jewish brothers and sisters have rejected Jesus Christ, we can still pray for God to give them the gift of faith to believe and also godly sorrow so they will repent.

Once we have received Christ, we have the challenge of walking in obedience to Him daily. Make no mistake, none of us can obey without the power of the Holy Spirit dwelling within us. Yes, people can obey the laws of God outwardly by not committing adultery, but Jesus made it quite clear that if a man lusts for a woman in his heart, he has committed adultery. He also said murder is committed if a man is angry against his brother. The law of God is only written on our hearts when we are born again. God's promise to write His law on the hearts of His chosen people tells us that there will be a day when many Jews are born again.

Jesus did not come to destroy the Law or abolish it. He came to fulfill the Law, and because He did fulfill the Law we now can have the law of God written on our hearts. When we receive Christ, God promises to no longer remember our sins and iniquities because we are now a covenant people. The old has passed away, and all things become new. One of the greatest new things that comes to pass when we are born again is that we now have a willing heart that seeks to please God and obey Him in both word and deed.

It was such a relief when I gave up trying to obey God in my own strength. When I realized it was God who worked within me both to will and to do of His good pleasure, I asked Him for grace (supernatural power and ability) to obey and please Him daily. The two laws God wants us to obey daily are first to love Him with all of our hearts, and to love our neighbor as ourselves. These laws are not grievous. On the contrary they give us great joy when we obey them.

We recently attended a meeting where a man who has fifteen children is fighting to get the Ten Commandments back into our public buildings and schools. When he was burdened with the fact the schools were not able to post the Ten Commandments, the Lord spoke to his heart and asked him if his own children could quote the Ten Commandments. When he tested them, none of his children passed the test. He had to ask the Lord's forgiveness for his own neglect in teaching the law to his children. We need to know the Ten Commandments, but more than that, we need to do them.

Thank You, Father, for sending the Obedient One, Jesus, to fulfill the Law so I can be empowered to keep Your law.

A Pattern of Prayer
Hebrews 9:1–12

David Yonggi Cho, who pastors a church of over a million Koreans, uses the tabernacle as a pattern of prayer. In today's reading we see the order of the tabernacle. This passage describes three of the parts of the tabernacle. Each division of the tabernacle included certain altars and emblems, which all represent the different parts of prayer we are to experience daily. Cho prays four *hours* a day, utilizing each of these parts of prayer. Here are the three parts of the tabernacle and what they represent in our own prayer life:

THE OUTER COURT
Enter His courts with praise (Ps. 100:4–5); praise and thanks.

~ **The Brazen Altar**—Offer your body as a living sacrifice and confess (Rom. 12:1)

~ **The Brazen Laver**—Wash your heart and mind with the WORD (Ps. 119)

THE INNER COURT OR HOLY PLACE
The veil is torn, and we can enter boldly.

~ **The Golden Candlestick**—Be filled with His Spirit (Isa. 11:1).

~ **The Table of Showbread**—Consider God's provision in His Word (Ps. 104:15).

~ **The Altar of Incense**—Your prayers and supplication are as a sweet incense (Rev. 8:4).

THE HOLY OF HOLIES
Worship God (Ps. 24:3, 46; Heb. 10:19–24; Isa. 57:15–21).

Cho reverses this pattern of prayer because now that Jesus has shed His blood for us, we can enter boldly into His throne of grace and find help in time of need. Jesus also reverses the order of the tabernacle when He gives His disciples His pattern of prayer:

Our Father which art in heaven, hallowed be Thy name
The Holy of Holies—Worship God

Thy kingdom come, Thy will be done on earth as it is in heaven
The Altar of Incense—Making our requests known unto the Lord

Give us this day our daily bread
The Table of Showbread—God's Word, our daily feeding

Forgive us our debts as we forgive debtors
The Laver—The washing of the water of God's Word and cleansing of our sin as we make confession for them

314

And lead us not into temptation
The Candlestick—We're now ready to go out into the world with our light shining brightly filled with the fresh oil of the Holy Spirit. We are the light of the world.

For Thine is the kingdom, and the power, and the glory forever.
The Outer Court—As we exit our prayers with thanksgiving and praise through the gates of praise into the world, we are reminded of our mission in life. We were created for the praise and glory of God.

Father, glorify Yourself in my heart (spirit) and soul (mind, will and emotion), and let me glorify You, Lord, today in attitude, word and deed. Amen.

God Has Willed All to Us

Hebrews 9:13–28

When my mother died, I could not come into my inheritance until all the legal requirements were met. Only then could I receive what she had willed to me many years earlier when she wrote her will.

In the very beginning of time God wrote a will for all of His children to inherit. Even though Christ had not yet been made flesh, He was present with the Father in the Spirit. Jesus was the very living Word of God that spoke the worlds into being. God intended for all who believed on His Son to inherit eternal and abundant life. The legal requirements had to be fulfilled first. For a will to be activated, the person who has written the will must be dead. Christ died once for all men, and because He died, we now can inherit all God intended for us to inherit from the beginning of time.

When my mother died, I had to go to the courthouse to claim my inheritance. I had to give proof of my identity and sign some papers. When Jesus died, the availability of His inheritance was there, but we now have to claim it. We claim our inheritance by believing and receiving by faith Jesus as our Lord and Savior. The sad part is that so many do not know anything about their great inheritance. If they never have heard the gospel, how can they claim their inheritance? What is even sadder is that some when they hear the gospel refuse to claim their inheritance. I have never understood this.

After the law was given to Moses, he sprinkled the blood of calves and goats upon the book, the people and the tabernacle. Without the shedding of blood there is no remission of sins. After Jesus died, His blood was made available to us to cleanse and sanctify our earthly tabernacles (our body, soul and spirit). Because Jesus said, "Lo, I come (in the volume of the book it is written of me,) to do thy will, O God," we now have the privilege of entering into all God has willed for us.

Father, I pray for all those today who have missed becoming a joint heir with Christ. I pray these lost people will have the eyes of their understanding opened, and I pray You will deposit the gift of faith to them so that they might believe and receive Jesus Christ, Your Son, as their Lord and Savior. I pray that soon they will be able to claim their full inheritance. Thank You, Father, for sending Your Son to earth, not only to live, but also to die and to live again.

November 10

READ: Ezekiel 21:1–22:31; Hebrews 10:1–17; Psalm 108:1–13; Proverbs 27:12

The Perfect Sacrifice
Hebrews 10:1–17

We studied about the tabernacle and the pattern of prayer. We saw that now we can begin our prayers instantly with worship, because Jesus through His shed blood on the cross purchased us the right to now go boldly to God's mercy seat and find help in time of need. Only the high priest in the first covenant could enter into the holy of holies where he saw the mercy seat with the cherubim over it. He could only enter through the veil of the holy of holies once a year on the Day of Atonement. We have the great privilege now of entering God's throne room daily to find help in time of need because of the authority we have in Jesus' name and through His shed blood.

The sacrifices offered by the early priests on the brazen altar were imperfect. Jesus truly is our all in all. He not only is our new High Priest, but He is also the Lamb of God slain from the foundation of the earth. When John saw Jesus, he said, "Behold the Lamb of God who takes away the sins of the world." The sacrifice the early priests made to atone for the sins of the people had to be done once every year, and the sins of the people were only covered, not taken away. The Bible tells us, "As far as the east is from the west, so far has the Lord removed our transgressions." This fact should make us want to enter every day with praise through the gates of thanksgiving. This great transaction on the cross when our sins, iniquities and transgressions were laid upon Jesus is aptly described in Hebrews 10:14: "For by one offering He has perfected forever those who are being sanctified."

Jesus was the perfect sacrifice who now gives us the hope of being presented blameless, without spot or wrinkle (perfect in every way) to the Father when we see Him face to face. Because Jesus was perfect, we now can be perfected in Him. Thank You, Jesus.

When I survey Your wondrous work on the cross, I stand in awe of what You purchased for me on that day. Help me, Lord, to allow Your Holy Spirit to conform me daily to Your image. Thank You for the hope that when I see You I will be like You—perfect and complete.

317

Hold Fast
Hebrews 10:18–39

R ecently I heard a message titled "What to do when you are going through hell. "The answer given in the message was this: "When you are going through hell, keep moving."

Over and over again in the Bible we see the exhortation to press forward, keep pressing toward the goal and the high calling of God. This is the season of the summer Olympics, and as I watch the athletes, it is evident they enter every event with a certain goal. The goal is to win the gold. These athletes work tirelessly for years to prepare themselves for even one Olympic event. They, however, never work alone in their training. They always have a trainer, and sometimes they have more than one trainer to exhort them to keep pressing for the goal of a gold medal. In this reading in Hebrews we hear this exhortation: "Let us hold fast the confession of our hope without wavering, for He who promised is faithful. And let us consider one another in order to stir up love and good works" (v. 23). The gold medal in God's eyes is for us to love as He loves and do the same works He did.

As you read through Hebrews this month, underline or circle every time you see the phrase "Let us." Holding fast to the faith is impossible if we are trying to hold on to our faith without the help of others. This is why the next verse exhorts, "Not forsaking the assembling of ourselves together, as is the manner of some, but exhorting one another, and so much the more, as you see the Day approaching" (v. 24).

We are nearing the finish line of the event of our life. Jesus is coming soon, so more than ever we need the help of our brothers and sisters in Christ and the training of the Holy Spirit to get us in shape for the finish line of our lives. Jesus said, "When I come again, will I find faith on the earth?" Jesus will find faith on the earth if we hold fast to our faith by holding fast to one another in faith in these End Times.

Lord, help me to take every opportunity to fellowship with fellow believers. I need their help and the help of Your Holy Spirit to hold fast as the days draw near to Your Second Coming.

READ: Ezekiel 24:1–26:21; Hebrews 11:1–16; Psalm 110:1–7; Proverbs 27:14

The Frame of Faith
Hebrews 11:1–16

We recently purchased some beautiful oil paintings painted by some Israeli art students. These students were temporarily in the United States selling their paintings to earn money for their art school in Jerusalem. They went door to door and also had a few shows in the U.S. The paintings were not framed, but we had the promise of these students that a fellow student would call us who could give us a good price on framing the pictures for us. We waited and waited for this call. Meanwhile our beautiful pictures were gathering dust while they were stored under our bed. No one knew we had such beautiful paintings because they were not framed yet and we could not display them on our walls.

Our reading in Hebrews today describes the beautiful lives painted through history by men and women of faith. As we read about those heroes of our faith, we can picture in our minds the scene of Noah who by faith prepared the ark; Abraham who by faith left his homeland to go to a strange land; Sarah who by faith gave herself to Abraham when she was ninety because of the promise of a child; and on and on the scenes pass through our minds.

We learn in Hebrews 11:3 that there is a very special frame for these pictures of faith: "By faith we understand that the worlds were framed by the word of God, so that the things which are seen were not made of things which are visible."

Through faith the Word of God framed the worlds. God sees to it that when we are presented with His artwork there is already a frame for each masterpiece. Just as our paintings could not be displayed until they were framed, these scenes of great faith painted by our Bible heroes could not be displayed without the Word of God framing these scenes. It is through the Word of God that we are able to read these wonderful stories that inspire us to greater faith. In every scene of faith conveyed in chapter 11 of Hebrews, we see how these men and women of faith received and acted upon the Word of God. They attached themselves firmly to the frame of God's Word and then displayed His Spirit, character, power and works to the world. Faith comes by hearing and hearing by the Word of God. God has framed the masterpiece of your life in the golden frame of His Word. Without His Word, we could never display the faith that works by love and moves mountains to the world.

Lord, help me to attach myself firmly to the frame of Your Word so that my life will display the beauty of Your character and love to others.

November 13

READ: Ezekiel 27:1-28; Hebrews 11:17-31; Psalm 111:1-10; Proverbs 27:15-16

Looking at the Unseen
Hebrews 11:17-31

As we continue our travels through the Book of Hebrews, underline or circle the phrases *looking at* or *looking towards*. Faith always looks at the eternal rather than the temporal. We can see the temporal, but we cannot usually see the eternal. In this chapter we see more stories from the Hall of Faith, and each story has one thing in common. These heroes of our faith were able to see the unseen by faith. We see the faith of Moses in the following passages: "By faith Moses, when he was come to years, refused to be called the son of Pharaoh's daughter; choosing rather to suffer affliction with the people of God, than to enjoy the pleasures of sin for a season. Esteeming the reproach of Christ greater riches than the treasures in Egypt: for he had respect unto the recompense of the reward. By faith he forsook Egypt, not fearing the wrath of the king: for he endured, as seeing him who is invisible" (vv. 24-27, KJV).

Moses saw Christ with his spiritual eyes. He even saw the rewards Christ would give him on that great day when Jesus will reward the saints for their deeds and words on earth. Moses, like David, Job and Isaiah, saw Jesus Christ in the Spirit even though it was years before Jesus would be born on earth. These heroes of our faith were able to look into the unseen realm of the Spirit.

When Moses asked God to show him His glory, I believe Moses at that time saw much more than God the Father. I believe he saw the Trinity. He could only see the backside of God, who does have form even though He is a Spirit. He also saw Jesus and the Holy Spirit. The Spirit was represented by the fire in the burning bush, as the Spirit is often represented by fire. The golden candlestick in the tabernacle of Moses represented the sevenfold Spirit of God. I believe Moses also saw Jesus. God honored Moses' faith by allowing him to see Jesus not only in the Spirit but also in the flesh. This happened on the Mount of Transfiguration when Moses and Elijah appeared with Jesus on the Mount.

If we want our lives to display the same kind of faith Moses and these other Bible heroes displayed, we must wear our spiritual glasses every day. These glasses correct our nearsightedness and allow us to see into the realms of God's glory.

Are you wearing your spiritual glasses today, or are you still blinded by the problem and trials of this world? Put on your glory glasses this morning and see into the unseen by faith. You will never be the same.

Lord, show me Your glory.

November 14

Looking Unto Jesus
Hebrews 11:32–12:13

These heroes of the faith pressed forward to the goal, and they received the gold. As we see by the lives mentioned in this passage of Hebrews 11, many were martyred and tortured for their faith. How did they get through these great trials of faith, which are even more precious to the Lord than gold? The answer is simple: They kept their focus on the Provider, not the problem. We read in Hebrews 12:2, "Looking unto Jesus, the author and finisher of our faith, who for the joy that was set before Him endured the cross, despising the shame, and has sat down at the right hand of the throne of God."

Jesus knew the joy we would all experience because of His sacrificial death and resurrection. He knew the joy He would experience every time someone was liberated from rejection, disease, sickness and bondage of all kinds. He saw the joy we would receive when we repented of our sins and received His forgiveness and cleansing. He saw the joy we would encounter when we would be translated from the kingdom of darkness into His kingdom of light where there is peace, right standing with God and joy. This joy provided Him strength to get through every trial and to even endure the torture of the cross for our sakes. What got Jesus through every trial was His focus. He kept His eyes ever on the Father. What will get us through every trial is our focus. We must keep our eyes upon Jesus.

We all will experience trials, troubles and temptations. Some of the promises in the Bible we seldom claim are, "In the world you will have tribulation," and "Many are the afflictions of the righteous, but the Lord delivers them out of them all." The righteous are also promised persecution. Only as we look unto Jesus will we be able to endure these last days. The following prayer was shared with me today, and I thought I would pass it on to you:

Lord, help me to look at my problems in the light of Your power instead of looking at You in the shadows of my problems.

November 15

READ: Ezekiel 31:1–32:32; Hebrews 12:14–29; Psalm 113:1–114:8; Proverbs 27:18–20

Looking Heavenward
Hebrews 12:14–29

The great theme of faith continues as we study the Book of Hebrews. We have learned that faith sees the unseen, and we endure in faith and hope when we keep our eyes focused on Jesus Christ, the author and finisher of our faith. Now we turn our eyes heavenward to look into realms of glory in heaven.

I have often wondered why some great men and women of faith die young. Recently a great servant of the Lord named Ruth Heflin died. I personally felt she had many more years of service to offer the Lord here on earth. She wrote a book called *Glory*. As I thought about her death, I felt the Lord had revealed the fullness of His glory and the glories that awaited her in heaven. The realms of glory she saw in the Spirit made this earth grow strangely dim to her, so the light of her life was transferred into the light of that city where there is no need of light—the City of Our God, Zion, the New Jerusalem.

The early heroes of our faith could not get near the glory of God. Moses had to be hidden in a rock while God's glory passed him. When God's glory burned on the mountain, the children of Israel were warned not to come near the mountain, because truly our God is a consuming fire. Because of the cross, however, we can now all be friends with God just as Moses was counted as a friend to God. We now have entrance into the city of the living God, the heavenly Jerusalem, and we are welcomed in the assembly of the saints. The thought of seeing some of these great heroes of our faith face to face blows me away. We also experience now the great cloud of witnesses on earth, and an innumerable company of angels surrounds us. Even though we cannot see these things with our natural eyes, the truth is the kingdom of God is at hand. When we reach our hands up in praise to God, we are able to touch the kingdom of God.

Glimpses of God's glory are available to us daily. Have you taken a peak lately?

> *Lord, I know the things that keep me from experiencing Your glory daily are my concerns and cares. There are so many things on this earth to think about, and these things seem to dull my eyesight. Help me not to be nearsighted. Help me to catch glimpses of Your glory daily. I think I caught a glimpse yesterday as I looked at the smiling face of my eleven-month-old grandson. Thank You, Lord. Show me Your glory.*

A House Full of Angels
Hebrews 13:1–25

This chapter begins with an interesting two verses: "Let brotherly love continue. Do not forget to entertain strangers, for by so doing some have unwittingly entertained angels."

In thinking over our lives I recall several encounters with what I am sure were angels. I just finished reading a book called *Awakened by Angels,* so these two verses in Hebrews particularly interest me. In this book the author had his eyes opened to see into the spirit realm, and he had ongoing encounters with angels. I must caution the reader to be careful about what kind of material he reads about angels as there are many counterfeits out there, especially in the New Age Movement. We have to remember there are two kinds of angels—the ministering spirits sent by God to minister to the saints and the angels of darkness that clothe themselves and make themselves out to be angels of light. This book on angels, however, I felt was valid because Jesus was always lifted up. The author received no teachings from the angels. He only received short messages from the angels. The Holy Spirit, who is the Great Teacher, gave all the teachings to the author, and they were all scripturally based.

One of the encounters the author had is described in the book, and I have heard many similar stories. He and his wife were traveling home by car when they saw a stranger wanting a ride. They almost picked him up, but were hesitant, so they drove to their home. Only fifteen minutes later this stranger appeared at their door. He asked for food, so they allowed him to come in and fed him. He then left. The Holy Spirit told the author later that this was not a man, but was an angel sent by the Lord to test their hospitality.

I had an encounter with what I am sure was an angel. It was right after Martin Luther King was assassinated. I had started an interracial prayer group in the inner city. As I was driving from this meeting, an African American man dressed in a gray suit was thumbing a ride. I gave him a lift, and when he entered the car, I asked him if he was a pastor. He said, "No," and then he delivered this message to me: "The day is coming when there will be people standing in line to get into the churches in Atlanta to hear the gospel preached and to experience the power of God." He then asked me to drop him at the next corner. When I looked in my rearview mirror to see where he was going, he was no longer there.

One of the End-Time exhortations is to be given to hospitality. I understand now why we are urged to open our doors to people more than ever as the day draws close to the Lord's return. I believe God will send more and more angels our way to minister to us because the days are going to be hard before He returns. We may face persecution as many are already facing this. Don't hesitate to be hospitable, because you never know whom you may be hosting.

November 17

READ: Ezekiel 35:1–36:38; James 1:1–18; Psalm 116:1–19; Proverbs 27:23–27

God Is Good
James 1:1–18

I saw a bumper sticker that said "Good God; Bad Devil." This is a statement most Christians should understand, but often we give God credit for doing bad things in our lives. We have to recognize that God is not evil, neither can He tempt us with evil. Whatever God does or allows in our lives will always be good. The author of sickness, confusion, disease, misery and strife is the devil. James makes it very clear in his letter that God cannot tempt us with evil. Only the devil tempts us with evil. James says, "Do not err, my beloved brethren. Every good gift and every perfect gift is from above, and cometh down from the Father of lights, with whom is no variableness, neither shadow of turning" (vv. 16–17, KJV).

If we are seeking to walk with the Lord daily, we can rest assured that whatever He allows in our life will ultimately be for our good. God allowed Satan to tempt Job, but at the end of the testing Job had everything restored to him double over what the enemy stole. Paul tells us that all things work for the good of those that love the Lord and are called according to His purpose. If we are rebellious against God and refuse our call in life, we cannot expect for everything to work for the good even though we are saved.

I loved the illustration a Bible teacher gave about life. She shared that God creates our lives as a homemaker makes a cake. First the homemaker collects all the ingredients in the recipe: Baking soda, which has a salty taste; salt; flour, which has no taste at all; eggs, which are tasteless; milk, etc. are all added at different times. The cake is stirred and finally baked. Only after the cake is baked are we able to taste these blended flavors and enjoy the results. Throughout our lives we will experience the bitter with the sweet, the flavorful and the flavorless, but if our hearts are determined to serve the Lord, the end result will be good. None of us like to think about being put into a hot oven, but we all will experience fiery trials. Peter even said for us not to be surprised when this happens.

Our reading today says the man who endures temptation will receive a crown of life. It is no fun to be tempted of the devil. However, if every time we are tempted we seek the way of escape, that is Jesus, we will have the victory. The fact God allows temptation has always puzzled me. We pray in the Lord's Prayer, "Lead us not into temptation." We have to remember that the Holy Spirit, not Satan, led Jesus into a time of temptation. The reason God allowed this temptation of Jesus was so He would win the victory over the tempter for us. Now the reason that God allows us to be tempted is to prove to the enemy that we too have the victory over him because of what Jesus did for us on the cross. We can endure temptation and receive the crown of life because Jesus endured and overcame every temptation Satan presented Him. Even trials, troubles, temptations and testings will work for our good if we love Jesus and are living our days fulfilling His will and His calling on our lives.

November 18

READ: Ezekiel 37:1–38:23; James 1:19–2:17; Psalm 117:1–2; Proverbs 28:1

The Speed of the Spirit
James 1:19–2:17

This passage in James talks about the speed we need to set to cruise in the Spirit. We have a cruise setting on our car. When we set it at the right speed, we are able to take our foot off the gas peddle and the car will continue at the right speed. James tells us exactly what speed we should set our hearing, speaking and anger to allow the Spirit to go forward at a great cruise level as we travel the road of life. He says, "So then, my beloved brethren, let every man be swift to hear, slow to speak, slow to wrath; for the wrath of man does not produce the righteousness of God" (James 1:19–20).

James says we should set the level of our hearing on high speed and the level of our speaking and anger on slow speed. We were given two ears and one mouth for a reason. We should listen twice as much as we speak. Proverbs tells us that he who keeps his lips keeps his soul from trouble. Most of the trouble we encounter in this life is caused by our not being able to bridle our tongues. When we are willing to listen to instruction and learn from others, we are wise. When we are quick to listen, we also can hear the still quiet voice of the Holy Spirit prompting us, inspiring us and instructing us.

We also need to set the speed of our anger on slow. An angry man stirs up strife, and strife never yields good fruit. When we get into strife, our tongues become uncontrollable, and we run the risk of damaging our own soul and the souls of others. Some people really have a problem with anger, and they are called "rageaholics." When people allow anger to rise up within them and flow out of them, sometimes they experience the same sensation a drunk feels. They are out of control and cannot even remember what they said during their rage. James tells us to be slow to wrath.

Today before you leave to travel through life's journey, check your speed. Be careful to be quick to listen, slow to speak and slow to anger. When you set these controls at the proper speed, you are then ready to cruise with the Holy Spirit all day.

> *Lord, help me to set the controls of my life at the right speed. I want the Holy Spirit to be in control of my life, but if I am too quick to speak, I will run ahead of His still quiet voice prompting me to be still and quiet. Lord, I need to put my mind in gear before I start the motor of my mouth. Help me to listen more than I speak, and help me to seek peace and pursue it. I know if I allow myself to lose it with my anger, I have also lost the control of my life by the Holy Spirit. Forgive me, Lord.*

READ: Ezekiel 39:1–40:27; James 2:18–3:18; Psalm 118:1–18; Proverbs 28:2

Two Kinds of Wisdom
James 2:18–3:18

There are two kinds of wisdom we can experience here on earth. We can experience the wisdom of this world or heavenly wisdom. Earlier in this letter James tells us that if any man lack wisdom, he should ask God, and God will grant him wisdom. The kind of wisdom God gives is described as follows: "But the wisdom that is from above is first pure, then peaceable, gentle, willing to yield, full of mercy and good fruits, without partiality, and without hypocrisy" (James 3:17).

If we could daily walk in such wisdom, we would be great ambassadors for Christ. The world needs such wisdom, but most people in this world are bound by the wisdom from below. James tell us "But if you have bitter envy and self-seeking in your hearts, do not boast and lie against the truth. This wisdom does not descend from above, but is earthly, sensual, demonic. For where envy and self-seeking exist, confusion and every evil thing are there" (James 3:14–16).

Any time we get into strife, we are operating in the wisdom of this world, which is demonic. If we are jealous or confused, we also are experiencing the wisdom of this world. The fruit of worldly wisdom is always bad.

If we think ourselves to be wise, we can easily become fools the moment we get into strife. We are exhorted in God's Word to cease from anger and strife and to seek peace and pursue it. God loves a peacemaker, and whenever we bring His peace into a strife-filled situation, we have pleased the Lord. Those who make peace always sow the fruit of righteousness in peace.

Lord, help me to operate in Your wisdom today and help me to be a peacemaker.

November 20

Rejoicing Every Day
Psalm 118:19–29

No matter what each day holds for us, we can rejoice in it. But you may say, "I don't feel like rejoicing." Often when a new day dawns, our bodies don't want to get up and greet the day with cheerfulness because we just simply may not feel good. Our souls, however, can always rejoice in the Lord. When we greet the day with gratefulness instead of grumbling, we will set the sails of the ship of our lives to receive the wind of the Holy Spirit.

David tells us exactly how we can rejoice daily. He gives us three ways to rejoice:

1. Praise the Lord.
2. Exalt the Lord.
3. Give thanks to the Lord.

If we will do the above, we will always have a blessed day no matter what we may encounter. Have a blessed day. REJOICE IN THE LORD ALWAYS!

Lord, forgive me for the times I have not greeted a new day with joy in my heart. Starting tomorrow morning, when I awaken I want to praise and give thanks to You for a new day. Then as I touch my feet to the floor to start sailing with the wind of the Holy Spirit, help me to exalt and glorify You in both word and deed. Thank You, Great Helper, for helping me today and every day.

November 21

READ: Ezekiel 42:1–43:27; James 5:1–20; Psalm 119:1–16; Proverbs 28:6–7

The Cure-All
James 5:1–20

Much research is being done to find cures for diseases like AIDS and cancer. These are diseases that so far have no cure-all. These are also diseases that are affected by the strength of our immune system. This passage in James gives a cure-all for ill health, but few avail themselves of this cure. James lists four things in this passage that will help bring healing to our bodies:

1. Call for the elders.
2. Let them anoint you with oil and pray with faith for you.
3. Confess your faults one to another so you may be healed.
4. Pray for one another that you may be healed.

When we are sick, usually the first thing we do is run to the doctor. Doctors treat the symptoms of our illness, but if the root cause is not determined, we may be vulnerable to another attack of illness. Often when we are bitter toward someone, our immune system becomes defiled. We are more vulnerable to disease. This is not to say that a root of bitterness causes all illness, because we live in a fallen world where disease germs are easily transmitted. We can, however, make sure there is no unforgiveness or bitterness in us, and thereby we can help our immune system to fight off disease.

Often I find that if I have opened myself to strife with another person, I have also opened myself to sickness. By praying for others more, I believe we are less subject also to hypochondria, which also can lead to real sickness.

When I become ill, I usually ask the Lord if I need to get right with another person. If I receive no response from the Spirit as I seek Him, then I hit the vitamin C and ask for others to pray for me. My usual last resort is to call the doctor. I want to give Doctor Jesus every chance to heal me.

Lord, I try to take good care of my body by eating healthy and exercising, but often I neglect what needs to be even more healthy than my body—my own heart. If there is anything in my heart today such as bitterness or unforgiveness, please show me. If You will help me keep my heart in good condition, I know this will also help the condition of my body. Thank You, Father, for Your provision for health. His name is Jesus.

A Great Inheritance
1 Peter 1:1–13

My mother died last year, and I received a small inheritance of $1,000. This inheritance has already been spent. Imagine having an inheritance that never disappears. I had a friend who wanted to leave her precious antiques to her daughter. Some of these antiques dated back to before the Revolution. They were priceless. Her daughter, however, said she did not want these pieces of furniture. I have heard stories where people received the contents of their mother or father's home, and in the process of cleaning the homes to sell them, they found thousands of dollars tucked in mattresses and cracks in walls. I have seen items given to sons and daughters by their beloved departed that have been allowed to mildew, dry rot and become worthless. If these people had taken care of those things they inherited, they probably could have sold them for a good price.

Peter tells us about our great inheritance in our reading today: "Blessed be the God and Father of our Lord Jesus Christ, who according to His abundant mercy has begotten us again to a living hope through the resurrection of Jesus Christ from the dead, to an inheritance incorruptible and undefiled and that does not fade away, reserved in heaven for you, who are kept by the power of God through faith for salvation ready to be revealed in the last time" (vv. 3–5).

The whole world is able to claim this inheritance, but few in the world choose to receive or claim it. This inheritance is reserved in a place where moth and rust will never corrupt it and where thieves cannot enter in to steal it. This inheritance is reserved for every one who believes in the Lord Jesus Christ. Just as the daughter refused to receive her inheritance of those lovely antiques, many people never claim and therefore cannot receive this great inheritance.

The Bible clearly tells us that we are joint heirs with Christ. Everyone who is born again can receive all that Jesus has inherited. This inheritance includes the kingdom of God, which is righteousness, peace and joy in the Holy Ghost. It also includes all the promises of God, which are all yes and amen through Jesus Christ, the Word of God with all of its wisdom, the fruit of the Spirit and the gifts of the Spirit. Many Christians even fail to receive their full inheritance. The thing that blocks them from receiving their inheritance in full measure is unbelief.

Today you can avail yourself of this inheritance. All that Jesus has is yours. You can access this inheritance simply by faith. Everything we receive from God is by faith, as we learned in our study of Hebrews. If you do not have enough faith to believe for your total inheritance, then ask God to give you the gift of faith so you can enter into your full inheritance.

Living Stones
1 Peter 1:14–2:10

Peter compares believers in Jesus Christ to living stones that are built into a spiritual house. So many people come for a season to our church and then move on to another church. Such people never have the beautiful experience of forming a spiritual house. I have heard some refer to such people as rolling stones instead of living stones. If we are always hopping from one church to another simply because things just do not suit us, we run the risk of never maturing in our walk with the Lord. It takes living stones rubbing other living stones even the wrong way for a season to bring each stone into the position where they fit into the building of a spiritual house. If we leave one fellowship before we have found our place of service there, chances are we will never fit into any other spiritual house or body of believers as the Lord wants us to do. Love is not easily offended, and if we run away every time we are offended without dealing with the situation, love will never be perfected (matured) in our lives. As living stones we have to learn to fit together and work together to build a spiritual house.

Our church supports a ministry in France that had the challenge of rebuilding an eleventh-century village into a retreat area. Most of the structures were in shambles when they began their work. The ancient stones were in piles here and there over the properties, and often they had to search for these ancient stones so they could be used in the rebuilding process. The scripture that inspired this couple to begin this work in France over twenty-five years ago was Isaiah 58:12: "And they that shall be of thee shall build the old waste places: thou shalt raise up the foundations of many generations; and thou shalt be called, The repairer of the breach, The restorer of paths to dwell in" (KJV).

As this couple worked with others to rebuild this village, they had to lay the stones out and determine exactly which ones would fit most tightly into the next space that was available. Sometimes they had to shape the stones to fit by chiseling a little on the edges. Their goal was to have as little mortar as possible between each stone because they knew this would make a stronger building. In other words, they had to close up the gaps and get rid of any spaces or breaches between the stones. God wants to do the same with the living stones in His body.

During the building of this village, those who worked on the restoration learned so many spiritual lessons and understood clearly why the body of Christ is compared to living stones. Every summer different teams of young people would come to work on the restoration. This couple noticed that the teams that accomplished the most in the least bit of time were those teams that had little bickering and strife. The teams that were best were made up of individuals who esteemed and respected one another. There was no competition or jealousy between the members of the team, and they were all working for a common goal, not their own agenda. The results of such teams were nearly miraculous. May this be the case in every church.

November 24

READ: Ezekiel 47:1–48:35; 1 Peter 2:11–3:9; Psalm 119:49–64; Proverbs 28:12–13

Covering Up
Proverbs 28:12–13

In recent years we have seen in our own country what happens when we try to cover up our sins. There was Watergate, and then the unfaithfulness of a president. There is a verse in the Bible that says that everything done in darkness will be brought to light.

Whenever we try to cover our sins rather than confess them, we will not prosper. We may prosper outwardly, but inwardly covering our sin will cause our souls to be damaged. Our minds will become confused, our emotions will experience torment and fear, and our wills will become unsurrendered and rebellious to God. John writes in one of his letters, "I would that you all prosper and be in health as your soul prospers." The person who covers his sin will never prosper. Proverbs also tells us that he who hides iniquity in his heart will not prosper.

If we want to prosper both outwardly and inwardly, we must be honest with God and others about our sins. I can remember one time in my life (thank God I can only remember one time) when I told a boldface lie to my husband. I did not sleep well until this sin was out in the open. Unfortunately I got caught before I confessed my sin to my husband. Thank God he was forgiving and understanding. Rest assured that whatever we do will eventually be uncovered; if not in this life, it definitely will be uncovered in the next life. When our son was on drugs he told us many lies, but everything he tried to hide from us was eventually uncovered. God in His mercy saw to that. Life is so wonderful when we are able to be open and honest and confess our sins. The Bible says we are to confess our sins, not cover our sins, to one another so that we might be healed. We foolishly think sometimes we can hide our sins from God, but He knows all and sees all.

The next time you are tempted to cover your sins rather than confess them, think about the consequences. The torment, confusion and fear this brings is not worth it. The sooner we confess our sins, the sooner we can be liberated from the bondage that caused us to sin.

Lord, I remember all too well the torment I was in when I tried to cover my sin. Please do not let me ever do this again. I want my soul to prosper.

Adding Days to Your Life
1 Peter 3:10–4:6

So many people in the world are almost hyper about adding days to their lives. They go from one health fad to another, hoping against hope that their longevity will be increased. We see the fitness freaks, the joggers, dieters, vitaholics, weight lifters all trying to beat old Father Time.

In this passage Peter tells us one sure way we can lengthen our days here on earth. Listen to his advice: "For he that will love life, and see good days, let him refrain his tongue from evil, and his lips that they speak no guile: Let him eschew evil, and do good; let him seek peace, and ensue it" (1 Pet. 3:10–11, KJV).

Here Peter lists four ways we can lengthen our days on earth and insure they will be good days:

1. Refrain our tongues from evil
2. Speak no guile
3. Hate evil
4. Pursue peace

Think about it a moment. What would your day be like if you never spoke evil of anyone, but instead you sought to live at peace with all men? That would be a good day! What would your day be like if you refused to enter into any evil practices or even entertain evil thoughts in your mind? That would be a good day! If you lived this way, you would always have a measure of peace that would see you through any amount of stress from your job, church or family.

Even as I write this, my son is under unbelievable stress because of a job situation, but I know he will get through this stressful time because the Prince of Peace lives in his heart. We can be under tremendous stress from outside factors, but if we have peace in our hearts, our bodies and minds will not crumble under the pressure.

If we refuse to entertain evil and hate evil, we would be more careful to keep the laws of the land. So many deaths occur on the highways because of drunk drivers. I must confess I have often gone above the speed limit, and at those times I know I have walked out of God's protection. I read recently that we have four guardian angels—two who go with us wherever we go and two who remain in our dwelling place to protect it. I also read that our guardian angels cannot break the law, so when I speed in my car, my angels are left behind. This has made me slow down, and this small obedience to the law may also add years to my life. Peter shared timeless truths that will help us all experience good days. Obedience to our heavenly Father and those in authority is a major way we can insure we will live out our appointed days and experience good days.

End-Time Exhortations
1 Peter 4:7–5:14

As Peter wrote this letter he had a sense of urgency. He felt the Lord's return was imminent, and he wanted his fellow believers to be ready for His return. He says, "But the end of all things is at hand: therefore be serious and watchful in your prayers" (1 Pet. 4:7). It is interesting that his End-Time exhortations were exactly what Jesus told us to do as the day of His return drew near. He told us to watch and pray. None of us know the exact time of the Lord's return, but we all need to be ready. Each of us will have our appointed day to die, and Peter's day came shortly after he wrote this letter. We should all, however, live every day of our lives as if it might be our last day on earth.

In this passage Peter mentions many End-Time exhortations that would be beneficial to each of us if we fulfilled them.

1. Be sober.
2. Be watchful.
3. Be prayerful.
4. Be loving.
5. Be cheerful, not grudging.
7. Be good stewards.
8. Be bold to speak often about the Lord.
9. Be operating in your God-given gifts and abilities.
10. Glorify God in all things.

If we are careful to do the things listed above, we will be ready for the Lord's return, and our lives will produce much fruit for God.

Lord, I want to fulfill these exhortations, but I know I need the help of Your Holy Spirit to do it. Help me daily to glorify You in word and deed.

November 27

READ: Daniel 4:1–37; 2 Peter 1:1–21; Psalm 119:96–112; Proverbs 28:17–18

Stop the World; I Want to Get Off!
2 Peter 1:1–21

Often when our family is gathered at the dinner table, someone will say, "Things are really getting tough out there." The world is definitely waxing worse and worse, but the good news is those who walk uprightly will get better and better.

After watching the evening news, I usually want to say, "Lord, please come quickly." The world is so corrupt, and it will be even more corrupt before the Lord comes again. We do not have to fret about this, however, because there is a way right now we can escape the corruption of this world. Listen to what Peter shares: "Grace and peace be multiplied to you in the knowledge of God and of Jesus our Lord, as His divine power has given to us all things that pertain to life and godliness, through the knowledge of Him who called us by glory and virtue, by which have been given to us exceedingly great and precious promises, that through these you may be partakers of the divine nature, having escaped the corruption that is in the world through lust" (vv. 2–4).

The world is corrupt because of the lusts in it. Even as Christians we too have lusts that have the potential of corrupting our private worlds. This is why Peter exhorts us many times in his letters to be watchful, sober and prayerful. We have an enemy who would love to bite into our fleshly lusts and cause us to be drawn away into sin. Seducing spirits have an assignment to draw every Christian away from their calling while they are on earth. Listen to the high calling we have. We are called to glory and virtue. We will only be able to fulfill this calling if we watch out for the temptations and enticements of the enemy in our lives. We have to pray constantly and stay totally dependent upon God during these last days. In Paul's letter to Timothy, he made it clear that seducing spirits will be on the prowl more than ever in the last days.

The way to submit ourselves to God and effectively resist the devil is to be sure that we live in the Spirit every day instead of the flesh. Sometimes I am quite aware that my flesh is showing, and when it does, the enemy begins to salivate. He would love to bite and devour me, but he only will have success if I continue to expose my flesh to him. When I am walking in the Spirit, I will not fulfill the lusts of my own flesh.

Lord, help me to walk in the Spirit daily so I do not let the enemy see my flesh. I want Satan to see Jesus when he looks at me.

READ: Daniel 5:1–31; 1 Peter 2:1–22; Psalm 119:113–131; Proverbs 28:19–20

You Are My Hiding Place
Psalm 119:113–131

David in this psalm reveals the secret of getting through trying circumstances. He says, "You are my hiding place and my shield; I hope in Your word" (v. 114). Corrie ten Boom wrote the story of her experience in the concentration camps where she lost all of her family. She titled the book *The Hiding Place*. She was arrested for hiding Jewish people during the war, but she was able to get through those trying times because she hid herself in the Lord.

Just yesterday I heard the testimony of a precious saint who lost two of her children in a tragic accident in a one-week period. As she shared her story, I knew she had discovered David's secret. A policeman showed up at their door to tell her that her son had been killed in an automobile crash. When she received the news, she shared that quietness settled over her heart. The Lord Himself was shielding her from the shock. One week after her son's death she received the news that her husband and daughter were in a terrible crash. They were on the way to meet her at a conference. Her husband survived, but her daughter did not. Once again she hid herself in Jesus, and He quieted her troubled soul.

She did grieve, but even during those weeks of grief, the Lord shielded her from being overwhelmed with grief. The Bible tells us that Jesus was a man of sorrows who was acquainted with grief. He can identify with grief, but because of His sacrifice on the cross for us, we now have the strength through Him not to be overwhelmed with grief.

During the trying times of our life we need to remember this verse of scripture in Colossians 3:3: "For you died, and your life is hidden with Christ in God." What a safe place to be. I like to demonstrate this verse by letting my thumb represent me. As I fold my thumb into the same hand, I say, "I am hidden with Christ." Then I take my other hand, which I say represents God, and as I enfold my left-fisted hand with my right hand, I say, "I am hidden with Christ in God." The security and peace we have when we see our position in Christ Jesus will get us through whatever storms of life we will experience. Christ is the rock of our salvation, and we can hide ourselves in Him daily. How do we do this? We can pray a prayer like this:

> *Lord, You are a shield round about me. I hide myself today in the pavilion of Your love far away from the strife of tongues and the fiery darts of the enemy. I abide in You today, and I receive my nourishment and protection from You. Help me to remain in this safe place all the day long. I never want to leave Your side, and You have promised never to leave me or forsake me.*

READ: Daniel 6:1–28; 2 Peter 3:1–18; Psalm 119:132–155; Proverbs 28:21–22

Hope in God's Word
Psalm 119:132–155

David says several times in this psalm that his hope is in God's Word. Faith is the evidence of things not seen, the substance of things hoped for as we learned earlier in our study of Hebrews. The substance that gives us hope is the Word of God.

I've always pictured in my mind a highway to heaven. That highway is called faith. Prayer is the vehicle I must place myself in to reach the destination of God's throne room. This highway is paved with hope. Hope is the substance of the highway of faith.

David tells us to hope in God's Word. We can never hope in God's Word if we do not read God's Word. Reading the Word of God, however, will not instill faith and hope in us. We must hear God's Word. Paul tells us that faith comes by hearing and hearing by the Word of God. As we read God's Word, we must let the Holy Spirit be our narrator. He wants to teach us and instruct us through the Word of God, but this will not happen unless we are carefully listening to His voice. The Holy Spirit speaks in a still, quiet, voice so we also must be still and quiet to receive His gentle instructions, corrections, reproofs and teachings as we read through the Bible.

We are almost finished another year of reading the Bible through. If you are like me, you may have missed a few days. At the end of each year I pray the Lord will teach me by His Holy Spirit anything I may have missed in my journey through the Bible that year. We are in the classroom of life, and the goal of our teacher, the Holy Spirit, is to instill faith and hope in us every day. Will you continue to attend class next year faithfully? There are always new lessons to learn. The Holy Spirit is waiting daily to teach you. Listen to David's words: "Your testimonies, which You have commanded, are righteous and very faithful" (v. 138). "Your word is very pure: therefore Your servant loves it" (v. 140).

As you are faithful to read God's Word daily, you will love it more and more and love Him more and more.

Lord, I want to keep reading the Bible through every year. Each time I do I learn more about You, and I grow to love You more. Thank You, Holy Spirit, for being my faithful teacher who makes God's Word exciting and life changing.

Fellowship
1 John 1:1–10

Fellowship is a Christian buzz word, but what does it mean? I heard one definition: "Fellowship is fellows in the same ship on the sea of life." This is not a bad definition, because we usually fellowship with people who are going on the same journey we are. There is nothing sweeter than Christian fellowship. If we miss fellowship with those in the body of Christ, we are risking falling away from the faith. As we learned in Hebrews, we are not to forsake the assembling of ourselves together. So often when people leave a Christian fellowship or church, they do not attach themselves to another. When asked where they are going to church now, too often the response is, "I'm having church at home now." If we cut ourselves off from the body of Christ, our Lord soon has nothing to direct in our lives. Jesus is the head of the body and if we detach ourselves from the body, we will be cut off from the wisdom and the mind of Christ. We will not be able to see how the body can function together under the headship of Jesus.

Satan loves to cut people off from the body of Christ because he knows then that they are open prey for him. If we choose to be loners in our walk with Christ, we have opened ourselves up to great deception. John clearly shares in this passage the importance of staying in fellowship. He says, "If we say that we have fellowship with Him, and walk in darkness, we lie and do not practice the truth. But if we walk in the light as He is in the light, we have fellowship with one another, and the blood of Jesus Christ His Son cleanses us from all sin" (vv. 6–7).

We release ourselves from the effective cleansing of Christ's blood if we refuse to fellowship with those who are walking in the light. When two of my boys attended college, they quit attending church. I shared with them I didn't care whether or not they were in an institutional church, but they needed to be in a fellowship of believers that met together at least once a week.

When we fellowship on a regular basis with fellow believers, we become accountable to one another and we come out of hiding. When people get to know us, it is hard to hide our lives from them. The Christian walk is never a walk alone.

Lord, I pray for all those who have not found a regular place to fellowship weekly. Help them to attach themselves once again to the body of Christ so they will be able to abide in You daily.

December 1

READ: Daniel 8:1–27; 1 John 2:1–17; Psalm 120:1–7; Proverbs 28:25–26

Stop the World! I Really Want to Get Off!!
1 John 2:1–17

In these last days before the Lord returns, it seems the world is increasing in evil. The Bible tells us this will happen. Timothy tells us that in the last days seducing spirits will be everywhere. We have this hopeful word in God's Word that says where sin abounds, grace does much more abound. Sometimes my husband and I sit at our peaceful dinner table and remark to one another, "Things are really getting bad out there." One only has to watch the news to see the corruption in our world and the steady descent into more darkness. Sometimes after watching the news I want to say, "Stop the world! I want to get off!!" Today's reading gives us the reason the world is such a mess. We cannot blame it on God or even the devil. We only have to look at ourselves to find the answer to our predicament. Listen to what John says: "Love not the world, neither the things that are in the world. If any man love the world, the love of the Father is not in him. For all that is in the world, the lust of the flesh, and the lust of the eyes, and the pride of life, is not of the Father, but of the world. And the world passeth away, and the lust thereof: but he that doeth the will of God abideth for ever" (vv. 15–17, KJV).

The world is waxing worse simply because more people are giving into their own lusts—the lust of the flesh (seeking to fulfill their five senses in an overindulgent way—drugs, alcohol, overeating, etc.); the lust of the eyes (greedy longings in the mind such as covetousness, greed, fantasies, pornography, etc.); and the pride of life (trusting in ourselves more than we trust in God). There is no question that our own lusts are the problem. The Bible says that in the last days men will be lovers of pleasure more than lovers of God (the lust of the flesh) and lovers of self more than lovers of God (the lust of the eyes and the pride of life).

The good news is that the world will pass away and all of its lusts with it. There will be a day when the Lord Himself will stop the world, and we will be able to get off. Let's pray earnestly that all of our loved ones will be in a position to get off when things come to an end here on earth. The position we all need to be in when the Lord returns and stops the world as we know it today is on our knees humbly bowing and acknowledging that Jesus Christ is Lord of all even this corrupt world, and most of all, He is Lord of our lives.

Lord, I confess my own selfish lusts. So often I do put my own pleasure ahead of spending time with You. Many times I place more trust in myself and my own abilities rather than depending upon You and Your supernatural ability (Your grace). Forgive me for the prideful times in my life when I chose to put self on the throne rather than You. Help me to humble myself daily.

You Will Be Like Him!
1 John 2:18–3:6

When we went to India in 1980, I met a young man who I had a hard time loving. He was a manipulator, and I did not care for his mode of operation. During our visit to India I managed to be civil toward this young pastor, but it was not easy. Frankly on many occasions I wanted to tell him off, but the Holy Spirit helped me hold my tongue.

Upon our return from India, I was in the kitchen preparing dinner, and I said to the Lord, "Lord, I don't think I can look forward to seeing this young Indian man in heaven because I just simply do not like him. Then I heard the Lord speak to my heart the following: "When you get to heaven and see this young man, you will simply love him because he will be just like Me."

There are probably people you know today whom you are not looking forward to seeing in heaven. The words I received on that day in the kitchen offer wonderful hope. What is even a better hope is that I too will be like Jesus. This means all my character flaws, insensibilities and lack of love will be replaced by His perfect love. JOY!! Listen to John's words in our reading today: "Beloved, now we are children of God; and it has not yet been revealed what we shall be, but we know that when He is revealed, we shall be like Him; for we shall see Him as He is. And everyone who has this hope in Him purifies himself, just as He is pure" (1 John 3:2–3).

Knowing I will be like Jesus when I see Him face to face does not give me an excuse to sin willfully here on earth. On the contrary, I am challenged to lean more upon His righteousness and perfect love than ever by daily abiding in Him. Only by abiding in Him will I be able to purify myself. I'm not that good, but He is!! GLORY!!

Lord, help me to love everyone with Your love as I live out my days here on earth. I blow it so often, but You are the perfect One who can help me daily to not sin in my heart. My heart is to love as You love, and I know this will only happen as I daily abide in You. Your love far exceeds any I would have to offer anyone.

No Name It and Claim It!
1 John 3:7–24

During my lifetime, there was a movement that many coined as "name it and claim it." Many preachers and teachers were saying you could have anything you asked God for—all you had to do was believe and claim it by faith. It is true that even Jesus says whatever you pray about, believe that you have it and you will receive it. However, one must read this promise in context. Jesus also shares that for this to come to pass in our lives, we must fulfill a condition. That condition is to abide in Him and allow His love and Word to abide in us. Jesus tells us we must keep his commandments. He says, "If ye abide in me, and my words abide in you, ye shall ask what ye will, and it shall be done unto you... This is my commandment, That ye love one another, as I have loved you. Greater love hath no man than this that a man lay down his life for his friends" (John 15:7, 12–13, KJV).

In our reading today John again gives the major condition for answered prayer. "And this is His commandment: that we should believe on the name of His Son Jesus Christ and love one another, as He gave us commandment" (v. 23).

All of us want to see our prayers answered. Our prayers will all be answered if we pray according to God's will. John in another letter shares that if we pray anything according to God's will, He hears us, and we have the petitions we require of Him. Do you realize one of the main reasons for unanswered prayer is that we are not praying according to God's will?

What is God's will? His will is simply that we love Him with all our hearts and keep His commandment to love one another. I have yet to see a bitter, unforgiving, jealous, prideful person receive answers to his prayers. Why? God never even hears his prayers. When we pray with unforgiveness in our hearts, God cannot forgive us, and our prayers fall to the ground. There is one prayer, however, that God always hears. That prayer is the prayer of repentance. Is there any unforgiveness, bitterness, resentment, jealousy or lack of love in your heart today? Confess it to God, and He will not only forgive you, but He also will cleanse you of all unrighteousness. After you are cleansed, daily abide in His Word and in His love, and you will begin to see God answer your prayers because God will pray through you the prayers that are according to His will.

Lord, I realize today You hear my heart before You hear my prayers. Cleanse my heart so my prayers will soar into Your throne room.

The Love Test
1 John 4:1–21

The whole counsel of God's Word exhorts us not to judge others. However, we can give the love test to others. The Bible says you shall know them by their fruits. The fruit of the Spirit is love. John talks about the love test. "Beloved, if God so loved us, we also ought to love one another. No one has seen God at any time. If we love one another, God abides in us, and His love has been perfected in us" (vv. 11–12).

When we see someone who does not walk in love, we can rest assured that person does not know God because God is love. Every day I pray, "Lord, help me to love as You love." His love is gentle, kind, longsuffering, full of faith, joyful, peaceful, patient and self-controlled.

No human being is capable of having love like this, but this love can flow through us if we daily abide in the love of Jesus and His Word. We have to admit honestly to God that without Him we can do nothing; especially we cannot love. He is love (true love), and only as we submit ourselves daily to Him for a fresh infilling of His love will we be able to even begin to love as He loves. The Bible tells us that the love of God is shed abroad in our hearts by the Holy Spirit. We must depend upon the Holy Spirit to conform us to the image of Jesus daily and to perfect within us the love of Christ. Once we receive a fresh infilling of His Spirit daily, we have to make sure we do not leak. How can we do this? Ephesians 5:18–21 shares the answer. "And be not drunk with wine, wherein is excess; but be filled with the Spirit; speaking to yourselves in psalms and hymns and spiritual songs, singing and making melody in your heart to the Lord; giving thanks always for all things unto God and the Father in the name of our Lord Jesus Christ; submitting yourselves one to another in the fear of God" (KJV).

The above exhortation does not seem to be a tall order. On the contrary, it is quite doable, and if we sing and speak to ourselves in psalms, hymns and spiritual songs and make melody in our hearts, we will be filled not only with the Spirit, but also with His love, peace and joy.

Today, when you are stopped at a traffic light, try singing some of your favorite hymns aloud. The moment you awaken in the morning, read and sing some of the psalms. If you do this faithfully, you will be able to pass the love test. Remember, always it is the love of Jesus within you, not your own love, that will make an impact on others.

Lord, I give You thanks for Your Word that says You will perfect Your love within me. I submit myself to Your Spirit of love today.

The Priestly Role
1 John 5:1–21

Few know the power God has given them through Jesus Christ to confess and remit the sins of others. This is the ministry of reconciliation. God was in Christ Jesus reconciling the world to Himself. The possibility of the whole world being reconciled to God was extended on the cross when Jesus died not only for your sin, but also for the sins of the whole world. When Jesus said, "Father, forgive them for they know not what they do," Jesus was entering into the ministry of reconciliation.

What does this ministry of reconciliation involve? Just after Jesus breathed the Holy Spirit into His disciples, He said these words: "Whose soever sins ye remit, they are remitted unto them; and whose soever sins ye retain, they are retained" (John 20:23, KJV).

At this time the disciples and all those who would believe in Jesus after them were given the power to remit sins. John speaks of this power in this letter. He says, "If any man see his brother sin a sin which is not unto death, he shall ask, and he shall give him life for them that sin not unto death. There is a sin unto death: I do not say that he shall pray for it" (v. 16, KJV).

When we see a brother sin, we are to cover that sin and not talk about it to others. We also have the great privilege of confessing that sin to the Father in Jesus' name for our brother. Then we can ask God to have mercy and not count this sin against our brother. Jesus set the example of the ministry of reconciliation on the cross. We also see Stephen minister reconciliation when he was being stoned. He said, "Father, lay this not to their charge." What a great privilege we have as priests of the Lord. Priests confess the sins of others for them to God.

Wouldn't you want someone talking to God about your sin rather than talking to others about your sin? Much more is gained through prayer than through talk. The promise in this scripture is that as we ask for mercy for our brother who sins, God will give him life. Death is always the result of sin. Something in our soul dies. Our mind, will and emotions are affected by sin. God promises to bring life once again to the one who has sinned, and where sin brought death, the Lord can bring life. Remember always that the same Spirit that raised Christ Jesus from the dead is able to quicken our mortal bodies (able to give life to us). When we confess the sins of others, we are releasing them to the work of the Holy Spirit. The Holy Spirit will then be able to bring conviction to this person about his own sin, and the Holy Spirit can also soften this person's heart so he will confess his own sin and repent.

December 6

READ: Hosea 4:1–5:15; 2 John 1:1–13; Psalm 125:1–5; Proverbs 29:9–11

Security in the Lord
Psalm 125:1–5

We have led many tours to Israel, and sometimes people are hesitant to go because they are fearful of terrorists and possible war in Israel. When they express those fears, Tom and I always share that we feel safer walking the streets of Jerusalem than we do walking the streets of Atlanta. There is a sense of God's peace and presence in Israel that supersedes the threat of war and terrorism.

This psalm is one of the psalms of ascent that the Israelites sang as they made their pilgrimage three times a year to Jerusalem for the feasts of the Lord. This psalm especially expresses the security we have in the Lord, even though there may be trouble all around. Listen to these comforting words: "As the mountains surround Jerusalem, so the LORD surrounds His people from this time forth and forever" (v. 2).

We had the opportunity after the Scud missile crisis to have a Jewish couple share about their experiences during this time. They were living in Jerusalem, and they said they would speak Psalm 91 aloud during the times when the Scud missiles were soaring over Jerusalem to Tel Aviv. When all hell is breaking loose, we find ourselves trying to find comfort with heavenly thoughts. There are so many heavenly thoughts in the psalms that bring peace to us in the midst of troubled times. This psalm promises such security to all who put their trust in the Lord and abide in Him. When we trust in the Lord we do not have to run in terror, and our hearts can be fixed upon the Lord. We do not have to fear evil tidings. Listen to these comforting words: "Those who trust in the LORD are like Mount Zion, which cannot be moved, but abides forever."

We are going through a time in history when everything that can be shaken is being shaken. There is a hiding place we can run to during these times. That hiding place is the presence of the Lord, and the path to this hiding place is the Word of God, praise and worship. We enter His gates with thanksgiving and into His courts with praise. A good way to do this is to begin to sing some of the psalms. David was on the run most of his life, but he found a place of safety and security—a place where the shaking around him would not shake him. That place is a place of trust. He said, "When I am afraid, I will trust in the Lord." We all experience fearful times, but now we know how to overcome fear. We overcome fear by trusting in the Lord and remaining in His presence. Try singing some of the psalms today.

Lord, sometimes I get in a panic over things that are happening in my life. Forgive me. I choose today to put my trust in You instead of being afraid.

The Prosperous Soul
3 John 1:1-14

Not too long ago there was a lot of prosperity teaching. One of the examples given to try to prove God wanted to bless our giving was the promise of the hundredfold return for the gifts we give to God. Some of these evangelists preaching such a return on gifts were expecting the gifts of money to be given to them. They wanted the hundredfold return, and often were manipulating people by putting guilt trips on them to give monies to their ministry. These evangelists never told the whole truth about the hundredfold return. We are only promised the hundredfold return if we forsake certain things. Listen to what the Bible actually says about the hundredfold return. "Verily I say unto you, There is no man that hath left house, or brethren, or sisters, or father, or mother, or wife, or children, or lands, for my sake, and the gospel's, but he shall receive an hundredfold now in this time, houses, and brethren, and sisters and mothers, and children, and lands, with persecutions; and in the world to come eternal life" (Mark 10:29-30, KJV).

Did you see anything in the promise of the hundredfold return about money? God wants us to prosper financially, spiritually and every way. Jesus said, "I came to give you life and life more abundantly." When we hear this verse, our minds immediately think, *Show me the money.* Because we live in such a materialistic society, we think prosperity means more money. The abundance Jesus promises has very little to do with money. The hundredfold return speaks of the return we will experience in the true treasures of life—people. Whenever we forsake anything for the gospel's sake, God's promise is to return to us hundredfold for our loss, and He promises this in this life, not just the world to come in eternity.

The prosperity that will always be ours here on earth and also in heaven is the prosperity of the soul and the souls we have touched for the Lord. John writes, "Beloved, I pray that you may prosper in all things and be in health, just as your soul prospers" (3 John 1:2).

Whenever we put the Lord first in our lives, we invest in His storehouse of souls. Our own souls are strengthened, and we receive much more than worldly riches. We receive peace, joy and righteousness. We also receive the joy of knowing we will live eternally with those people with whom we have shared the gospel. Our soul truly prospers when we think of the possibility of seeing hundreds in heaven who will say, "I'm here because you cared enough to share God's truth of the gospel with me." Doesn't this make you want to invest today into God's storehouse? His storehouse is filled with souls who are now prospering because Jesus has given them abundant life.

December 8

READ: Hosea 10:1–14:9; Jude 1:1–25; Psalm 127:1–5; Proverbs 29:15–17

Sharp Arrows
Psalm 127:1–5

The fruit of my forty-plus years of marriage has been three marvelous sons with their beautiful wives and children. God has promised us at least ten grandchildren before Jesus returns, and I kid people a lot by telling them, "Never mind all the signs of the times mentioned in the Bible that usher the return of our Lord. Just know that when the tenth grandchild is born, Jesus is on the way." God's heart is concerned with people, and He always rejoices when births occur (physical births of new babies and spiritual births of new babes in Christ). God loves to add to His family because He is a family God. This psalm speaks of children as the heritage of the Lord and the Lord's reward. Listen to these words: "Behold, children are a heritage from the LORD, the fruit of the womb is a reward. Like arrows in the hand of a warrior, so are the children of one's youth. Happy is the man who has his quiver full of them; they shall not be ashamed, but they shall speak with their enemies in the gate" (vv. 3–5).

People (not just any people, but people who love the Lord and obey His commandments) are God's greatest weapon against the enemy. Such people are forming a mighty army, and they are like arrows sent to wound the enemy. All of our own children have been fashioned into sharp arrows that will penetrate the enemy's camp. Our middle child will penetrate the enemy's camp in China, and our youngest son is penetrating the enemy's camp in Hungary. Our oldest son is penetrating the enemy's camp in the corporate world.

When my husband retired, we felt God would send us full time to either China or Russia to penetrate the enemy's camp there with the gospel. Instead, God sent China to us in the form of a precious Chinese daughter who lived with us for five years and a handsome Russian son who lived with us seven years. These additions to our family made a quiver of children for us. I heard a quiver is five or more. What a joy to know these five arrows are doing effective warfare against the enemy. They are not only talking to the enemy at the gate; they are invading his camp and taking back what he has stolen.

Maybe you are not married, so you may think you have no sharp arrows to send against the enemy. The truth is you can have many thousands of sharp arrows. Every time you share the gospel with another person, God is fashioning a sharp arrow that can create great destruction in the enemy's camp. Is your quiver full?

345

December 9

Children's Children
Psalm 128:1–6

What a blessing it is to be grandparents. This psalm promises the children of Israel that they will see their children's children. "Thy wife shall be as a fruitful vine by the sides of thine house: thy children like olive plants round about thy table" (v. 3, KJV). "Yea, thou shalt see thy children's children, and peace upon Israel" (v. 6, KJV).

We are so grateful for the fruitfulness of God in our lives. We are going to have to expand our dining table because the olive plants are already crowding the table.

As we shared yesterday, the Father loves to be surrounded by many children. David in this psalm speaks of God's faithfulness to give us fruitful lives on this earth. He says, "Blessed is every one who fears the Lord, who walks in His ways. When you eat the labor of your hands, you shall be happy, and it shall be well with you" (vv. 1–2).

David is telling us of God's provision to those who fear Him. His provision to all who serve Him is fruitfulness to us as we birth physical births and spiritual births, fruitfulness because of the labor of our hands, and fruitfulness to our souls. Our souls will demonstrate the fruits of the spirit—joy, peace, love, patience, kindness, gentleness, meekness, temperance and faithfulness. The words *faithfulness* and *fruitfulness* are closely related. As we are faithful to fear the Lord, He is faithful to produce fruit in our lives, and we will live abundant, happy (blessed) lives. This does not mean we will never have troubles. It means we will remain in His joy, and our joy will be full as we abide in the vine no matter what circumstances we are experiencing. After all, fruit receives nourishment from the vine, and Jesus is that strong vine who supplies daily all we need to be fruitful.

> God, I know You are a firstfruit God. As I seek You first in my life, I know You will bless every aspect of my life with fruitfulness. Thank You for supplying such a wonderful nourishing vine (Jesus Christ) that I can receive from daily all I need in this life.

Hasty Words
Proverbs 29:19–20

I remember my mother's instructions, "Put your mind in gear before you start the motor of your mouth." I've tried to follow that advice all my life, but sometimes I forget. When I do, I usually find that what I say in haste hurts others. Someone told me to roll my tongue around in my mouth twenty times before I speak. That also is good advice.

The Holy Spirit moves in a gentle way and speaks in a quiet voice. He does not press us into action. Instead He impresses our spirit with a gentle leading. Whenever we move in haste we are going the way of the enemy. Often our tongues are the weapon Satan uses to invade our souls. There is a proverb that says, "He that keeps his lips keeps his soul from troubles."

When we speak in haste, we supply the enemy with a rapid-firing machine gun that does not even need reloading. Our mouth drives on before our minds get in gear. When our spirits are provoked, we speak unadvisedly. Psalm 106:32–33 says, "They angered Him also at the waters of strife, so that it went ill with Moses on account of them; because they rebelled against His Spirit, so that he spake rashly with his lips."

If you have provoked someone to anger, that situation can be defused right away if you say, "Wait a minute; I spoke in haste, and I ask your forgiveness for causing you to be upset." A good scripture to meditate on before we begin our day is Ecclesiastes 5:2: "Do not be rash with your mouth, and let not your heart utter anything hastily before God. God is in heaven, and you on earth; therefore let your words be few."

This scripture tells us that God has a lot more to say than we do, so we had better listen to Him before we speak. If we are listening to God before we speak, then our words will be few. He wants us to speak only those things that are true, lovely, of good report, pure and virtuous. This limits our conversation, doesn't it? It also keeps us from speaking foolish words. "Do you see a man hasty in his words? There is more help for a fool than for him" (Prov. 29:20).

> Lord, help me to hold my tongue. Sometimes I just rattle on and on, and when I do, I always say something wrong. Help me today to listen to You before I speak. You have things You want me to say to others.

347

December 11

Forgiving Iniquities
Psalm 130:1–8

Where would we be if God marked our iniquities? We have all sinned and fallen short of the glory of God. God's plan has always been to redeem us, not condemn us. Redemption is extended to us through Jesus, and the possibility of having our sins, transgressions and iniquities all forgiven is offered to all who believe in the Lord Jesus Christ.

This psalm says with the Lord there is mercy and plenteous redemption. How sad it is that men refuse such an offer to have their sins washed away so they can receive a fresh start—newness of life. Why would anyone reject such an offer? People refuse to believe in Jesus Christ because they are blinded by Satan. He deceives many and convinces them that they do not need a Savior.

Pride is often the stumbling block to receiving Jesus Christ as Lord and Savior. Some people actually believe they have no sin, and therefore they do not need a Savior. Before redemption can take place, we must first believe our lives need to be changed. We must admit that our nature is to sin, and we need a second nature—the very nature of Jesus Christ who was sinless.

God promises to redeem all who will believe in His Son Jesus Christ. His invitation to us all is to receive His precious gift to earth given two thousand years ago. Now that Christmas is coming, I have been cleaning out the basement to ready it to receive the Christmas gifts I purchase. Every year when I do this, I discover there are some presents remaining from last year that were never wrapped or given. So I simply wrap them up and give them to someone this Christmas.

Two thousand years ago God wrapped Himself in an earthly suit, and Jesus was born to give us life and life more abundantly. He died and was resurrected to set us free from the bondage of sin and death. Listen as this great gift on the first Christmas is described: "God so loved the world, that he gave his only begotten Son, that whosoever believeth in him should not perish but have everlasting life. For God sent not his Son into the world to condemn the world, but that the world through him might be saved" (John 3:16–17, KJV).

Have you failed to receive God's gift to you given on the very first Christmas, or have you shelved this gift and refused to open it? The only way we can know God personally is to come to know His Son who was freely given to you. Don't let another Christmas go by without receiving this precious gift, and when you do, be sure to pass this gift on to others.

December 12

The Keys of David

Revelation 3:7–22

Jesus holds the keys of David that can open the doors that no man can shut, and He also can shut the doors that no man can open. Often I have prayed for Jesus to go ahead of me and open the doors no man can shut and to close the doors no man can open. Jesus holds the keys to our future, and we need to release our future to Him. I am praying for the employment of one of my friends now, and I am praying that Jesus will use these powerful keys to open or close doors for her future job.

We so often try to force doors open. It is a part of our nature to sometimes go ahead of the Lord, and when we do, we miss His best. Things usually work out much better when we are willing to wait upon the Lord and allow Him to be the one to prepare the way for us.

When our Russian son was interviewing for jobs, I prayed for the Lord to open the doors for him and to close any doors to jobs that would not be a good match for him. I also prayed that he would be led to the job where he could produce the most fruit for the Lord. God desires for us to be fruitful, and He has a way of placing us in the right place at the right time where we can be the most fruitful.

Whenever we see a change of locations or jobs coming our way, that is the time we need to commit our way to the Lord. He leads us in paths of righteousness for His name's sake. He wants us to be His righteous representatives in a place where our witness will cause many to come into His kingdom. Promotion does not come from the east or west. It comes from the Lord. Maybe His plan for you is even to promote you into a position where you will have a deeper impact and influence on many more lives. God is after people, not position. Rest assured if you commit your way to Him, He will bring His will to pass in your life. His will is that you will be fruitful and multiply (fruitful in your witness so souls will be multiplied into His kingdom).

Lord, help me to trust You to go ahead of me to prepare the way. You know what is best for me. Thank You for putting me in the right place at the right time today.

349

Snared by the Fear of Man
Proverbs 29:24–25

When I first married, I was so bound by the fear of what others thought of me. I wondered if my mother thought I was a good mother. Did my husband think I was a good wife? Did my neighbors think I was a good neighbor? I remember my next door neighbor coming to my home and telling me how she cleaned her oven and range every day. From that day forward I made sure my oven and range were spotless just in case "Mrs. Clean" dropped by uninvited. Before I was delivered from the fear of man, I never really listened to what people were saying. I was too busy thinking about what I would say to them when they finished talking.

One day I was listening to a teaching tape on my back patio. The subject was "The Fear of Man." As I listened and discovered how the fear of man is a snare, I asked God to deliver me from that fear. That day I was delivered, and now I can honestly say I fear God more than I fear man. I desire to please God first in all of my ways and honor Him instead of trying to please man.

Since that significant prayer of deliverance from the fear of man, I have been free to esteem others higher than myself, to think of others rather than myself, and I don't seek to impress people. Instead, I now want to make a spiritual impact for God upon people. I seek now to put His best foot forward instead of my own. What a blessing to be free from the tension and pressure of trying to please others. Now I just want to please God.

Has the fear of man been a snare in your life? If it has, maybe you would like to get set free of that wicked snare today. If you do, you can pray with me the following:

> *Father, set me free from the fear of man, and fill me with the fear of You only. In the name of Jesus Christ, I bind the spirit of fear of man in my life and command it to leave me this moment and never return. I refuse to ever receive the fear of man again. I will no longer be concerned with what people will think of me. Instead I will only be concerned with what You think about me. Thank You, Lord, for delivering me from the snare of the fear of man.*

December 14

READ: Jonah 1:1–4:11; Revelation 5:1–14; Psalm 133:1–3; Proverbs 29:26–27

Blessed Unity
Psalm 133:1–3

One of God's greatest desires is that we dwell together in unity. One of Satan's greatest desires is that we would be divided. God hates it when men come against each other with accusations and strife. This psalm talks about the sweetness of unity. It compares unity of the brethren to the oil that flowed from Aaron's beard upon his garments. Oil usually symbolizes God's anointing and His Holy Spirit. When the priests were anointed for service, oil was poured over their heads. This oil flowed freely and soaked even their garments.

The only way unity of the brethren will ever be achieved is through the anointing of God's Holy Spirit. Natural man seeks his own agenda, and pride rules over him. If we, however, submit ourselves to be filled daily with the Holy Spirit, there is that possibility we will not even strive at all during the day. We will instead seek peace and pursue it.

When there is division in our families or church, we first should pray for God's anointing. This anointing includes the spirit of wisdom and understanding, might and counsel, knowledge and the fear of the Lord, which are all aspects of the Spirit of the Lord. Daily I pray for a double portion of this anointing because I know the anointing is my only hope of being able to love and help others the way Jesus does. This anointing is my only hope of living in peace and harmony with those around me. Perhaps you would like to pray with me this morning as I ask for this anointing:

Father, today I ask for a double portion of Your anointing—the spirit of wisdom and understanding, counsel and might, knowledge and the fear of the Lord. Let the Spirit of the Lord rest upon me this whole day. Thank You for the unity of heart with You and with others this anointing always produces.

Learning War No More
Micah 1:1–4:13

The Bible is clear about what causes war. James tells us that wars exist because of our own lusts. I am so thankful that no one in my immediate family ever had to fight in a war, because "war is hell." I heard the testimony of a Christian who was shot down in Vietnam and held prisoner for over a year. His testimony was inspiring, but just think of a day when there will be no more testimonies like his. One day there will be no more war. Micah looks forward to that day when he says, "But in the last days it shall come to pass, that the mountain of the house of the LORD shall be established in the top of the mountains, and it shall be exalted above the hills; and people shall flow unto it. And many nations shall come, and say, Come, and let us go up to the mountain of the LORD, and to the house of the God of Jacob; and he will teach us of his ways, and we will walk in his paths: for the law shall go forth of Zion, and the word of the LORD from Jerusalem. And he shall judge among many people, and rebuke strong nations afar off; and they shall beat their swords into plowshares, and their spears into pruninghooks: nation shall not lift up a sword against nation, neither shall they learn war any more" (Mic. 4:1–3, KJV).

This will come to pass in the last days when Jesus comes to rule and reign on earth. During this time of the millennial reign of Jesus Christ, nations will drop their weapons and there will finally be peace on earth. This period of peace, however, will not last forever, because during this time Satan once again will be released and wars will again begin. The good news is that the army of God wins the final war, and then there will be a new heaven and a new earth.

Does this seem like a fairy tale that is too good to come true? This prophecy will take place, rest assured. Does this seem to be so far distant that it has no affect upon your behavior now? Remember, one thousand years is as a day with the Lord, and we are about to begin our third day. Jesus was raised on the third day, and there is a coming day soon when we all will be raised with Jesus to live forever in His presence. In the meantime, we can do our part to keep the wars in our relationships from happening. We can choose to lay down right now the mighty weapon of our tongues that wounds and hurts others with the bullets of words fired rapidly from our mouths. We can choose to cease from strife and speak only those things that edify. If you will make a covenant with your mouth as David did when he said, "I purposed that my mouth shall not transgress," the wars in our personal relationships will cease. The major cause of strife is pride.

Humble yourself today by submitting your tongue to the Prince of Peace.

December 16

READ: Micah 5:1–7:20; Revelation 7:1–17; Psalm 135:1–21; Proverbs 30:5–6

Sing to the Lord
Psalm 135:1–21

When we praise the Lord with singing, it is pleasant to Him, and He will make our days pleasant if we will sing throughout every day. David spent most of his days singing songs of praise. He was a psalmist. We do not have to be an expert as David with his song writing, but we can sing in the Spirit and sing some of David's psalms all the day long. In fact, this is the way to stay filled with the Spirit. Paul exhorts us in Ephesians to sing spiritual songs, psalms and hymns and to always make melody in our hearts. He shares that this is the secret to staying filled with the Spirit. It is hard to fulfill the lusts of our own carnal nature when we are constantly making melody in our hearts unto the Lord.

God rejoices over us with singing, so we in return should rejoice over Him with our singing. He loves it when we raise our voices to Him with songs of praise and worship, and He also hears every song we sing in our hearts.

Have you ever thought of the fact that Jesus is not only our chief rabbi (the teacher who teaches the keys to living), but He is also the chief cantor. Whenever we sing songs of praise and worship in our church, He sings right along with us. We learn this in Hebrews 2:11–12: "For both he that sanctifieth and they who are sanctified are all of one: for which cause he is not ashamed to call them brethren, saying, I will declare thy name unto my brethren, in the midst of the church will I sing praise unto thee" (KJV).

The next time you enter praise and worship with others, picture Jesus singing in the midst of your church. He is singing songs to the Father as we sing songs to Him. If you listen carefully, you may tap into some new songs in the Spirit.

Today as you go about your daily tasks, sing aloud when you can, and be sure to always make melody in your heart. Your day will be a blessed day because the Lord will bless you, and you will be a blessing to others. You also will stay filled with the Spirit.

Lord, give me a new song to sing to You today.

His Mercy Endures Forever
Psalm 136:1–26

There are many aspects of God's love, but four are particularly outstanding. When I was seeking the Lord one day about the height, depth, breadth and length of His love Paul relates to us in his letter to the Ephesians, I learned something very special about His love. Paul in this letter said we could know the height, depth, breadth and length of God's love even though such knowledge cannot be discerned without the help of the Holy Spirit. Paul said he wanted us all to comprehend these precious dimensions of the love of Jesus. I asked the Lord just what were the height, depth, breadth and length of His love, and the following is what I heard with my spiritual ears: "The height of My love is My grace. It is poured out upon you from above. The depth of My love is My forgiveness. My forgiveness goes deep within the recesses of your soul and cleanses and restores you. The breadth of My love is My truth. My truth is able to set you free to walk in all the fullness of My love. My truth is able to expand your mind so you can experience My boundless love. The length of My love is My mercy. My mercy extends forever and ever to every generation."

This psalm speaks of God's mercy. Each verse in this psalm ends with the response, "His mercy endures forever." This psalm speaks of the wonderful works of the Lord that have demonstrated His mercy throughout history.

Whenever we go through times of stress and pressure, when we fret and worry, we need to say over and over again just as this psalm says, "His mercy endures forever." If we will do this, the peace that passes all understanding will mount guard over our hearts and minds.

Today give thanks to the Lord because His mercy endures forever and to all generations.

> *Lord, forgive me for the times I have fretted over things I have no control over. Help me to always remember You are on Your throne no matter what is going on here on earth, and Your throne is a throne of mercy where I can always find grace in the time of need.*

How to Wait for Your Vision
Habakkuk 1:1–3:19

The Bible tells us that without a vision the people will perish. It is so important to have a vision or several visions throughout our lifetime. God calls us to be visionaries. He created the imagination to be used for His glory. Satan, however, ever since the Fall seeks to use our imaginations for his dirty work. Satan has the power to plant images in our minds that will tempt us to sin. We see this clearly when so many today are involved in pornography. When we set our eyes on anything that is not holy, good, pure, virtuous and lovely, those images we receive will be played over and over again in our minds. The spiritual battlefield is our minds and we must use the mighty weapons of God (His Word, the blood of Jesus, prayer and the name of Jesus) to pull down those vain imaginations that Satan would use to destroy us. God desires our minds to be stayed upon Him, and when they are, we will have perfect peace. The visions and images God wants us to have are of Him and His plans for our lives.

Just recently as someone was counseling my son, he was asked the question: "What is your dream?" This is a good question to ask ourselves, because often we will find the calling God has on our lives when we answer this question. Perhaps God has given you a vision. You may have a recurring dream or a thought that brings images to your mind of God's plans for you. Maybe He gave this vision to you many years ago, and it has not yet been fulfilled. What do you do while you are waiting on the fulfillment of the vision of visions God has given you? This passage in Habakkuk gives us the answer to this question.

I was in a meeting with Marilyn Hickey when she singled me out of the crowd and gave this verse from Habakkuk to me: "For the earth will be filled with the knowledge of the glory of the LORD, as the waters cover the sea" (Hab. 2:14) She said, "There is an area in your life you have been praying for years about, but your vision of completeness in this area has not yet been fulfilled. Know and rest assured that this area of your life shall be filled with the glory of God." I instantly knew the area she was speaking about, and I thought this fulfillment would happen the next day. The truth is, I had to wait nearly twenty years for this vision to be fulfilled. What did I do while I waited for this vision to be accomplished? I learned what to do in this passage in Habakkuk. The prophet Habakkuk writes that although we do not see the tree blossoming or the fruit on the vine and the fields are yielding nothing, we still rejoice in the Lord. We wait with confident expectation of what has been promised. We declare the Lord is our strength, and He makes our feet like hind's feet to walk on the high places. Deer jump using the strength of their feet, and they can leap great distances in the air because of the springing ability of their feet. Rejoicing in the Lord continually even though we do not see our vision fulfilled right away will keep the spring in our steps as we wait for the vision to be fulfilled. Rejoice in the Lord always, and again I say rejoice.

He Perfects Those Things That Concern Us
Psalm 138:1–8

Through the years I have used this scripture many times as different situations and relationships became a concern to me. It is so comforting to know that the Lord knows everything that concerns us. He knows every person that we are concerned about. It is so exciting to realize that He not only knows all my concerns, but His plan is to perfect everything that concerns me. Listen to these comforting words again "Though I walk in the midst of trouble, thou wilt revive me: thou shalt stretch forth thine hand against the wrath of mine enemies, and thy right hand shall save me. The LORD will perfect that which concerneth me: thy mercy, O LORD, endureth for ever: forsake not the works of thine own hands" (vv. 7–8, KJV).

We have God's promise never to leave us or forsake us. We are His workmanship created to accomplish His good works throughout our lifetime. God knows every detail about our lives. He even knows the number of hairs each one of us has on our heads. God not only sees the things I see, but He also knows the end from the beginning. He knows all about the hidden things in me that need the touch of His resurrection power even when I am not aware of my own need. His plan is always to revive us daily. There are some days I really need His right hand to touch me and strengthen me with His grace, mercy and energizing power.

As we near this Christmas season, I am reminded of a precious vision I had one day when I was praying. I was overwhelmed with cares and concerns for my three sons, who were not married yet. I once again was praying for their mates, and once again I released this concern to the Lord in prayer. When I did this, I saw the following in the spirit: My cares and concerns were wrapped with gold ribbon in silver packages. As I prayed, each care was ascending heavenward and Jesus was receiving them all. When He received them, He said, "Thank You." Then I saw Him holding all those packages of my cares and concerns to His chest as He danced around heaven with them. Then He said, "I love you because you cast all of your cares upon Me."

Peter tells us to humble ourselves under the mighty hand of God by casting all of our cares upon Him because He cares for us. Our cares and concerns are gifts to Him, because once He receives them He can then do something about them. Today wrap all of your cares in prayer and send them soaring into His throne room. He is waiting eagerly to receive them so He can be about performing His plan and will concerning each of your concerns.

December 20

READ: Haggai 1:1–2:23; Revelation 11:1–19; Psalm 139:1–24; Proverbs 30:15–16

His Thoughts Toward Me
Psalm 139:1–24

This psalm declares clearly how much God is thinking about us. We have an expression in the Christian community we use when we are concerned about someone. We say, "You have really been on my heart." We are on God's heart every day of our lives. Listen quietly and You can hear Him say, "Today, My child, you are on My heart, and I am praying for you." This psalm says, "How precious also are Your thoughts to me, O God! How great is the sum of them! If I should count them, they would be more in number than the sand: when I awake, I am still with You" (vv. 17–18).

Not only is God thinking about you today, His thoughts were absorbed with you even before you were born. This psalm tells us that God was watching us when we were formed in our mother's womb, and He wrote down the members of our body.

If you feel today, that God has somehow abandoned you or forgotten that you exist, read this psalm. After you read it, you can then praise and give thanks to the Lord because you are fearfully and wonderfully made. He loves you, and you are in His thoughts today. Jesus is making effective intercession for you right now at this very moment.

Thank You, Lord, for thinking about me today. I know in Your thoughts is a plan for me today. Father, let what is in Your mind and heart for me today be accomplished according to Your will. I submit myself to Your way, which is much higher than my own way. Help me by Your Holy Spirit to tap into what Jesus is praying for me today and to what You have planned for me each minute of this day.

Peace Be on Jerusalem
Zechariah 1:1–21

As we come nearer to the celebration of Jesus' birth, our thoughts go back to that still, quiet night in Bethlehem when the shepherds were startled by a heavenly host that sang, "Glory to God in the highest, and on earth, peace, good will to men." I had the opportunity to stay in a kibbutz in Bethlehem that overlooked the shepherds' fields. As I sat quietly on the balcony I could hear in the distance the tinkling of the bells on the shepherds' staffs as the shepherds led their sheep to a place of rest for the evening. It was a star-filled night very much like the one when heaven came down and glory filled our hearts.

There is anything but peace in Jerusalem and in the world right now. The evening news is filled with scenes of the battles between the Palestinians and the Jews. We see stones flying, helicopters dropping firebombs on buildings and we wonder, "Will there ever be peace in Jerusalem?" Our passage in Zechariah tells us of such a day. Listen. "Therefore thus saith the LORD. I am returned to Jerusalem with mercies: my house shall be built in it, saith the LORD of hosts, and a line shall be stretched forth upon Jerusalem. Cry yet, saying, Thus saith the LORD of hosts; my cities through prosperity shall yet be spread abroad; and the LORD shall yet comfort Zion, and shall yet choose Jerusalem" (vv. 16–17, KJV).

God is telling us to not give up on praying for Jerusalem. We are to keep crying out for the peace of Jerusalem because He will fulfill His plan for this city. When we pray for the peace of Jerusalem, we are also praying for the Lord's return. Jerusalem will not be in a state of total peace until the Lord comes again to rule and reign from this city. The Lord has chosen this city to be the seat of His millennial government, and His plans will not be thwarted by the devil or anyone else. Our prayers, however, help to hasten this day, and this is why we continue to cry out in our prayers for the peace of Jerusalem. When the Prince of Peace comes to set up His throne in the city of Jerusalem, the prophecy the angels declared on that first Christmas Eve, "Peace on earth, good will toward men," will be fulfilled. Lord, hasten the day!

Thank You for reminding me to daily pray for the peace of Jerusalem. Don't let a day go by that I do not do this, because more than ever I see what this prayer will accomplish. Thank You for showing me one of the things I can faithfully do to prepare the way for Your Second Coming. I can daily pray for the peace of Jerusalem.

December 22

READ: Zechariah 2:1–3:10; Revelation 13:1–18; Psalm 141:1–10; Proverbs 30:18–20

Shut Your Mouth
Psalm 141:1–10

In this psalm David prays a prayer we all need to pray. He prays, "Let my prayer be set before You as incense, the lifting up of my hands as the evening sacrifice. Set a guard, O Lord, over my mouth; keep watch over the door of my lips" (vv. 2–3).

Our mouths were created to praise and worship the Lord. Every part of our being was created to glorify God here on earth. Our hands are to lift in praise to Him daily. Even the trees of the fields rejoice and clap their hands. So often, however, we use these God-given, fearfully and wonderfully made bodies to do things that Satan wants us to do. Remember, Satan has no power to make you do anything, even sin. Sin happens in our lives because we are led astray by our own lusts. We learned earlier the way to keep us from giving into our own lusts and fulfilling them is to stay filled with the Spirit. One of the ways to stay constantly filled with the Spirit is to use our mouths to praise, sing spiritual songs and hymns, to give thanks and to make melody in our hearts. If we are busy praising and worshiping the Lord, we will not have time to give into our own lusts.

One of the ways I like to keep myself filled with the Spirit is to have good praise music and hymns playing throughout the day when I am home doing my chores. I sing along with the hymns, and I also love to play classical music that lifts soul and spirit. I mostly concentrate on Handel and Bach. The world tries to drag us down, and can easily do it if we set ourselves in front of the boob tube all day long or even have it playing while we are doing other things. Remember, Satan is the prince and power of the air. He loves to use TV and radio to gain an advantage over us.

Another way we can stay filled with Spirit is to refuse to allow anything to come out of our mouths that would wound or hurt others. Our mouths were created to praise God and also to praise and edify others. David knew his own weakness in the matter of the tongue, and he calls upon the help of God to set a watch over his mouth. This morning let's pray a prayer that David prayed. "Lord, let the words of my mouth and the meditations of my heart be acceptable in Your sight. Set a watch over my mouth, and may my mouth, be used today only to praise You and to edify and praise others."

359

Not by Might, nor by Power, but by My Spirit
Zechariah 4:1–5:11

We sing a song in our church based on this scripture. This song is saying it is not by our own might or strength that we do God's will. It is by the might and power of the Spirit that we are able to do anything for the Lord on this earth. The Holy Spirit is the might and power of God. The Holy Spirit manifests God's works and wonders on this earth, and these wonders and works reveal God's might and power. We can only see the wind by watching the trees rustle their leaves and sway to and fro. God's Spirit manifests God's power and might throughout the earth and also through our own lives. We are vessels of the Lord created to contain His Spirit. We have to remember, however, we are not to keep this treasure to ourselves. We are to manifest God's glory (His might, light and power) to others by allowing the Holy Spirit to rustle us, to stir us up and to pour the oil of His anointing from these earthen vessels to all those we encounter throughout the day.

God intends for us to do mighty exploits for Him today, but we must be filled with the Spirit and anointed by the Spirit for this to become a reality in our lives. Whenever I try to do things in my own strength I fail miserably. So often I overcommit myself to people and to doing things, and I feel overwhelmed. When this happens the Holy Spirit whispers this gentle reminder in my ears. "You can do all things through Christ who gives you the strength." Suddenly the pressure and stress of what I am facing is removed, and joy replaces worry. His joy begins to strengthen me for whatever task I am facing.

One of the prayers I pray often in the morning is the one below. Maybe you would like to join me as I pray this today:

> *Lord, give me strength to face whatever this day may bring. Empower me by Your Spirit to walk in Your ways and to do Your will. I depend upon Your might and power totally and refuse to do things in my own strength. Thank You, Lord, for the Holy Spirit who is Your might and power.*

Thirsting for Fellowship
Psalm 143:1-12

In this psalm David said, "I spread out my hands to You; my soul longs for You like a thirsty land" (v. 6). Recently we have gone through a severe drought where I live. As I looked on our land, I saw cracks in the earth, and they seemed to be crying out, "Fill me, fill me." The earth was cracked because there was no moisture to spare it from the burning rays of the sunshine. David was going through a dry time, and the land of his soul felt parched, dry and cracked for lack of the rain of God's Spirit.

Sometimes God allows a dry time in our lives just so we can have a new appreciation for the work of His Spirit as He refreshes us and quenches our thirst as we read God's Word. Thank God the dry times in my life never lasted too long. I don't think I could have survived if they did. During those dry times, it seemed I could receive nothing from God. I knew He was still with me, but my prayer life and my Bible reading became duties instead of delight. In most of these dry times, I discovered the Lord was longing to restore fellowship with me. He had not moved, but I was allowing my lack of feeling to dictate my relationship to the Lord. It is at the dry times of our lives when we honor God the most if we continue to read the Word, pray and commit our days to Him because this takes great faith. We don't have the delight, but we still are willing to discipline ourselves to a time daily with the Lord. If we are faithful not to abandon our quiet times during dry times, suddenly the river will begin to flow to fill and refresh those cracked, parched areas of our soul.

Do you realize that God thirsts for you? He longs to fellowship with you daily. When Jesus cried out "I thirst" on the cross, He was crying out for the Spirit of God to quench His thirst. At that moment in time it seemed all had forsaken Him, and even God for a moment turned away from Him. Jesus was thirsting for fellowship with the Father and for fellowship with you and me. Jesus said "I thirst" just after He cried out, "My God, My God, why have You forsaken Me?" John records these words about the cross: "After this, Jesus, knowing that all things were now accomplished that the Scripture might be fulfilled, said, 'I thirst'" (John 19:28).

Jesus on the cross accomplished everything for our sakes that we will ever need to overcome the world. Healing, forgiveness, salvation and wholeness in every way were accomplished. Now Jesus thirsts for us to come to Him daily to obtain and receive all He has promised. He longs to fellowship with you. Even when you are in a dry place, your prayers are welcomed and your praise delights the heart of the Lord. If you continue in the discipline of a daily quiet time when you are in a dry land, you will soon feel the arms that have been around you all the time—the precious arms of Jesus. Will you quench His thirst for fellowship with you today?

Lord, I come in faith to You, and even though I feel nothing, I know You are near.

True Joy
Psalm 144:1–15

One of my favorite Christmas hymns is "Joy to the World." True joy can only come from Jesus, and on this Christmas morning we are more aware than ever of this fact. All over the world people are celebrating the birth of Jesus, and their joy is not based upon their circumstances. Their joy is based on the fact Jesus has come to touch their circumstances and every area of their lives.

So many on this day go to the bars to celebrate, and often they celebrate Christmas by getting loaded because of overdrinking. Such people are seeking joy in the wrong kind of drink. These people will only be satisfied temporarily. Jesus offers to us all the drink of living water that will cause us never to thirst again. He told us the secret to true joy, which is to abide in Him and allow His words and love to abide in us. Jesus is the source of lasting joy. He said, "These things have I told you that your joy might be full and that My joy might remain in you."

So many get depressed right after Christmas because the glow has vanished and they are faced once again with the mundane daily job and duties. They have forgotten that Christmas Day is passed, but Jesus Christ has not. He lives and is praying for us on the day after Christmas and on every day for the rest of our lives. Jesus is the true joy who is the glory and lifter of our heads. He is the day spring that causes us to spring with His Spirit daily. This psalm says, "Happy are the people whose God is the LORD."

Today you will be happy if you make Jesus the Lord of your life. He is waiting to receive those special gifts of your cares and concerns wrapped in prayer. As you are giving gifts to others, be sure to cast all of your worries, cares and everything that concerns you into the arms of Jesus. He can't wait to receive your cares because He cares for you. When you cast all of your cares upon Him, you can enter into the exhortation, "Be happy, don't worry." Joy is waiting you this Christmas day as you rest your burdens into His hands. Joy to the world! The Lord has come not just once, but He lives now and is praying for you, and soon He will come again. What a day that will be when our Jesus we will see. We will look into His face and see the majesty of His grace. It will be better than Christmas. JOY! JOY! JOY !!!

Happy birthday, Jesus! I give You all my cares and concerns as gifts to You on Your birthday. Thank You for touching each one.

December 26

READ: Zechariah 9:1–17; Revelation 17:1–18; Psalm 145:1–21; Proverbs 30:32

God Is Great!
Psalm 145:1–21

I remember as a child praying this blessing before every meal: "God is great! God is good! Let us thank Him for our food! Amen." This psalm expresses the greatness of God. David says, "Every day will I bless You, and I will praise Your name forever and ever. Great is the LORD, and greatly to be praised; and His greatness is unsearchable" (vv. 2–3).

It would take our whole lifetime to search out God's greatness, but at the end we would realize we had not even begun our search. His greatness is truly unsearchable.

Today I am thanking Him for the great life He has given me with my husband as we celebrate our wedding anniversary together. Today we celebrate also the birth of Jesus in our marriage and in the marriages of all of our three sons. Jesus lives in each of their hearts, and Christmas is celebrated every day of their lives. Christ lives within us, and He is our hope of glory. He is the light of the world that does not go out when the Christmas lights are turned off. He is and was and ever more will be the great I Am, Emmanuel—God with us—the Great Potentate of all time, the King of glory who touches our lives with His glory and causes our light to shine before others.

Every day can be Christmas day if we will bless the Lord and praise His name. Joy will flood our souls, and no man will ever be able to steal this joy. Today I not only celebrate my marriage to my husband, and the joy it brings, but I also celebrate my marriage to Jesus Christ who gives me joy now and forever more, even into eternity. Great is the Lord and greatly to be praised.

> *Lord, I give thanks and praise to You today. Don't let a day go by that I do not praise Your holy name. Thank You for the generations after me in my own family who will praise Your name and declare Your mighty works to others. You are truly good. You are gracious, full of compassion, slow to anger and of great mercy, and You are good to all. Your tender mercies today are over me and all my loved ones. Thank You for Your everlasting greatness.*

December 27

READ: Zechariah 10:1–11:17; Revelation 18:1–24; Psalm 146:1–10; Proverbs 30:33

Happy New Year
Psalm 146:1–10

We are fast approaching the new year, and soon we will hear the age-old phrase, "Happy New Year!" Everyone wants a happy New Year. The Greek word for *happy* also means "blessed." In fact, the Beatitudes in some modern translations say, "Happy is the man who..." instead of "Blessed is the man who..." Let's think a moment about the word *Beatitudes*. When we break this word down, we see it means the attitude of our being. This psalm states the attitude we should have daily as we live on earth. Listen to the words of David: "While I live I will praise the LORD, I will sing praises to my God while I have my being" (v. 2).

If we want to have a "Happy New Year," then our attitude daily needs to be one of thanksgiving and praise to the Lord. David continues revealing the secrets to experiencing a happy new year when he says, "Happy is he who has the God of Jacob for his help, whose hope is in the LORD his God" (v. 5).

The way to have a happy new year is to trust the Lord to help us when we have a need and to place our hope not in circumstances in this world, but in the Lord.

Do you want to have a happy (blessed) new year? There are things you can do in this next year that will insure you will experience a blessed, happy new year. Here are three simple things you can do:

1. Praise the Lord daily and sing praises to Him.
2. Trust in Him to help you instead of putting your trust in man or yourself.
3. Hope in the Lord instead of hoping in circumstances or this world's system.

HAVE A BLESSED NEW YEAR!!!

> *Lord, help me to do these three things in this next year. They are not vain resolutions. They are things I can do each day with Your strength and grace, and I know when I do them faithfully, each day of this new year will be blessed.*

December 28

READ: Zechariah 12:1–13:9; Revelation 19:1–21; Psalm 147:1–20; Proverbs 31:1–7

Mourning For Messiah
Zechariah 12:1–13:9

This scripture in Zechariah is a powerful prophecy of when the veil of the Jewish people will be dropped and Israel will be saved in a day. Zechariah prophesies, "And I will pour upon the house of David, and upon the inhabitants of Jerusalem, the spirit of grace and of supplications: and they shall look upon me whom they have pierced, and they shall mourn for him, as one mourneth for his only son, and shall be in bitterness for him, as one that is in bitterness for his first born" (Zech. 12:10, KJV).

The sentence "and they shall mourn for him, as one mourns for his only son" has special meaning for me today because it is the birthday of my firstborn son, Russell. What a delight he has been to me, and I cannot even begin to comprehend the grief and mourning I would experience if he left this earth before his appointed time.

Most Jewish people today recognize Jesus as a prophet, but they do not believe that He is God in human flesh. This passage speaks of the day when Jesus' own Jewish brethren will look upon Him and recognize Him because they will see the nail prints in His hands and the wound in His side. On that day it will be like Joseph revealing himself to his own brothers. At first they did not recognize him, but after he wept privately over his brothers, Joseph made himself known to them. The brothers were afraid and probably thought, *We tried to kill him, and now, he will kill us.* They, however, were so wrong because Joseph had no animosity toward them. He forgave them and said, "What you meant for evil, God meant for good." I believe Jesus will say these same words when He reveals Himself to His Jewish brothers.

Our Lord has a great plan to redeem and restore all His Jewish brothers and sisters who will believe on Him. There will be great rejoicing in the house of Israel on that day after these precious Jews have their time of mourning.

Father, thank You for drawing me to Your Son Jesus. I pray You will do the same for all of my Jewish friends.

Called to Excellence
Psalm 148:1–14

From the time our three sons were very young until this day I prayed this prayer for them: "Father, I pray our sons will have the same excellent spirit Daniel had. Daniel was filled with Your Spirit, and Your Spirit is excellent."

This psalm declares that only the name of the Lord is excellent. The word *excellent* is usually attached to the attributes of the Lord. In the love chapter of 1 Corinthians 13 Paul speaks of a more excellent way. Whenever we allow God's Spirit to flow through us and demonstrate the fruit of the Spirit (God's love), we are walking in the most excellent way.

Several years ago I was partaking of communion in church when my eyes were drawn to Vladimir, our Russian son. I heard the Lord speak to my heart, "I have called Vladimir to excellence."

I shared this with Vladimir after church, and I was blessed to know the Lord had inspired me to extend my prayer for my three natural sons to this fine young Russian who is like a son to us. Then my mind flashed back to the time when Vladimir first came to us as an exchange student. At that time he was not a Christian. I was driving him to register him for school when out of my mouth came these words: "Vladimir, you have an excellent heart, and God will use you."

This was prophetic as Vladimir one year later accepted Jesus as his Lord and Savior. We have rejoiced as we have seen his growth over the seven-year period he has lived in our home.

Do you want to live an excellent life? Then allow the excellent love of Jesus Christ to be shed abroad from your heart daily by the power of His Holy Spirit.

> *Lord, help me to remember that the most excellent thing I can do today is to love others as You love them. Empower me by Your Spirit to do this today and every day.*

The New Jerusalem
Revelation 21:1–27

As we draw near to the end of our yearly readings, this passage in Revelation should cause our hearts to leap. If you know your name is written in the Lamb's Book of Life, you can look forward to living in the New Jerusalem. The description of this holy city is mind boggling, but I believe every word of it. Yes, we will walk streets of gold, and there will be gates made of pearl. There will be no need of the sun or the moon because the light will emanate from the glory of God.

As I read this passage, I can hear the words of that great song "The Holy City." My mother sang it many times in many churches all over this city. As I meditate on the words, I can almost hear her singing this great hymn now, but this time she has a hosts of saints and angels joining her in the chorus "Jerusalem, Jerusalem!!" Mother died May 17, 1999, but she lives today in heaven and is singing with the saints who have gone before her. I can almost hear her beautiful contralto voice now.

Just after my mother had her stroke, she shared a vision she had with us. Her life was in the balance, and she could hardly talk, but we managed to hear what she described as she had a vision of heaven. She said, "I see a man standing by a huge lake. He is reading a book. He said, 'It is not your time.' I hear music, beautiful music." Then my mother added these words as she looked into our eyes. She said, "Prayer is very important."

God was using my mother's vision to give us this message. Our prayers on earth do make a great difference, and God has chosen prayer to be His mode of operation while earth exists. Nothing is done in the realm of earth if we do not give God's Word voice on earth through our prayers and declarations. We pray, "Thy kingdom come, thy will be done on earth as it is in heaven." When we pray this, we are hastening the day when the holy city will descend from heaven to earth and Jesus will rule and reign forever. Even so, Lord, come quickly!

Lord, help me to make prayer a top priority daily in my life.

December 31

READ: Malachi 3:1–4:6; Revelation 22:1–21; Psalm 150:1–6; Proverbs 31:25–31

The Book of Remembrance
Malachi 3:1–4:6

I trust you have been blessed by reading through the Bible with me this year. I pray your first New Year's resolution will be to read the Bible through next year and every year until you go to be with the Lord. Perhaps you would like to write devotionals of your own as you read through the Bible in this next year. I plan to write devotionals on those passages that I did not cover this year.

It has been a joyful experience for me to share my heart with you as certain passages spoke to me. One of the greatest inheritances we can give to our children are the words we have written down as we study God's Word. Every time we speak about the Lord or even think about Him, a sentence or paragraph is written in the Book of Remembrance in heaven. Listen to what Malachi says: "Then they that feared the LORD spake often one to another: and the LORD hearkened, and heard it, and a book of remembrance was written before him for them that feared the LORD, and that thought upon his name" (Mal. 3:16, KJV).

My desire is for my book to have thousands of chapters because of the many times I have spoken and thought of the Lord. I trust your book will also be loaded with chapters. Right now God is writing down in this book every thought you have of Him. Daily you have the opportunity to add to this Book of Remembrance as you think and speak about Jesus. I challenge you this year to write down your thoughts as you read through the Bible once again. You will leave a legacy for your children and their children they will treasure forever.

God bless you in the New Year as you add to your own Book of Remembrance.

> *Lord, thank You for caring enough to record Your words through the pen of men so I can be changed by these words. Thank You for sending Your Son, the living Word, to abide with me always. Thank You for sending Your Holy Spirit, who teaches me as I read Your Word. Thank You also for recording my words in a book as I think upon You and share Your Word with others. I am looking forward to reading my book of remembrance in heaven. I love You.*

To contact the author:

LINDA SOMMER
6716 Wright Road
Atlanta, GA 30328
Phone: (404) 252-3187
Email: trsommer@aol.com